Business Groups and the Thailand Economy

Business Groups and the Thailand Economy examines the role of business groups, specifically state, local, and foreign capitals in the economic development of emerging economies and highlights why business groups are essential in helping a country break out of the middle-income trap.

Wailerdsak reviews Thailand's industrial and economic growth strategies through the local and international investors and explains why business groups are one of the key drivers of economic advancement and why they help to avoid the middle-income trap. The author also examines their business power expansion methods, including selection and specialization, political influence, mergers and acquisitions, outward FDI and business alliances. The book concludes with policy recommendations of how the government can engage business groups to accelerate high-tech industrialization and create jobs.

The middle-income trap issue faced by Thailand would be of interest to many emerging economies, especially scholars and policymakers researching on Asian business and management, Asian economies, developmental economics, political economy, policy studies, corporate governance, entrepreneurship, and private company strategic management in emerging countries.

Natenapha Wailerdsak is currently an associate professor at Thammasat University in Thailand. She holds an economics PhD from the University of Tokyo. She was an assistant professor at the University of Tokyo's Institute of Advanced Studies on Asia and a visiting scholar at the University of the Philippines' School of Economics.

Routledge Focus on Business and Management

The fields of business and management have grown exponentially as areas of research and education. This growth presents challenges for readers trying to keep up with the latest important insights. *Routledge Focus on Business and Management* presents small books on big topics and how they intersect with the world of business research.

Individually, each title in the series provides coverage of a key academic topic, whilst collectively, the series forms a comprehensive collection across the business disciplines.

Proposal Writing for Business Research Projects
Peter Samuels

Systems Thinking and Sustainable Healthcare Delivery
Ben Fong

Gender Diversity and Inclusion at Work
Divergent Views from Turkey
Zeynep Özsoy, Mustafa Şenyücel and Beyza Oba

Management and Visualisation
Seeing Beyond the Strategic
Gordon Fletcher

Knowledge Management and AI in Society 5.0
Manlio Del Giudice, Veronica Scuotto and Armando Papa

The Logistics Audit
Methods, Organization and Practice
Piotr Buła and Bartosz Niedzielski

For more information about this series, please visit: www.routledge.com/Routledge-Focus-on-Business-and-Management/book-series/FBM

Business Groups and the Thailand Economy

Escaping the Middle-Income Trap

Natenapha Wailerdsak

Routledge
Taylor & Francis Group
LONDON AND NEW YORK

First published 2023
by Routledge
4 Park Square, Milton Park, Abingdon, Oxon OX14 4RN

and by Routledge
605 Third Avenue, New York, NY 10158

Routledge is an imprint of the Taylor & Francis Group, an informa business

British Library Cataloguing-in-Publication Data
A catalogue record for this book is available from the British Library

Library of Congress Cataloging-in-Publication Data
A catalog record for this book has been requested

ISBN: 978-1-032-44114-6 (hbk)
ISBN: 978-1-032-44115-3 (pbk)
ISBN: 978-1-003-37053-6 (ebk)

DOI: 10.4324/9781003370536

Typeset in ITC Galliard Pro
by Apex CoVantage, LLC

To Sombat, Saijai, and Yabushita family

Contents

Figures

Tables

Preface

This book examines the role of business groups, specifically state, local, and foreign capitals in the economic development of emerging economies and highlights why business groups are essential in helping a country break out of the middle-income trap.

The book reviews Thailand's industrial and economic growth strategies through the local and international investors and explains why business groups are one of the key drivers of economic advancement and why they help to avoid the middle-income trap. The author also examines their business power expansion methods, including selection and specialization, political influence, mergers and acquisitions, outward FDI and business alliances. The book concludes with policy recommendations of how the government can engage business groups to accelerate high-tech industrialization and create jobs.

The middle-income trap issue faced by Thailand would be of interest to many emerging economies, especially scholars and policymakers researching on Asian business and management, Asian economies, developmental economics, political economy, policy studies, corporate governance, entrepreneurship, and private company strategic management in emerging countries.

Natenapha Wailerdsak is an associate professor at the Thammasat Business School, Thammasat University in Thailand. She holds a PhD in economics from the University of Tokyo. Her research interests lie in the area of business groups and economic development, labour markets, and human resource management. Her research output has been published in leading peered review journals such as *Asia Pacific Journal of Management, Journal of Asian Business & Management, Journal of International Human Resource Management, Journal of Southeast Asian Economies*, and also in academic books such as *the Oxford Handbook of Business Group, the Oxford Handbook of Asian Business System, and the Changing Face of Management in Thailand.* She also worked as an assistant professor at the Institute of Advanced Studies on Asia, the University of Tokyo, and was a visiting scholar at the School of Economics, the University of the Philippines.

Acknowledgements

I deeply thank Prof. Peera Charoenporn, coordinator of the Project Series on Escaping the Middle-Income Country Trap of the Office of the Thailand Science Research and Innovation (TSRI), for providing a research grant (contract number SRI6251202). Research project advisors are Dr. Cholachit Vorawangso Virakul, of the Office of the Eastern Economic Corridor (EEC), and Prof. Akira Suehiro of the University of Tokyo.

I would like to acknowledge the four anonymous reviewers arranged by the TSRI, three anonymous reviewers arranged by the Business Research Center, Thammasat Business School, and two anonymous reviewers arranged by the Routledge editorial team, for their valuable suggestions on my proposal. Deep appreciation goes to Prof. Pasuk Phongpaichit, Prof. Asli M. Colpan, and Prof. Akira Suehiro for their time to review my manuscript and provide the endorsement quotes.

Special thanks to Professors Sununta Siengthai, Supranee Srichatrapimuk, Suwanna Thongpradit, Attachak Sattayanurak, Pavida Pananon, Kriangkrai Techakanont, Chaturong Napathorn, Suthinee Rurkkhum, Benjamin Ivry, Ho-Don Yan, Luis Alfonso Dau, Emily Sims, Antonio Tencati, Chayanich Thamparipattra, Yukako Ono, Hajime Yamamoto, Phramaha Supee Thitametho, Casey Hall, Bank Ngamarunchot, Thanapol Eawsakul, and research assistant Pornlert Sukonpathip for their continuous supports. Bonggot Anuroj, Sudhasinee Smitra, and Thumrong Ampornratana of Thailand Board of Investment, executives of Thai private companies, and Japanese investors who took the time to interview and exchange ideas. Thammasat Business School, which allowed the author to take sabbatical leave to write this book for one year (August 2021–July 2022) and attend international seminars and conferences overseas almost annually.

I would like to express my gratitude to Yongling Lam and Kendrick Loo, book editors for business, economics, and law at Routledge, Payal Bharti and Alice Maher, editorial assistants, and the production team for their speedy and helpful work on this volume. Finally, I would like to thank my family, especially

Sombat and Saijai Wailerdsak, my parents, Tomohiro, Tomone, and Yasuhiro Yabushita, for their unwavering support.

The research results have been approved for ethical conduct in research involving humans by the Human Research Ethics Subcommittee of Thammasat University No. 2 in accordance with Certificate No. 060/2562, Research Project No. 043/2562 (between 17 September 2019–17 September 2021).

Abbreviations

ADB	Asian Development Bank
AEC	Asian Economic Community
AIIB	Asian Infrastructure Investment Bank
APO	Asian Productivity Organization
BCG	bio-circular-green economy
BOI	Board of Investment
BOT	Bank of Thailand
BUILD	BOI Unit for Industrial Linkage Development
CLMV	Cambodia, Laos, Myanmar, and Vietnam
COVID-19	coronavirus Disease 2019
CPTTP	Comprehensive and Progressive Agreement for Trans-Pacific Partnership
EEC	Eastern Economic Corridor
EMDCD	Emerging Markets and Developing Countries Dialogue
EOI	export-oriented industrialization
EPAs	Economic Partnership Agreements
ESDP	Eastern Seaboard Development Program
FBGS	family business groups
FDI	foreign direct investment
FETCO	Federation of Thai Capital Market Organizations
FTA	free trade agreement
GDP	gross domestic product
GERD	gross expenditure on R&D
GFC	global financial crisis
GLCs	government-linked companies
GNI	gross national income
GVC	global value chain
HDD	hard disk drives
HPAEs	high-performing Asian economies
IFF	infrastructure fund
IOD	Institute of Directors
IQF	individual-quick-freeze

JPPSCC	Joint Public and Private Sector Consultative Committee
KTMF	Kingdom of Thailand Modernization Framework
LCRs	local content requirements
LTP	Lewis return point
M&A	merger and acquisition
MIT	middle income trap
MNC	multinational corporations
MVA	manufacturing value added
NAIC	newly agro-industrialized country
NCPO	National Council for Peace and Order
NESDB	National Economic and Social Development Board
NESDC	National Economic and Social Development Council
NICs	newly industrialized countries
NIEs	newly industrialized economies
NSRF	New Silk Road Fund
NVDRs	non-voting depository receipts
OBOR	One Belt, One Road Initiative
ODM	original design manufacturer
OECD	Organization for Economic Co-operation and Development
OECF	Overseas Economic Cooperation Fund
OEM	original equipment manufacturer
PPP	public-private partnership
PVLT	passenger vehicle and light truck
REIT	real estate investment trusts
SDGs	sustainable development goals
SET	Stock Exchange of Thailand
SEZs	special economic zones
SMEs	small and medium-sized enterprises
SOE	state-owned enterprise
TFP	total factor productivity
UNCTAD	United Nations Conference on Trade and Development
UNFCCC	United Nations Framework Convention on Climate Change
WIPO	World Intellectual Property Organization

Introduction

I.1 Background of the book

This book, *Business Groups and the Thailand Economy: Escaping the Middle-Income Trap*, was written to complement three previous books: *Capital Accumulation in Thailand 1855–1985* (published in 1992), *Catch-Up Industrialization: The Trajectory and Prospects of East Asian Economies* (2008), and *Thai Family-Owned Business Groups Before and After the 1997 Crisis* (in Thai) (2006). The first two volumes were written by University of Tokyo professor Akira Suehiro, a specialist on Asian economy. The last-mentioned book was written by the author.

All these studies examine the role of business groups in economic success of latecomer nations. East Asia, Latin America, and other emerging economies exhibit comparable capital accumulation and business group formation. The author bases explanations on empirical study with Professor Akira Suehiro and original data gathered over two decades.

The first two books examine the role of business groups in accumulating capital and driving the economy and the evolving political and social background of Asian latecomer nations, including Thailand, throughout industrialization. Several techniques proposed comprise import substitution; export-oriented industrialization; economic integration to promote international trade, foreign direct investment (FDI) promotion, and local investment. All help the transition from low- to lower-middle- to upper-middle-income nation.

However, the 1997 Asian financial crisis slowed these engines. Thailand's persistent decline in economic growth affixes it in the middle-income category. The World Bank, international organizations, and academia have debated this problem since the early 2000s. The economic crisis devastated influential local business groups, as described in the third volume. Eventually, the Thai economy began to stagnate. Unfortunately, premature deindustrialization occurred. To achieve high-income nation status, Thailand shifted to attempts to penetrate the service sector, travel, reprimatization (return to exporting agricultural goods), outbound FDI, and strategic alliances with foreign partners who provided superior technology.

DOI: 10.4324/9781003370536-1

In the 2020s, Asian economics researchers argued that major technological disruptions such as digital technology, Industry 4.0, artificial intelligence (AI), the internet of things (IoT), and the metaverse should help Asia finally escape the middle-income trap. As developed nations, they would import and develop related advanced technology and encourage new startups generating innovative businesses. This is a clear blueprint for Asia to catch up with more sophisticated industrialized nations (Goto et al., 2020; Lee et al., 2020). Yet this new cycle of catching up does not guarantee escaping the trap or creating branded technology. Dependency theory experts assert that Asia must continue to rely on foreign firms (Carroll et al., 2020; Mahoney & Rodríguez-Franco, 2018).

The literature (Dau et al., 2020, 2021a, 2021b) affirms that latecomer nation business groups as key players in latecomer industrialization depend on business group governance and therefore must struggle to advance. Asian economists sometimes overlook this difficulty. As long as the family business trap or family capitalism persists, still more rounds of catch-up continue, no matter how advanced technology is introduced by purchase or investment with foreign partners. In this sense, there are parallels between automobiles and electrical appliances in the 1980s and 1990s, and 2020s-style electronic device production, digital technology, and Industry 4.0.

This book suggests that while Thai private firms remain ensnared in the family business trap with concentrated shareholding based on holding companies and pyramidal structures, owners or large shareholders dominate corporate management through operations frequently for private gain rather than public good. There are few capable family executives. Succession plans are drawn up for family executives, but non-family executives remain apprehensive due to a lack of development framework. Hence, for Thai private firms, accumulating and developing branded technology remains a challenge.

At the same time, capital monopoly, state-inner-circle benefits (neglecting outer business groups), and dual society inequity (between large business groups and small and medium-sized enterprises (SMEs) persist. Thai business groups prioritize economic rents and excess profits from monopolies or government ties instead of research and development (R&D) investment to build their own technology and create breakthroughs. This is evident in the Eastern Economic Corridor (EEC) plan, which invites multinational corporations (MNCs) to import new modern technology and invest in specific business groups, in a step awaiting fulfilment.

Some Thai business groups are able to expand abroad, but most have restricted growth. The sole pathway to developed nation status is to embrace corporate governance or managerial capitalism (Dau et al., 2020, 2021a, 2021b; Morck, 2005):

- Diversifying shareholdings to become widely-held corporations in which majority shareholders are difficult to discern, and a robust monitoring mechanism supervises the top management team.

- Separating ownership and control, with companies aiming to benefit society, not owners or specific groups.
- Training non-family professional managers, vital for transmitting technology generationally within a firm until branded technology is created.

These are difficult challenges for family-owned firms, requiring the relinquishment of ownership and administrative power. Latecomer nations that have followed this path demonstrated that managerial enterprise corporate governance may help distribute wealth and ultimately reduce economic inequality (Dau et al., 2021b).

Finally, Thai business groups are mostly family-owned, with no ownership dispersion or control separation (Suehiro & Wailerdsak, 2004; Wailerdsak & Suehiro, 2010, 2014). This has hampered technological transfer and progress, limiting Thailand to middle-income nation status. Without progress on this point, whatever the target industry, imported technological advancement, or degree of startup and innovation, Thailand's development model will continue to be obsolete. The Kingdom's middle-income status will remain, and in the worst-care scenario, technological backwardness may lead to deterioration in status.

1.2 Book objective

This book serves four purposes:

1. Assessing if a latecomer country is trapped in middle-income nation status, using indicators such as economic growth rate, export value by industry, productivity level, R&D activities, and to identify escape methods based on catch-up industrialization, the middle-income trap, and developmental state theories.
2. Reviewing Thailand's industrial and economic growth strategies as articulated by local and international investors, especially Japan that promotes Thailand Plus One policy, and China that southern move with One Belt One Road Initiative, and the Eastern Economic Corridor (EEC) project, based on a tripod structure of business group, dependency theories, and Chinese and Japanese rivalry.
3. Showing that business groups are essential for economic advancement and preventing the middle-income trap. Business groups must be boosted to reduce industrial monopoly and separate major corporate ownership and control, according to latecomer business group theory. Their business power expansion methods, including selection and specialization, political influence, mergers and acquisitions, outward FDI, and business alliances with foreign partners, are also analysed.
4. Indicating the route to the subsequent developed nation status, stimulating the transition from family to managerial capitalism, outstanding

intra-organizational labour relations to absorb foreign technology and build dedicated technology, and move from family firms to managerial enterprises. According to the management critical point notion (organizational resource limits) and family business traps, professional executives may replace family executives.

1.3 Book content

The content is structured into three sections and eleven chapters: (1) theories and issues; (2) policies, target industries, and foreign investors; and (3) Thai firm case studies and policy recommendations. Chapters may be read out of sequence, although sequential reading is encouraged.

The initial section (Chapters 1–4) explores theories and issues, starting by explaining why the Thai government proclaimed the Thailand 4.0 strategy and set a goal to escape the middle-income trap by highlighting business group involvement with three categories of ideas:

- Catch-up industrialization, strategies to avoid the middle-income trap, and structural changes.
- Developmental state political economy and dependence theory.
- Organizational resource limitations and family business traps.

The second section (Chapters 5–6) consists of policies. Through a review of economic growth rates, export sales by sector, and Thai labour productivity and innovation activities, it highlights Thailand's slow deterioration in competitiveness and inability to attain developed nation status during a prolonged stasis while being stuck for a long time. Next examined are economic measures enacted by several governments following the 1997 Asian financial crisis to avoid the middle-income trap, including the creative economy policy, the new S-curves, and the bio-circular-green (BCG) economic model.

Chapter 7 covers target industries and foreign investors, investigating investment promotion data and the EEC plan to boost domestic investment, with its implementation challenges. This section concerns the Belt and Road Initiative and growth of Thai-Chinese strategic alliances. Since 1986, Japanese investors have lured Thailand into Japan's flying geese value chain. After the 2011 flood, the Thailand Plus One program was developed, diversifying risks by boosting reserve production bases in neighbouring nations and demonstrating that foreign business groups continued to impact the Thai economy.

Thai business case studies are in the third section (Chapters 8–10), analysing Thai business groups with industrial business concentrations and monopolies, Thai firm competitiveness from domestic and international investor perspectives, and business power expansion methods, including selection and specialization, political influence, mergers and acquisitions, outward FDI, and business alliances with foreign partners. It also looks at inadequate management resources (funds, technology, and human resources), lack of ownership and management separation, and ownership concentration through a holding company and cross shareholding. Thailand has few managerial enterprises. Thai businesses grow slowly and remain stunted due to the aforementioned conditions.

Lastly, Chapter 11 offers a summary and recommendations. The chapter concludes that the business group governance system was highly effective during Thailand's development into an upper-middle-income country and the era of population bonuses providing many young workers, allowing resources to be allocated to high-wage industries. Despite this, the business group governance system hinders technology and innovation in high-income countries. It requires corporate governance for managerial enterprises to prevent industrial monopolies and foster startup formation. If a large company is of national significance, it should be owned, dispersed, and managed for the public, not just a family or group. The people approach emphasizes strong labour relations and hiring non-family professional managers.

The book suggests three paths to high-income-nation status:

- Thailand might imitate the growth of other industrialized nations or follow the German Industry 4.0 model. Rich countries foster advanced research and technology and benefit from strong innovation systems. High-technology industrial exports have increased, especially automobiles and auto parts, electrical appliances, electronics, information technology (IT), and digital products. Along this pathway, Thailand relies on foreign business groups because no relevant Thai enterprises have been established.
- Agro-industrialization and Thainization. Industry has merged with agriculture from early stages of industrialization. In the 1970s and 1980s, newly agro-industrialized countries (NAICs) evolved into creative economies that conceptually sought to build added value for export products with a focus on Thainess, where Thai companies competed in global markets for agricultural products, processed foods, and consumer goods. However, to replace high-tech industrial items, value must be provided and adequate income earned.
- Marketing 4.0, focusing on middle-class oriented businesses that employ domestic resources and services, including medical services, real estate, retail, travel, hotels, stand-alone restaurants, banking, and insurance. These companies expand through the Association of Southeast Asian Nations (ASEAN) community by mergers and acquisitions and overseas partners, especially China and Japan. Thai business groups pioneered this approach as Thailand outperformed middle-income nations in several areas.

I.4 Definitions

Middle-income trap

The middle-income trap describes a nation that might advance from low-income to higher middle-income but is caught in an intermediary phase. It cannot achieve wealthy nation status (Asian Development Bank, 2011, p. 9). Much research has been done on what makes countries developed and what hinders their progress. Most focus on their own technology and innovation, industrial goods exports, industry policy, and public education policy (Goto et al., 2020; Lee et al., 2020). The roles of business groups and private companies have attracted little research in terms of avoiding the middle-income trap (Colpan et al., 2010).

Capital and capital accumulation

Capital refers to business groups in an economic sense. Based on the Marxist concept of capital, real sector investments are investment instruments in additional capital, focusing on factory-based capitalism. Entrepreneurs spend excess profits (surplus, windfalls) gained from workers on diverse forms of primitive accumulation (Suehiro, 1989).

Governmental power or local influence is used to capture or dominate land or property belonging to weaker owners, then converting it into private property and investing the earnings. In accordance with early economic development plans, the state gives concessions, business licenses, and investment promotion permits to state enterprises and private companies (including foreign companies) in return for specific benefits, including lowered income taxes and reduced fees for importing machinery (Suehiro & Wailerdsak, 2013). Later, the concept of surplus profit became known as "economic rent"[1] (Khan & Jomo, 2000; Phongpaichit & Treerat, 2003).

Entrepreneurs also use social capital to accumulate capital by employing local kinships or peers as well as contacts with more prominent individuals to build their company, which is called crony capitalism, nepotism, or the state-business relationship (Phongpaichit, 2006).

Business groups

Business groups is defined as "collections of firms bound together in some formal and/or informal ways" (Granovetter, 1994, p. 454). Business groups play a key role in Latin America and Asia's governance landscape, but there are significant differences between them, and they are known under a variety of designations: *grupos economicos* in Latin American countries; *grupos* in Spain; the *zaibatus* and *keiretsu* of Japan; *chaebol* of Korea; *qiye jituan* in China; *business houses* of India; the *hongs* of Hong Kong; *quanxi quiye* in Taiwan; government-linked groups of Singapore; ethnic Chinese business groups in

Thailand, Malaysia, Indonesia, and the Philippines; the *bumiputera* groups of Malaysia and Indonesia; and *family holdings* in Türkiye (Carney, 2008; Guillén, 2010).

Khanna and Yafeh (2007) studied diversified business groups that are ubiquitous in emerging markets (such as Brazil, Chile, China, India, Indonesia, South Korea, Mexico, Pakistan, and Thailand) and even in some developed economies (Italy, Sweden). These groups typically consist of legally independent firms, operating in multiple, often unrelated, industries united by persistent formal and informal ties such as equity or familial relations, respectively. They provide a novel taxonomy for business groups in three dimensions:

- Group structure: the extent of horizontal diversification, vertical integration, and financial sector involvement.
- Group ownership and control: the extent to which the group is pyramidal in structure or family controlled.
- Group interaction with society: the nature of interaction between business groups and the state, the extent of monopolistic power wielded by groups.

This taxonomy highlights reasons for business group formation, their prevalence in different economic environments, and welfare implications associated with their presence. In conclusion, two opposed viewpoints exist. Diversified business groups are "paragons" driving economic progress. Diversified corporate groups are perceived negatively as "parasite"[2] potentially harmful to societal welfare by rent-seeking or monopolistic power[3] (Carney et al., 2018; Khanna & Yafeh, 2007).

Thai business groups

Thai business groups (*klum thun thai*) are Thai private companies thriving in all industries. Their subsidiaries may be listed or unlisted. For listed companies on the Stock Exchange of Thailand (SET), the owners' families or primary shareholders (the Ministry of Finance as state entity) must own over 20 percent of company shares (the World Bank's 20 percent criterion). Financial statements, investment plans, and corporate management must be made public. Non-listed companies should submit financial statements and shareholder accounts to the Ministry of Commerce's Department of Trade Registration (Suehiro & Wailersak, 2004; Wailerdsak, 2006, 2008; Wailerdsak & Suehiro, 2010, 2014).

Company size is measured by incomes or sales, comprising a variety of conglomerates and pyramidal ownership arrangements. Thai business groups include state enterprises (such as PTT, THAI, and Krungthai Bank) and family business groups like the Crown Property Bureau (such as Siam Cement group/SCG, Siam Commercial Bank/SCB), Charoen Pokphand/CP, TCC/ThaiBev, Bangkok Bank, Osotsapa, Sahapat, Central, and Land & House.[4]

Foreign business groups

The term "foreign business group"[5] refers to private enterprises that maintain a foreign identity by owning 100 percent of company shares; alternatively, they create a joint venture with Thai investors, despite foreign companies retaining control of manufacturing technologies and international markets (Suehiro, 1989).

Historically, most foreign companies operating in Thailand were European. Japanese and Chinese companies with bases in Hong Kong, Singapore, and Taiwan eventually took over. They are engaged in procuring and producing goods for export from Thailand. Some have become import-substituting manufacturers and services. This book focuses on foreign companies involved in EEC projects, especially Japan and China, which are vying for supremacy in Asia.

I.5 Target readership

This book is intended for use in social science–related undergraduate and graduate courses in Asian business and management, Asian economies, developmental economics, political economy, policy studies, corporate governance, entrepreneurship, and private company strategic management in emerging countries.

It also encourages academics, researchers, policymakers, and journalists to conduct additional research to better understand the role of business groups in economic development and business administration. It is hoped that this will result in policies that place middle-income nations such as Thailand on a progressive path to developed nation status.

I.6 Preliminary accord

- The book is divided into 11 subchapters, according to researchers propounding each separate theory and topic to facilitate reading, researching, and teaching and learning used by students and readers from all social sciences, in addition to economics.
- Each chapter begins with study goals outlining principal ideas.
- Each chapter has keywords reflecting relevant theme.
- Each chapter contains a concluding synopsis and questions to encourage independent thinking and comprehension.
- End-of-chapter references are offered to encourage research. Some works may be cited in several chapters.
- Endnotes supply reliable foundational theory for non-economists to understand topics.
- Tables and figures are original, created by the author, not reproduced from older publications, to inspire scholars and students to construct visual supports for their own future research.

Notes

1 Economic rent, or rent, refers to compensation or revenue in excess of normal profit. It uses the situation of a perfectly competitive market, divided into six groups, as a normality criterion: (1) Monopolistic rents are more lucrative than usual because monopolies exist to produce or sell products or services, possibly due to economies of scale, production technology, brand loyalty, or the state granting one manufacturer the right to limit output and set prices without competition, such as concessions and licensing; (2) rents based on transfer with revenue derived from the transfer of resources through political processes such as taxes and subsidies, or transferring public resources to private property; (3) natural resource rents with income derived from access to scarce or restricted natural resources, leading to potentially arduous or quasi-impossible reconstruction over decades; (4) income generated from innovation or Schumpeterian rents with profits generated by new item producer ingenuity unmatched by rivals. Intellectual property rights are protected for an interval to prevent competition in a system encouraging entrepreneurial investment in innovation; (5) educational rents with profit surpluses resulting from improved manufacturing efficiency. Through the process of receiving foreign technology and adapting it for use, more fresh breakthroughs are created. For a scheduled time, the government may support enterprises in chosen industries to boost export productivity; (6) superior governance and management rents, resulting in surpluses due to outstanding management skills (Khan & Jomo, 2000; Phongpaichit & Treerat, 2003).

2 A similar term, "rentier capitalist (*thun kafak*)," was defined by Phongpaichit (2006) and Bresser-Pereira (2020) as a group of entrepreneurs profiting from property speculation without participating in production activities, such as inheriting land, renting it to others as a sleeping tiger, collecting rent, or waiting for land prices to rise before selling it, taking money that has been invested in the bank, earning interest on it, or purchasing stocks on the SET, receiving dividends, and trading shares back and forth. Rentier capital impedes others, causing land prices to rise and attempts to use its power to promote laws encouraging speculation. It is detrimental to real manufacturing builders, as opposed to "industrial entrepreneurs."

3 For other words, such as heroes or villains (Claessens et al., 2000), red barons or robber barons (Perotti & Gelfer, 2001), and anachronisms or avatars (Granovetter, 1994).

4 Before 1997, Thai commercial bank family owners (known as *Chao Sua* bank capitalists) held over 30 percent of their banks and were always protected by the state. After the crisis, they sold parts of their enterprises to foreign partners, merged with state banks, and raised money until share proportions plummeted, but the heirs still held control (Polsiri & Wiwattanakantang, 2006; Satitniramai, 2013; Wailerdsak, 2006, 2008). Notably, during the novel Coronavirus 2019 (COVID-19) pandemic, some family-managed banks transferred control to widely held managerial enterprises (see Chapter 10).

5 Long-term foreign residents and workers in Thailand, such as the Chinese. Most have already assimilated into Thai culture. Commercial activities of these individuals, as well as those of other nationalities, such as B. Grimm (German), Minor International (American), Indorama Ventures (India), less numerous than Thai Chinese, are not deemed foreign (Wailerdsak & Suehiro, 2010).

References

Asian Development Bank. (2011, August). *Asia 2050: Realizing the Asian century*. Asian Development Bank.

Bresser-Pereira, L. C. (2020). A new theoretical framework: New developmentalism. *Challenge*, *63*(3), 114–132.

Carney, M. (2008). The many futures of Asian business groups. *Asia Pacific Journal of Management*, *25*(4), 595–613.

Carney, M., Van Essen, M., Estrin, S., & Shapiro, D. (2018). Business groups reconsidered: Beyond paragons and parasites. *Academy of Management Perspectives*, *32*(4), 493–516.

Carroll, T., Hameiri, S., & Jones, L. (Eds.). (2020). *The political economy of Southeast Asia: Politics and uneven development under hyperglobalisation*. Springer Nature.

Claessens, S., Djankov, S., & Lang, L. H. P. (2000). *East Asian corporations: Heroes or villains?* World Bank Discussion Paper No. 409. The World Bank Group.

Colpan, A. M., Hikino, T., & Lincoln, J. R. (2010). *The Oxford handbook of business groups*. Oxford University Press.

Dau, L. A., Morck, R. K., & Yeung, B. (2020). *Corporate governance, business group governance and economic traps*. NBER Working Paper No. 28069. National Bureau of Economic Research.

Dau, L. A., Morck, R. K., & Yeung, B. (2021a). Corporate governance versus business group governance, part 1: The low-income trap. In K. Sogner & A. Colli (Eds.), *The emergence of corporate governance: People, power, and performance* (Chapter 6, pp. 103–120). Routledge.

Dau, L. A., Morck, R. K., & Yeung, B. (2021b). Corporate governance versus business group governance, part 2: The middle-income trap. In K. Sogner & A. Colli (Eds.), *The emergence of corporate governance: People, power, and performance* (Chapter 7, pp. 121–134). Routledge.

Goto, K., Endo, T., & Ito, A. (2020). *The Asian economy: Contemporary issues and challenges*. Routledge.

Granovetter, M. (1994). Business groups and social organization. In N. J. Smelser & R. Swerdburg (Eds.), *The handbook of economic sociology* (Chapter 19, pp. 429–450). Princeton University Press.

Guillén, M. (2010). Capability building in business groups. In A. M. Colpan, T. Hikino, & J. R. Lincoln (Eds.), *The Oxford handbook of business groups* (Chapter 27, pp. 743–762). Oxford University Press.

Khan, M. H., & Jomo, K. S. (Eds.). (2000). *Rents, rent-seeking and economic development: Theory and Evidence in Asia*. Cambridge University Press.

Khanna, T., & Yafeh, Y. (2007). Business groups in emerging markets: Paragons or parasites? *Journal of Economic literature*, *45*(2), 331–372.

Lee, K., Wong, C., Intarakumnerd, P., & Limapornvanich, C. (2020). Is the fourth industrial revolution a window of opportunity for upgrading or reinforcing the middle-income trap? Asian model of development in Southeast Asia. *Journal of Economic Policy Reform*, *23*(4), 408–425.

Mahoney, J., & Rodríguez-Franco, D. (2018). Dependency theory. In C. Lancaster & N. van de Walle (Eds.), *The Oxford handbook of the politics of development* (Chapter 2, pp. 22–42). Oxford University Press.

Morck, R. (Ed.). (2005). *A history of corporate governance around the world: Family business groups to professional managers*. University of Chicago Press.

Perotti, E. C., & Gelfer, S. (2001). Red barons or robber barons? Governance and investment Russian financial-industrial groups. *European Economic Review*, *9*, 1601–1617.

Phongpaichit, P. (2006). Thaksinomics ca yang yuu kap rao yaangnoi 10–20 pii (Thaksinomics will persist for at least ten to twenty years). *Same Sky Journal*, *4*(4), 78–93 (In Thai).

Phongpaichit, P., & Treerat, N. (2003). Corruption, rents, and economic development. *Thammasat Economic Journal, 21*(4), 1–28 (In Thai).

Polsiri, P., & Wiwattanakantang, Y. (2006). *Corporate governance of banks in Thailand.* Center for Economic Institutions Working Paper Series No. 2005–20. Institute of Economic Research, Hitotsubashi University.

Satitniramai, A. (2013). *Rat Thai kab kan patiroop settakit: Chak kamnerd toonniyom nai tanakaan tung wikrit settakit 2540 (The Thai state and economic reform: From the establishment of banking capitalism to the Asian financial crisis).* Same Sky Books (In Thai).

Suehiro, A. (1989). *Capital accumulation in Thailand, 1855–1985.* UNESCO The Centre for East Asian Cultural Studies.

Suehiro, A., & Wailerdsak, N. (2004). Family business in Thailand: Its management, governance, and future challenges. *ASEAN Economic Bulletin, 21*(1), 81–93.

Suehiro, A., & Wailerdsak, N. (2013). Thailand: Post-developmentalist capitalism. In M. Witt & G. Redding (Eds.), *The Oxford handbook of Asian business system* (Chapter 13, pp. 258–280). Oxford University Press.

Wailerdsak, N. (2006). *Klumthun turakit krubkruathai koon lae lang wikrit pii 2540 Thai family-owned business groups before and after the 1997 crisis.* BrandAge Books (In Thai).

Wailerdsak, N. (2008). Family business in Thailand: Ownership structures and stock Market. In V. Gupta, N. Levenberg, L. Moore, J. Motwani, & T. Schwarz (Eds.), *Culturally-sensitive models of family business in Southern Asia: A compendium using the GLOBE paradigm* (Chapter 5, pp. 108–136). ICFAI University Press.

Wailerdsak, N., & Suehiro, A. (2010). Business groups in Thailand. In A. M. Colpan, T. Hikino, J. Lincoln, & D. Musson (Eds.), *Oxford handbook of business groups* (Chapter 9, pp. 237–266). Oxford University Press.

Wailerdsak, N., & Suehiro, A. (2014). Family business groups in Thailand: Coping with management critical points. *Asia Pacific Journal of Management, 31*(4), 997–1018.

Part I

Theory and issues

Chapter 1

Catch-up industrialization theory

1.1 Advantages of backwardness and technological leap

In the aftermath of World War II, when African, Latin American, and Asian nations were liberated from colonial dependence, the concept of economic development in less-developed countries emphasizing the key strategies of industrialization and liberalization became widespread. Western international organizations such as the World Bank, United Nations, and International Monetary Fund spearheaded policies for developing countries (Suehiro, 2008).

In each, the industrialization process appeared similar. From being an agricultural country producing and exporting agricultural goods while importing industrial products, nations eventually developed to import substitution and produced labour-intensive industrial products for export. Then, each nation individually produced and exported industrial products through advanced technology (Jimenez & Ricardo, 2019). A key theory describing this process is catch-up industrialization, which has been successful in many developing Asian and Latin American countries, including Japan and the so-called Four Asian Tigers (the economies of South Korea, Taiwan, Singapore, and Hong Kong) as well as newly industrializing economies (NIEs), including Argentina, Brazil, Chile, and Mexico (Amsden & Wan-wen, 2003; Balassa, 1981, 1986; Kehoe & Felipe, 2011; Paula & Jabbour, 2020; Zheng, 2020).[1]

The term "catching-up" is defined as the process by which a national latecomer reduces gaps in income (economic catch-up) or technological (technological catch-up) capabilities compared to leading economies by taking advantages of technological backwardness[2] (Asian Development Bank, 2015). The core concept, as posited by the economic historian Alexander Gerschenkron, is that by importing modern technologies from leading industrialized countries and investing in cutting-edge machinery and equipment, latecomers to the development process may skip modernization stages that had been deemed necessary by previous researchers such as Walt Rostow in any successful path to economic development (see next section).

By skipping or taking shortcuts, Gerchenkron argued, late-developing economies could generate faster and more capital-intensive industrial growth

DOI: 10.4324/9781003370536-3

unhindered by societal constraints, as orchestrated by a strongly dirigiste state, because latecomers can build on knowledge and technology already developed by incumbents without having to go through costly processes of trial and error to develop them on their own. Late developers have witnessed the development of early industrializers and know what to emulate and what to avoid, but taking shortcuts by emulating good experience and avoiding mistakes requires the organizing power of institutions (Gerschenkron, 1962; Nayyar, 2013; Nolan & Lenski, 1985).

Gerschenkron showed that as a late developer, late-nineteenth-century Germany developed by using banks and large industrial firms as coordinators and promoters for rapid industrial growth. When Russia began to develop later, the government became directly involved in economic development (Gerschenkron, 1962). Similarly, the success of developmental states such as Japan and South Korea during the Cold War era is attributed to cooperative state – business relationships maintained by selective industrial policies (Amsden, 1989, 2001; Hsiao & Hsiao, 2017).

Arguments akin to Gerchenkron's are currently being revived in the flourishing discourse of technological leapfrogging (Lee, 2019), suggesting that less-developed countries could reap benefits from skipping intermediate stages in technological progress, such as by jumping straight into mobile-phone-based e-payment systems without first building an ATM infrastructure, automated train and subway systems or self-checkout and e-kiosk systems in retail and food services (Schlogl, 2020).

Advantages of backwardness are windows of opportunity for all latecomer countries in industrialization, but opportunity offers no guarantee that latecomers will fully enjoy the advantages of backwardness. To do so, they must meet a number of preconditions (Asian Development Bank, 2015; Nolan & Lenski, 1985). Abramovitz (1986) was among the first researchers to observe that endogenous capabilities to attract, absorb, and improve technologies are indispensable for exploiting opportunities of international knowledge transfer. These "social capabilities," as he terms them, largely explain whether countries will catch up or fall behind.

Were it not so, developing countries internationally would have achieved industrialization long ago, and economists would not be arguing about economic development in developing countries today. Therefore, the middle-income trap shows that not every developing country can advance further to developed nation status. The significant reason is a lack of social capabilities in industrialization (Nayyar, 2020; Suehiro, 2014), including:

- Government leadership capable of changing policies to strive seriously for economic development and inequality reduction.
- Administrative abilities of local private companies.
- Skilled workers.

In addition, although latecomers have the aforementioned advantages of backwardness, they also face related disadvantages. Countries in latecomer positions of economic development prioritize industrial development rather than resource conservation and environmental protection. More importantly, compressed development occurs quickly, or so-called "thin industrialization." Time confinement is a key feature of compressed development. Development over the past 150 years in the United Kingdom, and 50 years in Japan, was compressed into ever-shorter time frames by more recent developing nations (Sturgeon & Whittaker, 2019; Whittaker et al., 2020).

This results in fatigue and consequent social problems such as stress, depression, and higher suicide rates. Less visibly, social relations and values associated with agricultural or early industrial societies, such as high value placed on male children, may overlap with late or postindustrial emphases on equality and higher education opportunities for women. These in turn may worsen gender tensions and accelerate trends towards later marriage, reducing childbirth rates and increasing societal aging that typically occurs with economic development, as it has in Thailand (Suehiro & Wailerdsak, 2013; Sturgeon & Whittaker, 2019; Whittaker et al., 2020). These widespread tensions are powerful, yet little academic attention has been directed to the phenomenon of compression.

1.2 Flying-geese pattern and limitations

In fact, early development theories tried to uncover common paths or sequential stages that all industrializers follow to achieve industrialization. For example, Rostow (1960) specified five stages of industrialization: traditional society, preconditions to takeoff, takeoff, drive to maturity, and age of high mass consumption. In his later work, Rostow added a sixth step for sustainable development: the search for quality (Rostow, 1971). This approach influenced post–World War II concepts of economic development, concretely following contemporaneous US foreign policy towards developing countries (Suehiro, 2008).

The term "flying geese" is often used to describe metaphorically East Asian economies because they adopt similar development strategies by imitating an earlier developing neighbour (Akamatsu, 1962). This concept, as presented by the Japanese economist Kaname Akamatsu, suggested that innovation occurring in Nation A would result in spectacular development in that country over some years (differentiating it from other countries through heterogenization), before the pace of development slowed to stagnation. By this time, Nation B would introduce technology from Nation A, resulting in homogenization with increased similarity of the two countries. A nation might start by importing innovative products, then shift to self-production, before finally exporting products to third nation markets, or the nation that made the initial innovation. Thus, homogenization of the world economy proceeded in a pattern resembling the flight of geese (Akamatsu, 1962, p. 20).

In the 1980s and 1990s, this theory was used to describe relocation of manufacturing bases from Japan to Asian NIEs, and then advancing to the Association of Southeast Asian Nations (ASEAN), China and India respectively, illustrating the international division of labour across Asia. Japan led the V-formation for over three decades, but economic stagnation after the 1992 Japanese asset price bubble and the 2007–2008 global financial crisis (GFC) as well as the Fukushima Daiichi nuclear disaster and other ongoing natural disasters, Japan's position as a super-aged society is seen as weakening. China and India can assume leaderships roles in Asia, replacing Japan (Hayter & Edgington, 2004, 2021; Kenderdine, 2018).

Later, arguments against catch-up industrialization theory appeared from several perspectives. For example, the theory was unable to rationalize industrialization processes in large population countries such as China or India. Industrialization in South Korea or Taiwan, focusing on rapid developments in the information technology (IT) industry, did not follow the flying-geese pattern emphasizing basic industries such as television, clothing and textiles, or agriculture. Many South Korean, Taiwanese. and Chinese companies developed cutting-edge technology by shifting from stages of catch-up to leapfrog rather than being path-dependent on established technologies according to theoretical precedent (Amsden & Wan-wen, 2003; Hsiao & Hsiao, 2017).

The two-stage catch-up industrialization argument (Sato & Sato, 2016) opines that catching up should be divided into two phases: firstly, a learning process or duplicative imitation. In a stylized way, latecomer countries start by borrowing technology through foreign direct investment or licensing agreements; then they gradually create capabilities to use technologies efficiently by adapting them to local conditions. Using reverse engineering, latecomer countries focus on producing a few product types that are cheap and easy to use through mass production. After some development, limitations in learning will be encountered.

The second step is process innovation or creative imitation, building capabilities for indigenous innovation. During this phase, governments must offer clear supportive policies. After importing technologies, private companies must try to compile organizational capabilities to create indigenous innovation.

Current innovation management allows latecomer companies to industrialize, facilitating technological pursuit by forward-thinking, component, or architectural product innovations. These need not be radical or thoroughly disruptive innovations.[3] Participation in the global production supply and value chains using the modular production system (modularization) reduces redundancy and increases flexibility. Growing automation and open innovation systems facilitate access to product knowledge more than prior closed innovation systems (Apaitan et al., 2017; Suehiro, 2014; Vivarelli, 2016).

1.3 Catch-up theory revisited and technological creep

Although some researchers admit that catch-up industrialization theory is outdated, but it has been advanced again to analyse economic developments in China during the globalization era, as seen in the World Bank report *From Flying Geese to Leading Dragons: New Opportunities and Strategies for Structural Transformation in Developing Countries* (Lin, 2011) and in studies by Ang (2018), Jimenez and Ricardo (2019), Kenderdine (2018), and Zheng (2020).

China's rapid industrial catch-up, due in part to an aggressive strategy of accessing and copying foreign technology, on the other hand, lends apparent credibility to Gerschenkron's optimistic thesis. Traditional industrial production technology for garments and textiles, electrical appliance, electronic products, automobiles, and machinery has made China into the so-called factory of the world (Kenderdine, 2018). In addition, modern technology such as digital and green technologies for energy and the environment are also seen as catch-up phenomena. The United States has giant technology companies presenting new business models, such as Google, Amazon, Facebook, Apple, and Microsoft; China too has tech companies, such as Huawei, TikTok, WeChat, Alibaba, Tencent, and JD.com.

However, disadvantages of backwardness, or technological creeps as opposed to leaps, derived from early adoption of new technologies despite late development, impeding catch-up development. This phenomenon may be found across the developing world during the era of globalization. Results include forced liberalization of trade and industry and inability to protect domestic industries, premature deindustrialization/tertiarization, automation displacing abundant labour, jobless growth, value-added erosion due to global value chain (GVC) participation, technological dependency due to patents or lock-in effects, data colonies, and environmental issues such as growing energy consumption, electronic waste, and rising emissions (Schlogl, 2020).

In Thailand, some issues persist; no Thai national high-tech or unicorn company is listed on the Stock Exchange of Thailand (SET), suggesting that the Kingdom lacks catch-up social capabilities. The basic challenge for Thai companies is how to fully exploit advantages of backwardness and make the technology leap a reality. They must simultaneously confront disadvantages of backwardness that continue to impede catch-up development and prevent the nation from falling into the middle-income trap (Kanchoochat, 2018).

1.4 Unravelling structural change challenges

1.4.1 Structural change in gross domestic product and employment

For a decade, Thailand has been trapped in a middle-income country growth slowdown, exacerbated by the novel coronavirus 2019 (COVID-19) outbreak. The Kingdom can no longer compete with latecomer competitors in standardized, labour-intensive products, since wages are relatively high. Yet it has not attained the ability to compete with developed countries in higher value-added activities, as productivity is relatively low (Kanchoochat, 2018; Kanchoochat & Intarakumnerd, 2014; Paus, 2020).

Industrialization positively affects distribution by creating jobs in manufacturing and related sectors, thereby eradicating poverty. Two key indicators are manufacturing share in gross domestic product (GDP) and in total workforce. The industrial upgrading processes from basic to high-quality products in the manufacturing sector and structural change from agriculture to manufacturing and services are essential for transitioning from middle to high income (Agénor, 2017; Asian Development Bank, 2015).

The Lewis two sector model is a well-known example of the structural-change approach, dividing societies into rural and urban portions. During an initial phase of development, low income countries can compete in international markets by producing labour-intensive, low-cost products with imported technology. These nations can achieve large initial productivity gains by reallocating unrestricted labour surplus from low productivity rural (agriculture-dominant) to high-productivity urban (manufacturing and service-orientation). Businesses may boost profits without paying additional wages. When the economy develops to the point that the pool of underemployed rural workers decreases, further investment will increase wages, eroding competitiveness (Jimenez & Ricardo, 2019; Lewis, 1954).

At this Lewis return point (LTP), finding additional workers becomes more difficult, and gains from importing foreign technology significantly diminish. This results in decreased marginal returns on investment in physical capital and related growth slowdowns (Agénor, 2017). To continue to thrive, nations require new growth sources for maintaining sustained per capita income increases, such as new workforces in the form of beginning or migrant workers. Yet such increases do not usually occur dramatically (Foster-McGregor & Verspagen, 2016).

Another way to increase productivity is by changing machinery and production processes or innovating with high-tech and high-value-added products. But these approaches are more difficult than shifting additional workers from agriculture to industry.

1.4.2 Agriculture – Dutch disease and reprimatization of exports

Thailand is trapped by the natural resource curse as well as the Dutch disease. Many Thais still believe that the Kingdom's agricultural sector is a major comparative advantage in international trade. Since the 1980s, Thailand was deemed a newly agro-industrialized country (NAIC) with development based on agro-industrial exports. Japan and the Asian Tigers, mostly resource-poor, declared themselves newly industrializing economies (NIEs) focusing at the onset on exports of manufactured products (Kanchoochat, 2018; Kanchoochat & Intarakumnerd, 2014).

By 2021, Thai annual agricultural export value was up to 1.0 trillion baht, ranked thirteenth in the world. But agricultural products fell to the tenth ranking in total export value. Rice was no longer a main export product. Thailand is still in a transition period, with a 30–40 percent decline in agricultural employment. Agriculture value added has also declined over the past three decades, accounting for only 10 percent of GDP (Dayley & Sattayanurak, 2016; Warr, 2008). The path to developed country status requires that fewer than 10 percent of the total workforce be employed in agriculture, whose contribution to the GDP should drop to below 10 percent. Such developments might dismay some Thai observers.

Nevertheless, the agriculture sector remains vital in offering food security and upstream company units, especially during crises. Thailand is never obliged to import food, and a full range of nationally produced consumer products remains available. In reality, this belief facilitates fixture at a low productive agriculture sector (Dayley & Sattayanurak, 2016). If productivity was high, Thai farmers would prosper and not be indebted as they are today.

Reprimatization of exports is another reason why Thailand is trapped in a resource curse. Thailand reverted to comparative advantages in natural resources, innovating with edible fruits, nuts, citrus fruit peel to supplement previous mainstays such as rice, tapioca, and rubber (Kanchoochat & Intarakumnerd, 2014). Since the year 2000, China's high growth and rising natural resource demands have been key factors in the commodity price boom. China has become an important trading partner of Thailand in agricultural exports as well as services such as tourism and real estate.

In 2020, Thailand became the world's largest durian exporter in volume and export value, with a continuously expanding global market share that reached 75.9 percent. Yet the export value of fresh Thai durian is only USD 2.8–2.9 billion (average price 90–130 baht per kilogram), far cheaper than high-tech or high-value-added manufactured products.

In the near future, Thailand anticipates significant productivity growth through the bio-circular-green (BCG) economy, incorporating advanced technology such as smart farming, precision agriculture, and renewable energy. But higher technology requires fewer workers, and employees must have advanced skills to master new technology. High-tech agriculture is not a source of employment for low-skilled people or to absorb lower-level workers, as low-tech farming was in the past (Foster-McGregor & Verspagen, 2016). Where surplus agricultural workers will be allocated remains a major problem in future.

Significantly, Thailand faces annual natural disasters, with alternating drought and floods, due to climate change and water mismanagement. The Global Climate Risk Index by German Watch ranks Thailand ninth of 180 world countries vulnerable to climate change. Effectively managing water and the natural environment in a way conducive to increasing agricultural productivity will be time-consuming.

In addition, there is a lack of fair land reform policy, a political and social problem to be overcome by every middle-income country. For an example, in the Eastern Economic Corridor (EEC), dilemmas over land use as industrial zones, farmlands, or tourist sites are increasing. Revised city plans for the three provinces involved, Rayong, Chon Buri, and Chachoengsao, will enlarge the industrial zone and consume areas of fertile farmland, displacing farmers of durian and other economic fruit crops. Popular tourist destinations such as Bang Sean Beach and Pattaya Beach are also located nearby. More importantly, EEC regulations will allow foreign property ownership, as projects target foreign purchasers, leading to social conflict and resistance from local residents (see Chapter 7).

In sum, to match and forge ahead of developed nations, Thailand must escape the resource curse and progress in land reform and redistribution, thereby contributing to sustainable development.

1.4.3 Industrial – deindustrialization and national innovation system

Moving from factor-driven to innovation-driven growth is fundamental for transitioning from middle-income to high-income economy status. The key is developing domestic technological and innovation capabilities to ascend the value chain thoroughly enough to generate sustained productivity growth (Asian Development Bank, 2017; Vivarelli, 2016).

Some researchers have proposed a Schumpeterian national innovation system. Some attributed to the state a dynamic role in shifting to greater innovative-based growth. Government institutions may need to pioneer prioritizing innovation areas because private producers deem initial risks excessive, requiring Schumpeterian rent. So governments must leverage macro policies, tax incentives, and protect intellectual and property rights, a difficult challenge (Apaitan et al., 2017; Lee, 2013).

Over the past half century, few nations have achieved this transition, among them the Asian Tigers, the economies of South Korea, Taiwan, Singapore, and Hong Kong. By contrast, many Latin American and Southeast Asian countries have been fixed at the middle-income level for decades.

In the late 1980s, several Thai companies jointly invested in foreign companies, especially Japanese multinational corporations (MNCs) in such areas as automotive assembly, auto parts, electrical and electronic products, textiles and clothing. These joint-venture firms reinforced Thailand's import substitution and export-oriented industrialization, to aspire to upper-middle-income nation status by 2010. But the 1997 Asian financial crisis transformed corporate strategy (Ouyyanont, 2019; Wailerdsak, 2008).

Premature deindustrialization occurred, in which a country shifts its economy from manufacturing production before having extracted full productivity gains from industrialization. This phenomenon had four main causes.

Firstly, Thai companies were insufficiently successful in technological spillovers to create indigenous innovations. After the 1997 Asian financial crisis, the Board of Investment (BOI) removed restrictions in foreign shareholding to help affected companies improve liquidity positions. Before this, majority ownership had to be held by a Thai national in using domestic elements, as in the automobile industry. This resulted in a certain level of technology transfer. Later, foreign partners in 164 automotive firms changed their shareholding structure from minority to majority shares. This caused Thai partners to withdraw from joint-venture firms, but Thai companies were unable to launch their own car manufacturing concerns (Intarakumnerd, 2020; Intarakumnerd & Techakanont, 2016).

Instead, they moved away from core businesses. For example, MMC Sittipol Company, Limited (Ltd.), a partner with Mitsubishi Motors, turned to elastomer products and rubber tires (Inoue Rubber (Thailand) PLC) and lighting equipment for vehicles (Thai Stanley Electric PLC). Siam Motors Co., Ltd., a partner of Nissan Motor Co., Ltd., turned to auto parts (Siam GS Battery Co., Ltd., Yuasa Battery (Thailand) PLC), machinery (Komatsu Ltd.), musical instruments (Yamaha Thailand), motorcycle-leasing (Thitikorn PLC), and hotels and golf courses (Siam@Siam). Until now, no Thai company has been listed on the Stock Exchange of Thailand (SET) among high-tech industries.

Secondly, the International Monetary Fund (IMF) and World Bank introduced adoption of a market-led model, or so-called Washington Consensus (trade liberalization), to the economic recovery process after the 1997 Asian financial crisis. This was followed by a strong free trade agreement (FTA) trend, along with the rise of China and other developing countries such as India and Vietnam (Kenderdine, 2018; Samphantarak, 2020). When the Thai government liberalized imports and moved to a market-led model, many domestic producers found themselves unable to compete (Wailerdsak, 2008).

And many domestic and foreign producers switched from domestic to international suppliers, destroying national value chains and ushering in rapid deindustrialization. This brought on a concomitant rise of the informal sector, a decline in export sophistication, poor innovation performance, and underinvestment in social capabilities required for broad-based upgrading within, and across, sectors (Chuntongvirat, 2020; Paus, 2017).

Thai companies began to import intermediated inputs, such as machinery and equipment, electronic and optical products from China, instead of continuously trying to upgrade domestic production technology. Industrial product production remained only in certain industries relying on the following:

- Low-salaried migrant workers maintaining low-priced products such as processed foods, textiles and clothing, and jewellery.
- Domestic market monopoly power with different state concessions, including telecommunications, beer and liquor, construction, and consumer products.
- Those burgeoning with the national middle-class boom, including real estate, housing, and shopping mall development.

Thirdly, since the 2015 ASEAN Economic Community (AEC) launch, Japanese companies investing heavily in Thailand gradually moved operations to neighbouring countries paying lower wages, instead of increasing investment. Japan was behind the AEC movement because Japanese MNCs benefited most from tariff reduction and eliminating intra-regional trade in the ASEAN community. They were able to build cross-border production networks, encouraging horizontal labour divisions among ASEAN countries (Ouyyanont, 2019; Samphantarak, 2020).

The model of shifting operational bases, which Japanese companies termed "Thailand Plus One," amounted to investing in Thailand and another neighbouring country to diversify risks. It accelerated by increased minimum daily wage to 300 baht during the Yingluck Shinawatra government, ending the era of cheap labour. Further momentum was increased by the 2011 Thailand floods and the COVID-19 pandemic.

Fourthly, the state role in the national innovation system was weak and incoherent, whereas few private companies realized the importance of expenditure on research and development (R&D) (Intarakumnerd, 2020). As a result, Thailand's gross expenditure on R&D (GERD) increased slowly from 2002, when it was 0.25 percent of GDP, totalling 12 billion baht, to 2020, when it was 1.09 percent of GDP, totalling 166 billion baht. The private sector contributed 71 percent, with the remainder from the government sector (Ouyyanont, 2019). The Office of National Higher Education Science Research and Innovation Policy Council (NXPO) forecasted that by 2027, national R&D spending would reach 400 billion baht, or 2 percent of GDP. This prediction might be unrealistic, as it took over two decades to reach 1 percent of GDP. Attaining 2 percent of GDP in only six to seven years would require an unprecedented effort.

In democratic and authoritarian regimes, political leadership goals for securing power often encourage focus on short-term economic strategies designed to bring quick political returns. These might include growth strategies, emphasizing mobilization of existing production factors or clientelist arrangements designed to channel largesse to key constituencies interested in quick profits through rental or speculation (Doner et al., 2009). Developing innovation competencies through national innovation system demanding risk, time, and multiple partners may not suit politicians seeking to win political support through short-term policies.

Therefore, Thailand must escape premature deindustrialization and strive for industrial upgrades by increasing R&D expenditure to avoid the middle-income trap.

1.4.4 Services – from labour-intensive sectors to the digital economy

Depreciation of the Thai baht after the 1997 Asian financial crisis made Thai export products more competitive abroad, accelerating the deindustrialization process (Chuntongvirat, 2020). But Thailand's main export industries had already fallen into the hands of foreign companies. While exports accounted for 45 percent of GDP, few Thai companies were among the top 20 exporters, including Western Digital Storage Technologies (Thailand) Ltd. (US), Toyota Motor Thailand Co., Ltd. (Japan), AutoAlliance (Thailand) Co., Ltd. (Thai), IRPC PLC (Thai), and Samsung Electronics Co., Ltd. (South Korea).

Meanwhile, Thai companies elected to dominate small manufacturers of auto parts, electronic parts, food and agricultural products, and the tourism and service sector. The last-mentioned category boomed due to overvalued exchange rates and progressive low-cost airlines (Asian Development Bank, 2022).

Evidently, Thailand cannot escape the middle-income trap through the service sector alone. This is because the old service sector model, focusing on tourism, which accounted for over 10 percent of Thailand's GDP, was labour-intensive and based on mass/cheap products (Ouyyanont, 2019). It is unsure if and when international tourism to Thailand will returns to pre-pandemic levels of 40 million annual visits.

In the post-pandemic world, tourism is likely to be more costly due to different health and hygiene measures. The tourism sector has been repositioned in response to the new tourism demand. Thailand's competitive landscape includes medical tourism for treating treatments that are more costly elsewhere, medical retreats, and green and community-based tourism. By contrast, adventure tourism should decrease. How to retrain and reallocate unemployed tourism sector workers is an important recovery challenge (Asian Development Bank, 2022).

In the meantime, the emerging technology revolution may serve as a window of opportunity for latecomers to increase the stakes for catching up in terms of expertise. Since the 1990s, analogue technology has been replaced by digital technology in the Third Industrial Revolution, serving as a window for Korea and Taiwan (Hsiao & Hsiao, 2017). Similarly, the Fourth Industrial Revolution (4IR) can be a window for the next tier of Asian economies. ASEAN economies are seen as uniquely benefiting from double dividends: demographically, through a young population, and digitally, insofar as the young population has a high digital literacy rate.

At this stage of development, a persistent effort is needed to promote digital technologies generally and high-speed communications networks specifically, including Big Data, artificial intelligence (AI), 5G, and the Internet of Things (IoT), automation, and cloud computing extended reality to boost economic growth, build indigenous capabilities, and improve well-being.

However, some observers suggest that national innovativeness indicators must alter according to new innovation paradigms. In addition to the innovation component (the Twelfth Pillar) of the Global Competitiveness Index, composed of indicators such as capacity for innovation, company R&D spending, and university-industry R&D collaboration, further new indicators should be added.[4]

A 2019 report, *Innovation in East Asia*, edited by Koichiro Kimura, studied innovation development of leading Asian companies, including startups,[5] especially unicorns, in digital technology, IoT, and AI. New indications were introduced as follows:

- Number of startups in different fields.
- Connectivity between startups and universities, such as universities where startup founders graduated, number of incubation projects for startups (incubator) in cooperation with universities.
- Number of financial institutions and venture capital/private equity businesses investing in startups.
- Number of startups that can develop into unicorns.
- Number of coworking spaces and memberships.
- Number of companies in which universities invested through university-established holding companies.[6]

These indicators reflected the focus of innovation policies on Silicon Valley–like startup clusters, stemming from the assumption that new firms expand the technology frontier due to willingness to engage in radical innovation. By contrast, incumbent firms focus on incremental product and process innovations.

However, Thailand must increase competitiveness on a number of domestic restrictions, including the following:

- Wage rises and a super-aged society resulting in labour shortages and fiscal burden on elder care. Other developing countries such as Vietnam are entering the demographic window or sweet spot in an economy's history where a prominent portion of the population is of working age, but Thailand is entering a super-aged society (30 percent of the population aged 60 and over (Poonpolkul et al., 2022; Sasiwongsaroj & Burasit, 2019). The demographic window of Thailand closed in 2015.
- Political instability caused by socioeconomic inequality will be multiplied by a K-shaped economic recovery. Survivors will be richer, but losers even poorer (Luangaram & Sethapramote, 2018).
- Opting out of several FTAs, including the EU-Thailand FTA, Comprehensive and Progressive Agreement for Trans-Pacific Partnership (TPP11), will close export opportunities (Samphantarak, 2020).
- Increased social problems due to compressed industrialization such as mental health problems (depression, rising suicide rates), stress, and family issues (Suehiro, 2014).

There are also problems from external effects difficult to control, such as new epidemics, a trade war between the United States and China, tensions in the Pacific Ocean, global warming and climate change, air pollution in the form of particulate matter (PM) 2.5, and terrorist threats.

The question remains how Thailand will pursue new structural change. From which sectors will the GDP emerge? What adequate jobs will be created for young workers to maintain the middle-income level and continue to ascend the value chain? How should surplus low-skilled workforce, particularly those in informal sector (54.3 percent of employment, totalling about 20 million workers), be reallocated?

Only by promoting a job-rich recovery will inequalities be lessened and inclusive and a sustainable post-COVID era of growth be made possible.

Notes

1 Béla Alexander Balassa, a Hungarian economist at Johns Hopkins University and consultant for the World Bank, coined the word "newly-industrializing developing countries (NICs)," defined to include developing countries that had per capita incomes in excess of $1,100 in 1978 or 27,500 Thai baht (exchange rate 25 baht = US$1) where the manufacturing sector share in gross domestic product (GDP) was 20 percent or higher in 1979 (Balassa, 1981, 1986).

2 Technological catch-up is mostly associated with decreasing income gaps, yet economic catch-up may be driven by other factors, such as resource rents (Nolan & Lenski, 1985).

3 Product innovations may be categorized into four types according to the Henderson – Clark model of innovation in 2x2 grid form. The horizontal dimension captures the impact of innovations on components, while the vertical captures impact on linkage between components. Firstly, radical and incremental innovation are extreme points along both dimensions. Radical innovation establishes a new dominant design. Hence, a new set of core design concepts are embodied in components linked to a new architecture. Incremental innovation refines and extends established designs. Improvement occurs in individual components, but underlying core design concepts, and links between them, remain constant. Modular innovation changes product architecture but leaves components, and core design concepts that they embody, unchanged. One example is the replacement of analogue by digital telephones. Finally, architectural innovation is often triggered by change in components, whether size or other subsidiary design parameter; this creates new interactions and linkages with other components in the established product. The key point is that core design concepts behind each component and associated scientific and engineering knowledge remain identical (Apaitan et al., 2017; Henderson & Clark, 1990, pp. 2–3).

4 In the past, there was a ranking of countries owning the fastest and most supercomputers, because the ability to calculate and process millions of instructions per second reflects work efficiency in many fields. Currently, this indicator is of lesser importance.

5 In 2017, alma maters of most startup founders included National University of Singapore (NUS) at 254, followed by Nanyang Technological University (NTU Singapore) at 138, Institut Européen d'Administration des Affaires (INSEAD) at 75, Stanford University at 62, Harvard University at 22, the University of Cambridge at 21, Massachusetts Institute of Technology (MIT) at 17, and the University of Sydney at 11 (Koichiro, 2019).

6 There has been a trend for innovation universities to set up individual holding companies by separating funding and administration from universities for investing in high-tech companies. For example, holding companies might run a university science park and invest in deep technology startups (Koichiro, 2019).

References

Abramovitz, M. (1986). Catching up, forging ahead, and falling behind. *The Journal of Economic History*, *46*(2), 385–406.

Agénor, P. (2017). Caught in the middle? The economics of middle-income traps. *Journal of Economic Surveys*, *31*(3), 771–791.

Akamatsu, K. (1962). A historical pattern of economic growth in developing countries. *The Developing Economies*, *1*, 3–25.

Amsden, A. H. (1989). *Asia's next giant: South Korea and late industrialization*. Oxford University Press.

Amsden, A. H. (2001). *The rise of the rest: Challenges to the West from late-industrializing economies*. Oxford University Press.

Amsden, A. H., & Wan-wen, C. (2003). *Beyond late development: Taiwan's upgrading politics*. MIT Press.

Ang, Y. Y. (2018). Domestic flying geese: Industrial transfer and delayed policy diffusion in China. *China Quarterly*, *234*, 420–443.

Apaitan, T., Ananchotikul, N., & Disyatat, P. (2017). *Structural transformation in Thailand: A perspective through product innovation*. Discussion Paper No. 72. Puey Ungphakorn Institute for Economic Research.

Asian Development Bank. (2015). *Thailand: Industrialization and economic catch-up*. Asian Development Bank.

Asian Development Bank. (2017). *Asian development outlook 2017: Transcending the middle-income challenge*. Asian Development Bank.

Asian Development Bank. (2022). Thailand: Recharging the future of tourism. In *Southeast Asia rising from the pandemic* (Chapter 6, pp. 66–77). Asian Development Bank.

Balassa, B. (1981). Trade in manufactured goods: Patterns of change. *World Development*, *9*(3), 263–275.

Balassa, B. (1986). The employment effects of trade in manufactured products between developed and developing countries. *Journal of Policy Modeling*, *8*(3), 371–390.

Chuntongvirat, K. (2020, May 1). A study of deindustrialization and its implications on Thailand's private investment. *Focused and Quick*, *166*. Monetary Policy Group, Bank of Thailand.

Dayley, R., & Sattayanurak, A. (2016). Thailand's last peasant. *Journal of Southeast Asian Studies*, *47*(1), 42–65.

Doner, R. F., Hicken, A., & Ritchie, B. K. (2009). Political challenges of innovation in the developing world. *Review of Policy Research*, *26*(1–2), 151–171.

Foster-McGregor, N., & Verspagen, B. (2016, March). *The role of structural transformation in the potential of Asian economic growth*. ADB Economics Working Paper Series No. 479. Asian Development Bank.

Gerschenkron, A. (1962). *Economic backwardness in historical perspective: A book of essays*. The Belknap Press of Harvard University Press.

Hayter, R., & Edgington, D. W. (2004). Flying geese in Asia: The impacts of Japanese MNCs as a source of industrial learning. *Journal of Economic & Social Geography*, *95*(1), 3–26.

Hayter, R., & Edgington, D. W. (2021). Panasonic in China: A search to overcome the liability of foreignness. *Journal of Asia-Pacific Business*, *22*(1), 58–83.

Henderson, R. M., & Clark, K. B. (1990). Architectural innovation: The reconfiguration of existing product technologies and the failure of established firms. *Administrative Science Quarterly*, *35*(1), 9–30.

Hsiao, F. S. T., & Hsiao, M. W. (2017). *Economic development of emerging East Asia: Catching up of Taiwan and South Korea*. Anthem Press.

Intarakumnerd, P. (2020). Industrialization, technological upgrading, and innovation. In P. Chachavalpongpun (Ed.), *Routledge handbook of contemporary Thailand* (Chapter 17, pp. 214–225). Routledge.

Intarakumnerd, P., & Techakanont, K. (2016). Intra-industry trade, product fragmentation and technological capability development in Thai automotive industry. *Asia Pacific Business Review*, *22*(1), 65–85.

Jimenez, P., & Ricardo, J. (2019). Mainstream and evolutionary views of technology, economic growth and catching up. *Journal of Evolutionary Economics*, *29*(3), 823–852.

Kanchoochat, V. (2018). Thailand trapped: Catch-up legacies and contemporary malaise. *TRaNS: Trans-Regional and -National Studies of Southeast Asia*, *6*(2), 253–277.

Kanchoochat, V., & Intarakumnerd, P. (2014). *Tigers trapped: Tracing the middle-income trap through the East and Southeast Asian experience*. Working Paper No. 04/2014, Berlin Working Papers on Money, Finance, Trade and Development. University of Applied Science.

Kehoe, T. J., & Felipe, M. (2011). Catch-up growth followed by stagnation: Mexico, 1950–2010. *Latin American Journal of Economics*, *48*(2), 227–268.

Kenderdine, T. (2018). Death of the East Asian goose and the rise of China's geoindustrial policy. *Journal of Chinese Political Science*, *23*(3), 437–453.

Koichiro, K. (Ed.). (2019). *Higashi ajia no inobeeshon: Kigyou seijou o sasae, kigyou o umu (Innovation of East Asia: Supporting firm growth, creating entrepreneurship)*. Sakuhinsha (In Japanese).

Lee, K. (2013). *Schumpeterian analysis of economic catch-up: Knowledge, path-creation, and the middle-income trap*. Cambridge University Press.

Lee, K. (2019). *The art of economic catch-up: Barriers, detours and leapfrogging in innovation systems*. Cambridge University Press.

Lewis, A. W. (1954). Economic development with unlimited supplies of labour. *The Manchester School*, *22*(2), 139–191.

Lin, J. Y. (2011). *From flying geese to leading dragons: New opportunities and strategies for structural transformation in developing countries*. The World Bank Group.

Luangaram, P., & Sethapramote, Y. (2018). *Economic impacts of political uncertainty in Thailand*. Discussion Paper No. 86. Puey Ungphakorn Institute for Economic Research.

Nayyar, D. (2013). *Catch up: Developing countries in the world economy*. Oxford University Press.

Nayyar, D. (2020). Can catch up reduce inequality? In P. A. G. van Bergeijk & R. van der Hoeven (Eds.), *Sustainable development goals and income inequality* (Chapter 9, pp. 169–191). Edward Elgar.

Nolan, P. D., & Lenski, G. (1985). Technoeconomic heritage, patterns of development, and the advantage of backwardness. *Social Forces*, *64*(2), 341–358.

Ouyyanont, P. (2019). Thai economic growth: Retrospect and prospect. In M. J. Montesano, T. Chong, & M. Heng (Eds.), *After the coup: The National council for peace and order era and the future of Thailand* (Chapter 13, pp. 335–356). ISEAS – Yusof Ishak Institute.

Paula, L. F., & Jabbour, E. (2020). The Chinese catching-up: A developmentalist approach. *Journal of Economic Issues*, *54*(3), 855–875.

Paus, E. (2017). *Escaping the middle-income trap: Innovate or perish.* Asian Development Bank Institute Working Paper No. 685. Asian Development Bank Institute.

Paus, E. (2020). Innovation strategies matter: Latin America's middle-income trap meets China and globalization. *The Journal of Development Studies, 56*(4), 657–679.

Poonpolkul, P., Porapakkarm, P., & Wasi, N. (2022). *Aging, inadequacy and fiscal constraint: The case of Thailand.* Discussion Paper No. 182. Puey Ungphakorn Institute for Economic Research.

Rostow, W. W. (1960). *The stages of economic growth: A non-communist manifesto.* Cambridge University Press.

Rostow, W. W. (1971). *Politics and the stages of growth.* Cambridge University Press.

Samphantarak, K. (2020). Thailand's corporate sector and international trade. In P. Chachavalpongpun (Ed.), *Routledge handbook of contemporary Thailand* (Chapter 16, pp. 204–213). Routledge.

Sasiwongsaroj, K., & Burasit, Y. (2019). Features and challenges of an ageing population in Thailand. In M. J. Montesano, T. Chong, & M. Heng (Eds.), *After the coup: The National council for peace and order era and the future of Thailand* (Chapter 14, pp. 357–380). ISEAS – Yusof Ishak Institute.

Sato, Y., & Sato, H. (Eds.). (2016). *Varieties and alternatives of catching-up: Asian development in the context of the 21st century.* Palgrave Macmillan.

Schlogl, L. (2020). *Leapfrogging into the unknown: The future of structural change in the developing world.* UNU-WIDER.

Sturgeon, T. J., & Whittaker, D. H. (2019). Compressed development. In S. Ponte, G. Gereffi, & G. Raj-Reichert (Eds.), *Handbook on global value chains* (Chapter 28, pp. 452–465). Edward Elgar.

Suehiro, A. (2008). *Catch-up industrialization: The trajectory and prospects of East Asian economies.* National University of Singapore Press.

Suehiro, A. (2014). *Shinkou ajia keizai-ron: Kyacchi-appu wo koete (Newly emerging Asian economies: Beyond the catch-up industrialization approach).* Iwanami (In Japanese).

Suehiro, A., & Wailerdsak, N. (2013). Thailand: Post-developmentalist capitalism. In A. M. Witt & G. Redding (Eds.), *The Oxford handbook of Asian business system* (Chapter 13, pp. 258–280). Oxford University Press.

Vivarelli, M. (2016). The middle-income trap: A way out based on technological and structural change. *Economic Change and Restructuring, 49*, 159–193.

Wailerdsak, N. (2008). Companies in crisis. In P. Phongpaichit & C. Baker (Eds.), *Thai capital after the 1997 crisis* (Chapter 1, pp. 17–57). Silkworm Books.

Warr, P. (2008). Trade policy and the structure of incentives in Thai agriculture. *ASEAN Economic Bulletin, 25*(3), 249–270.

Whittaker, D. H., Sturgeon, T. J., Okita, T., & Zhu, T. (2020). *Compressed development: Time and timing in economic and social development.* Oxford University Press.

Zheng, Y. (2020). Globalization, industrialization and economic catch-up. *China Economist, 15*(6), 27–38.

Chapter 2

Middle-income trap

2.1 Definition of middle-income trap

Recent years have witnessed a re-emergence of interest on the part of economists and the general public in issues relating to the middle-income trap, a term often used in discussions about emerging Asian countries by international institutions and American think tanks since the 2000s[3] (Charoenporn, 2017; Suehiro, 2019). Dating back to the East Asian Miracle era in the early 1990s, several East Asian economies have provided a template for success, continuing to grow rapidly after attaining middle-income status due to export-oriented industrialization, thereby attaining per capita income levels comparable to those of advanced countries (World Bank, 1993).

Later, while Northern East Asian economies or Asian newly industrializing economies (NIEs)/four Asian tigers (relatively small countries) successfully transitioned from middle income to rich, Southeast Asian economies as well as China stagnated at middle-income levels and failed to graduate into the ranks of high-income countries (Aiyar et al., 2013). Therefore, this section examines when each country attained middle-income, followed by high-income, status and how the middle-income trap is defined. The following chapter explains strategies for overcoming the trap to becoming a high-income country.

The term middle-income trap was first used by Indermit Gill and Homi Kharas of the World Bank in *An East Asian Renaissance: Ideas for Economic Growth* (Gill & Kharas, 2007). They argued that in modern growth theory, three transformations were required for emerging (middle-income) Asian countries to continue growth:

- Transformation from diversification to more specialization in production and employment (based on economies of scale).
- Transformation from focusing on investment to innovation.
- Educational systems shifting from equipping workers with skills permitting them to adjust to new technologies to shape new products and processes.

DOI: 10.4324/9781003370536-4

These would be observable outcomes associated with a successful shift in strategy as countries progressed through middle-income status. Gill and Kharas sounded a warning that economic growth in such countries would be sluggish without steady progress through these three transformations and that emerging Asian countries would be caught in a middle-income trap, as is the current situation for many middle-income countries in Latin America and the Middle East. This was because strategies based on factor accumulation are likely to deliver steadily worse results, a natural occurrence as marginal productivity of capital declines (Gill & Kharas, 2007, 2015; Paus, 2014, 2017).

They further argued that the pattern of trade, flow of ideas and innovations, new financial architecture, and performance of cities are all consistent with East Asian economies displaying a shift toward growth founded on economies of scale. In addition, distributional consequences (a change from growth with equity to rising income inequality within countries and concerns about urban congestion and corruption) were also symptomatic of economies of scale. These drawbacks, which they termed "friction," resemble the aforementioned concept of disadvantages of backwardness (Gill & Kharas, 2007, pp. 11, 17–18).

Following the argument of Gill and Kharas, the Asian Development Bank (ADB) published a report, *Asia 2050: Realizing the Asian Century*, clearly defining the middle-income trap (Asian Development Bank, 2011, 9 box 2; and 34 box 1):

> They are caught in the Middle-Income Trap – unable to compete with low income, low wage economies in manufacturing exports and unable to compete with advanced economies in high skill innovations. Put another way, such countries cannot make a timely transition from resource driven growth, with low cost labour and capital, to productivity-driven growth.

Conventional arguments suggest that the middle-income trap means decline of economic growth in developing countries due to limitations of traditional development patterns, depending mainly on low-cost advantages such as cheap labour forces and low-cost capital, including foreign direct investment. A slowdown of economic growth was caused by a rise in real wages inconsistent with increased labour productivity and decreased investment efficiency (Khoo et al., 2017).

A middle-income country failing to boost output centring on high-value market segments and growth and increasingly relying on productivity improvements through innovation will fall into the middle-income trap. On the one hand, it cannot compete with low wages of low-income countries; on the other, it cannot compete with innovation and high-value production of high-income countries. It is trapped between the two (Zhuang et al., 2012, p. 11).

Therefore, as long as labour productivity cannot be increased by dramatic improvements in educational levels and increased worker efficiency due to better management and more technological progress, East Asian economy growth rates will decline. For this reason, the term middle-income trap used by international institutions is synonymous with limitations of "input-driven growth" (Krugman, 1994; Suehiro, 2014, p. 131).

In this report, the Asian Development Bank provided two long-term forecasts for all of Asia, constructing an optimistic scenario (the Asian Century) and a pessimistic scenario (the risk of getting caught in a middle-income trap). The optimistic scenario anticipated that by 2050, Asian gross domestic product (GDP) would reach US$148 trillion, or 51 percent, compared to Europe at 18 percent, and North America at 15 percent of global GDP. However, under the pessimistic middle-income trap scenario, Asian GDP per capita in purchasing power parity (PPP) terms would be about half (US$20,300) that under the Asian Century scenario (US$38,600). By 2050, Asian GDP would only reach US$61 trillion, or 32 percent, compared to Europe at 26 percent, and North America at 23 percent of global GDP (Asian Development Bank, 2011, p. 10 and 119).

2.2 From East Asian miracle to innovative East Asia

If the definition of middle-income trap coincides with the aforementioned, previous warnings have existed about limiting East Asian growth without using the same terminology. After the World Bank report *East Asian Miracle: Economic Growth and Public Policy* (1993) noted extraordinary annual East Asian growth rates from 7 to 13 percent, Paul Krugman, a Princeton University economist and later Nobel Prize winner, was among the first to challenge the World Bank economist assertions. Krugman's article *The Myth of Asia's Miracle* (1994) stated that previous rapid growth in East Asia definitely did not comprise a new growth model:

> It is a tautology that economic expansion represents the sum of two sources of growth. On one side are increases in "inputs": growth in employment, in the education level of workers, and in the stock of physical capital (machines, buildings, roads, and so on). On the other side are increases in the output per unit of input; such increases may result from better management or better economic policy, but in the long run are primarily due to increases in knowledge. . . . Economic growth that is based on mere increases in inputs, without an increase in the efficiency with which those inputs are used – investing in more machinery and infrastructure – must run into diminishing returns; input- driven growth is inevitably limited.
>
> (Krugman, 1994, pp. 66–67)

Krugman argued that East Asian growth, like that of the Soviet Union a half century before during a high-growth era that alarmed the West with the launch of Sputnik, was apparently driven by extraordinary growth in inputs such as labour and capital (input-driven growth) rather than efficiency gains. Sustained growth in national per capita income can only occur with a rise in output per unit of input. Only technological advances lead to continual increase in total productivity factor, with a continual rise in national income for each unit of input. But there was startingly little evidence of efficiency improvement in East Asia, except for Japan.[4] So the input-driven growth was an inherently limited process, and East Asian growth was virtually certain to slow, and the so-called miracle age would end.

Three years later, Krugman's prediction was realized. The Asian emergent economy bubble burst, leading to the 1997 Asian financial crisis, known in Thailand as the *Tom Yam Kung* crisis. Krugman's article achieved sudden renown, but analysing the real causes of the Asian currency crisis revealed a combination of international factors, including large speculative movements of short-term international funds and domestic factors such as fragile financial systems and poor corporate governance, rather than any consequence of input-driven growth, as Krugman charged (Suehiro, 2008: Chapter 4).

Nevertheless, it was true that input-driven growth became a bottleneck for East Asian economies to later overcome the middle-income trap (Felipe et al., 2017; Kabe et al., 2016). World Bank economists saw the Asian financial crisis as a turning point, considering all East Asian economic development henceforth as input-driven growth to emphasize its negative aspects. For example, Yusuf and Evenett (2002, pp. 3–4) noted in *Can East Asia Compete?*:

> Except for the low-income economies, innovation will be the engine of growth for much of East Asia now that the initial resource-intensive phase of industrialization is ending. Innovation in a broad range of areas, from products to services and business organization, will be the principal source of increases in productivity and in export competitiveness.

Yusuf and Evenett (2002) and Yusuf (2003) underlined the importance of solving these three challenges:

- Creating an environment stimulating research and development (R&D) by public and private entities forming innovative fundamentals.
- Integrating manufacturing sectors with financial and services sectors.
- Leveraging information and communications technology.

In terms of R&D, they stress creating an R&D-friendly environment such as corporate clusters of networked firms based on open competition rather than government-driven policies. Arguments presented in these reports were virtually identical as the middle-income trap argument that won popularity in the early 2010s. By then the diagnosis was over a decade old.

2.3 When was Thailand caught in the middle-income trap?

World economists have offered diverse arguments about the middle-income trap. One important issue was how to gauge if a country was stuck in the middle-income trap or has not yet reached high-income status (Ozturk, 2016). Two observations were essential:

- Classification of middle-income and high-income countries.
- Years elapsing in transition from middle-income to high-income nation status.

Three indicators were used: income thresholds/cut-offs, economic growth rate, and duration. If varying indicators differentiated slow from fast transitions, identification of adherence to the middle-income trap changed immediately (Suehiro, 2019).

From 1987 onward, World Bank income classification has been the most widely used. The World Bank classifies economies into low, lower-middle, upper-middle, and high incomes based on economy per capita gross national income (GNI) with current pricing. The World Bank updates original thresholds annually, adjusted for international inflation, average inflation of the eurozone, Japan, the United Kingdom, and the United States. According to the 2010 classification, countries were classified into four groups (Felipe et al., 2012, p. 11):

- Low income: US$1,005 or less.
- Lower-middle income: US$1,006–US$3,975.
- Upper-middle income: US$3,976–US$12,275.
- High income: US$12,276 or higher.

In 2010, the World Bank upgraded China and Thailand from lower-middle-income to upper-middle-income country status. At that time, Thailand had a per capita GNI of US$4,210 (Suehiro, 2009). To understand how long it takes an economy to move from lower-middle to upper-middle-income country status, and from upper-middle to high-income country, we must analyse long-term economic experience to reach high-income status and the time it took to do so.

Felipe et al. (2012) explored this issue with two major criteria: income range used to distinguish a middle-income country (per capita GDP in 1990 PPP dollars) and average duration in median number of stagnation years in the same category of middle-income country on the basis of past experiences; 124 countries and economies were surveyed for 61 years (1950–2010) with consistent data and divided into four groups according to per capita GDP (see Table 2.1):

- 40 low-income countries; below US$2,000;
- 38 lower-middle income countries (LM); between US$2,000 and US$7,250;
- 14 upper-middle income countries (UM); between US$7,250 and US$11,750;
- 32 high-income countries; above US$11,750.

Table 2.1 Country classification by income level comparing World Bank and Filipe et al.

(\$US, Number of year)

	GNI per capita		Classification		Number of year 1980-2010 (61 yrs)			
	2021	2010	World Bank	Felipe et al.	low income	lower middle	upper middle	high income
Hong Kong	54,450	32,434	high income	high income	-	26	7	28
Singapore	64,010	30,830	high income	high income	-	28	10	23
Taiwan	33,708	22,461	high income	high income	17	19	7	18
Japan	42,620	22,260	high income	high income	1	17	9	34
Korea	34,980	20,724	high income	high income	19	19	7	16
Malaysia	10,930	10,567	upper middle	upper middle	19	27	15	-
Thailand	7,260	9,143	upper middle	upper middle	26	28	7	-
China	11,890	8,019	upper middle	upper middle	42	17	2	-
Indonesia	4,140	4,790	lower middle	lower middle	36	25	-	-
Myanmar	1,140	3,301	low income	lower middle	54	7	-	-
Vietnam	3,560	3,262	lower middle	lower middle	52	9	-	-
Philippines	3,640	3,054	lower middle	lower middle	27	34	-	-
Cambodia	1,550	2,529	low income	lower middle	55	6	-	-
Laos	2,520	1,864	lower middle	lower middle	61	-	-	-
Mongolia	3,760	1,015	lower middle	low income	61	-	-	-

Note: Countries/economies are ranked by GNI per capita (current US\$) of 2010. In July 2021, World Bank defined high-income economies with a GNI per capita of \$12,695 or more; upper-middle-income economies with a GNI per capita between \$4,096-\$12,695; lower-middle-income economies with a GNI per capita between \$1,046-\$4,095; and low-income economies with a GNI per capita of \$1,045 or less.

Sources: Compiled by the author based onFelipe, Abdon and Kumar (2012, pp. 51-53) for 2010 and World Development Indicators for 2021 https://data.worldbank.org/indicator/NY.GNP.PCAP.CD?view=chart

As the World Bank income classification series (GNI per capita) was only available since 1987, longer data series were needed to examine traps. Therefore, Maddison's (2010) historical per capita GDP estimates for 124 countries from 1950 to 2008 were studied, extending the series to 2010 by using per capita GDP growth rates in local currency measured in constant prices from the IMF World Economic Outlook database.

Then, the threshold number of years for a country to be in the middle-income trap were calculated. To become lower-middle-income, a nation must attain an average annual per capita income growth rate of at least 4.7 percent to avoid falling into the lower-middle-income trap; a nation becoming upper-middle-income must attain an average annual per capita income growth rate of at least 3.5 percent to avoid falling into the upper-middle-income trap. Avoiding the middle-income trap is therefore a question of how to grow fast enough to cross the lower-middle-income segment within 28 years, and the upper-middle-income segment within 14 years.

Analyses indicate that in 2010, 35 of 52 middle-income countries were in the middle-income trap, while 30 of 38 lower-middle-income countries remained as such for over 28 years (lower-middle income trap). Five of 14 upper-middle-income countries remained in the same income range for over 14 years (upper-middle income trap). Eight of the remaining 17 middle-income countries (untrapped in 2010) were at the risk of falling into the trap. Of 35 countries in the middle-income trap in 2010, 13 were Latin American, 11 in the Middle East and North Africa, six in Sub-Saharan Africa, three in Asia, and two in Europe. Therefore, the phenomenon mostly affected Latin America, the Middle East, and Africa.

East Asian countries were into several groups. Firstly, five were already high-income: Hong Kong, Japan, South Korea, Singapore, and Taiwan. Five Asian economies had been low-income since 1950. Three were in the middle-income trap in 2010: Sri Lanka, Philippines, and Malaysia. The remaining eight Asian economies were middle-income, but not in lower or upper-middle-income traps. Indonesia and Pakistan were at risk of soon falling into the lower-middle-income trap. However, China and Thailand were upper-middle-income countries for only two years by then. Therefore, claims that they might be approaching the trap were premature (Chareonwongsak, 2015).

Comparing analyses between the World Bank and Felipe et al., the World Bank GNI per capita categorized Thailand as a middle-income country in 2010, similar to China (see Table 2.1). Thailand would have until 2024 or 14 median years to attain high-income status above US$12,475, without yet being entirely trapped (Chareonwongsak, 2015). However, 2018 per capita GNI was just US$6,610 and was expected to decline in 2021 due to the novel coronavirus 2019 (COVID-19) pandemic (Tangkitvanich, 2021).

Using per capita GDP in 1999 PPP as outlined by Felipe et al., Thailand would have been classified as a middle-income country by 2004, or five years faster than China, which achieved that status in 2009 (Felipe et al., 2012). This suggests that Thailand fell into the middle-income trap (Suehiro, 2009).

In addition, Thailand's per capita GNI one year before the 1997 Asian financial crisis was at middle-income country level, however briefly. But baht depreciation against the US dollar during the crisis caused Thailand's status to decline into a lower middle-income country. Using the baht as currency, Thailand's per capita GNI did not decline much. Thai upper-middle-income lifestyles began in 1996 before the Tom Yam Kung crisis rather than in 2010 or 2004, as mentioned previously. Therefore, Thailand attained upper-middle-income status over 25 years ago, more reason for it to be considered as stuck in the middle-income trap (Charoenporn, 2017; Suehiro, 2009, 2017).

Likewise, Eichengreen, Park, and Shin's *Growth Slowdown Redux: New Evidence on the Middle-income Trap* (2013) defined countries in the middle-income trap as those that had undergone average annual GDP growth of at least 3.5 percent for several years and subsequently declined by at least two percentage points during successive seven-year periods. Similar observations were shared by the IMF group (Felipe et al., 2012; Kanchoochat, 2015, p. 56).

Analysing growth slowdown correlates, they discovered that slowdowns were positively associated with high growth in earlier periods (suggestive of mean reversion), with unfavourable demographics (especially high old-age dependency ratios), with high investment ratios (as if growth fuelled by brute-force capital formation eventually became unsustainable), and with an undervalued exchange rate (as if countries with undervalued currencies had less incentive to ascend the technological ladder from unskilled-labour-intensive, low-value-added sectors and therefore making rapid growth more difficult to sustain). They also found that slowdowns were less likely in countries where the population had a relatively high level of secondary and tertiary education and where high-technology products accounted for a relatively large share of export (Eichengreen et al., 2013, pp. 2–3).

As a result, to escape from the middle-income trap, nations should not adhere to past successes which apparently no longer work, such as exporting low value-added products, mobilizing cheap labour (including foreign workers), and depending on foreign direct investment as main engines to drive export sectors. By contrast, nations should find new strength and competitive advantage, such as increasing human capital potential and innovation capabilities needed to stay competitive (Chareonwongsak, 2015; Harrison et al., 2018). Strategies to overcome the middle-income trap will be discussed in the next chapter.

2.4 Catching-up problems

2.4.1 Pursuing technological innovation

The MIT problem is not solely of academic interest; MIT implies income stagnation for 70 percent of the world's population, most of whom are currently living in middle-income countries. Such growth stagnation has major human and global consequences. Understanding correlates of successful middle-income growth helps indicate future approaches for developing policy framework (Bulman et al., 2017, p. 7).

We may divide into two groups the definitional debate about the trap, involving the question of when each country is forced into an MIT trap. One group sees the trap as growth slowdown or weak growth disease from experiencing high growth rates to recession (see Eichengreen et al., 2013; Felipe et al., 2012). Another focuses more on catching-up problems that make middle-income countries unable to pursue technological innovation and advanced developed country status (e.g., Paus, 2014, 2017; Ohno et al., 2017). This chapter embraces the latter definition.

The World Bank and other researchers are scrutinizing China to see whether it will be trapped or escape the MIT. The Asian Development Bank first addressed this issue in a report, *Growing beyond the Low-cost Advantage: How the People's Republic of China can Avoid the Middle-income Trap* (Zhuang et al., 2012). It offered detailed analysis and warnings that while China adhered to a growth model dependent on low-cost advantages, China's economic prosperity era would end. They suggested a path for China to take to emerge from upper-middle-income to high-income-nation status by combining four elements (Zhuang et al., 2012, p. 11):

- Technically advanced domestic firms.
- High-value goods and services.
- Developed markets.
- Innovation in products and processes.

That year, the World Bank raised the same issue in a report, *China 2030: Building a Modern, Harmonious, and Creative High-income Society* (World Bank, 2013). It underlined the difficulty of shifting from middle-income to high-income nation status. Indeed, of 101 middle-income countries or economies designated in 1960, only 13 of them reached high-income status by 2008: Equatorial Guinea, Greece, Hong Kong, Ireland, Israel, Japan, South Korea, Mauritius, Puerto Rico, Portugal, Singapore, Spain, and Taiwan (Zhuang et al., 2012, p. 12). Four of these (Hong Kong, South Korea, Singapore, and Taiwan) belong to the so-called Asian newly industrialized economies (NIEs) (Suehiro, 2008, 2019).

ADB identified seven risks and problems for the Chinese economy (Zhuang et al., 2012):

- Labour productivity gaps compared to advanced countries.
- Labour market changes and rapid wage hikes.
- A growth pattern relying excessively on public investment (high savings) and exports.
- Widening domestic income inequality.

- Exploitation of natural resources and environmental degradation.
- International backlash against the growth in Chinese presence in the world economy.
- Institutional weakness for supporting long-term growth.

These approximately overlap factors outlined in China 2030. The measures most stressed by the World Bank included productivity improvement through innovation and upgrading industrial structure. The report also proposed adopting three strategies:

- Inclusive growth to reduce income inequality.
- Shifting from a growth path overly reliant on industrial goods investment and export to one based on increasing domestic demand and developing the service sector.
- Environmentally friendly (green) growth, conserving resources, and protecting the environment.

China's transition to high-income status is not necessarily as smooth as its government had foreseen. The state-led policy of developing science and technology was insufficient as a sole measure. Notably, a contentious institutional issue remains over whether China must transition to a Western-style political system or some form of democracy to avoid the MIT. If so, political measures will be necessary to eradicate many social economic problems, including corruption, income disparity, and monopoly. These in turn may affect conflicts of interest among elite classes under the socialist system. In the future, China will be challenged by democratic movements accompanying economic growth (Huang et al., 2017; Zhou & Hu, 2021).

In addition, Felipe et al. (2012) pointed out that a product trap causes countries to remain lastingly in the MIT, insofar as not all products have the same consequences for growth. For example, countries in the lower-middle-income trap export a significant share of products that are unsophisticated and not especially well-connected to other products. Countries in the upper-middle-income trap are better positioned, but nevertheless, the share of well-connected products in their overall export basket is limited.

Another explanation for what happens to some middle-income countries is that they never fully industrialized the way most developed countries did, due to less sophistication, diversification, and product connectedness; later, they may undergo early deindustrialization (see next section), with downward shifts of manufacturing value added (MVA) and employment share in gross domestic product (GDP) and total employment, respectively, with increased service share.

2.4.2 Premature deindustrialization[5]

Premature deindustrialization refers to the recent trend in developing countries to become more dependent on services without a full industrialization experience (Felipe et al., 2017; Fujimoto & Whittaker, 2021). According to Rodrik (2016, 2018), while deindustrialization in advanced economies, especially real output, derives from continuous improvement of manufacturing efficiency, premature deindustrialization of middle- and low-income countries may stem from premature manufacturing productivity growth stagnation. Rodrik believes that the manufacturing sector is characterized by rapid technological advancement and unconditional labour productivity convergence as a major employer of unskilled labour and a tradable sector. Due to these characteristics, manufacturing has become a perfect ladder structure for developing economies to catch up with advanced economies. Therefore, premature deindustrialization is akin to blocking a major avenue of rapid growth.

Declining MVA and manufacturing employment share in many developing countries was not caused by changes in sector development potential but instead resulted from globalization, automation (less labour-intensive production), and shifts in manufacturing activities to a relatively small number of populous countries (for example, China, Vietnam, and Indonesia). This resulted in a concentration of manufacturing activities in specific developing countries. Although some service businesses, such as information technology and finance, may play a role similar to those in industrial economies, they require highly skilled workers and cannot absorb unskilled or low-skilled labour like the manufacturing sector (Huang et al., 2018).

Baumol et al. (1989) argued that deindustrialization is a consequence of the differential in labour productivity between manufacturing and services. For developed countries, deindustrialization is the product of successful economic development. This poses a problem for developing countries because, according to Baumol, economies arrive at a situation of "asymptotic stagnancy,"[6] where long-run growth is essentially determined by service sector productivity growth lower than in manufacturing. If some middle-income countries prematurely enter this lower growth phase, it becomes necessary to implement policies to reverse it (Felipe et al., 2012, p. 43).

That is, nations must turn back to refocus on manufacturing industries by striving to produce complex, diverse, and connected export products and use firm capabilities to leap forward to growth, instead of reducing the prominence of manufacturing industries and fleeing to the service sector, thereby increasing entrapment.

This concurs with Haraguchi et al. (2017), who explain that if middle-income countries seek to move towards high-income status, they should develop manufacturing industries creating higher value-added, better labour absorption, and take fuller advantage of backwardness.

In the case of Thailand, bypassing the technical debate over when Thailand fell into the MIT, policymakers realized that the Thai economy has approached its growth limit under low-cost advantages. Both the Bank of Thailand (BOT) and the National Economic and Social Development Council have discussed the matter and consider the deterioration of Thailand's competitiveness since 2011 as a serious problem (Charoenporn, 2017; Jitsuchon, 2012).

Thai businesspeople have also attempted to develop high-technology industrial products for export by joint ventures with multinational corporations in the automobile, auto parts, electronic product, petrochemical and chemical product, and home appliance sectors. Thailand could become an upper-middle-income country for a short period of time in 1996 (Suehiro, 2009; Wailerdsak & Siengthai, 2016).

But after confronting the 1997 Asian financial crisis, Thai entrepreneurs turned to export agricultural and low-value-added industrial products rather than attempt to continuously upgrade high-technology products as in the past. In addition, by taking advantage of baht depreciation after the crisis, relatively low wages, and cheap foreign labour, manufacturing has tended to concentrate on a relatively narrow range of subsector industries and activities. These have grown spectacularly through global value chain engagement but often without depth or inter-industrial links created by earlier developers over time (Suehiro, 2009; Virakul et al., 2021; Wailerdsak & Siengthai, 2016).

In addition, over the past two decades, the tourism sector saw unprecedented growth, accounting for 10 percent of GDP. However, tourism-related sectors still rely heavily on the attractiveness of national nature destinations, inducing relatively low tourist spending and therefore contributing minimally to GDP. From the labour market perspective, the sector mainly employs low-skilled labour, and therefore wages offered are still far below those in the manufacturing sector (Makohin et al., 2020). In short, the growing services sector in Thailand has not contributed sufficiently to overall growth to offset potential decline in the manufacturing sector. This is because traditional, relatively low value-add services remain in the majority (Sakwit, 2020).

After the 1997 Asian financial crisis, Thai investors withdrew from the manufacturing sector, especially for high-value-added industrial products. This was not because economic development was successful compared to the situation for developed countries, but it was easier to create jobs and gain income in service sectors. This caused Thailand to enter asymptotic stagnancy, according to Baulmol et al., in which the economic growth rate deteriorated prematurely.

Some Thai observers misread premature deindustrialization as a positive phenomenon, implying that Thailand is following the same path as developed countries. But they might consider that the economy began to deindustrialize while labour productivity remained low, and the nation had already entered aging society status. As long as such underlying fragility remains addressed, the deindustrialization process is liable to be unhealthy. To sustain longer-term economic growth, the government must prioritize structural policies in two main areas: undertaking infrastructure investment in strategic manufacturing and revisiting competition policies to encourage firms to innovate and invest in technology (Chuntongvirat, 2020; Virakul et al., 2021).

2.5 Comparing China, Malaysia, and Thailand

In this section, the strategies of escaping the MIT of three countries (Malaysia, China, and Thailand) are compared, or more precisely, their growth pattern strategies to transcend low-cost advantages.

For several decades, Malaysia has witnessed strong economic growth, becoming among Asia's newly industrialized countries. Per capita GDP grew annually by an average of 2.8 percent from 1970 to 2010, reaching US$10,830 per capita in 2005 purchasing power parity (PPP) terms. By World Bank standards, Malaysia transitioned to an upper-middle-income country in 1979. It subsequently dropped back to lower-middle-income status, regaining upper-middle-income status in 1991 (Lee, 2017; Yusuf & Nabeshima, 2009). But until now it has been unable to join the group of high-income countries.

Over the past four decades, Malaysia has clearly remained at an MIT standstill compared to Taiwan, which took 15 years to transition to a high-income country after becoming an upper-middle-income country in 1973, and South Korea, which took 16 years to transition to a high-income country after becoming an upper-middle-income country in 1978 (Suehiro, 2014, p. 128).

Nevertheless, Malaysia diversified its export base and substantially increased export sophistication. High growth increased living standards. Human development indicators improved significantly, average years of schooling increased, and infant mortality decreased while life expectancy was augmented. Despite overall good performance, crucial questions remain whether Malaysia can attain high-income status and which policies it should implement for success (Cherif & Hasanov, 2015; Yusuf & Nabeshima, 2009).

Cherif and Hasanov (2015) suggest that Malaysia relied substantially on electric and electronic goods as export products, accounting for 70 percent of manufactured exports and over 50 percent of total exports by the end of the 1990s. Malaysia's exports comprised those similar to other Asian countries, with severe competition from China, but little progress was made towards diversification. Instead, Malaysia relied on multinational corporations and foreign direct investment for technological transfer. Despite persistent attempts to increase local content and export upgrading, tangible results remained limited. Technology creation and diffusion did not occur to any hoped-for extent, and industry linkages and agglomeration were not widespread. More importantly, human resource training to develop new technologies and products did not occur (Lee, 2017).

After Seagate, the world's leading manufacturer and exporter of hard disk drives, closed its Malaysian plants in 2000, Intel, Motorola, and Dell either shrunk their operations or closed their factories there in 2001, shifting production bases to China (Yusuf, 2003, p. 294). The Malaysian economic growth rate began to falter. The most serious issue for Malaysia was the high proportion of manufacturing sector migrant workers, mostly from Indonesia, Bangladesh, and Nepal, in decreasing order of significance (Yusuf & Nabeshima, 2009).

By contrast, China and Thailand joined the group of upper-middle-income countries in 2010, although only for 15 years. Any direct comparison to Malaysia might be misleading due to challenges facing individual nations as well as Indonesia, itself about to become an upper-middle-income country. Instead, it is essential to clarify the policies necessary for transitioning into high-income-nation status (Lee, 2017).

Meanwhile, in 2007 and 2008 India and Vietnam both escaped low-income statuses, respectively, so can no longer be discussed in the same terms as China and Thailand. This is because India and Vietnam must identify policies needed for future transition into upper-middle income, rather than a high-income, country. Some Thai commentators are concerned that Vietnam's economy might overtake Thailand's two to three decades from now.[7]

If comparing to Latin American national trends, after previously being a high-income country, Argentina dropped back to upper-middle-income status in 1968. Brazil and Mexico are both termed middle-income countries, fluctuating between upper and lower middle-income levels (Krasilshchikov, 2022). Such vacillation was not uncommon in Asia, apart from Malaysia.

It is clearly ill-advised for international institutions to group emerging Asian countries as middle-income nations despite differing per capita income levels and assert that they are all caught in comparable traps. Instead, concealed problems in growth patterns common to these countries should be evaluated, especially growth limitation issues grounded in the low-cost advantage.

In addition, according to Kanchoochat and Intarakumnerd (2014) and Kanchoochat (2015), patterns of avoiding the MIT trap are classified into three major groups by concentrating on the "role of the state":

- Group A countries: getting education and institutions right.
- Group B countries: changing export composition by following comparative advantage.
- Group C countries: industrial upgrading by the proactive state.

Firstly, they note that some cross-country studies find relationships between education and economic growth to be weak or even irrelevant. That is probably due to past equalizing experiences of Asian NIEs. Governments prioritized education, producing high-quality workers manufacturing exports with advanced technology and innovation, resulting in higher economic growth rates.

However, a literature review demonstrates that human capital increases resulting from improvements in workforce educational attainment have not positively affected economic growth or the rate of individual worker output growth. Although a positive correlation between education and economic growth is palpable, any causal relationship is likely to run in the opposite direction: in fact, economic growth leads to higher educational quality and quantity. Therefore, the time-honoured belief that education is a key factor in economic growth is insufficiently documented (Maitrarat et al., 2021).

To contribute substantially to economic growth, educational policy must be tailored to support national development strategy to build a workforce to meet market needs, rather than simply increasing literacy rates, average years of schooling, or even gross tertiary enrolment. This includes upgrading existing industrial workforce abilities through learning by doing and on-the-job training in addition to improving formal training provided by educational institutions.

Thailand has experienced a labour market supply and demand mismatch (Suehiro, 2009). While the private sector requires high-skilled workers, they cannot be found in the market. University graduates with bachelor's degrees are widely unemployed. Many industries have tried to resolve this issue by improving cross-industry collaborations, educational institutions, and governmental partnerships through job shadowing, apprenticeships programs, and curriculum design with employers as well as technical and vocational training programs (Maitrarat et al., 2021; Tangkitvanich, 2021).

Differences among the three groups result from different roles played by governments in instituting innovative measures. Group C is characterized by the most active governmental role in innovation and industrial upgrading, while group A reflects minimal state participation in industrial promotion; instead, the state is expected to facilitate infrastructure as an educational system to promote innovation. Group B maintains a position between groups A and C, wherein private firm efforts (supply side) and world market (demand side) conditions predominate. A shift to higher-value-added exports is realized through market mechanisms, rather than state intervention (Kanchoochat, 2015, pp. 56–57).

China is intended to represent group C, while Malaysia and Thailand belong to group B. Indeed, the Malaysian and Thai governments have constantly intended to play significant roles in industrial upgrading and export composition change. But multinational corporations (MNCs) invested in the two nations to develop new industries and products, eventually introduced by foreign companies. In addition, local private companies apparently discovered competitive advantages in resource-based industries and the service sector, rather than core manufacturing industries. They have also visibly focused on niche products and markets rather than new products and production technology (Suehiro, 2017; Zhou & Hu, 2021).

To compare the two nations in terms of governmental role in formulating national economic plans, Malaysia follows the group C approach. Its government was empowered to supervise the private sector under the administrations of Prime Minister Mahathir from 1981 to 2003 and again from 2018 to 2020. Conversely, in Thailand from 2001 to 2005, the Thaksin administration empowered the government to support targeted industries through tax incentives and semi-government institutions (*sathaban*).[8]

After the military coup d'état of 2006, the Thai government's role necessarily declined. However, as will be discussed later, since 2014, the Prayut Chan-ocha government has attempted to restore state leadership in economic development by proposing an ambitious national Thailand 4.0 strategy. In this sense, Thailand revealed a shift from group C to group B, before returning to group C more recently (Suehiro, 2017). However, the role of Thai private companies, including state-owned enterprises, in the global market may not rival those of China.

Notes

1 The geographical notion of East Asia is defined diversely, referred to as the Far East, Northeast Asia for Japan and Asian NIEs (including Hong Kong, South Korea, Taiwan, and Singapore) and Southeast Asia (Malaysia, Indonesia, the Philippines, and Thailand). Here the notion of East Asia signifies the eastern part of Asia, including Northern and Southeast Asia (Kumagai, 2019).
2 The analytical focus is on manufacturing rather than industry. In addition to manufacturing, the latter definition encompasses mining and construction insofar as most deindustrialization debate has been about loss of manufacturing jobs. Mining is significant only to a small number of advanced economies, and employment in the construction sector is volatile, causing difficulties in making international industrial sector comparisons.
3 Pioneer literature includes the World Bank (Yusuf & Evenett, 2002; Gill & Kharas, 2007), International Monetary Fund (Aiyar et al., 2013), Asian Development Bank (Zhuang et al., 2012), the National Bureau of Economic Research (Eichengreen et al., 2013), and the Levy Economics Institute of Bard College (Felipe et al., 2012).
4 Krugman mentioned that Japan, unlike the East Asian tigers, apparently grew through high rates of input and efficiency growth. Today's fast-growth economies were nowhere near convergent on US efficiency levels, but Japan was staging an unmistakable technological catch-up. In addition, Japan's experience had much less in common with other Asian nations than is generally imagined (Krugman, 1994, pp. 73, 75).
5 In most advanced economies, the manufacturing employment share has declined continuously for over two decades, a phenomenon referred to as deindustrialization. Early contributions in this area by Baumol (1967) and Fuchs (1968) were later expanded more systematically by Rowthorn and Wells (1987) and Baumol et al. (1989), arguing that advanced economy deindustrialization may be the desirable natural consequence of industrial dynamism displayed by economies.
6 Published research indicates that service sector productivity is currently lower than in the manufacturing sector, including the challenge posed by Baumol growth disease to service economies. See more in Rowthorn and Ramaswamy (1999), Fernandez and Palazuelos (2012) for the European Union (EU), Oh and Kim (2015) for South Korea, and Coricelli and Ravasan (2017) for China.
7 In 2019, Thailand's economy was valued at 16.4 trillion baht, ranking 22nd in the world. Its population earned an average annual income of 236,000 baht, ranked 82nd internationally. Vietnam's economy was worth 7.9 trillion baht, ranked 44th in the world. Its population earned an average annual income of 82,000 baht, 135th in the world. Thailand is a middle-income country, but Vietnam is a lower middle income one. In brief, Thailand's economy generates twice the GDP and three times the per capita average income than Vietnam's. Thailand's annual growth rate is about 3 percent, while Vietnam's is 6 percent, suggesting that it will take Vietnam 24 years to overtake Thailand.
8 Not until the Thaksin government (2006) were explicit vertical industrial policies tailored to specific sectors first deployed. The government targeted five sectors: food,

automotive, fashion, software, and tourism. Clear corresponding visions were attributed to them: Kitchen of the World, Detroit of Asia, Asia Tropical Fashion, World Graphic Design and Animation Centre, and Asia Tourism Capital. Eligible firms in these sectors were value chain suppliers as well as final product makers. In addition, special Board of Investment–initiated investment packages promoted science, technology, and innovation (STI). Nonetheless, the Thaksin government largely failed to create consistency and continuity for those policies or establish mechanisms to enforce, monitor, and evaluate their outcomes (Kanchoochat & Intrakumnerd, 2014).

References

Aiyar, S., Duval, R., Puy, D., Yiqun, W., & Zhang, L. (2013, March). *Growth slowdowns and the middle-income trap.* IMF Working Paper No. 13/71. International Monetary Fund.

Asian Development Bank. (2011). *Asia 2050: Realizing the Asian century.* Asian Development Bank.

Baumol, W. J. (1967). Macroeconomics of unbalanced growth: The anatomy of urban crisis. *The American Economic Review*, *57*(3), 415–426.

Baumol, W. J., Blackman, S., & Wolff, E. N. (1989). *Productivity and American leadership: The long view.* The MIT Press.

Bulman, D., Eden, M., & Hguyen, H. (2017). Transitioning from low-income growth to high- income growth: Is there a middle-income trap? *Journal of the Asia Pacific Economy*, *22*(1), 5–28.

Chareonwongsak, K. (2015). Ookaad lae uppasak khong thai naikanpen prathed thii mii settakit raidaisoong (Opportunities and obstacles of Thailand to become a high-income economy). *Academic Journal of Burirum Rajabhat University*, *7*(1), 1–23 (In Thai).

Charoenporn, P. (2017). *Seminar on Thailand and overcoming the middle-income trap.* At Faculty of Economics, Thammasat University, on October 10 (In Thai).

Cherif, R., & Hasanov, F. (2015). *The leap of the tiger: How Malaysia can escape the middle- income trap.* IMF Working Paper No. 15/131. International Monetary Fund.

Chuntongvirat, K. (2020, May 1). A study of deindustrialization and its implications on Thailand's private investment. *Focused and Quick*, *166*. Monetary Policy Group, Bank of Thailand.

Coricelli, F., & Ravasan, F. R. (2017). *Structural change and the China syndrome: Baumol vs trade effects.* CEPR Discussion Paper No. DP12069. Centre for Economic Policy Research.

Eichengreen, B., Park, D., & Shin, K. (2013). Growth slowdowns redux: New evidence on the middle-income trap. *Japan and the World Economy*, *32*, 65–84.

Felipe, J., Abdon, A., & Kumar, U. (2012, April). *Tracking the middle-income trap: What is it, who is in it, and why?* Working Paper No. 715. Levy Economics Institute of Bard College.

Felipe, J., Kumar, U., & Galope, R. (2017). Middle-income transitions: Trap or myth? *Journal of the Asia Pacific Economy*, *22*(3), 429–453.

Fernandez, R., & Palazuelos, E. (2012). European Union economies facing Baumol's disease within the service sector. *Journal of Common Market Studies*, *50*(2), 231–249.

Fuchs, V. R. (1968). *The service economy.* National Bureau of Economic Research.

Fujimoto, K., & Whittaker, H. (2021). *Premature deindustrialization, inter-sectoral shifts, and accelerated servicization*. Working Paper No. 530. Centre for Business Research, University of Cambridge.

Gill, I., & Kharas, H. (2007). *An East Asian renaissance: Ideas for economic growth*. The World Bank Group.

Gill, I., & Kharas, H. (2015). *The middle-income trap turns ten*. World Bank Policy Research Working Paper No. 7403. The World Bank Group.

Haraguchi, N., Cheng, C. F. C., & Smeets, E. (2017). The importance of manufacturing in economic development: Has this changed? *World Development, 93*, 293–315.

Harrison, R., Scheela, W., Lai, J., & Vivekarajah, S. (2018). Beyond institutional voids and the middle income trap: The emerging business angel market in Malaysia. *Asia Pacific Journal of Management, 35*(4), 965–991.

Huang, B., Morgan, P. J., & Yoshino, N. (Eds.). (2018). *Avoiding the middle-income trap in Asia: The role of trade, manufacturing, and finance*. Asian Development Bank Institute.

Huang, Q., Liu, G., He, J., Jiang, F., & Huang, Y. (2017, June). *The middle-income trap and the manufacturing transformation of the People's Republic of China (PRC): Asian experience and the PRC's industrial policy orientation*. ADBI Working Paper No. 752. Asian Development Bank Institute.

Jitsuchon, S. (2012). Thailand in a middle-income trap. *TDRI Quarterly Review, 27*(2), 13–20.

Kabe, S., Ushiyama, R., Kinkyo, T., & Hamori, S. (2016). *Moving up the ladder: Development challenges for low and middle-income Asia*. World Scientific Publishing.

Kanchoochat, V. (2015). The middle-income trap and East Asian miracle lessons. In A. Calcagno et al. (Eds.), *Rethinking development strategies after the financial crisis, Vol. 1: Making the case for policy space* (pp. 55–66). United Nations.

Kanchoochat, V., & Intarakumnerd, P. (2014). *Tigers trapped: Tracing the middle-income trap through the East and Southeast Asian experience*. Working Paper No. 04/2014, Berlin Working Papers on Money, Finance, Trade and Development. University of Applied Science.

Khoo, B. T., Tsunekawa, K., & Kawano, M. (Eds.). (2017). *Southeast Asia beyond crises and traps: Economic growth and upgrading*. Palgrave Macmillan.

Krasilshchikov, V. (2022). *Brazil – Emerging forever?: A case study of middle-level development trap*. Springer.

Krugman, P. (1994). The myth of Asia's miracle. *Foreign Affairs, 73*(6), 62–78.

Kumagai, S. (2019). The middle-income trap in the ASEAN-4 countries from the trade structure viewpoint. In K. Tsunekawa & Y. Todo (Eds.), *Emerging states at crossroads* (Chapter 3, pp. 49–70). Springer.

Lee, H. (2017). Malaysia's transformations: High income, middle capability. In B. Khoo, K. Tsunekawa, & M. Kawano (Eds.), *Southeast Asia beyond crisis and traps: Economic growth and upgrading* (Chapter 5, pp. 131–166). Palgrave Macmillan.

Maddison, A. (2010). *Statistics on world population, GDP and per capita GDP, 1–2008 AD*. Online. www.ggdc.net/maddison/oriindex.htm

Maitrarat, P. K., Openshaw, R., & Walshaw, M. (2021). *The history of higher education in Thailand: Confronting challenges*. Palgrave Macmillan.

Makohin, Z., Atamanchuk, Z., & Mitiushkina, K. (2020). The role of tourism in escaping the middle-income trap. *Management Theory and Studies for Rural Business and Infrastructure Development, 42*(3), 295–302.

Oh, W., & Kim, K. (2015). Baumol effect and the Korean economy. *Emerging Markets Finance and Trade*, *51*(S1), 214–223.

Ohno, K., Ohno, I., & Intarakumnerd, P. (2017). *Mismanaging innovation systems in Thailand and the middle-income trap*. Routledge.

Ozturk, A. (2016). Examining the economic growth and the middle-income trap from the perspective of the middle class. *International Business Review*, *25*(3), 726–738.

Paus, E. (2014). *Latin America and the middle-income trap*. Financing for Development Series, No. 250. The Economic Commission for Latin America and the Caribbean (ECLAC).

Paus, E. (2017). *Escaping the middle-income trap: Innovate or perish*. ADBI Working Paper 685. Asian Development Bank Institute.

Rodrik, D. (2016). Premature deindustrialization. *Journal of Economic Growth*, *21*(1), 1–33.

Rodrik, D. (2018). *New technologies, global value chains, and developing economies*. NBER Working Paper No. 25164. National Bureau of Economic Research.

Rowthorn, R. E., & Ramaswamy, R. (1999). Growth, trade, and deindustrialization. *IMF Economic Review*, *46*, 18–41.

Rowthorn, R. E., & Wells, J. R. (1987). *De-industrialization and foreign trade*. Cambridge University Press.

Sakwit, K. (2020). *Globalisation, tourism and simulacra A Baudrillardian study of tourist space in Thailand*. Routledge.

Suehiro, A. (2008). *Catch-up industrialization: The trajectory and prospects of East Asian economies*. National University of Singapore Press.

Suehiro, A. (2009). *Tai: Chushinkoku no mosaku (Thailand: Challenge of a middle income country)*. Iwanami Publisher (In Japanese).

Suehiro, A. (2014). *Shinkou ajia keizai-ron: Kyacchi-appu wo koete (Newly emerging Asian economies: Beyond the catch-up industrialization approach)*. Iwanami (In Japanese).

Suehiro, A. (2017). New growth strategies of Thailand's big firms in the ASEAN economic community era. In B. Khoo, K. Tsunekawa, & M. Kawano (Eds.), *Southeast Asia beyond crisis and traps: Economic growth and upgrading* (Chapter 2, pp. 35–69). Palgrave Macmillan.

Suehiro, A. (2019). Responses to the middle-income trap in China, Malaysia, and Thailand. In K. Tsunekawa & Y. Todo (Eds.), *Emerging states at crossroads* (Chapter 2, pp. 27–47). Springer.

Tangkitvanich, S. (2021, November 10). Thailand needs a new growth pathway. *Bangkok Post.*

Virakul, C. V., et al. (2021). *Thailand labour market restructuring*. Bank of Thailand (In Thai).

Wailerdsak, N., & Siengthai, S. (2016). Business network in Thailand: From import substitution, export oriented to expansion in AEC. In J. Nolan, C. Rowley, & M. Warner (Eds.), *Business networks in East Asian capitalisms: Enduring trends, emerging patterns* (Chapter 10, pp. 211–233). Chandos Publishing, Elsevier.

World Bank. (1993). *The East Asian miracle: Economic growth and public policy*. Oxford University Press.

World Bank. (2013). *China 2030: Building a modern, harmonious, and creative high-income society*. The World Bank Group.

Yusuf, S. (Ed.). (2003). *Innovative East Asia: The future of growth.* The World Bank Group.

Yusuf, S., & Evenett, S. J. (2002). *Can East Asia compete? Innovation for global markets.* The World Bank Group.

Yusuf, S., & Nabeshima, K. (2009). *Tiger economies under threat: A comparative analysis of Malaysia's industrial prospects and policy options.* The World Bank Group.

Zhou, S., & Hu, A. (2021). *China: Surpassing the middle-income trap.* Palgrave McMillan.

Zhuang, J., Vandenberg, P., & Huang, Y. (2012). *Growing beyond the low-cost advantage: How the People's Republic of China can avoid the middle-income trap.* Asian Development Bank.

Chapter 3

Developmental states and business groups

3.1 Developmental state political economy

3.1.1 Developmental states

After World War II, most latecomer countries set economic development as a national goal in line with US foreign policy urging developing countries to advance to oppose communism as a challenge to liberal democracy. To foster high national growth rates, neoclassical economists created prevailing theoretical assumptions about market-led strategies, opposing government intervention or state-led strategies (Paus, 2017).

However, in the 1970s and 1980s, Japan and newly industrializing economies (NIEs) such as South Korea, Taiwan, and Singapore attained high growth, matching the pace of developed nations (Amsden, 1989, 2001; Johnson, 1982, 1996; Wade, 1990, 2018). They adopted developmental theory akin to Gerschenkron's (1962) analysis of late development in Germany. Government officials directed lending to industries considered of strategic importance to boost the nation on the development ladder through export-oriented industrialization (Evans, 1995).

National governments were categorized as either "strong" or "weak," with strong states in France and Japan considered models of success, while Britain's weak state was regarded as a laggard (Carney & Witt, 2010). Developmental states actively intervened in market activities, particularly in drafting and executing industrial policies as well as promoting reverse engineering, selective tariff protectionism, devalued and favourable exchange rates, joint ventures for foreign technology transfers, and scale gains so that nascent companies could find favourable export conditions (Haggard, 2018).

By contrast, Latin America, which also attempted to match developed countries, remained fixed in middle-income traps. Latin American researchers explained that developmental states in Latin America and Southeast Asia (except Singapore and India) historically became, at least partially, predatory states (Evans, 1989, 1995; Reno, 2014).

DOI: 10.4324/9781003370536-5

Despite imitating Northeast Asia by adopting industrial policies and focusing on import-substitution industrialization (ISI) and protectionism, typically this form of state features a high concentration of economic benefits for a relatively small group whose members are usually intimately connected to top political leaders by family or kinship ties. With politics predominantly used as an instrument for self-enrichment, corruption and political favouritism are common (Carney & Witt, 2010).

Later in the 2000s, Latin American researchers proposed the concept of "new developmentalism" in response to the inability of classical developmentalism and post-Keynesian macroeconomics to lead middle-income countries to resume growth. New developmentalism sees the state as an economic actor that, besides guaranteeing private property and contracts, should coordinate noncompetitive industries and five macroeconomic rates (interest, exchange, profit, wages, and inflation) and two major macroeconomic accounts: fiscal and current, which the market is unable to regulate (Bresser-Pereira, 2020; Tijerina, 2020).

In addition to the state role in economic development, political economists also investigated the nexus between the state and business groups (Carney et al., 2020; Hamilton-Hart & Wai-chung Yeung, 2021). They collaborate effectively for national advancement with some degree of inclusive politics (Weberian bureaucracies and bureaucracy's embedded autonomy from political pressure). These help spearhead nationwide development (Doner & Schneider, 2016; Evans, 1995). But if the state promotes only private entrenched interests of dominant groups (such as politicians, the armed forces, bureaucrats, or influential private groups) with strong lobbying powers, it may impede the next step of economic growth (Morck & Yeung, 2004; Suehiro & Wailerdsak, 2013). This leads to fixture in the middle-income trap and social conflicts over inequality.

The next section identifies private companies of latecomer countries and analyses controversies over domestic business groups, monopolies, and concentrated ownership and control.

3.1.2 Business group tripod structure theory

There are two types of private companies in developed countries:

1) Large, globally influential corporations or big business with monopoly power over manufacturing technology, services, markets, and brands. These global companies or multinational corporations (MNC) own subsidiaries in many countries internationally.
2) Small- and medium-sized enterprises (SMEs), including emerging startups.

However, private companies in latecomer countries consist of three types: domestic, state, and foreign, or the so-called tripod structure of business

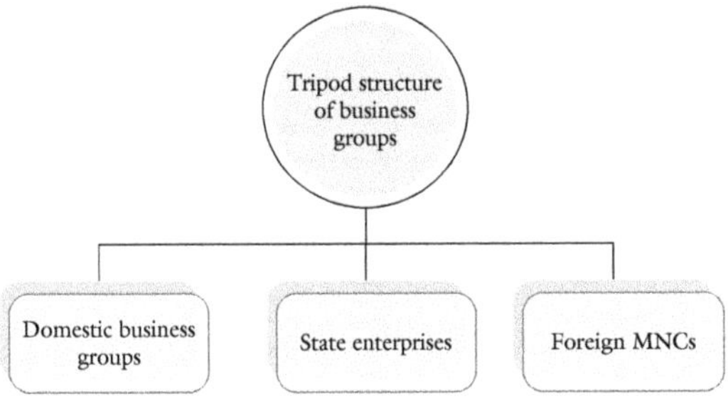

Figure 3.1 Tripod structure of business groups

Source: Compiled by the author based on Suehiro (1992)

groups (see Figure 3.1). They constitute individual legs of a three-legged chair underpinning economic development.[2]

In the first case, developmental states effectively deploy domestic business groups as industrialization vehicles (Amsden, 1989, 2001; Carney et al., 2018; Leff, 1978). Some research believed that FBGs achieve stronger resilience both during and after an economic crisis, compared with non-family businesses. They resist the downturn better, recover faster, and continue exhibiting higher performance and stronger financial structures over time (Amanna & Jaussaud, 2012; Suehiro, 1993). However, the value of domestic business group contributions to industrialization is tempered by the fact that they often become political businesses (or oligarchies) engaging in rent collection and corruption. Therefore, developmental state research has focused on calibrating proper state-business relations (Carney et al., 2020; Kang & Jo, 2021).

The second group is state-owned enterprises due to the success of Northeast Asian countries in adopting the concept of developmental states. In addition to governmental policymakers guiding industrialization, private companies were also established in the form of state-owned enterprises (the state holds all or a majority of shares) to operate in accordance with stated industrial policies (Carney, 2018; Haggard, 2018). State-owned enterprises are often established by statute or special law, divided into two types:

1) State enterprises[3] operating under the national budget.
2) Public enterprises established under corporate law with 100 percent ownership by the government, or acting as major shareholder.

In South Korea, Thailand, and Indonesia, several state-owned enterprises are privatized and listed on stock exchanges, following conditions for loan assistance from the International Monetary Fund (IMF) and the World Bank after the 1997 Asian financial crisis. These former state-owned enterprises were termed government-linked companies (Carney, 2018; Suehiro & Wailerdsak, 2013; Wisuttisak & Rahman, 2021).

The third group is foreign companies, or those in which foreigners hold half or more of shares, or less than that, but with power to make business decisions. Most foreign companies investing in Asia are MNCs with headquarters in the United States or Japan and operate by spreading production bases abroad. The role of MNCs will be discussed in detail in Chapter 7.

Governments in developing countries usually target foreign direct investment (FDI) in areas with the greatest potential for technological spillovers, given location-specific assets. This also means working with MNC affiliates producing nationally to upgrade productive capabilities through complementary advances (Kang & Paus, 2020).

3.2 Latecomer nation domestic business groups theory

3.2.1 Three periods of study

Studies of domestic business groups in latecomer countries may be divided into three periods:

(1) The 1980s and 1990s, when Northeast Asia achieved high economic growth. Evidence included the formation of zaibatsu in Japan, chaebol in South Korea, and SME networks in Taiwan. Developmental states strategically select particular industries by sector and foster them with a wide range of industrial policies such as policy finance, subsidies, and tax incentives. They encourage the private sector to allocate credit to strategic sectors, especially export-oriented ones (Amsden, 1989, 2001; Johnson, 1982, 1996, Wade, 1990, 2018).

On the other hand, according to Kunio Yoshihara's book on *The rise of ersatz capitalism in Southeast Asia* (Yoshihara, 1988, p. 2), Southeast Asian capitalists are unlike the capitalist class in Europe and the United States, who began investing in R&D to improve the quality of their products in the early stages of the production process. This R&D process enables capitalists to become modernization agents for their nation. As Yoshihara has indicated, the greatest obstacles Southeast Asian capitalists confront are capital ownership, access to overseas markets, and mastery of advanced technologies. Ersatz capitalism has been shaped by business practices based on the four crucial factors listed in the next section:

- The practice of rent-seeking between capitalists and bureaucrats.
- The reluctance of capitalists to invest in technical innovation. Capitalists are overly concerned that they will not be able to compete with established capitalists from developed nations.
- Foreign principals' commitment to technological development and local capitalists' lack of technological innovation.
- Capitalists' role as a mere comparator who seeks only immediate high-profit returns.

Based on the concept, ersatz capitalists include all business owners who rely on foreign capital and technology to operate their businesses and who act merely as traders with distributorship licenses for foreign-manufactured products.

(2) Study of business groups augmented in the aftermath of the 1997 Asian financial crisis. These were largely owned and managed by ethnic Chinese for ASEAN-5, previously admired as the main driver of the so-called East Asian miracle and, conversely, blamed as the culprit for the onset of crises. Almost all strong points turned out to be weaknesses.

Generally, close government-business collaboration in developmental states was accused of moral hazard, favouritism, endemic corruption, and crony capitalism, basically causing the crisis. More specially, the financial system was a bank-oriented fund funnel approach and imprudent banking system, because the legal system was too weak to permit a correctly performing stock market to develop. As a consequence, corporate ownership remained concentrated in the hands of families, the state, or through cross shareholdings forming part of a business group, used to benefit a clientelist group (Carney & Witt, 2010; Claessens et al., 1999; Dhnadirek & Tang, 2003).

Government-initiated export-oriented industrialization was innately fragile and lacking in sustainability because East Asian countries were obliged to rely on low wages, labour-intensive manufacturing, MNC dominance of manufacturing (MNC concentrating on domestic R&D), and the United States as market of last resort for manufactured goods. The Asian economic crises have been described as marking the end of the Asian developmental state (Doner & Schneider, 2016; Satitniramai, 2020).

Moreover, Khanna and Yafeh (2007) and Carney et al. (2018) tried to examine the extent to which business groups should be viewed as "paragons" (groups playing a positive role by compensating for underdeveloped economic institutions) or "parasites" (groups detrimental to social welfare because of rent seeking or monopoly power).

(3) In the 2010s, intra-capital contestation was transformed into what might be termed "inner-outer circles." Conglomerates closely connected with government parties and the military junta in Thailand, for example, could amass fortunes in telecommunications, automobile, media, agro-business, and food and beverage industries. The inner circle of political clientelism was redrawn with a small group of allied Sino-Thai conglomerates granted major lucrative state concessions. These concessions were for mega-infrastructure projects allowing them to outperform the competition (Kanchoochat et al., 2021; Naknoi, 2020).

Even major Thai business groups, from an international perspective, appear small and laggard. A single Thai company appeared on the 2020 Fortune Global 500 survey of the world's largest companies, PTT (Petroleum Authority of Thailand), consolidating all affiliate assets, ranked 140[4] (Wisuttisak & Rahman, 2021).

3.2.2 *Monopoly issues*

In countries with compressed industrialization, the more economies develop, the more big business group monopolies occur. Essentially, business groups emerge to reduce risks from institutional voids – infrastructural imperfections in doing business in emerging countries, such as underdeveloped capital markets, legal and judicial institutions, and labour markets for skilled employees and executives (Khanna & Yafeh, 2007).

Business groups diversify into many fields by relying on internal capital markets distinguished by pyramidal and cross shareholding structures, vertical integration and intragroup trading, and internal labour markets featuring interlocking directorates (Hamilton-Hart & Wai-chung Yeung, 2021; Huneeus et al., 2021; Wailerdsak & Suehiro, 2010).

From the start of the first National Economic and Social Development Plan (1961–1966) until the Twelfth Plan (2017–2021), significant economic sectors in Thailand have had high concentration. During a major phase of Thai economic development, the Kingdom emerged from an impoverished nation status with per capita GDP of US$80 in 1950 to an upper-middle-income ranking with per capita GDP of US$7,066 by 2021. A few conglomerated, family-owned business groups controlled considerable proportions of the Thai economy through Board of Investment (BOI) promotion policies and developmental guidelines (Satitniramai, 2020; Suehiro & Wailerdsak, 2013).

Most domestic conglomerates concentrated in commodities (natural resources, basic metals, and other semi-processed goods), regulated sectors (especially banking and utilities), natural oligopolies (such as cement and beer), and occasionally, low-tech manufacturing (blocked from high-tech manufacturing by MNCs) (Doner & Schneider, 2016).

As a result, the Thai economy has grown slowly and yields are distributed unevenly, increasing inequality. Two questions arise about how trickle-down economics[5] actually occurred and how to make business groups with monopoly power more socially responsible (Phongpaichit, 2016).

According to modern corporation theory, ownership and control play determinant roles in defining corporate social responsibility. If owners-managers are the same persons or groups, social responsibility at this type of business is minimal because businesses profits will be sought as much as possible and individually owned. This will incite businesses to exploit others more, such as by selling goods and services to consumers at monopolistic prices. Business rent seeking will inevitably increase (Carney & Child, 2013; LaPorta et al., 1999).

3.2.3 Concentrating ownership and control

However, if ownership and control are separated or owner-managers are not the same persons or groups, corporate social responsibility may increase. Because executives are not business owners, their compensation is in the form of salary and bonuses. Therefore, they need not seek maximum profit by exploiting people but manage businesses to create profits and satisfy business owners, while also benefiting from their jobs. This type of business is generally more responsible to society as a whole (Dhnadirek & Tang, 2003; Morck, 2005; Morck & Yeung, 2004; Sood, 2021).

But when considering how concentration or monopoly of businesses affect society, we must examine the state's role in business regulation, including laws related to shareholding distribution and business ownership (such as a public companies or commercial banking act), laws providing protection to individuals (such as a pricing and antitrust or consumer protection act) (Wisuttisak & Rahman, 2021). In some nations, governments require senior executives in certain types of businesses, such as financial and infrastructure endeavours to meet qualifications, abilities, and ethics standards set by the government (Satitniramai, 2020).

To advance on the path to more inclusive growth and national competitiveness, Thailand must reduce the monopoly of conglomerate-led regimes and promote separation of ownership and control to ensure that private companies, the spearhead of economic development, operate for the benefit of society rather than for individuals and their families. This should start by dispersing ownership (or shareholding), posing a serious threat to wealth accumulation by Thai elite groups (Dhnadirek & Tang, 2003).

3.3 Four types of Thai family business groups

Conventional wisdom suggests that cross-national patterns of corporate organizations are converging or will converge on the Anglo-Saxon model, the "managerial enterprise" or "managerial revolution," characterized by a sharp separation between (dispersed) ownership and (managerial) control, which is inevitably more efficient than alternative organizational models. In relation to this argument, this section refers two classic models, the Berle and Means model (1932) and the Chandler model (1977, 1990), and develops a new model.

We developed a 2×2 dimensional model to classify FBGs into four types. The first dimension, on the vertical axis, focuses on the management structure or the professionalization of management, by examining the rate of appointments of employed managers to the board of directors. This replaces the development of managerial hierarchies in the Chandler model (Suehiro & Wailerdsak, 2004).

We divided 215 Thai FBGs into three different types,[6] including the unreformed or authoritarian type, which stands for FBGs controlled closely by an owner family (116 groups, 54 percent); the hybrid type, which is where an owner family partly appoints employed managers but continues to play a significant role in the top management structure (63 groups, 29 percent); and the modernized (or managerial enterprise-oriented) type, where the FBGs are keen to allow non-family managers to hold key positions within the company (hired from the external labour market) to prepare their organizations for the new global economy (36 groups, 17 percent).

The second dimension on the lateral axis shows business diversification by examining the degree of expansion in the size of businesses and by examining the variety of major industrial bases. This replaced the advance in economies of scope and scale in the Chandler model (Chandler, 1990). There were three different types, including 87 (41 percent) of the specialized or single type, which were firms that had specialized in one core business, such as agricultural product export, agro-industry, or telecommunications. There were 104 (48 percent) semi-conglomerate types, which had one core business, plus one or two non-core businesses (particularly in the property or finance sectors), and 24 (11 percent) were full-blown conglomerates.

Based on these two dimensions, four types of Thai FBGs were generated, as demonstrated in Figure 3.2:

A) Unreformed single business.
B) Authoritarian conglomerate.
C) Modernized single business (including the hybrid type).
D) Modernized conglomerate (including the hybrid type).

Type A belongs to a traditional style of family business, while types C and D, accounting for 99 FBGs (46 percent of the total FBGs in Thailand), can be called modernized family businesses (not managerial enterprises) because they have succeeded in transforming their management style to clearly distinguish

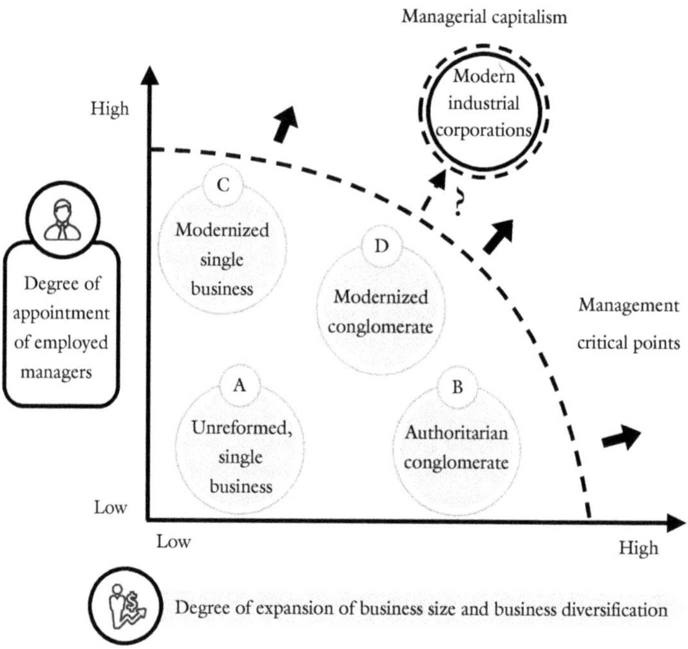

Figure 3.2 Management critical points

Source: Wailerdsak and Suehiro (2014)

it from the traditional management style, based on the closed control of ownership and management (see details in Wailerdsak, 2008).

Thai FBGs do not appear to have gravitated towards a supposedly modern corporation, as assumed by the conventional views held by Chandlerian scholars. Some FBGs have evolved into "modernized family businesses" by restructuring and innovating management systems inside their groups. In their pursuit of growth and diversification, owners of such business groups have continuously worked to overcome serious limitations in management resources, or – as this chapter terms them – "management critical points." It is suggested that these efforts of owner families have alleviated the implicit pressures of management limitations found in the traditional type of family business.

3.4 Theory of management critical points[7]

According to the official definition, the word critical point means the point at which a substance has the physical nature to change discontinuously, similar to the point at which boiling water becomes steam. Therefore, the management critical point of FBGs should be the most extreme limit at which an FBG is able to sustain a certain form of business type. In other words, though the critical point can be raised, depending on the conditions, it cannot be overcome or cleared. Clearing does not mean that a family business evolves by overcoming limitations; at that point, it stops being a family business (discontinuous change).

It would be interesting to note at what stage the management critical point surfaces, and according to what specific situations does it occur in each country? In Thailand, the time it took for some businesses to reach critical point was unexpected; also, their upper limits were unexpectedly high. In other words, in line with Figure 3.2, we can suppose that domestic and international economic conditions, government policies, and initial efforts of owner families themselves can extend the upper limits (or boundaries) of the critical points, thus relaxing the limitations of the expected management resources, enabling further development of the family business.

3.4.1 *Investment fund limitation*

Three limitations of management resources include investment fund, production technology and market knowledge, and human resources. Here, we examine sample cases of FBGs that were chosen to represent either modernized single businesses (Type C) or modernized conglomerates (Type D), in order to illustrate their self-sustained efforts to overcome the limitations of their management resources.

Private ownership limits access to capital, forcing privately, family-owned, and family-managed firms to rely on internal resources to fund investments.

Traditionally, FBGs do not dilute family ownership to fund growth. They are unwilling to involve non-family investors and, thus, are limited to the internal financing (e.g., retained earnings, and internal capital market) and debt financing (funds borrowed from commercial banks) to finance growth, while capital markets are undeveloped (Charumilind et al., 2006; Chrisman et al., 2011).

At this point, the corporate financial strategies of these firms move from costly, bank-oriented systems (indirect finance), to cheaper, market-oriented systems (direct finance) when the capital markets have substantially developed. Thai FBGs that want to perpetuate the business for future generations will follow suit. Thus, we must now focus on the following three practices – the internal capital market and tax incentives, bank borrowing/debt financing, and equity financing.

3.4.1.1 Internal capital market and tax incentives

The use of internal capital market represents the use of control pyramids and pyramidal/cross shareholding. Investment companies or holding companies act as the vertices of the pyramidal structures of groups like this one. They control the first-tier firms with dominant voting stakes. Each first-tier firm controls several second-tier firms, each one controlling yet more firms, and so on.

Control pyramids let these families control not just one large firm but many large firms collectively, which are worth substantially more than the family's actual wealth. The owner family can generate the needed capital for numerous affiliated firms and can retain majority control rights through miniscule actual investments in firms they control. Controlling families also wield control by placing family members in executive positions in key firms throughout a pyramidal group (Almeida et al., 2015; Buchuk et al., 2014; Chrisman et al., 2011).

Also, the cross shareholding structure creates mutual dependence among member firms in a business group and enables firms to exert profits and internal reserves of the group while protecting them from market uncertainties, particularly takeover threats and competition. The use of control pyramids and cross shareholding is widely observed in conglomerate-type family businesses in East Asia and Latin America, as well as in big business groups in Japan (Claessens et al., 1999; LaPorta et al., 1999). By using these strategies, owner family members have successfully maintained their substantial control over both capital ownership and management during business expansion. For more details about the various types of pyramidal structures within Thai FBGs, see Charumilind et al. (2006), Suehiro (2006), and Wailerdsak (2005, 2008).

Apart from the use of internal capital market, another major strategy is the use of tax incentives. Thai investment promotion laws grant privileges and benefits (exemption or reduction of import duties on machinery and raw materials, and corporate income tax exemptions – tax-based incentives) to promote companies, in principle, only once. As a result, the companies that aim to maximize their internal reserves by using investment privileges develop a policy that aims to establish many new companies (even if they are similar businesses or produce similar products) in order to receive repeated tax-based privileges and benefits. This is the main reason for the increased rate of growth of Thai FBG-affiliated firms within a short period of time.

3.4.1.2 Debt financing/bank borrowing

In Thailand, commercial banks (except government-owned banks) take an overdraft account, which is a financing method that holds the deposits of customers as mortgages and loans to them 120–130 percent of their deposits. The banks also provide loans to large depositors at significantly lower interest rates than the market rate in order to fund working capital and also to fund factory and equipment investments.

As a result, there are close ties between certain commercial banks and certain FBGs. Bank-centred FBGs can also partially ease the problem of accessing external funds because the banks act both as sources of equity and as sources of debts to the firms in the business groups, the so-called "connected lending"[8] (Charumilind et al., 2006; Wailerdsak, 2005). Recently, bank borrowing has remained an imperative funding source in the acquisition of established companies.

3.4.1.3 Equity financing and the stock market

Other sources of funding for FBGs include the use of initial public offerings (IPO), seasoned equity offerings, and capital gains obtained by selling the shares they own through the stock market. These capabilities were extended when the Thai government launched financial liberalization in the late 1980s. It was also at that time when Thailand entered an unprecedented economic boom, stock boom, and land boom (the so-called bubble economy) (Wailerdsak & Suehiro, 2010).

The new funds were derived from the enormous amounts of premium income and capital gains, which were created by listing companies during the stock boom. The new funds were also gained from the debts from local banks that had assumed high prices of land as mortgages (owing to the land boom) and from the acceptance of the foreign currency fund from foreign countries, in line with the liberalization of capital transaction (Suehiro, 2006).

By going public, companies can gain enough strength to reach the size required to keep up with the current dynamic and fiercely competitive business environment. They also gain a positive public image since listed firms are thought of as being financially healthy and as having high standards for transparency and information disclosure. Having a public profile boosts a company's credibility, increases its bargaining power, and enhances employee loyalty (Carney, 2005).

These benefits to listing a company can offset the disadvantages that come with going public. One of the biggest concerns is a potential loss of control that could result from bringing in outside shareholders. However, this will not necessarily be the case because the family business can restrict the trading of shares or can use privately held holding companies to fully control subsidiaries that might be publicly owned.

3.4.2 Production technology and market knowledge limitation

The second limitation is insufficient accumulation of production technology and market knowledge for new products, which is required for market strategies, such as diversification and internationalization. Generally, FBGs in late industrializing countries can acquire the technological capacities to break into new markets through licensing arrangements, original equipment manufacturing (OEM), original design manufacturing (ODM), JVs, and strategic alliances. In this way, they, as latecomers, or as the "second movers" in growing industries, are able to catch up and sometimes leapfrog competition in the production of high-quality, low-cost goods, as typically seen in the development of the Taiwanese personal computer industry (Amsden & Chu, 2003).

In the case of Thai FBGs, when advancing into a new type of industry, they have often introduced cutting-edge technology and necessary knowledge through family successors, who are usually better educated (have a college degree or MBA degree and are educated abroad), and professional managers, hired from outside (Chua et al., 2009); this is a topic mentioned later in the paper. However, JVs with foreign partners have proved the most important external technology source for expansion and diversification of local firms. This is very different from the experiences of business in developed countries such as the United States, Germany, and Japan, as they must invest heavily to develop new technologies.

Thai FBGs, particularly those in manufacturing, emerged from 1960 onwards. They sought JVs with foreign partners in favour of acquiring production technology (mostly standardized technology), market knowledge, and managerial know-how. For example, when the commerce-based groups, which engaged solely in import and domestic sales of commodities in certain specific fields, decided to advance into the manufacturing sector of the same products (e.g., construction material, beverages, synthetic fibres, household electrical appliances, chemical fertilizers, sheet glass, and auto assembly) as the government launched the industrial policy of import substitution (Suehiro, 1992). At the same time, they diversified business into new areas, such as steel, petrochemical, and telecommunications, as the policy of upgrading the industrial structure was initiated. The modern retail business sector was also affected, which also appeared to mature in the domestic consumer market (Suehiro, 2006, pp. 199–203).

Also, local businesses probably developed their own know-how, which was limited to real estate, agro-industry, finance, and insurance. Nevertheless, even in the case of agro-industry, it is true that they must have relied on some specific production technology that was developed by foreign firms, like those in the United States and Japan – particularly in important sectors, for example, the production of hybrid chickens for broilers, the cultivation of breeding prawns, and the "Individual-Quick-Freeze (IQF)" technology, which enabled the export of agricultural and fishery livestock products.

Recently, many Thai companies have expanded their business domestically and within the ASEAN region. Creating JVs with foreign partners, particularly Japanese companies, is an alternative to invading international markets or relocating the manufacturing base.

3.4.3 Human resource limitation

The third limitation was a scarcity of well-trained human resources, in particular, the professional management class that supports business expansion and innovation. There were three basic options to counteract this problem: to professionalize members of the owner family, professionalize existing non-family employees (internal labour market), and recruit professional managers from outside the family and the business groups (external labour market) (Chrisman et al., 2011; Chua et al., 2009; Huneeus et al., 2021).

3.4.3.1 Owner family members – planned succession of business

Succession is a crucial matter for family businesses in order for them to survive and develop. As Rose (1995, pp. 133–134) pointed out: succession, although by no means the only factor determining business performance or survival, forms the critical foundation upon which the future prosperity of a family firm. Conversely, failure to provide for a smooth and effective succession can be detrimental to future performance of otherwise successful business, or lead to its disappearance. Indeed, since it is possible to plan creatively for leadership succession, such provision should be seen as being as much part of entrepreneurship as technological or organizational innovation.

Rose called this failure in leadership succession the "Buddenbrooks syndrome" (from Thomas Mann's novel), while Church (1993, p. 25) labelled it the "third generation hypothesis," or the third-generation entrepreneurial weakness, which was seen as a factor contributing, to a significant degree, to Britain's relative industrial decline.

It is very important to distinguish between the problem of the succession of office (or leadership succession in Rose's definition) and the problem of the succession of property. If all children have equal rights to property/inheritance (co-parcenary), the succession of office becomes a crucial matter to the continuity of the family business.

For that reason, the eldest son is intentionally selected as president/CEO, despite the fact that they may not be given a larger share of ownership than their siblings. We found that the tendency in Thai FBGs – with Chinese backgrounds – followed the principle of primogeniture (in which leadership and control of the voting stock passes to the first-born) for the succession of office, which was contrary to the traditional business culture in mainland China, where business leadership has customarily been handed down to the able-male family member (Bunkanwanicha et al., 2013, p. 628; Suehiro, 2006, Chapter 2). This primogeniture principle helps avoid acrimonious succession battles and intergenerational rivalry and friction in a large extended family (Wailerdsak, 2008).

A common characteristic of family businesses is the concentration of decision-making and senior management in the hands of family members and trusted associates. Decisions on important issues are rarely delegated to non-family managers (Suehiro, 2006). Even the case of modernized conglomerates, although many groups were transformed into listed companies and aggressively hired non-family employees to manage their core firms, founding families often maintained strong control over strategic management of the group.

This scenario does not necessarily lead to the separation of ownership and control. Family influence on business operations still significantly affects strategic development. Detailed information about the senior management of listed companies in Thailand was compiled by Wailerdsak (2005).

In general, there are very few founders of FBGs who hold a bachelor's degree or higher. Most of these founders started their businesses just after junior high school or even after primary school in Thailand or in mainland China. In contrast, there is a clear trend toward the professionalization of second and later generations, who are often sent to engineering and business schools in the United States and European countries.

This is because Thailand's higher education and external markets for the managerial classes are poorly developed. There are countless cases where founders have targeted their offspring as successors at an early stage (typically their sons) and constantly invested in professional education. Some families are particularly effective at instilling in their offspring a spirit of entrepreneurship from an early age. These founders often plan to reform the management of their organizations and diversify into new areas when their children return with new ideas about the future.

In many cases, it is not the founder of the company but rather the well-educated second and subsequent generations who are the ones who expand the family-owned firm and convert it into a business group. Until now, it seems that most of Thai FBGs still have a pool of willing-to-work, full-time family members and are able to gain the necessary management skills.

The planned succession observed in Thailand's FBGs is very different from the Chandlerian depiction of family members in the family firm. Chandler (1977, p. 492) stated that because family members were assured of large incomes, they had little financial incentive to spend years working up the managerial ladder, and within two generations, family members did not participate in the management of the firm.

3.4.3.2 Internal labour market and "Luukmo"

As a family business grows and becomes a conglomerate (diversified business group), it is unlikely that the family will be able to staff all the key positions and have all the necessary skills to run it effectively. Therefore, the family will hire non-family managers to fulfil this function (Huneeus et al., 2021).

The first group of employed managers is the so-called "trueborn managers" (or *luukmo* in Thai) or internal labour market, which comprise two sub-groups: those who have worked since the launch of the business or joined the firm after graduation (without work experience outside the firm) and those early, mid-career managers who have worked outside for only a few years before joining the firm. All have gradually climbed the corporate ladder while accumulating the firm-specific skills until being promoted as executives, based upon their abilities.

Huneeus et al. (2021) argued that business groups may overcome external labour market frictions by using internal labour markets. Internal placement of employees is less expensive and more effective than external placement. In response to international shocks, a greater proportion of top management shifts should occur between firms in the same group than between unaffiliated businesses. Internal labour flows also increase firm-level productivity, consistent with the hypothesis that internal labour markets may provide group firms with an edge over standalone firms.

This trend towards trueborn managers is evident in the commercial bank and financial groups in Thailand. For example, early on, the Thai Farmers Bank (renamed Kasikornthai Bank in 2004) used the intra-company scholarship system to send fast-track elites (selected among non-family employees) to study aboard. The company appointed them as managers later on, after they had learned from a wide range of experiences and endured a number of screening procedures.

Major FBGs have attempted to create a cadre of managerial talent and develop efficient internal labour markets by providing internal management-development programs, which help counteract the rigidities and variations of the external labour market. The companies also reap the benefits of the long-term, company-specific training of employees. It suggests that the managerial internal labour market in Thailand has already emerged, providing more flexibility in exploiting new business opportunities and dealing with business downturns. In other words, managerial talents are internalized within the company group due to the absence of efficient external markets (Sood, 2021; Wailerdsak, 2005).

3.4.3.3 Managers hired from outside

The second group of employed managers is the ready-made professional managers. Thai FBGs have been active in promoting managerial reform, including the recruitment of able professionals from external labour markets, to meet increasing demands for professional managers. For example, the Bangkok Bank (since the 1950s) and the CP group (since the 1960s) hired "specialist-type managers" from foreign firms who were proficient in certain fields, such as finance and accounting (e.g., Shell, Exxon, Unilever), large local firms (e.g., SCG, Bangkok Bank), international accounting offices, universities, and government agencies. Then, there developed a tendency to actively hire professional managers and engineers from outside, especially when they advanced into new businesses, such as electronics, petrochemicals, telecommunications, and TV program production.

Since the late 1980s, there has been a movement towards the professionalization of family successors who have aggressively pursued higher education and specialist skills. Also, there has been a combination of owner managers, trueborn managers (who have been promoted from within), and ready-made managers (who have been hired from outside). It is obvious that family businesses can reap benefits from this triple alliance in the composition of the top management echelon and further alleviate the pressures due to the scarcity of well-trained human resources. Furthermore, this triple alliance has helped extend the upper limits of the critical points of family businesses, as illustrated in Figure 3.2.

In summary, facing these limitations, FBGs have tended not only to utilize retained family earnings but also to mobilize fresh money from local stock markets or from international financial institutions. Furthermore, when advancing into new types of industry, they often introduce cutting-edge technology and vital knowledge through second- or third-generation family members, who have been educated abroad, and from foreign partners in joint ventures. Finally, these businesses are active in promoting managerial reform, including the recruitment of able professionals from outside the family, to meet increasing demands of management. Thanks to these self-sustained efforts, they succeed in transforming their traditional managerial style (based on closed and exclusive control of ownership and management) into a more modern style.

Notes

1 Family business groups (FBGs) are conglomerations of legally independent firms operating in multiple strategically unrelated activities that are under common administrative and financial control and are managed by particular families. These FBGs continue to play a vital role in the economic development of both East Asian and Latin American countries (Grosse, 2007; Khanna & Yafeh, 2007; Suehiro, 2006).

2 Each nation defines private companies differently. In China, many foreign companies have invested in the telecommunication and computer industries. However, in South Korea and Taiwan, local companies are key players in the information technology (IT) industry. Apart from foreign and large local companies, China, Thailand, Malaysia, and Indonesia host many state-owned enterprises in oil refining, petrochemicals, electric power, telecommunications, and finance (commercial banks) (Suehiro, 1992).

3 As of 2020, there are 52 state-owned enterprises in Thailand, including eight public companies. In September, the Cabinet approved a budget of 1.51 trillion baht for 44 state-owned enterprises supervised by 15 ministries, with a net profit of 73,503 million baht expected (Wisuttisak & Rahman, 2021).

4 *Fortune* magazine's 2020 ranking of the world's 500 largest companies featured 133 companies from China, 121 from the United States, and 53 from Japan. The United States maintained No. 1 ranking for the seventh consecutive year and for the fifteenth time since 1995. PTT had revenues in 2019 of $71,502 million, ranked 140th, declining from 130th the previous year.

5 Trickle-down economics is a concept of mainstream economics that believes that societal economic growth will cause income distribution. The flow of benefits will be passed on from major capitalists to SMEs and eventually to impoverished urban and rural dwellers. This must begin by promoting major capitalist profits from innovation (Schumpeterian profits) growth, attracting more retail investors to become trading partners. In turn, jobs are created and real wages increased, improving the overall economy and quality of life for the entire population. This theory led to policy issuances favouring large business groups by cutting progressive taxes under US President Ronald Reagan. However, this concept is increasingly criticized for aggravating inequality between rich and poor citizens. Interests remained entrenched in a few large business groups, described as the rich and the scattered. Lower-level people had to scramble for remaining resources, without much choice (Akinci, 2018; Stiglitz, 2003).

6 In order to draw a complete picture of business groups in Thailand, we gathered information from five database sources: (1) *Thai Business Groups: A Unique Guide to Who Owns What, 5th edition* (Brooker Group, 2003); (2) Professor Akira Suehiro's database on FBGs in Thailand; (3) Forbes Asia's rankings of Thailand's 50 richest businesspeople between 2005 and 2020; (4) the top 500 millionaires and families on the Stock Exchange of Thailand, as ranked by *Money and Banking* magazine between 2005 and 2020; and (5) Business Plus's Top 1,000 Companies. Additionally, information regarding the ownership structure, financial data, business expansion and diversification activities, and management style of each FBG has been collected by the authors from the companies' annual reports and their annual registration statements (Form 56-1) submitted to the Stock Exchange of Thailand, as well as from newspapers, business magazines, and in-depth interviews with executives.

These data enabled us to identify 215 FBGs that were influential economic groups or families controlling the Thai economy. Regarding type of nationality, these business groups comprised six Thai-owned groups (including the Crown Property Bureau (CPB) owned by Thailand's royal family), three Indian-owned groups, three Western-owned groups (who had settled in Thailand), and three groups with missing data. The remaining 200 groups were Chinese-Thai-owned groups. These figures validate the overwhelmingly dominant position of Chinese-Thai families who occupy large business groups in Thailand. In 2020, the combined revenues of these companies made up approximately 60 percent of Thailand's total GDP, while the combined revenues of the 20 largest FBGs were equivalent to 31 percent of the GDP.

7 The first version of this chapter was published in Wailerdsak and Suehiro (2014). "Family business groups in Thailand: Coping with management critical points," *Asia Pacific Journal of Management, 31*: 997–1018.

8 Connected lending explains that strong connections with banks and finance companies provide firms preferential access to long-term loans. Banks have incentive to provide more long-term financing to firms with which they have close personal connections or board ties because these connections help limit information asymmetry and moral hazard problems (Charumilind et al., 2006).

References

Akinci, M. (2018). Inequality and economic growth: Trickle-down effect revisited. *Development Policy Review*, *36*, O1–O24.

Almeida, H., Kim, C. S., & Kim, H. B. (2015). Internal capital markets in business groups: Evidence from the Asian financial crisis. *The Journal of Finance*, *70*(6), 2539–2586.

Amann, B., & Jaussaud, J. (2012). Family and non-family business resilience in an economic downturn. *Asia Pacific Business Review*, *18*(2), 203–223.

Amsden, A. H. (1989). *Asia's next giant: South Korea and late industrialization.* Oxford University Press.

Amsden, A. H. (2001). *The rise of the rest: Challenges to the West from late industrializing economies.* Oxford University Press.

Amsden, A. H., & Chu, W. (2003). *Beyond late development: Taiwan's upgrading politics.* MIT Press.

Berle, A. A., & Means, G. C. (1932). *The modern corporation and private property.* Commerce Clearing House.

Bresser-Pereira, L. (2020). A new theoretical framework: New developmentalism. *Challenge*, *63*(3), 114–132.

Buchuk, D., Larrain, B., Muñoz, F., & Urzúa, F. (2014). The internal capital markets of business groups: Evidence from intra-group loans. *Journal of Financial Economics*, *112*(2), 190–212.

Bunkanwanicha, P., Fan, J. P., & Wiwattanakantang, Y. (2013). The value of marriage to family firms. *Journal of Financial and Quantitative Analysis*, *48*(2), 611–636.

Carney, M. (2005). Corporate governance and competitive advantage in family-controlled firms. *Entrepreneurship Theory and Practice*, *29*, 249–265.

Carney, M., Van Essen, M., Estrin, S., & Shapiro, D. (2018). Business groups reconsidered: Beyond paragons and parasites. *Academy of Management Perspectives*, *32*(4), 493–516.

Carney, R. W. (2018). *Authoritarian capitalism: Sovereign wealth funds and state-owned enterprises in East Asia and beyond.* Cambridge University Press.

Carney, R. W., & Child, T. B. (2013). Changes to the ownership and control of East Asian corporations between 1996 and 2008: The primacy of politics. *Journal of Financial Economics*, *107*(2), 494–513.

Carney, R. W., Child, T. B., & Li, X. (2020). Board connections and crisis performance: Family, state, and political networks. *Journal of Corporate Finance*, *64*, 101630.

Carney, R. W., & Witt, M. A. (2010). The role of the state in Asian business systems. In M. A. Witt & G. Redding (Eds.), *The Oxford handbook of Asian business systems.* Oxford University Press.

Chandler, A. D., Jr. (1977). *The visible hand: The managerial revolution in American business.* Belknap Press, Harvard University Press.

Chandler, A. D., Jr. (1990). *Scale and scope: The dynamics of industrial capitalism.* Belknap Press, Harvard University Press.

Charumilind, C., Kali, R., & Wiwattanakantang, Y. (2006). Connected lending: Thailand before the financial crisis. *The Journal of Business*, *79*(1), 181–218.

Chrisman, J. J., Chua, J. H., & Steier, L. P. (2011). Resilience of family firms: An introduction. *Entrepreneurship Theory and Practice*, *35*(6), 1107–1119.

Chua, J. H., Chrisman, J. J., & Bergiel, E. (2009). An agency theoretic analysis of the professionalized family firm. *Entrepreneurship Theory and Practice*, *33*, 355–372.

Church, R. (1993). The family firm in industrial capitalism: International perspectives on hypotheses and history. *Business History*, *35*(4), 17–43.

Claessens, S., Djankov, S., & Lang, H. P. (1999). The separation of ownership and control in East Asian corporations. *Journal of Financial Economics*, *58*(1–2), 81–112.

Dhnadirek, R., & Tang, J. (2003). Corporate governance problems in Thailand: Is ownership concentration the cause? *Asia Pacific Business Review*, *10*(2), 121–138.

Doner, R. F., & Schneider, B. R. (2016). The middle-income trap: More politics than economics. *World Politics*, *68*(4), 608–644.

Evans, P. B. (1989). Predatory, developmental, and other apparatuses: A comparative political economy perspective on the third world state. *Sociological Forum*, *4*(4), 561–587.

Evans, P. B. (1995). *Embedded autonomy: States and industrial transformation*. Princeton University Press.

Gerschenkron, A. (1962). *Economic backwardness in historical perspective: A book of essays*. Belknap Press, Harvard University Press.

Grosse, R. (2007). The role of economic groups in Latin America. In R. Grosse & L. F. Mesquita (Eds.), *Can Latin American firms compete?* (Chapter 2, pp. 29–44). Oxford Academic.

Haggard, S. (2018). *Developmental states: Politics of development*. Cambridge University Press.

Hamilton-Hart, N., & Wai-chung Yeung, H. (2021). Institutions under pressure: East Asian states, global markets and national firms. *Review of International Political Economy*, *28*(1), 11–35.

Huneeus, F., Larrain, B., Larrain, M., & Prem, M. (2021). The internal labour markets of business groups. *Journal of Corporate Finance*, *69*, 102017.

Johnson, C. (1982). *MITI and the Japanese miracle: The growth of industrial policy, 1925–1975*. Stanford University Press.

Johnson, C. (1996). *Japan: Who governs? The rise of the developmental state*. W. W. Norton & Company.

Kanchoochat, V., Aiyara, T., & Ngamarunchot, B. (2021). Sick tiger: Social conflict, state – business relations and exclusive growth in Thailand. *Journal of Contemporary Asia*, *51*, 737–758.

Kang, N., & Jo, K. (2021). State – business relations in flux: Capturing the structural power of business in South Korea's green industrial policy. *Journal of Contemporary*, *51*, 713–736.

Kang, N., & Paus, E. (2020). The political economy of the middle income trap: The challenges of advancing innovation capabilities in Latin America, Asia and beyond. *Journal of Development Studies*, *56*(4), 651–656.

Khanna, T., & Yafeh, Y. (2007). Business groups in emerging markets: Paragons or parasites? *Journal of Economic Literature*, *45*(2), 331–372.

LaPorta, R., Lopez-de-Silanes, F., & Shleifer, A. (1999). Corporate ownership around the world. *Journal of Finance*, *54*(2), 471–517.

Leff, N. H. (1978). Industrial organization and entrepreneurship in the developing countries: The economic groups. *Economic Development and Cultural Change*, *26*(4), 661–675.

Morck, R. (Ed.). (2005). *A history of corporate governance around the world: Family business groups to professional managers*. University of Chicago Press.

Morck, R., & Yeung, B. (2004). Family control and the rent – seeking society. *Entrepreneurship Theory and Practice*, *28*(4), 391–409.

Naknoi, K. (2020). *The Thai military as a business group, 1940–2016 (No. 2019–14)*. Center for Economic Institutions, Institute of Economic Research, Hitotsubashi University.
Paus, E. (2017). *Escaping the middle-income trap: Innovate or perish*. ADBI Working Paper No. 685. Asian Development Bank Institute.
Phongpaichit, P. (2016). Inequality, wealth and Thailand's politics. *Journal of Contemporary Asia*, *46*(3), 405–424.
Reno, W. (2014). Predatory states and state transformation. In S. Stibfried (Ed.), *The Oxford handbook of transformation of the state*. Oxford University Press.
Rose, M. B. (1995). *Family business*. Edward Elgar.
Satitniramai, A. (2020). Thai state formation and the political economy of the middle-income trap. In P. Chachavalpongpun (Ed.), *Routledge handbook of contemporary Thailand* (Chapter 15, pp. 189–203). Routledge.
Sood, B. (2021). The emergence of managerial capitalism in Europe. *International Journal of Research in Engineering, Science and Management*, *4*(11), 169–177.
Stiglitz, J. E. (2003). *Globalization and its discontents*. W. W. Norton & Company.
Suehiro, A. (1992). *Capital accumulation in Thailand, 1855–1985*. UNESCO The Center for East Asian Cultural Studies.
Suehiro, A. (1993). Family business reassessed: Corporate structure and late-starting industrialization in Thailand. *The Developing Economies*, *31*(4), 378–407.
Suehiro, A. (2006). *Famiri bijinesu-ron: Kohatsu kogyoka no ninaite (Family business: Agents of late industrialization)*. Nagoya University Press (In Japanese).
Suehiro, A., & Wailerdsak, N. (2004). Family business in Thailand: Its management, governance, and future challenges. *ASEAN Economic Bulletin*, *21*, 81–93.
Suehiro, A., & Wailerdsak, N. (2013). Thailand: Post-developmentalist capitalism. In A. M. Witt & G. Redding (Eds.), *The Oxford handbook of Asian business system* (Chapter 13, pp. 260–282). Oxford University Press.
Tijerina, W. (2020). Developmentalism as a comparative-historical model: From Friedrich List to Bresser-Pereira. *Brazilian Journal of Political Economy*, *40*(3), 484–492.
Wade, R. H. (1990). *Governing the market: Economic theory and the role of government in East Asian industrialization*. Princeton University Press.
Wade, R. H. (2018). The developmental state: Dead or alive? *Development and change*, *49*(2), 518–546.
Wailerdsak, N. (2005). *Managerial careers in Thailand and Japan*. Silkworm Books.
Wailerdsak, N. (2008). Companies in crisis. In P. Phongpaichit & C. Baker (Eds.), *Thai capital after the 1997 crisis* (Chapter 1, pp. 17–57). Silkworm Books.
Wailerdsak, N., & Suehiro, A. (2010). Business groups in Thailand. In A. Colpan, T. Hikino, J. Lincoln, & D. Musson (Eds.), *Oxford handbook of business groups* (Chapter 9, pp. 237–266). Oxford University Press.
Wailerdsak, N., & Suehiro, A. (2014). Family business groups in Thailand: Coping with management critical points. *Asia Pacific Journal of Management*, *31*(4), 997–1018.
Wisuttisak, P., & Rahman, N. B. A. (2021). Regulatory frameworks for reforms of state- owned enterprises in Thailand and Malaysia. In F. Taghizadeh-Hesary, N. Yoshino, C. J. Kim, & K. Kim (Eds.), *Reforming state-owned enterprises in Asia: Challenges and solutions* (Chapter 3, pp. 41–64). Springer.
Yoshihara, K. (1988). *The rise of ersatz capitalism in South East Asia*. Oxford University Press.

Chapter 4

Dependency theory and multinational corporations

4.1 Dependency theory

Since the 1980s, dependency theorists have studied the dominance of MNCs in East Asia. Countries in this region have actively sought to catch up with advanced countries economically and technologically by attracting inward FDI (Kabe et al., 2016); Japanese MNCs have invested in this domain to a greater degree overall than those based in the United States or Europe. These MNCs cohere in a Japanese-centred, dynamic division of labour that forms an Asian base for the global triad of dominant economic regions (Edgington & Hayter, 2013; Sato & Sato, 2016).[1]

However, whether Japanese MNCs significantly aid technological aspirations of other East Asian countries remains uncertain. East Asian latecomer countries share a recognition that technological advancement is facilitated by diverse institutional channels, such as original equipment manufacturing (OEM), licensing and joint ventures, and FDI. Consequently, host country attitudes towards Japanese MNCs are widely disparate (Sato & Sato, 2016).

By contrast, dependency theorists studying Latin America have expressed scepticism about East Asian economic growth, which they attribute neither to indigenous technological development nor to domestic market expansion or local business group growth. Instead, it is explicable by external factors such as world trade expansion and considerable foreign capital inflows in grants, public loans, and FDI, balanced on an unstable structure and vulnerable to changes in international economic environment as well as external shocks (Mahoney & Rodríguez-Franco, 2018; Paus & Gallagher, 2008).

Apparent national development that is underway is dictated by United States trade policy and MNC investment strategies as they enter East Asia. This concept is described as dependent development. Ultimately, local companies will be unable to develop autonomous technology and must remain dependent on MNCs indefinitely. This occurred on a domestic background of continuous political repression and deliberate repression of real wages and mass consumption (Mahoney & Rodríguez-Franco, 2018).

DOI: 10.4324/9781003370536-6

Later, East Asian economic growth dependency on external factors was confirmed by empirical research on American MNC activity. For example, Gerald K. Helleiner (1973) studied export-oriented industrial development in South Korea and Taiwan, including integrated circuits and markets for their products in the target country, the United States.

Helleiner concluded that in many cases, industrial products appear outwardly to be exported from one nation, such as Taiwan and South Korea, to the United States. But in fact, American MNCs used raw materials or intermediate products assembled in branch factories to benefit from low Asian labour costs, before the finished or semi-finished goods were exported to the United States. Therefore, export of industrial products from Asia to the United States increased merely as a result of MNCs relocating highly labour-intensive parts in the manufacturing process to sites where better trade terms might be obtained. Such exchanges should more accurately be characterized as intra-firm trade for each multinational concerned.

Indeed, debates about the effect of MNCs on local technology transfer are time-honoured; the conventional view of MNCs as sources of industrial learning and catalysts for technological upgrades has long been questioned. For example, Latin American dependency theorists saw MNCs as agents of underdevelopment (Paus & Gallagher, 2008), and Canadian nationalists have criticized MNCs for their truncating effects on domestic technology capacity (Hayter & Edgington, 2004).

Recently, these concerns were reinforced by regional fragmentation and cathedral in the desert hypotheses (Amin & Robins, 1990; Grabher, 1993). For now, the debate remains unresolved. In East Asia, Japanese FDI continues to be justified in terms of technological transfer as being technological capability defined as the endogenous ability to solve scientific and technological problems by following, assessing, and exploiting marketplace scientific and technological developments (Homklin et al., 2014).

However, this dependency theory was later contested. From the late 1990s onward, as East Asia economy developed, local business groups also grew. They occupied a portion of international trade and exports as well as expanding domestic markets due to urbanization and middle-class growth, not solely dependent on MNCs. Export destinations are more diverse, and US market dependency decreased correspondingly. High-tech industrial structure, such as heavy and chemical industries, was upgraded, and real wages rose exponentially (Haggard, 2018; Haggard & Kaufman, 2018; Ramstetter & Sjöholm, 2006).

The experience of Korea and Taiwan shows that developing domestic technology and firms at the technology frontier is key to escaping the middle-income trap. Relying on MNCs, even if positive spillovers exist, to incite local firms to develop autonomous technology is insufficient for achieving sustained high productivity gains (Ahmed & Kialashaki, 2019; Lee & Narjoko, 2015).

Moving into the 1990s, the focus of debate shifted from dependent economic development to how to interpret popular uprisings promoting democratization on the political front in South Korea, Taiwan, the Philippines, and Thailand. A definition of the causality between economic development and political democratization was sought (Carroll et al., 2020).

Conventional wisdom in developed countries was that political freedom was the only guarantee of economic development. Was this only the case for East Asian countries, or was there merit in the oft-heard argument that in latecomer countries, economic development should be pursued first under an authoritarian political regime, and political freedom could be enjoyed later, after an economic foundation for it had been established (Carroll et al., 2020; Suehiro, 2008).

In any event, today MNCs are among the most prominent big businesses in middle-income countries in East Asian and Latin America, where they usually account for one third to one half of the hundred largest firms. MNCs are especially dominant in manufacturing sectors of many middle-income countries. This typically translates into MNC dominance of manufactured exports, unlike East Asian high-income graduates, in which domestic firms account for most manufacturing exports. At a minimum, this MNC dominance excludes the largest domestic firms from manufacturing (Edgington & Hayter, 2013; Paus & Gallagher, 2008).

4.2 MNCs and human capital investment

Disagreements exist about the role of MNCs, one of the three supports of the dominant capital tripod, as the most significant vehicle for international technology transfer. Some believed that inward foreign direct investment (IFDI) increases export potential for a host nation, thereby increasing foreign exchange earnings. FDI may create jobs, facilitate technology transfer, and stimulate economic growth. The host nation obtains information as a result of FDI spillover, which occurs when multinational staff and management with superior training shift to domestic businesses (Ahmed & Kialashaki, 2019).

FDI promotes economic growth by adding external capital and spreading growth benefits. FDI delivers advanced technology as well as improved management and organization. Through global competitiveness, exports stimulate demand-side expansion and supply-side productivity. In these ways, FDI theoretically enhances national exports (Kalalang et al., 2022; Ramstetter & Sjöholm, 2006).

Also, it is recognized that MNCs undertake a major part of the world's private research and development (R&D) efforts and produce, own, and control most international advanced technology (Zhao et al., 2020). Therefore, foreign affiliates may help raise the human capital level in host countries and create productivity increases in local firms (Haworth, 2013; Kang et al., 2015).

In many cases, effects operate through forward and backward linkages, as MNCs provide training and technical assistance to local suppliers, subcontractors, and customers. The labour market is another important channel for spillovers, as almost all MNCs train operatives and managers who may subsequently accept employment in local firms or establish wholly new companies. This way, inward FDI may be a particularly valuable source of new technology (Haworth, 2013; Lee & Narjoko, 2015).

Thus, it is not surprising that most countries have liberalized policies to attract all sorts of foreign investment. Many governments have even introduced diverse forms of investment incentives to encourage foreign MNCs to invest in their jurisdictions (Intarakumnerd, 2019; Kang et al., 2015). However, productivity and technology spillovers are not automatic consequences of FDI (Ahmed & Kialashaki, 2019). In reality, MNCs are mostly sluggish in building host country human capital for three reasons:

Firstly, domestic firm and MNC interests and capacities differ. Many MNCs can shift investments to other countries with more human capital rather than investing in educational upgrades. MNCs that are less mobile, either because of natural resource investment or presence in countries with large domestic markets, usually have sufficient resources to pay internally to train typically small workforces.

Under the market-led model, latecomer country governments welcome FDI with open arms, expecting that at the macro level, capital infusions for which host country savings might not suffice, employment growth, foreign exchange, and tax revenue (Intarakumnerd, 2019). In addition, at the micro level, technology transfer and fiercer competition would generate stronger economic growth (Board of Investment, June, 2021; Homklin et al., 2014).

But the past three to four decades have shown that technology spillovers will only occur if domestic absorptive capacity exists; linkages will develop solely if domestic producers are already competitive; and foreign companies will invest in R&D exclusively in host countries that already possess an ecosystem sufficiently conducive for innovation firms (Kang et al., 2015). Latin American scholars have emphasized that technological benefits of FDI were limited or did not materialize. In contrast, FDI has put Latin American countries in a "dependency trap" (Paus & Gallagher, 2008; Paus, 2017).

Secondly, market-seeking MNCs might agree to join upgrading coalitions, but these firms have technological and marketing advantages in home markets protecting them from domestic competitors. These market advantages also permit them to pay workers higher salaries and recruit skilled employees from other jobs, thereby privately resolving the training problem (Fleming & Soborg, 2014).

Efficiency-seeking MNCs operating in global production networks (GPNs) might have strong interests in joining an upgrading coalition but also have other options: solving skill needs internally, relying on affiliated foreign suppliers, or simply moving higher value-added production to a country that already has the desired skills and infrastructure (Kabe et al., 2016; Kohpaiboon & Jongwanich, 2021).

On technology policy in particular, foreign and domestic firms rarely find common ground, especially for long-term, costly investments to build the institutional infrastructure needed for innovation. Although some domestic firms might favour such a push, foreign firms typically do not as they do most of their R&D at home. When MNCs do invest in R&D in developing countries, as happens increasingly in India and China, it is often for lower grades of technology and more routinized aspects of R&D. But MNCs invest little in R&D of any kind in large middle-income countries and show scant interest in paying for costly long-term upgrading for domestic innovation (Kang et al., 2015; Kohpaiboon & Jongwanich, 2021; Zhao et al., 2020).

Thirdly, it is evident that as industrialization develops, more raw materials and parts must be imported from abroad. This will increase problems in the balance of trade, or the well-known terms of trade (TOT) issue. Thailand has a continuous trade deficit with Japan and China. Therefore, the more Japanese and Chinese MNCs invest in Thailand, the greater the trade deficit with both countries will be.

It is unsurprising that MNCs did not serve as a conduit for technology diffusion to local firms. MNCs preferred their own suppliers and used in-house production or imported inputs, sourcing only simple content to local firms and repatriating profits. Local value added increased but not technology diffusion. Other explanations exist to discern why MNCs would not drive technology creation and diffusion locally.

Strong intellectual property environment and pertinent conditions for R&D may be lacking due to absence of skilled workers or other relevant support. MNCs might have less incentive to train or provide suboptimal training to local staff, with highly skilled scientists and engineers becoming mobile after training. In addition, company R&D departments tend to be located close to marketing departments, usually at corporate headquarters; less R&D occurs at foreign sites (Fleming & Soborg, 2014; Zhao et al., 2020).

4.3 BOI and target industries

FDI has played a key role in Thailand's industrialization process and global value chain (GVC) integration. At first, FDI in Thailand was dominated by US investors, but through the 1980s, Japanese foreign investment was over triple that of the United States. Foreign investment in the automobile, electronics and textile sectors led to rising exports, while some investments required assembly of imported components for domestic sale (Intarakumnerd & Techakanont, 2016; Topple et al., 2016). Inward FDI share in gross domestic product (GDP) increased to 50 percent by 2017. Investment is still dominated by Japanese manufacturing investors, with rising participation from other investors from within the ASEAN region, mostly Singapore, as well as outside the ASEAN community, for example China and Europe (OECD, 2021).

4.3.1 Number of projects by ownership

The Eastern Economic Corridor (EEC) Development Plan, a core strategy of the Thailand 4.0 economic model, aims to boost industrialization and competitiveness for ten target industries: half extant and half innovative high-tech. The plan includes complete transportation system design as well as incentives to attract international MNCs. Government investment plans totalling over 1.7 trillion baht ($49,900 million) for five years (2017–2021), consisting of 70 percent private investment and the remainder public investment.

The overall trend of projects approved for investment promotion may be examined by separating them into three categories, using BOI data.

- Proportion of foreign, as well as Thai, projects to total projects approved for promotion.
- Proportion of Thailand's ten target industries selected as part of Thailand 4.0.
- The proportion of three eastern provinces (Chonburi, Chachoengsao, and Rayong) to Thailand's total area (separated by region).

Tables 4.1 and 4.2 show the number of projects accepted for promotion and their anticipated investment value, respectively. There have been 5,987 projects approved for promotion over five years from 2016 to 2020. Project ownership may be divided into two groups based on ownership type: Thai- and foreign-owned.

- Entirely Thai-owned projects accounted for 2,279 projects, or 38.1 percent of the total.
- Foreign-owned projects (including 100 percent foreign-owned and joint ventures involving foreigners and Thais) accounted for 3,708 projects, or 61.9 percent of the total.

The proportion of foreign projects rapidly expanded annually: 57.6 percent in 2016, 62.3 percent in 2017, 66.6 percent in 2018, and 61.8 percent in 2019.

Distribution by target industry revealed 3,024 investment projects in ten target industries between 2016 and 2020, accounting for 50.5 percent of the total. The most projects (774) were digital, followed by agricultural and food processing (745), electrical appliance and electronics (380), petrochemical and chemical (367), and automotive and parts (297) respectively.

However, this figure merely represents the number of projects classified by industrial type, rather than determining if they were high-tech or cutting-edge developments. Most were standard projects, and new target industry initiatives are likely to be fewer.

Table 4.1 Approved investment projects by industry and location, 2016–2019 (number of projects)

	2016	2017	2018	2019	*2016-2019
(1) By ownership					
Number of projects	1,688	1,330	1,469	1,500	5,987
100% Thai (no. of projects)	715	501	490	573	2,279
***Proportion of 100% Thai**	42.4	37.7	33.4	38.2	38.1
100% Foreign (no. of projects)	603	501	576	622	2,302
Joint-venture (no. of projects)	414	328	404	305	1,451
(2) Ten target sectors as new engine of growth					
Automotive	55	46	102	94	297
Electrical and electronics	102	86	85	107	380
Tourism	16	24	32	27	99
Agriculture and food processing	247	150	155	193	745
Biotechnology	91	19	25	21	156
Automation and robotics	13	5	11	7	36
Aerospace	3	7	7	4	21
Petrochemicals and chemicals	112	64	98	93	367
Digital	270	209	142	153	774
Medical	24	33	46	46	149
Subtotal of ten target industries	933	643	703	745	3,024
Proportion of ten target industries	55.3	48.4	47.9	49.7	50.5
(3) Location: In EEC					
Eastern region	454	340	455	469	1,718
Chonburi	184	153	203	190	730
Chachoengsao	42	42	64	56	204
Rayong	164	105	148	179	596
Subtotal 3 provinces in EEC	390	300	415	425	1,530
Proportion of 3 provinces in EEC	23.1	22.6	28.3	28.3	25.6
Central region	833	665	704	671	2,873
Northeastern region	122	61	96	102	381
North region	107	93	71	72	343
West region	57	40	39	53	189
Southern region	85	82	63	94	324
Business without a permanent location	74	49	42	39	204

Source: Compiled by the author and Akira Suehiro based on the Board of Investment, Thailand, Investment Promotion Statistical Reports, Investment Promotion Summary (Thai only) January-December various years via www.boi.or.th, Foreign Direct Investment Statistics and Summary (Thai only)

Table 4.2 Approved investment projects by industry and location, 2016–2019 (value)

	2016	2017	2018	2019	*2016-2019
(1) By ownership					
Number of projects	867,530	631,080	549,500	447,360	2,495,470
100% Thai (mil. baht)	326,260	359,010	116,090	116,830	918,190
***Proportion of 100% Thai**	37.6	56.9	21.41	26.1	36.8
100% Foreign (mil. baht)	139,490	112,510	131,330	188,100	571,430
Joint-venture (mil. baht)	401,770	159,560	302,070	142,430	1,005,830
(2) Ten target sectors as new engine of growth					
Automotive	60,650	53,540	71,360	80,430	265,980
Electrical and electronics	64,500	38,270	38,690	57,530	198,990
Tourism	12,870	26,980	33,540	19,770	93,160
Agriculture and food processing	121,410	33,340	34,310	33,230	222,290
Biotechnology	45,670	6,480	25,040	20,210	97,400
Automation and robotics	770	780	1,460	860	3,870
Aerospace	140	2,760	2,740	7,220	12,860
Petrochemicals and chemicals	162,250	32,570	196,860	83,370	475,050
Digital	5,520	4,610	6,940	7,760	24,830
Medical	14,080	7,130	15,970	13,490	50,670
Subtotal of ten target industries	487,860	206,460	426,910	323,870	1,445,100
Proportion of ten target industries	56.2	32.7	77.7	72.4	57.9
(3) Location: In EEC					
Eastern region	409,510	334,610	352,610	265,400	1,362,130
Chonburi	113,260	118,250	225,500	79,770	536,780
Chachoengsao	19,510	30,780	23,100	41,050	114,440
Rayong	224,940	163,540	94,790	133,760	617,030
Subtotal 3 provinces in EEC	357,710	312,570	343,390	254,580	1,268,250
Proportion of 3 provinces in EEC	41.2	49.5	62.5	56.9	50.8
Central region	151,730	185,960	98,600	89,590	525,880
Northeastern region	78,300	13,950	13,860	23,200	129,310
North region	33,550	11,300	8,990	13,290	67,130
West region	28,980	13,780	5,330	7,900	55,990
Southern region	29,400	32,070	35,670	24,370	121,510
Business without a permanent location	136,060	39,410	34,440	23,620	233,530

Source: Compiled by the author and Akira Suehiro based on the Board of Investment, Thailand, Investment Promotion Statistical Reports, Investment Promotion Summary (Thai only) January-December various years via www.boi.or.th, Foreign Direct Investment Statistics and Summary (Thai only)

Figure 4.1 Approved investment promotion projects, 2016–2019

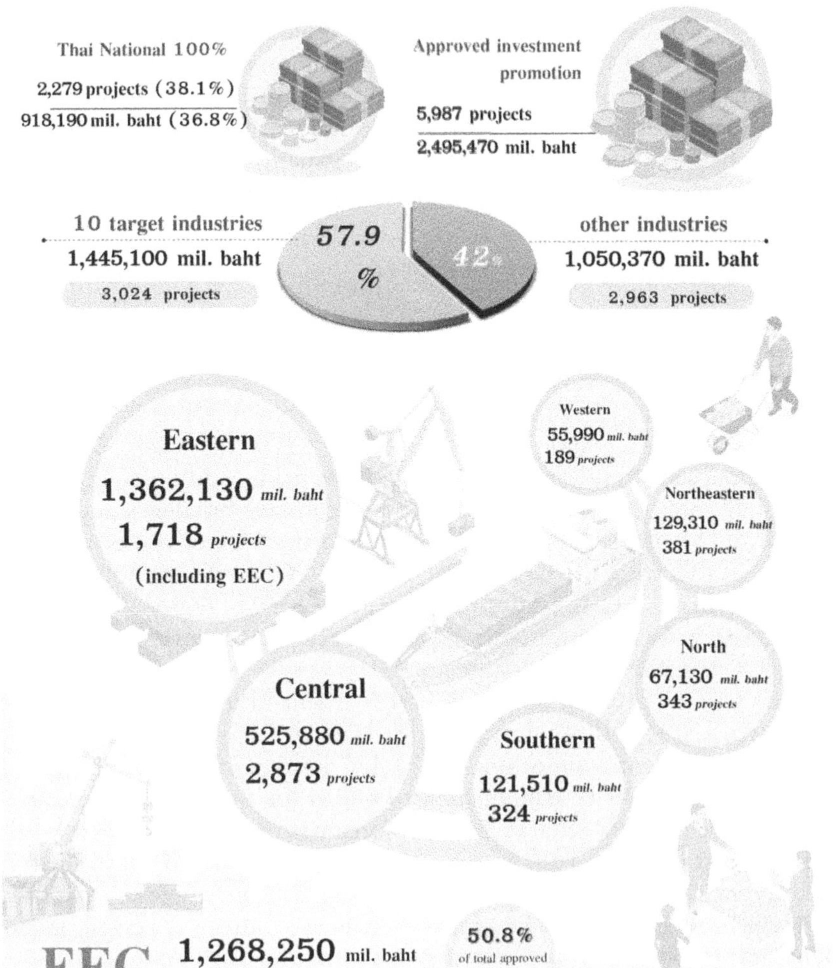

Source: Compiled by the author based on the Board of Investment, Thailand, Investment Promotion Statistical Reports, Investment Promotion Summary (Thai only) January–December various years via www.boi.or.th – > Foreign Direct Investment Statistics and Summary (Thai only)

4.3.2 Investment in EEC provinces

Between 2016 and 2020, in terms of geographic distribution, 1,530 projects were invested in three EEC provinces, accounting for 25.6 percent of the total. The investment value of 1.268 trillion baht was significant, or 50.8 percent of the overall investment value of 2.495 trillion baht, demonstrating focus on the three provinces. Rayong Province, the centre for large projects, had five times the amount of investment value of Chonburi and Chachoengsao Provinces (Teeramungcalanon & Chiu, 2020).

4.3.3 Investment in target industries

Foreign projects accounted for up to 63.2 percent of the total of 2.49 trillion baht in projects approved for promotion in Thailand between 2016 and 2020, according to BOI investment value data.

In terms of distribution by industry, investment value in ten target industries was 1.45 trillion baht, or 57.9 percent of the total. Many businesses refocused attention to investing in these fields. Additional goals were established in recent years in response to significant privileges and investment incentives provided by the BOI in the medical sector and eco-friendly investment following the bio-circular-green (BCG) economic policy underpinning Thailand 4.0. In addition, over half the total of regional investment distribution was concentrated in the three EEC provinces (Teeramungcalanon & Chiu, 2020).

Japan was the greatest source of FDI in Thailand over the past 40 years (Lauridsen, 2004, 2009). Intriguingly, from 2015 to 2020, the value of Chinese investment promotion was 12,457 million baht, ranking fifth in FDI, but Japan lost its leading rank to China for the first time in 2019. China offered investment in 203 projects worth 261,706 billion baht (including 160 billion baht in high-speed rail projects, up fourfold from 2018), while Japan offered 73,102 million baht. This suggests that Thailand will become increasingly reliant on China in future for trade, investment, and tourism.

Chinese investors are increasingly interested in investing in key industrial estates in Rayong, according to WHA Corporation PLC, which operates warehouses and sells or rents industrial estates. As yet less prominent than Japanese investors, the Chinese are playing an increasing role.

Industrial estate land is available for short- and long-term rental. Foreign investors continue to seek local Thai partners. Industrial estate management is responsible for utilities, including power, water, waste disposal, sewage, and digital communication systems. Also involved are accounting, staff recruitment, and labour relations management, all difficult for foreign investors to manage alone.[2]

4.4 Exploitation of foreign direct investment

4.4.1 Past experience

Thailand is now a net outward investor, with rapidly growing presence in neighbouring countries, as a pioneer in building development strategy around FDI and integration in global value chains. The Kingdom successfully attracted investment due to a combination of early liberalization of inward FDI for the manufacturing sector and proactive investment promotion and facilitation policies under a strong Board of Investment (BOI) (Lauridsen, 2004, 2009; OECD, 2021).

Since the 1985 Plaza Accord, Japanese MNCs moved production bases from Japan to Thailand and ASEAN for exports to the European Union and US markets. The goal was to reduce trade conflicts between Japan and Group of Five (G-5) nations. Japanese MNCs invested heavily in principal Thai industrial zones, especially the Eastern Seaboard Industrial Estate in Rayong Province. As a result, by the mid-1990s, Thailand appeared on the threshold of a new status as the fifth Asian Tiger (Topple et al., 2016).

For decades, Thailand's macro-level economic performance had been impressive. The Kingdom recorded sustained rapid growth rates, diversifying agricultural and industrial sectors. Deemed a newly agro-industrialized country (NAIC), it had the fastest-growing manufacturing exports of Asian economies from 1985 to 1996. At the same time, increasing concerns arose over whether the industrialization pattern was sustainable and especially whether new MNC-driven export industries truly contributed to long-term national competitiveness. This led in turn to formulation of policies on linkages between MNCs and SMEs as well as broader SME and supporting industry policies to supplement unfolding liberalization of trade and investment (Lauridsen, 2004, 2009).

Furthermore, foreign investments in the manufacturing industry mainly took the form of joint ventures (J/Vs) with an emphasis on assembly of final goods for the domestic market, while both capital goods industries and parts-producing industries remained relatively underdeveloped. Apart from a general high level of trade protection and local content requirements (LCRs), used most pervasively in the automobile industry, no specific policies induced local parts production, local spin-offs, or inter-industry linkages (Intarakumnerd & Techakanont, 2016; Kohpaiboon & Jongwanich, 2021).

In the automobile and electrical appliance industries, MNCs used localized suppliers, both related J/V and fully Thai-owned ones, typically with foreign technology contracts. Over the past four decades, locally it was believed that Thailand's vibrant automotive industry success resulted from a strategy of identifying as a regional automotive hub of one-ton pickup trucks or the Detroit of Asia. International MNCs were invited to establish plants in the Kingdom. The policy of using LCRs also helped Thai national manufacturers in supporting industry to develop and accumulate capabilities for international competition (Barnes et al., 2017; Intarakumnerd & Techakanont, 2016; Kuroiwa et al., 2021). Simultaneously, Malaysia's automotive industry developed but chose a strategy of designing a national car, the Proton, which ultimately failed.

These aspirations contrasted sharply with practical realities. Econometric and case studies show that hopes for technology transfer and spillover effects did not materialize in Thailand's automotive sector. No Thai companies were involved in developing new products or technologies led by foreign manufacturers (Homklin et al., 2014; Intarakumnerd, 2018). Statistically, Thailand had more local firms than foreign-owned ones, but mostly in the low-to-medium technology market.

In summary, Thailand has experienced a noteworthy economic development trajectory over the past four decades, and Japanese MNCs were pivotal to this success (Barnes et al., 2017; Topple et al., 2016). Yet unlike the PRC, Thailand had no complementary strategy of controlled opening to trade and FDI through aggressive promotion of domestic innovation capabilities. In this way, the Kingdom continues to rely on imported foreign technology and MNCs for the next development stage (Paus, 2017).[3]

Recipient governments frequently expect capital and technology transfers as a result of attracting FDI. Thailand's creative investment promotion program was forcefully backed by the military administration led by General Prayut Chan-ocha (founded on authoritarianism and nationalism, not liberalism as political economists would define it). Prayut, who assumed power in May 2014, directed the BOI to provide tax benefits for R&D investment. Since January 2015, the BOI has had new guidelines.

In June of that year, Yongyuth Yuthavong, who served as deputy prime minister and minister of science and technology during the Surayud (2006–2008) and Prayut (2014–2015) governments, announced a new policy to increase R&D expenditure from 0.37 percent of gross domestic product (GDP) in 2014 to 1.00 percent in 2016. This was done by creating special innovation zones at industrial estates and universities (Intarakumnerd, 2019).

Since 2011, Thailand has increased labour productivity with little R&D although real wages increased dramatically and despite cabinet support of the concept. As a result, Thailand's proposed 2016 target of 1.0 percent of GDP was not met. In response to rising wages, Thai private companies restructured businesses differently (Paweenawat, 2019).

BOI promotion policy on technology transfer anticipates foreign company investment and cooperation with Thai educational institutions. But no formal measures connect real technology transfer processes in factories, laboratories, or R&D centres (Board of Investment, June, 2021).

Incentives for in-house training, developing the internal labour market, and good labour relations were not included in investment promotion privilege packages. No concrete indicators demonstrate whether foreign corporations have transferred innovative technology or educated Thai employees. The BOI is responsible for FDI upstream, while the Ministry of Labour is responsible for it downstream (from interview).

In June 1992, a BOI Unit for Industrial Linkage Development (BUILD) was established to connect Thai SMEs and major manufacturers with parts and component suppliers. BUILD encourages Thai entrepreneurs to buy parts locally rather than importing them.

Since 2007, BOI has presented SUBCON Thailand, the largest international industrial part-sourcing and business-matching trade event in the Association of Southeast Asian Nations (ASEAN) community. It succeeded in allowing purchasers to meet vendors (suppliers) and assisting Thai companies to boost production and product quality to international standards (Board of Investment, September, 2021).

BOI executives explain that the creative economy policy has not vanished, but no single agency directs the policy, which is being reintroduced in alternate ways. The successful example of Thai entrepreneurs was clear. Company founders and their heirs, as well as employees, were devoted to working with skill to forecast or foresee the selection of correct technologies and products which might prove elusive if the wrong decisions are made.

The BOI is more adept at changing policies swiftly to satisfy the needs of foreign investors. Several BOI offices in Japan, as well as at the main office in Thailand, employ Japanese-speaking staff who are familiar with Japanese work culture. It is difficult to locate such skilled staff in other ASEAN countries.[4]

But problems arose when Japanese MNCs arrived in Thailand. Thailand's government regulators were undeveloped, making fair market competition harder to sustain. Most marketplaces and services were structured as monopolistic competition and oligopolistic markets. In addition, for many years Thailand was afflicted by a skills deficit as well as scarcity of skilled engineers and managers, preventing the economy from reaching its full potential. Thai employees were unable to surpass ASEAN levels of competency or beyond.

4.4.2 Future challenges

Thailand aspires to transition from upper-middle-income to high-income economic status by 2037, as outlined in its 20-year National Strategy (2017–2036). The government aims to achieve this objective by upgrading to a value-based green economy, as evidenced by the introduction of a Thailand 4.0 vision and bio-circular-green (BCG) economic model. This ambitious plan relies heavily on inward FDI and will therefore require continued concerted effort to reform and improve the investment climate (Chan-ocha, 2022).

New challenges related to the ongoing novel coronavirus 2019 (COVID-19) pandemic could delay achievement of this objective, interrupting Thailand's long stretch of growth. The economy is predicted to contract by approximately 1 percent in 2021, and exports and FDI are likely to decline even more (OECD, 2021). In July 2022, to tackle rising consumer and fuel prices, the government has designed a three-axis strategy. The first intends to launch the biggest infrastructure development project in Thailand. Prayut Chan-ocha, the prime minister, stated that projects including railways, highways, airports, and seaports promote prosperity, security, and connectivity.

The second core focuses on the industrial sector, including the Japan- and China-dominated automotive and related industries that are attempting to cut their fossil fuel consumption. The primer stated that the government is aiming to make electric vehicles more affordable and transform Thailand into a global manufacturing hub.

The third core is the banking sector, where the government intends to use modern digital technology to provide access to banking and financial services for 30 million people. He praised the public's cooperation that has helped Thailand survive the epidemic and become a leader in disease control practices (Chan-ocha, 2022).

Japanese MNCs have gradually reduced investment in labour-intensive manufacturing in Thailand and moved plants to neighbouring countries with higher growth rates and cheaper and younger workforces. Even Thai domestic business groups also tended to invest in neighbouring countries such as Vietnam, Indonesia, and Laos rather than Thailand. The Eastern Economic Corridor (EEC) project continually accelerated the MOU with foreign partners in twelve target high-tech industries.[5] Thailand actively seeks alternative foreign investors, such as China, Taiwan, India, Europe, and the United States. The success of the EEC project likely depends on MNC decisions over whether to invest in Thailand and any specific industry (Phuangketkeow, 2020).

According to empirical literature on productivity in Indonesia, Malaysia, the Philippines, Singapore, and Thailand (ASEAN-5), FDI spillover effects are nuanced. They differ among industries and depend on ownership patterns, whether joint venture, majority- or wholly owned, as well as the technology gap between local and foreign firms (Fleming & Soborg, 2014). Usually, productivity spillovers were potentially smaller in industries with high shares of foreign MNCs and wide technology gaps between local and foreign firms (Kalalang et al., 2022; Lee & Narjoko, 2015). Thus, in obtaining hoped-for technology transfer from MNCs, requiring foreign MNCs to enter in joint ventures with Thai companies would achieve more than allowing them to hold 100 percent of shares.

One main issue for the EEC project is to attract vast investment funding to build infrastructure, comprising a high-speed railway, international airports, industrial seaports, and digital park as well as state-of-the-art technology. National savings alone would be inadequate. The project was unambiguously announced as aimed at attracting foreign investment through a public-private partnership (PPP) model. This caused some local misunderstanding that Thai companies were uninvolved or that only a few large business groups with close ties to the government would participate. Subsequently, inward FDI and MNCs became indispensable engines driving Thailand to high-income country status (Phuangketkeow, 2020).

In addition to the PPP model, there is also a call to attract international talent to Thailand to help advance the nation.[6] The question arises whether the aforementioned development model will become dependent development. Dependency theorists fear that Thailand may achieve development by depending on MNCs and foreign talents, rather than the ability of local companies and its own citizens. Such a gamble might be worth considering. After all, the Kingdom is losing the educational race, has a severe demographic problem and economy caught in what is termed the middle-income trap, losing out to lower-cost competitors, nor does Thailand boast the cutting-edge knowledge or expertise of highly developed economies.

Notes

1 Edgington & Hayter proposed the concept of global localization, referred to as "glocalization (*dochakuka*)," in their 2013 study on regional headquarters (RHQ) strategies of electronics Japanese MNCs in ASEAN. Glocalization refers to the challenge of balancing the need to adapt foreign subsidiaries to local circumstances and to integrate corporate operations as a whole. RHQs are at the fulcrum of the idea of glocalization. RHQs are described in terms of the reciprocating relations between corporate structure and corporate strategy that change over space and time. This is often attributed to Sony Corporation's CEO Akio Morita. Sony used these terms in corporate advertising and branding campaigns during the 1980s and 1990s, and a related slogan to "think globally, act locally" encouraged its managers of overseas operations to respect cultural differences in workforces and local business practices.

2 Interview by the author with Thai executives of WHA Eastern Seaboard Industrial Estate, Rayong, on 29 May 2019.

3 During 2020–2021, Mediator Co., Ltd., a company specializing in Japan-Thailand business seminar and matching, held Zoom seminars about once monthly featuring senior executives from leading Thai companies such as Charoen Pokphand Foods, Mitr Phol, SCG, PTT, and Ichitan to discuss company history and future business plans with Japanese executives in Thailand and Japan. Japanese companies were invited to invest in new ventures for innovative technology transfer. Thai companies explained that conducting R&D by themselves was time-consuming and expensive, so they sought Japanese joint ventures as shortcuts.

4 Interview by the author with Sudhasinee Smitra, Bonggot Anuroj, and Thumrong Ampornratana, the Board of Investment, on 11 March 2020.

5 Interview by the author with Dr. Kanit Sangsubhan, Secretary-General of the EEC Office, on 22 August 2017.

6 Dhanin Chearavanont, chairman of Charoen Pokphand Group (CP), said that Thailand should import over 500,000 international employees with specific talents to enhance development of innovative industries, such as railway, automobile, and robotics sectors. This may be more rapid than sending Thai students to study abroad and educating them to become world-class executives, as Japan did in the Meiji era and before World War II, and China still does today (*Phucatkan Online*, 24 May 2020, in Thai).

References

Ahmed, E. M., & Kialashaki, R. (2019). FDI inflows spillover effect implications on the Asian-Pacific's catching up process. *Review of Development Finance*, *9*(2), 1–15.

Amin, A., & Robins, K. (1990). Industrial districts and regional development: Limits and possibilities. In F. Pyke, G. Becattini & W. Sengenberger (Eds.), *Industrial districts and inter-firm co-operation in Italy* (pp. 185–219). International Institute for Labour Studies.

Barnes, J., Black, A., & Techakanont, K. (2017). Industrial policy, multinational strategy and domestic capability: A comparative analysis of the development of South Africa's and Thailand's automotive industries. *The European Journal of Development Research*, *29*(1), 37–53.

Board of Investment. (June, 2021). *Thailand BOI approves enhanced incentives to promote R&D and HRD, and to attract semiconductor manufacturing, digital activities and smart packaging*. Investment Services Center, Board of Investment.

Board of Investment. (September, 2021). *BOI to host virtual edition of SUBCON Thailand subcontracting exhibition on Sept 20–27, 2021*. Investment Services Center, Board of Investment.

Board of Investment. (various years). *Raingan pawakanlongthun doytrong caak tangprathed nai prathedthai (Report on inward foreign direct investment situation in Thailand)*. International Affairs Division, Board of Investment (In Thai).

Carroll, T., Hameiri, S., & Jones, L. (Eds.). (2020). *The political economy of Southeast Asia: Politics and uneven development under hyperglobalisation*. Springer Nature.

Chan-ocha, P. (2022, October 27). *Accelerating Thailand*. A speech at the seminar on the National Infrastructure Development and Three-Axis Strategy, held by the Bangkok Post at Centara Grand at Central World (In Thai).

Edgington, D. W., & Hayter, R. (2013). Glocalization and regional headquarters: Japanese electronics firms in the ASEAN region. *Annals of the Association of American Geographers*, *103*(3), 647–668.

Fleming, D., & Soborg, H. (2014). Are emerging South-East Asian economies caught in a middle-income trap? Case: Malaysia paradoxes in provision of higher skilled labour. *Forum for Development Studies*, *41*(1), 115–133.

Grabher, G. (1993). *The embedded firm: On the socioeconomics of industrial networks*. Routledge.

Haggard, S. (2018). *Developmental states: Politics of development*. Cambridge University Press.

Haggard, S., & Kaufman, R. R. (2018). *The political economy of democratic transitions*. Princeton University Press.

Haworth, N. (2013). Compressed development: Global value chains, multinational enterprises and human resource development in 21st century Asia. *Journal of World Business*, *48*, 251–259.

Hayter, R., & Edgington, D. W. (2004). Flying geese in Asia: The impacts of Japanese MNCs as a source of industrial learning. *Journal of Economic & Social Geography*, *95*(1), 3–26.

Helleiner, G. K. (1973). Manufactured exports from less-developed countries and multinational firms. *The Economic Journal*, *83*(329), 21–47.

Homklin, T., Takahashi, Y., & Techakanont, K. (2014). The influence of social and organizational support on transfer of training: Evidence from Thailand. *International Journal of Training and Development*, *18*(2), 116–131.

Intarakumnerd, P. (2018). *Mismanaging innovation systems: Thailand and the middle-income trap*. Routledge.
Intarakumnerd, P. (2019). Thailand's middle-income trap: Firms' technological upgrading and innovation and government policies. *Seoul Journal of Economics*, *32*(1), 107–135.
Intarakumnerd, P., & Techakanont, K. (2016). Intra-industry trade, product fragmentation and technological capability development in Thai automotive industry. *Asia Pacific Business Review*, *22*(1), 65–85.
Kabe, S., Ushiyama, R., Kinkyo, T., & Hamori, S. (2016). *Moving up the ladder: Development challenges for low and middle-income Asia*. World Scientific Publishing.
Kalalang, R. J., Laorenza, E. V., & Canto, D. M. A. (2022). Stimulating global competitiveness: An economic analysis of the middle-income trap in the Philippines. *Journal of Economics, Finance and Accounting Studies*, *4*(1), 359–382.
Kang, B., Nabeshima, K., & Cheng, F. (2015). *Avoiding the middle-income trap: Indigenous innovative effort vs foreign innovative effort*. IDE Discussion Paper No. 509. The Institute of Developing Economies.
Kohpaiboon, A., & Jongwanich, J. (2021). Economic consequences of globalisation: Case study of Thailand. In S. Urata & H. T. T. Doan (Eds.), *Globalisation and its economic consequences: Looking at APEC economies* (Chapter 7, pp. 164–191). Routledge.
Kuroiwa, I., Techakanont, K., & Keola, S. (2021). Evolution of production networks and the localisation of firms: Evidence from the Thai automotive industry. *Journal of the Asia Pacific Economy*, December, 1–22. https://doi.org/10.1080/13547860.2021.2024361.
Lauridsen, L. S. (2004). Foreign direct investment, linkage formation and supplier development in Thailand during the 1990s: The role of state governance. *The European Journal of Development Research*, *16*(3), 561–586.
Lauridsen, L. S. (2009). The policies and politics of industrial upgrading in Thailand during the Thaksin Era (2001–2006). *Asian Politics & Policy*, *1*(3), 409–434.
Lee, C., & Narjoko, D. (2015). Escaping the middle-income trap in Southeast Asia: Micro evidence on innovation, productivity, and globalization. *Asian Economic Policy Review*, *10*, 124–147.
Mahoney, J., & Rodríguez-Franco, D. (2018). Dependency theory. In C. Lancaster & N. van de Walle (Eds.), *The Oxford handbook of the politics of development* (Chapter 2, pp. 22–42). Oxford University Press.
OECD. (2021). *OECD investment policy reviews: Thailand*. OECD Publishing.
Paus, E. A. (2017). *Escaping the middle-income trap: Innovate or perish*. ADBI Working Paper No. 685. Asian Development Bank Institute.
Paus, E. A., & Gallagher, K. P. (2008). Missing links: Foreign investment and industrial development in Costa Rica and Mexico. *Studies in Comparative International Development*, *43*, 53–80.
Paweenawat, S. W. (2019). Foreign direct investment and wage spillover in Thailand: Evidence from firm-level panel data. *International Journal of Social Economics*, *46*(10), 1198–1213.
Phuangketkeow, S. (2020). Thailand's eastern economic corridor: A bold strategic move. *ISEAS Perspective*, *13*, 1–11.
Ramstetter, E. D., & Sjöholm, F. (Eds.). (2006). *Multinational corporations in Indonesia and Thailand: Wages, productivity and exports*. Palgrave Macmillan.

Sato, Y., & Sato, H. (Eds.). (2016). *Varieties and alternatives of catching-up. Asian development in the context of 21st century*. Palgrave MacMillan.

Suehiro, A. (2008). *Catch-up industrialization: The trajectory and prospects of East Asian economies*. National University of Singapore Press.

Teeramungcalanon, M., & Chiu, E. M. (2020). The effects of foreign direct investment on income inequality of Thailand. *Southeast Asian Journal of Economics*, *8*(1), 107–138.

Topple, C., Lion, H., Vranic, V., Masli, E. K., & Donovan, J. D. (2016). FDI and development in Thailand. In J. D. Donovan, C. Topple, E. K. Masli, & T. Vanichseni (Eds.), *Corporate sustainability assessments: Sustainability practices of multinational enterprises in Thailand* (Chapter 2, pp. 15–39). Routledge.

Zhao, S., Papanastassiou, M., Pearce, R. D., & Iguchi, C. (2020). MNE R&D internationalization in developing Asia. *Asia Pacific Journal of Management*, *38*, 789–813.

Part II

Policies toward innovation-driven growth

Chapter 5

Upper-middle-income development model

5.1 The 1960s and 1970s import substitution industrialization

The evolution of Thai business groups propelled Thailand's economic development from low-income to upper-middle-income nation, divided into two eras: the 1960s and 1970s, and the 1980s and 1990s.

The 1961 National Economic Development Plan initiated Thailand's industrialization (the current 13th plan update runs from 2023–2027). During the Sarit Thanarat administration, Thai private companies began exporting agricultural products and importing manufactured goods. With aid from the World Bank, the government promoted import-substituting industrialization (ISI) with an emphasis on domestic sales. Before that, under the leadership of Field Marshal Plaek Phibunsongkhram (Phibun) and nationalist policy, over 100 state-owned enterprises were assigned responsibility for national security and public service (Hewison, 2006; Phipatseritham, 1981; Suehiro, 1989, 1992).

Heavy industry capitalists (for example, cement, appliances, and automobiles) and light industry capitalists (textiles and clothing) made up the business group. Local businesses benefited from import substitution. Since they lacked in-house technology, most owners formed joint ventures with Japanese partners (Goto & Endo, 2014; Phipatseritham, 1981). The Thailand Board of Investment (BOI) needed foreign direct investment (FDI) to transfer manufacturing and management technologies. The Foreign Business Act, B.E. 2542 (1999) prohibited foreign companies from holding over 49 percent of joint venture shares.

Despite efforts to minimize imports, Thailand was obliged to import capital goods, raw materials, and intermediate goods. Thailand's trade imbalance with trading partners, notably Japan, was chronic (Akbas et al., 2021). The corporate sector had intimate ties with the military and government officials. High-ranking personnel were typically requested to serve as company chairperson or director (Hewison, 2006; Phongpaichit & Baker, 1995).

For fund-raising, private firms relied on bank loans to launch and expand. Capital markets remained immature. The Bank of Thailand limited the number

DOI: 10.4324/9781003370536-8

Table 5.1 Evolution of business groups in Thailand: 1960s–1990s

Period	*1960s–1970s*	*1980s–1990s*
Strategy	Agriculture-based growth Import-substitution Industrialization	Economic reforms Export-oriented industrialization
Economic development	Exports dominated by rice, teak, tin, and rubber Infrastructure development BOI establishment 1966 Diversification away from agriculture (into textile, auto, pharma) Alien Business Law 1972	Declining terms of trade in agriculture, second oil shock 1979, public sector deficit Baht appreciation due to dollar peg, but then devaluation (Plaza Accord) FDI in low value-added manufacturing from Japan Manufacturing exports exceeded agriculture from 1985
Business networks	*Emerging business groups* Local capitalists Foreign MNCs (manufacturers) Government	*Diversified business groups* Local capitalists Foreign MNCs (manufacturers and trading partners) Government
Market	Domestic market	Domestic market and overseas markets (US, EU, Japan) M&A in domestic markets
Finance	Loans from commercial banks Financial conglomerate	Loan from commercial banks Financial conglomerate Listed on the stock exchange and pyramidal shareholdings
Technology	Joint ventures with foreign MNCs	Joint ventures with foreign MNCs
Human Resources	Personnel management Training and development	Human resource management Managerial education

of license-issuing banks and non-banking companies. The financial behemoth had links to the military, bureaucracy, and politics. Commercial banking groups dominated funding and flourished alongside the economic rise (Bualek, 2000). These commercial banking groups had transformed into financial conglomerates, including securities, insurance/life insurance, and nonfinancial sectors such as manufacturing and real estate firms. Four significant groups were Bangkok Bank, Thai Farmers Bank, Bangkok Metropolitan Bank, and the Bank of Ayudhya (Suehiro, 1989, 1992). After the 1997 Asian financial crisis, the financial conglomerate became unstable (Suehiro & Wailerdsak, 2004).

At the time, private sector human resource development was in its infancy. Only ten public universities administered admissions examinations. Therefore, the number of graduates remained modest. The major purpose was to educate government employees. The bulk of family-owned firms enrolled their offspring abroad for training about continuing operations in future as a sign of familial generational shift. Only private businesses had human resource (HR) departments (Wailerdsak, 2005; Siengthai et al., 2009).

5.2 The 1980s and 1990s export-oriented industrialization of and the Asian financial crisis

Since 1988, the growth of the new Thai business group was noteworthy. It was the principal source of foreign direct investment (FDI), especially from Japan, which had an inflated yen as a result of the 1985 Plaza Accord. Under the export-oriented industrialization (EOI) program, annual FDI between 1986 and 1991 averaged $1.3 billion, mainly in the manufacturing sector (Apaitan et al., 2019; Hewison, 2006).

Throughout this time, Thailand's industrial exports climbed by an average of 25 percent yearly, making the Kingdom one of the world's fastest-growing exporters. The nation shifted from dependence on imports to exporting agricultural and manufactured goods. In 1985, per capital income reached a lower-middle-income country level. Not until 2011 would Thailand attain middle-income nation status (Suehiro, 2009).

Thai companies grew, entering government-supported industries such as exports and related middle-class business involvements. Multinational corporations (MNCs) became increasingly present. Through the Pacific Trade Triangle, MNCs accelerated exports to the United States, Europe, and Japan. Thai companies acquired foreign technology by purchasing licenses, manufacturing original equipment manufacturer (OEM) products, and forming joint ventures. Thai officials were aware of export issues created by MNCs. Alongside efforts to ensure local content, MNCs were under pressure to assist Thai SMEs in supporting industries. In Thailand, SMEs currently contribute to global automotive, electrical appliance, and electronic supply chains (Busser, 2008; Doner, 2016: Kawakami & Goto, 2020).

The Stock Exchange of Thailand (SET) progressed as well. During the economic boom, many Thai business groups listed their primary firms or holding corporations on the SET. Business group governance facilitated pyramidal and cross-share ownership. Funding enabled firms to expand into business networks. On 4 January 1994, the SET achieved an all-time high of 1,735.73 points, a still-unsurpassed record. However, due to financial deregulation, the founding of Bangkok International Banking Facilities (BIBF) in 1992 added to Thai financial system instability, as a development distinct from acquisition of FDI (Wailerdsak & Siengthai, 2016).

BIBF facilitated substantial short-term capital entry into Thailand, including loans to major manufacturing firms and flows into non-manufacturing sectors such as land and real estate. Stock speculation and expensive real estate deals expanded. When property sales declined, signalling the bursting of an economic bubble, the

Figure 5.1 Upper-middle-income model of Thailand

financial sector was saddled with many bad loans. The BOT mishandled macroeconomic principles, while lacking supervision of nontransparent borrowing based on favouritism, as the Bangkok Bank of Commerce (BBC) did. Hedge funds attacked the Thai baht, and Thai foreign exchange reserves were drained. On 2 July 1997, the government floated the Thai baht, which had far-reaching consequences for Thai businesses and society (Hewison, 2006; Wailerdsak, 2008).

In a flourishing economy, the need for professionals and executives skyrocketed. MBA, Mini MBA, and XMBA programs became popular. People management transitioned to human resource management, emphasizing training and developing extant employees (internal labour market) to support corporate success, insofar as the external labour market was insufficient or failed to meet expectations (Wailerdsak, 2005).

5.3 Economic performance of Thailand

5.3.1 Economic growth rate

In 2010, Thailand and the People's Republic of China (later China) were promoted from lower to upper-middle-income countries by the World Bank.[1] Both countries have gained new potential to become high-income or developed countries in the near future. But Thailand's GDP growth rate has slowed for over a decade, averaging 3 percent annually compared to ASEAN countries with higher growth rates.

Retrospectively, Thailand transitioned from a low-income to lower-middle-income country in the early 1970s. The country began industrialization in the 1960s with an import-substitution strategy, then switched to an export-orientation approach in the mid-1970s. Thailand elicited investment from MNCs, particularly Japanese companies, due to its abundant natural resources, low labour costs, and macroeconomic stability. It has joined global value chains (GVCs) as part of an export-oriented strategy, especially in the automobile and electronics industries (Brown, 2004; Busser, 2008; Intarakumnerd, 2017, 2020).

As a result, Thailand's economy has been dramatically restructured. The agriculture sector's GDP share dropped from 31.1 percent in the 1960s to 10.5 percent in 2010 and 8.6 percent in 2020, while the manufacturing sector share climbed from 22.8 percent to 39.9 and 33.1 percent, respectively.[2] Thailand experienced an economic boom between 1987 and 1996, with annual GDP growth average of 9.5 percent (Phongpaichit & Benyaapikul, 2012). Political stability, a business-friendly regulatory framework, a large domestic market, open access to foreign investment, and participation in GVCs all contributed to this economic success (Kawakami & Goto, 2020). But the country experienced significant shrinkage when the 1997 Asian financial crisis erupted.

Between 2000 and 2015, Thailand experienced significant political turbulence, with two military coups d'état (September 2006 and May 2014) and four violent political clashes. But it would be an exaggeration to argue that the low growth rate was due to prolonged political turmoil. After the May 2014 military takeover, the political climate cooled, only to smoulder again after February 2020, following the dissolution of the Future Forward Party. But political activism has been hampered by the court system and the novel coronavirus 2019 (COVID-19) pandemic (Baker & Phongpaichit, 2021).

However, external shocks such as the 1997 Asian financial crisis, the Great Recession between 2007 and 2009, the 2011 Thailand floods, and the COVID-19 pandemic, all of which harmed the Thai economy more severely. Those events dampened investor confidence and affected domestic demand and growth performance. Also, due to rising wages, Thai worker productivity fell, compounding the problem of structurally low growth rates (Baker & Phongpaichit, 2021).

Table 5.2 shows GDP growth rates of Asian countries as announced by the Asian Development Bank (ADB; five-year average from 2015 to 2019). Thailand declined markedly to 3 percent or less, while ASEAN countries with annual growth rates of over 6 percent include Cambodia, Vietnam, China, Myanmar, Laos, Philippines, Indonesia with over 5 percent, and Malaysia with over 4 percent.

More significantly, based on World Bank national account data, Thailand's per capita GDP (current US$) rose by just 115 percent between 2010 and 2015 (from 5,076 to 5,840) and 123 percent between 2015 and 2020 (from 5,840 to 7,189), compared to 129 percent and 113 percent for upper-middle-income countries (from 6,324 to 8,156 to 9,178). While per capita GDP of high-income countries is 12,696 and more (according to World Bank criteria of 1 July 2021), evidently Thailand lags behind Malaysia with a GDP per capita at 10,402 in 2020.

Table 5.2 Growth rate of GDP in Asia, 2015–2021 (%)

		Actual Value						Projection	Average 5 years
		2015	2016	2017	2018	2019	2020	2021	*2015-2019
1	**Cambodia**	7.0	7.0	6.9	7.5	7.1	-3.1	4.0	7.1
2	**Vietnam**	6.7	6.2	6.8	7.1	7.0	4.8	6.8	6.8
3	**China**	6.9	6.8	6.9	6.7	6.0	2.3	8.1	6.7
4	**Philippines**	6.1	7.1	6.9	6.3	6.1	-9.6	4.5	6.5
5	**Lao**	7.3	7.0	6.9	6.2	4.7	-0.5	4.0	6.4
6	**Myanmar**	7.0	5.9	5.8	6.4	6.8	3.3	-9.8	6.4
7	**Indonesia**	4.9	5.0	5.1	5.2	5.0	-2.1	4.5	5.0
8	**Malaysia**	5.1	4.4	5.8	4.8	4.3	-5.6	5.5	4.9
9	**Thailand**	3.1	3.4	4.2	4.2	2.3	-6.1	3.0	3.4
	(Bank of Thailand)				4.1	2.4	-6.1	0.7	
10	**Singapore**	2.5	3.3	4.5	3.5	1.3	-5.4	6.0	3.0

Source: Author's compilation from ADB, Asian Development Outlook 2019 and 2021, annual growth rate of GDP, %.

Note: Ranking based on average annual growth rate from 2015 to 2019.

5.3.2 Export value by sector

Until now, Thailand's economic growth has been fuelled by two key factors:

- Rapid increase in exports
- Expansion of domestic consumption and tourism

Figure 5.2 depicts economic growth rate and export value changes between 1996 and 2021 (projected). Average annual growth rates between 2000 and 2015 were 3.84 percent, significantly lower than the 9.52 percent average annual growth rate (1988 constant price) experienced during the economic boom from 1987 to 1996. This figure is also inferior to other East Asian nation annual growth rates for the same period and less than half that of China.

Thai export values grew steadily, increasing 45-fold over the 31 years from 1981 to 2012, with the exception of 2009. Simultaneously in Thailand, development of consumer credit, automobile sales, and urban middle-class housing surged. Then, with 2012 as a turning point, Thailand's export value began to stabilize in the range of 7–8 trillion baht until 2020 (Kuroiwa et al., 2021). Domestic private consumption declined due to rising household loans and tight governmental monetary policy. Thailand was evidently facing limitations in traditional economic development.

Furthermore, the aforementioned statistics were compiled before the COVID-19 pandemic, indicating that an economic slowdown had already occurred. COVID-19 exacerbated a slowing growth rate, instantly impoverishing individual workers and lengthening the interval for transcending the middle-income trap[3] (Baker & Phongpaichit, 2021; Yusuf, 2017).

Another significant shift may be seen in export structure, divided into key commodity categories (Figure 5.3). The export value of agricultural, forestry, and fishery products such as rice, tapioca starch, and natural rubber dropped from 40.7 percent in 1985 to 7.9 percent in 2014, while export value has risen from 78.5 billion baht (193 billion baht × 40.7 percent) to 578 billion baht (7300 billion baht × 7.9 percent), a 7.7-fold increase over three decades.

Agro-industry export growth is even more noteworthy. Sugar, canned tuna, broiler chicken, and canned fruits increased from 24 billion baht in 1985 to 872 billion baht in 2014, for a 36-fold increase. These primary goods, relying heavily on domestic natural resources and low-cost labour, including migrant labour from neighbouring countries, contributed to market diversification and served as a buffer against the global recession's impact on the exporting manufactured goods such as information technology (IT) products (Apaitan et al., 2019).

From the start of Thailand's industrialization in the 1970s, it was proposed that the nation should adopt a NAIC mixed development model, combining manufacturing and agriculture. This differs from the manufacturing-focused NIC model. NAIC status, based on a substantial agricultural surplus and agricultural exports as central government tax revenue sources, is seen as a distinctive characteristic of Thailand (Suehiro, 2009).

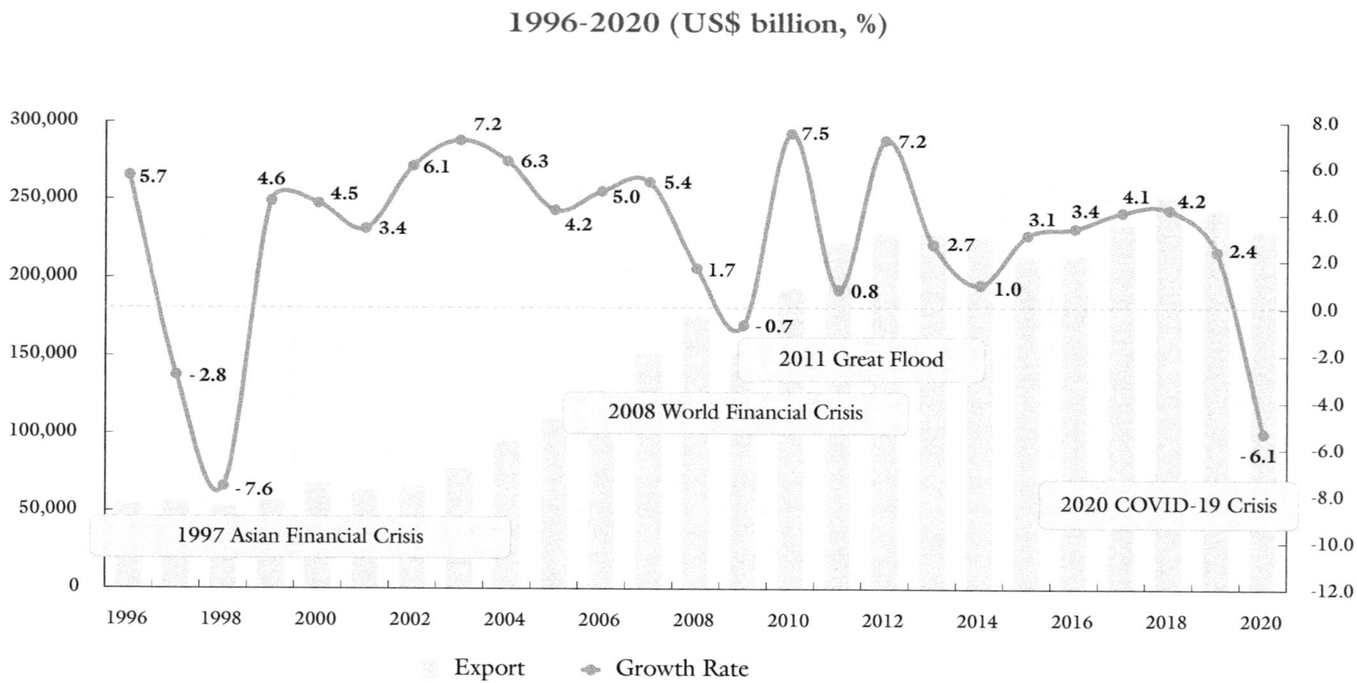

Figure 5.2 Overview of Thailand's economy

Sources: Author's compilation based on information from the Bank of Thailand's website

(1) Export value

www.bot.or.th/Thai/Statistics/EconomicAndFinancial/Pages/StatInternationalTrade.aspx

(2) Growth rate

www.bot.or.th/Thai/Statistics/EconomicAndFinancial/Pages/StatMacroEconomicIndicators.aspx

Note: The export volume is depicted on the left Y axis, while the growth rate is depicted on the right Y axis.

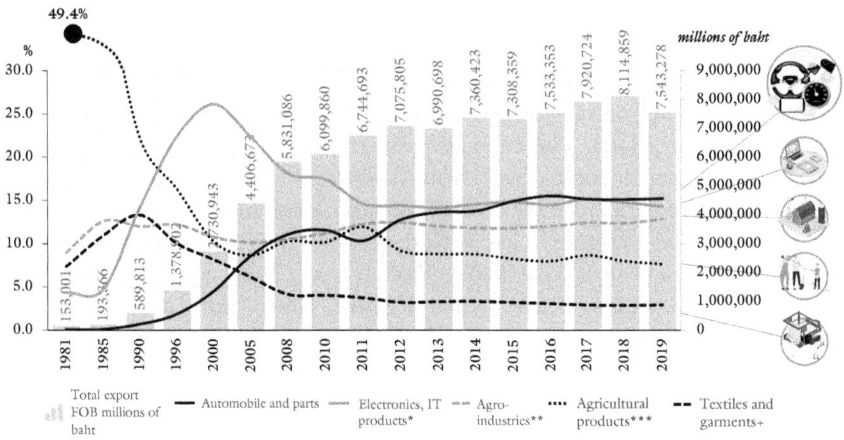

Figure 5.3 Changes in export structure by major commodity groups, 1981–2019

Source: Compiled by the author based on Ministry of Commerce website, http://tradereport.moc.go.th/TradeThai.aspx; Trade statistics and economic indicators of Thailand; and Total value and quantity of exports classified byproduct group; and from the Bank of Thailand websites, www.bot.or.th/Thai/Statistics/EconomicAndFinancial/ExternalSector/Pages/StatInternationalTrade.aspx

Remark: *Electronic, IT products include computer parts, integrated circuits, and telecommunication equipment. **Agro-industries include sugar, canned tuna, and canned fruits. ***Agricultural products include rice, tapioca, natural rubber, frozen chickens, and frozen shrimp. +Textiles and garments include yarns and fabrics.

Agro-industries dominated by powerful local conglomerates constantly pressure the Thai government to provide policy complacency and market intervention, such as the rice pledging or rice mortgage schemes, as well as price and export subsidy schemes for sugar, natural rubber, and palm oil, among other plans (Apaitan et al., 2020; Warr, 2008).

Textiles and clothing as labour-intensive products peaked in the late 1980s and early 1990s. Thai and foreign firms are primary manufacturers and exporters (Brown, 2004). The market share of these products has dropped from 13.3 percent in 1990 to 3.3 percent in 2014. Similarly, due to erosion of the low-cost advantage, sports shoes and wooden furniture, including wooden toys, have lost competitiveness in the global market.

By contrast, electric product exports rapidly grew during the 1990s, followed by automobiles and auto parts in the 2010s. Electronic goods exports, including integrated circuits (IC) and hard disk drives (HDD), expanded from 84 billion baht in 1990 to about 1,000 billion baht in 2005. Later, as China began to manufacture and export electronic products, Thai electronic exports started to decline (Ito, 2020a). Since 2014, Thailand's primary export products have shifted to automobiles and auto parts, particularly one-ton pickup trucks, with export value exceeding one trillion baht (Kuroiwa et al., 2021).

This growth reflects the prominent development of industrial clusters on the outskirts of the Bangkok Metropolitan Area (BMA), to which MNCs from Japan, the United States, Europe, and Asian NIEs have contributed by organizing production networks in collaboration with several local part suppliers (Intarakumnerd et al., 2016). Therefore, despite the "Made in Thailand" label on exports, real national income derives from corporate income tax, VAT, and wages totalling less than 10 percent of overall income. Most MNCs repatriated revenues to their home countries in line with the enclave industry concept[4] originally associated with the dependency theory (Apitan et al., 2020; Suehiro, 2008).

Many high-income countries, such as South Korea and Taiwan, targeted the electrical and electronics industry (Intarakumnerd & Liu, 2019). Less than 5 percent of South Korean and Taiwanese workers are in the agricultural sector, compared up to 40 percent of Thailand. In 2020, Thailand had the lowest export value share for electrical and electronic products compared to total export value among Asian countries at 16 percent, underperforming Singapore (52 percent), Taiwan (36 percent), the Philippines (34 percent), Malaysia (33 percent), and China (24 percent).[5] Thailand's participation in the global supply chain was jeopardized, lagging behind regional countries in international trade agreements and technology adoption.

Indeed, in the 1990s, Tanin Industries Co., Ltd., founded in 1946, was one of the few domestic Thai companies operating in the electrical and electronics industry as a leading consumer electronic equipment firm producing televisions, fans, radios, and rice cookers (Intarakumnerd, 2017). Already weakened by the emergence of global market competitors such as South Korea and Taiwan, which compromised its competitive status, Tanin folded after the 1997 Asian financial crisis, as did other indigenous Thai firms. Today, it would be difficult for Thailand to catch up to South Korea and Taiwan in industrialization by relying solely on local companies in the IT and electrical and electronics industries (Intarakumnerd, 2017; (Intarakumnerd & Liu, 2019).

When electrical and electronic products are exclusively considered as export products, Thailand is seen as having significant weaknesses. However, the export structure of Thai products reveals different product types and markets. Unlike Singapore and Malaysia, which rely heavily on electronics exports, or Indonesia, with oil and natural gas exports, Thailand can export electronic as well as non-electronic products competitively in the global market.

5.3.3 Export markets – from Pacific trade triangle to Asianization

Thailand's trade partners and export structure in commodity groupings altered considerably between 1995 and 2020. The G3 markets – Japan, the United States, and the European Union (EU, 27 countries) – all lowered their market share. For example, Japan's share dropped from 16.8 percent to 9.6 percent, while the United States share declined from 17.8 percent to 10.0 percent, and EU share lessened from 16.5 percent to 10.3 percent (see Figure 5.4).

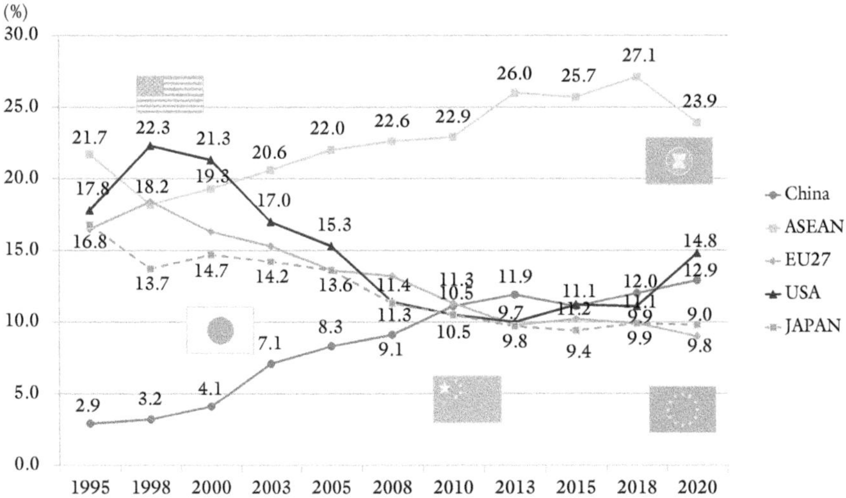

Figure 5.4 Major destination of Thailand exports, 1995–2020

Source: Author's compilation based on the Bank of Thailand website, EC_XT_003_S2 Trade Classified by Country/Economic Territories (US$)

By contrast, during the same time, the market share of ASEAN nations and China significantly increased. Thailand's largest market expanded from 21.7 percent to 26.1 percent due to ASEAN participation. Trade with China grew at a rate of approximately 20 percent. In 2009, China outstripped Japan in export value and, in 2010, outperformed the United States. As a result, since 2010, China has been Thailand's most significant trading partner (Ito, 2020a). In 2019, Thai-Chinese import and export trade totalled 2.48 trillion baht, accounting for 18 percent of Thailand's world trade. China was responsible for 12 percent of Thailand's exports and 21 percent of its imports. East Asia, in addition being the production base, is also an expanding consumer market. Therefore, the proportion of regional internal trading tends to increase.

In sum, the export structure shows how trading markets have shifted from the Pacific Trade Triangle (among Asia, Japan, and the West) to Asianization (among Asian countries) (see Figure 5.5) for two principal reasons (Goto & Oizumi, 2021; Moeller, 2021). Firstly, this reflects agricultural export reprimatization to the Chinese market, and consumer product exports to ASEAN markets, growing due to middle class growth (Ito, 2020b). Secondly, relocation of MNC supply chains and production networks within Asia, resulting from ASEAN Economic Community (AEC) free trade agreements (FTAs), such as the ASEAN-China FTA (Intarakumnerd et al., 2016; Wailerdsak &Siengthai, 2016).

Japanese company revitalization strategies in particular have shifted from products "made in Japan" to products "made by Japan," as part of a 2013 three-pronged strategy to boost Japanese growth, dubbed Abenomics. Japanese MNCs export

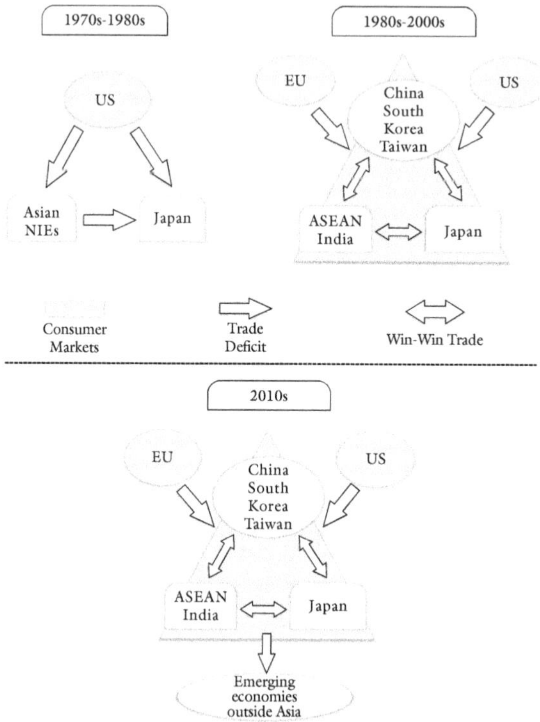

Figure 5.5 From pacific triangle to Asianization

Source: Suehiro (2014), p. 55

intermediate products from Japan to ASEAN countries, assemble and export them to partners such as the United States, EU, China, India, and South Korea. Japan strategically promotes different national Economic Partnership Agreements (EPAs) and Free Trade Agreements (FTAs) in the Asia-Pacific region and Europe (Moeller, 2021). In addition, after the 2011 Thailand floods, Japanese investment in Thailand decreased due to the Thailand plus one policy encouraging Japanese firms to invest in other ASEAN countries to mitigate risk.

5.4 End of the low-cost advantage era

5.4.1 The rise of wage rate

The noticeable growth in nominal wages that began in the late 2000s was the main reason that the Asian Development Bank and others saw China and Thailand in terms of the middle-income trap. Thailand experienced significant wage increases as well as the Lewis turning point (LTP)[6] (Phongpaichit & Benyaapikul, 2012). Minimum wage (baht per day) changed in the Bangkok Metropolitan Area and Chiang Mai in the north from 1989 to 2014. As consumer prices soared, the minimum wage in Bangkok jumped from 76 baht (69 baht in Chiang Mai) in 1989 to 132 (116) in 1994 and then to 157 (137) in 1996. The government and industrial organizations quashed calls for a higher minimum wage from 1997 to 2002 to limit the economic recession caused by the 1997 Asian financial crisis. In 2002, Bangkok's minimum wage remained at 165 (143 for Chiang Mai), just eight (six) baht above 1997 rates[7] (Suehiro, 2019).

To gain political support among industrial zone factory workers, the Thaksin government vowed to raise the minimum wage biannually after assuming office in February 2002. Even after Thaksin was deposed by a military coup d'état, new governments continued to follow the same agenda. In January 2011, the minimum wage in Bangkok was raised from 165 to 215 baht, while the minimum wage in Chiang Mai went from 143 to 180 baht (Suehiro, 2019).

Between 1989 and 2010, the increase in minimum wage was not seen as a crucial matter, but it became so after the Yingluck government (led by Yingluck Shinawatra, sister of Thaksin Shinawatra) raised the daily minimum wage to 300 baht in seven provinces in 2012 and nationwide in 2013, regardless of the difference in cost of living between Bangkok and the provinces (Samart & Kilenthong, 2020). This meant an 85 percent rise in labour costs for certain firms; in short, the minimum wage increased by over 60 percent during the past decade from 184 in 2006 to 215 in 2011 and then to 300 in 2013. It reflected the Thai government's desire to shift to an industrial structure leaning toward technology and knowledge-intensive industries by constraining the entry of foreign-owned companies seeking low-wage labour forces (Samart & Kilenthong, 2020).

The Thai government announced that starting from 1 October 2022, daily minimum wage for Thai nationals increased to 328–354 baht (USD 9.01 – USD 9.72), depending upon the province where the worker resided. After the headline inflation rate in July 2022 reached a 14-year high of 7.61 percent, Thailand's economy has been slowly recovering from three year-long impact of the novel coronavirus 2019 (COVID-19) pandemic. In addition to Russia's invasion of Ukraine, rising gasoline and food prices have increased economic instability in the Kingdom. Higher wages will burden the labour-intensive agriculture, retail, restaurant, construction, garment, and hotel industries.

Furthermore, starting in 2000, Thailand faced chronic skilled and unskilled labour shortages due to rapid demographic changes. The proportion of citizens over 60 years old more than doubled from 1975 to 2007, from roughly 5 percent to 11 percent of the population. The declining share of working-age population will create an economic growth gap potentially filled by automation. This situation adversely affected labour-intensive industries and SMEs. Consequently, many labour-intensive firms, including MNCs, turned to migrant labour or relocated to neighbouring countries with lower wage scales. Boosting worker productivity and automation appeared to be long-term solutions for restructuring the labour market (Paweenawat et al., 2017).

Later, the government issued work permits to foreign labourers from Cambodia, Laos, and Myanmar (CLM) who had legally entered Thailand and gave temporary work permits to illegal immigrants from CLM, following agreements with these nations. The foreign unskilled workers were employed in wide-ranging occupations, such as fishing, construction, paddy transport, and natural rubber and palm oil harvesting, as well as menial jobs in different manufacturing sectors and housework (Suehiro, 2019).

According to the Ministry of Labour, Office of Foreign Workers Administration data, as of 2011, Thailand had 580,000 legal workers and 1.25 million illegal immigrants and people with temporary work permits, for a total of 1.83 million foreign workers, of whom over 80 percent were from Myanmar. Naturally, a large contingent of foreign workers may impede labour productivity improvement in Thailand (Paweenawat et al., 2017). Meanwhile, Vietnamese wages are also rising. Unlike Thailand and China, Vietnam is not hampered by an overall labour force shortage but by the scarcity of highly skilled workers required in modern factories, a specific problem for underdeveloped countries (Suehiro, 2014).

Subsequently, the Thai government established a system for accepting more legal foreign workers, increasing from 1,373,388 in 2015 to 2,531,309 in May 2020.[8] Considering that just over nine million Thai workers are private sector employees, the proportion of foreign workers is significant.

5.4.2 Lower labour productivity

If labour productivity improves to offset the increase in nominal wage costs, a wage increase does not always translate to an economic growth slowdown. The nominal wage increase does not affect international competitiveness in this context but leads to greater domestic consumption (Yusuf, 2017). Before the 2000s, according to OECD definition of NIC and catch-up industrialization theory, international organizations and economists frequently used two metrics to indicate increased labour productivity.

- Growth of labour productivity, measured as annual growth rate in per capita production (amount of value added).
- Labour productivity differential, measured by taking the amount of per capita added value produced in the top developed country (the United States) as 100 and examining how the same figure for a given nation varies from that nation (aspiring to the United States economic development).

Significantly, Asian annual growth rate in labour productivity has consistently outperformed other world regions. The pertinent issue is change in the annual growth rate over time rather than annual labour productivity growth rate in general. This distinction is meaningful insofar as labour productivity growth rate tends to decline when capital stock increases with industrialization progress. Empirical data are published in the Productivity Databook of the Asian Productivity Organization (APO, 2021), providing data sets for nations by intervals (1990–1995, 1995–2000, 2000–2005, 2005–2010, 2010–2015, and 2015–2019) (see Table 5.3).

Table 5.3 Per-worker labour productivity growth in Asia, 1990–2019 (2017 PPP) (%)

	1990-1995	1995-2000	2000-2005	2005-2010	2010-2015	2015-2019
China	8.5	6.2	8.0	9.5	7.4	6.0
Vietnam	5.1	5.2	4.6	3.7	4.0	5.5
India	3.1	4.2	4.7	7.0	5.3	5.4
Thailand	6.5	0.3	3.8	2.5	3.4	3.9
Philippines	0.3	3.1	1.4	2.7	4.2	3.5
Singapore	4.4	4.2	3.3	1.3	1.8	2.9
Malaysia	6.7	1.0	3.8	1.3	1.7	2.4
South Korea	5.9	4.8	3.5	3.4	1.4	1.9
Indonesia	6.4	-1.6	3.6	2.6	4.1	1.7
Japan	0.6	1.2	1.4	0.1	0.7	0.0
EU15	1.9	1.4	0.9	0.3	0.6	0.4

Source: Compiled by the author from Table 16 Per-worker labour productivity growth, APO Productivity Databook, 2021, p. 185.

Note: GDP at constant basic prices per worker, using 2017 PPP.

According to this report, all nations apart from China and India are trending downward in per-worker labour productivity growth (using 2017 PPP).[9] For instance, Thailand experienced a sharp decline, from 6.5 percent in 1990–1995, to 2.5 percent in 2005–2010, and 3.9 percent in 2015–2019. While Malaysia showed a similar fall, from 6.7, 2.3, to 2.4 percent, during these years. South Korea (from 5.9, 3.4, to 1.9 percent) and Singapore (from 4.4, 1.3, to 2.9 percent), both high-income countries, also shared in this downward trend.

As workers in high-performing Asian countries tend to work longer hours on average than those in the US, the worker-based labour productivity gaps in this instance cast the Asian countries in a particularly favourable light (APO, 2021, p. 47). In addition, according to the data, after 2010, Thailand's manufacturing sector labour productivity stagnated.[10] Due to the political decision to set the minimum wage at 300 baht in 2012, the actual wage level rose significantly. Judging by quarterly instead of annual data, Thailand's labour productivity has stagnated since 2010 (Doner, 2016; Suehiro, 2019).

Another significant indicator of labour productivity is international comparison of value added per worker, with the figure for the United States at 100. Figure 5.6 presents the cross-country comparisons of per-worker labour productivity levels in 2019, measured as GDP per worker in US dollars as of 2019. On this measure,

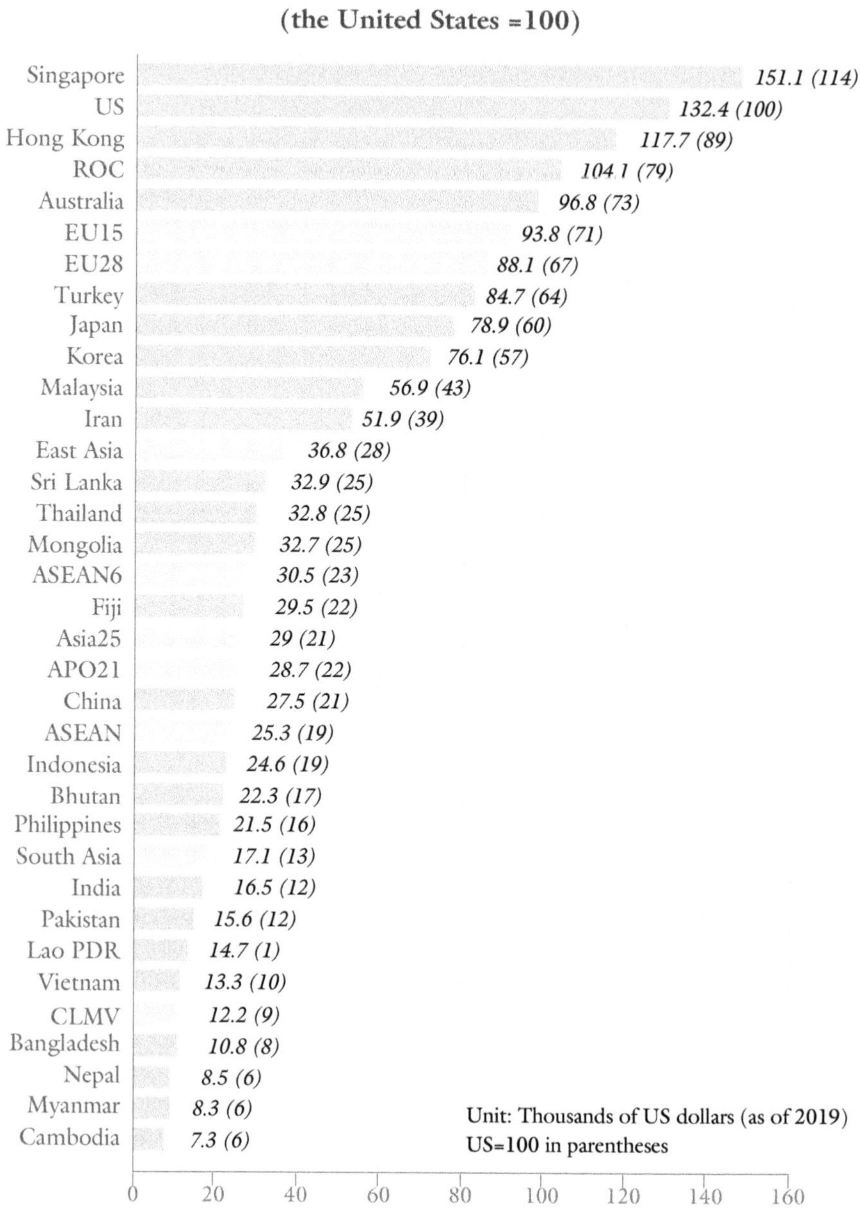

Figure 5.6 Per-worker labour productivity level by country, 2019

Source: Compiled by the author from Figure 28 Per-worker labour productivity level, APO Productivity Databook, 2021, p. 48

Note: GDP at constant basic prices per worker, using 2017 PPP, reference year 2019

Singapore is the leading economy, 14 percent higher than the US level. Hong Kong and ROC follow at some distance. The United States still largely outperforms even high-income Asian nations. Turkey, Japan, and Korea took the next tier, with productivity levels at 36–43 percent below the United States. Evidently, many countries among the Asia group have scarcely advanced in terms of matching US rates over the past three decades (less than 25 percent of the US). A productivity gap remains with the United States due to low service industry worker productivity.

One method to reduce the productivity gap with industrial developed countries would be to upgrade the national industrial structure by shifting the manufacturing sector from low-value-added industries to high-value-added ones. Another would be to switch from input-driven to innovation-led growth paths. If a middle-income country fails to encourage innovation, it may find itself on the verge of declining growth (Ito, 2020b; Kawakami & Goto, 2020).

5.5 Low R&D activity levels

Thailand's low labour productivity is associated with low public and private sector innovation and R&D expenditure levels on a national and corporate scale (Intarakumnerd, 2020). This section considers national level innovation. Metrics to measure national level R&D activities and assess whether a particular country is actively innovative include the following:

- R&D expenditure ratio to nominal GDP.
- Per capita R&D expenditure.
- Number of patent applications and acceptances.
- R&D personnel population density.
- Number of scientific articles published in international peer-reviewed journals.

Table 5.4 highlights the results of the first three metrics using data from the UNESCO Institute for Statistics (UNESCOSTAT) and the World Intellectual Property Organization (WIPO). R&D expenditure exceeding 2 percent of nominal GDP is an important criterion for judging active national innovation promotion. Thailand has not performed well, with 0.12 percent in 1999, 0.24 percent in 2010, and 1.1 percent in 2020.

By contrast, Japan and Asian NIEs (South Korea, Taiwan, and Singapore) have always exceeded 2 percent and as high as 3–4 percent in in some years. R&D expenditure is essential for boosting Japanese and Asian NIE economic status as high-income countries. This figure is higher than those of other nations deemed wealthy by the Organization for Economic Co-operation and Development (OECD) (Intarakumnerd & Liu, 2019).

In 2020, Malaysia R&D expenditure was at 1.30 percent, with Thailand at 1.33 percent,[11] and Indonesia under 0.28 percent. These three nations remain far from high-income status. Latin American countries have slightly better

Table 5.4 R&D activities in Asia, 2000 and 2020

Countries/ Economies	*R&D expenditure against nominal GDP (%)*		*R&D expenditure per capita ($)*		*International patent applications (cases)*	
	2000	*2020*	*2000*	*2020*	*2000*	*2020*
Japan	3.00	3.28	786	1,385	9,569	46,233
South Korea	2.18	4.82	401	2,179	1,582	18,671
Taiwan	1.90	3.63	419	2,034	N.A.	700
Singapore	1.82	1.89	767	1,931	222	1,020
China	0.89	2.40	26	413	781	61,030
Malaysia	0.46	1.30	60	344	5	267
Thailand	0.24	1.33	18	102	8	133
Indonesia	0.06	0.28	3.1	8.5	9	6
Philippines	N.A.	0.32	N.A.	9.1	0	27
Vietnam	N.A.	0.53	N.A.	19.5	1	21
India	0.74	0.66	15	38.3	190	1,412
Sweden	3.42	3.49	930	1,941	3,090	3,437
USA	2.62	3.45	953	2,183	38,015	55,708
France	2.08	2.35	555	1,096	4,137	7,060
Germany	2.39	3.13	640	1,736	12,581	18,568

Sources: Compiled by author based on the database of R&D expenditure per GDP and per capita (original data came from UNESCO STAT); number of patent applications (original data came from the World Intellectual Property Organization) from https://stats.oecd.org/Index.aspx?DataSetCode=GERD_TORD for OECD countries and from http://data.uis.unesco.org/for developing countries.

Note: R&D expenditure per capita includes both public and private sectors.

metrics than ASEAN countries but still lag behind Asian NIEs. Comparisons to Chinese rates (2.11 percent) reveal a striking contrast.

Thailand's backwardness in R&D is reflected in related indices such as per capita R&D expenditure,[12] amounting to US$101 in 2016, compared to US$1,655 in Singapore and US$222 in China. Likewise, the number of private sector R&D staff in Thailand remains small, with 130 per one million persons, only one in 50 for Taiwan (6,390 people) and less than one in 10 for China (1,400 people). All data points to a slow Thai government response from 1999 to 2020 to inadequate R&D activity and innovation.

Furthermore, publications in academic journals and worldwide patent registration statistics (World Intellectual Property Organization: WIPO) augment these findings. In these criteria, the United States has outdone Japan and China, although national disparities have shrunk in recent years.

In 2019, China seized first place in number of academic articles published since 2016 and international patent filings. There were 58,900 Chinese patents registered, with the United States a runner-up with 57,840 patents, followed by Japan, Germany, and South Korea with 52,660, 19,353, and 19,085 patents, respectively.

These figures suggest that China is working hard to dominate the world in science and technology. Unlike Malaysia and Thailand, which lack national policies in this area, Chinese technology promotion was established in 2006 with Guidelines on the National Medium-Term and Long-Term Program for Science and Technology Development (2006–2020) (Science Portal China, 2006; Reghunadhan, 2021). Indigenous innovation, leapfrogging in priority fields, facilitating development, and leading the future are key terms in these guidelines. Indigenous innovation refers to national innovation capability for developing new technologies within China, rather than borrowing technology (Kuroiwa et al., 2021; Song & Zhou, 2021).[13]

Based on Chinese experience, governments are anticipated to directly, rather than indirectly, contribute to innovation (Reghunadhan, 2021; Song & Zhou, 2021). Yusuf and Evenett (2002) and Yusuf (2003) explored different strategies, emphasizing government and business sector collaborations as well as networking between manufacturing and non-manufacturing sectors. China demonstrated that basic research, human development, and international network building were required to drive scientific, innovation, and R&D transformation. Off-the-shelf research might develop into a shopping mall with more product availability (Song & Zhou, 2021).

The Chinese ratio of R&D expenditure to GDP exceeded the national target of 2.0 percent in 2014, due to a science and technology promotion policy. As a result, since 2010, although China and Thailand periodically achieved upper-middle-income status, China gained apparent advantages in progression to high-income status.

Notes

1 In 2010, the threshold for upper-middle-income countries based on World Bank classifications is between $3,976 and $12,276 per capita gross national income (GNI).
2 See http://data.worldbank.org/data-catalog/world-development-indicators.
3 Tossaporn Sirisamphan, Secretary-General of the National Economic and Social Development Council (NESDC), formerly the National Economic and Social Development Board (NESDB), mentioned at a 2020 annual conference on "New Life in Thailand after COVID" that a review of the 12th National Economic and Social Development Plan (2018–2022) under the NCPO and Prayut government revealed that Thai household debt was up to 80 percent of GDP, or 13.6 trillion baht, with average per household debt of 200,000 baht. Income discrepancy between rich and the poor was as high as 20-fold, indicating wealth concentration in the upper class. The bottom line has not yet been reached in terms of sharing economic advantages. In 2018, 9.85 percent of the poor, or 6.7 million people, had earnings below the poverty line, up 1.4 million from 2017. He blamed disruptive technology, trade disputes, and a worldwide economic slowdown for the rise in poverty. Thailand anticipates confronting three highs and three lows following the COVID pandemic, with the former being high unemployment, governmental debt, and private debt, and the latter low economic growth, inflation, and interest rates (see "The impoverished have expanded throughout the NCPO government's six years in power, with a 20-fold overlap between the rich and the poor," *Thai Rath*, 24 September 2020).

4 When a group of foreign investors, all operating in the same industry, invest extensively in a specific region with the intent of manufacturing products for export, an enclave economy emerges. Governments promoting enclave economies, particularly based on foreign investment, frequently expect foreign investment and expertise to enhance the rest of the economy and domestic development. However, the hoped-for economic boost and domestic infrastructure development rarely materialize. Foreign companies frequently destroy domestic companies by raising domestic raw material costs or importing raw resources, which make it difficult for domestic companies to compete. Foreign companies also absorb the skilled labour pool. Profits from these economic enclaves are returned to the home countries of foreign investors, unconnected to the wider host-country economy (World Bank, 2017; Zeng, 2021).

5 Nine well-known IT companies are among the top 100 companies by revenue (including the finance and services sectors) in 2020: Western Digital (12th, the United States, HDD manufacturer), Cal-Comp Electronics (26th, South Korea), Seagate Technology (33rd, the United States, HDD manufacturer), and Thai Samsung Electronics (36th, South Korea). All nine businesses are foreign-owned. Among the top 1,000 companies by revenue, not one Thai company is listed.

6 A Lewisian turning point is a time at which real wages begin to rise as surplus labour from the farm sector (nonmodern sector) is absorbed by the city's modern sector (see Chapter 2).

7 For official minimum wage rates of each province, see the Ministry of Labour and Social Welfare (various years).

8 The National Statistical Office Population and Housing Census 2010 counted 1,796,633 Cambodian, Laotian, and Myanmar residents in Thailand. These workers and their families accounted for 66 percent of foreign workers and 5 percent of employees in Thailand. Several agencies have estimated the number of foreign workers in Thailand, but the Population and Housing Census statistics, compiled by survey, are seen as the most reliable. A 2020 decennial survey was postponed due to the COVID pandemic.

See www.doe.go.th/alien > Statistical Data> The Situation of Foreign Workers or Monthly Statistics.

9 In China, annual labour productivity growth rate was 10.6 percent from 1990 to 1995, 7.1 percent from 2005 to 2010, and 6.5 percent from 2015 to 2017. India's annual labour productivity growth rate was 3.1 percent, 7.0 percent, and 6.7 percent over the same years, respectively (APO, 2019, p. 170).

10 According to NESDB labour productivity survey (quarterly) for all sectors, including manufacturing, a slowdown began in 2007.

11 For government policies on promoting science and technology in Thailand, see BOI policy for promoting skill, technology, and innovation (STI) since 2004.

12 The Office of National Higher Education Science Research and Innovation Policy Council (NXPO) of the Ministry of Higher Education, Science, Research, and Innovation (MHESI) indicated that R&D expenditure has consistently grown since 2011. According to the 2019 report, Thailand spent 182,357 million baht on R&D in 2018, accounting for 1.11 percent of GDP, divided into 142,971 million baht in private investment, and 39,385 million baht in government investment, or 78 percent and 22 percent, respectively. Thailand has 159,507 R&D staff, or 24 per 10,000 inhabitants, with 33 percent of government employees and 67 percent of private sector employees working in this field. It still maintains a target of 2.0 percent of nominal GDP in 2027. (See "Explore Thailand's R&D budget and the path to achieving the 2 percent GDP target," *Prachachat Turakit*, 29 June–1 July 2020).

13 In 2016, the Beijing government adopted a long-term plan of promoting science and technology between 2006 and 2020 and addressed the national target of raising R&D expenditure to the level of 2.0 percent of nominal GDP as well as promoting self-reliance innovation (Suehiro, 2014, pp. 141–142).

References

Akbas, Y. E., & Sancar, C. (2021). The impact of export dynamics on trade balance in emerging and developed countries: An evaluation with middle income trap perspective. *International Review of Economics and Finance*, *76*, 357–375.

Apaitan, T., Banternghansa, C., Paweenawat, A., & Samphantharak, K. (2020). *Common ownership, domestic competition, and export: Evidence from Thailand*. Discussion Paper No. 140. Puey Ungphakorn Institute for Economic Research.

Apaitan, T., Disyatat, P., & Samphantharak, K. (2019). Dissecting Thailand's international trade: Evidence from 88 million export and import entries. *Asian Development Review*, *36*(1), 20–53.

Asian Productivity Organization. (2019). *APO productivity databook 2019*. Asian Productivity Organization.

Asian Productivity Organization. (2021). *APO productivity databook 2021*. Asian Productivity Organization.

Baker, C., & Phongpaichit, P. (2021). Thailand and the COVID-19 pandemic in 2020. In D. Singh & M. Cook (Eds.), *Southeast Asian affairs 2021* (pp. 356–378). ISEAS – Yusof Ishak Institute.

Brown, A. (2004). *Labour, politics and the state in industrializing Thailand*. RoutledgeCurzon.

Bualek, P. (2000). *The analysis on the major owners of Thai banks during 1932–1973* (2nd ed.). Siam Publisher (In Thai).

Busser, R. (2008). 'Detroit of the east'? Industrial upgrading, Japanese car producers and the development of the automotive industry in Thailand. *Asia Pacific Business Review*, *14*(1), 29–45.

Doner, R. F. (2016). The politics of productivity improvement: Quality infrastructure and the middle-income trap. *Thammasat Economic Journal*, *34*(1), 1–37.

Goto, K., & Endo, T. (2014). Upgrading, relocating, informalising? Local strategies in the era of globalisation: The Thai garment industry. *Journal of Contemporary Asia*, *44*(1), 1–18.

Goto, K., & Oizumi, K. (2021). Asianizing Asia: The rise of intra-regional trade and economic integration. In K. Goto, T. Endo, & A. Ito (Eds.), *The Asian economy: Contemporary issues and challenges* (Chapter 2, pp. 28–47). Routledge.

Hewison, K. (2006). Thailand: Boom, bust and recovery. In G. Rodan, K. Hewison, & R. Robison (Eds.), *The political economy of South-East Asia: Markets, power and contestation* (Chapter 3, pp. 72–106). Oxford University Press.

Intarakummerd, P. (2017). Industrial innovation in Thailand: The electronics, automotive and seafood sectors. In B. Khoo, K. Tsunekawa, & M. Kawano (Eds.), *Southeast Asia beyond crisis and traps: Economic growth and upgrading* (Chapter 6, pp. 167–192). Palgrave Macmillan.

Intarakumnerd, P. (2020). Industrialization, technological upgrading, and innovation. In P. Chachavalpongpun (Ed.), *Routledge handbook of contemporary Thailand* (Chapter 17, pp. 214–225). Routledge.

Intarakumnerd, P., Chairatana, P.-A., & Chaiyanajit, P. (2016). Global production networks and host-site industrial upgrading: The case of the semiconductor industry in Thailand. *Asia Pacific Business Review*, *22*(2), 289–306.

Intarakumnerd, P., & Liu, M. (2019). Industrial technology upgrading and innovation policies: A comparison of Taiwan and Thailand. In K. Tsunekawa & Y. Todo (Eds.), *Emerging states at crossroads* (Chapter 6). Springer.

Ito, A. (2020a). China reshaping Asia: economic transition and the rise of an economic superpower. In K. Goto, T. Endo, & A. Ito (Eds.), *The Asian economy: Contemporary issues and challenges* (Chapter 3, pp. 48–66). Routledge.

Ito, A. (2020b). Innovating Asia: Growth pattern changes in post-middle-income economies. In K. Goto, T. Endo, & A. Ito (Eds.), *The Asian economy: Contemporary issues and challenges* (Chapter 7, pp. 129–146). Routledge.

Kawakami, M., & Goto, K. (2020). Factory Asia: Global value chains and local firm development. In K. Goto, T. Endo, & A. Ito (Eds.), *The Asian economy: Contemporary issues and challenges* (Chapter 4, pp. 69–86). Routledge.

Kuroiwa, I., Techakanont, K., & Keola, S. (2021). Evolution of production networks and the localisation of firms: Evidence from the Thai automotive industry. *Journal of the Asia Pacific Economy*, December, 1–22. https://doi.org/10.1080/13547860.2021.2024361.

Moeller, J. (2021). *Asia's transformation: From economic globalization to regionalization*. ISEAS – Yusof Ishak Institute.

Paweenawat, A., Chucherd, T., & Amarase, N. (2017). *Uncovering productivity puzzles in Thailand: Lessons from microdata*. Discussion Paper No. 73. Puey Ungphakorn Institute for Economic Research.

Phipatseritham, K. (1981). *Wikrao laksana kanpen chaokhong turakit khanaadyai nai prathedthai (Analysing the ownership structure of the Thai big business groups)*. Thammasart University Press (In Thai).

Phongpaichit, P., & Baker, C. (1995). *Thailand, economy and politics*. Oxford University Press.

Phongpaichit, P., & Benyaapikul, P. (2012). *Locked in the middle-income trap: Thailand's economy between resilience and future challenges*. Friedrich-Ebert-Stiftung.

Reghunadhan, R. (2021). *Political economy of science, technology and innovation diplomacy of the People's Republic of China*. Cambridge University Press.

Samart, W., & Kilenthong, W. (2020). *Effect of minimum wage on changes in the Thai labour market*. Discussion Paper No. 137. Puey Ungphakorn Institute for Economic Research.

Science Portal China. (2006). *National outline for medium and long term science and technology development planning (2006–2020)*. Ministry of Science and Technology of the People's Republic of China.

Siengthai, S., Dechawatanapaisal, D., & Wailerdsak, N. (2009). Human resource management: Future trends. In T. G. Andrews & S. Siengthai (Eds.), *The changing face of management in Thailand* (Chapter 6, pp. 115–145). Routledge.

Song, L., & Zhou, Y. (2021). *China's challenges in moving towards a high-income economy*. ANU Press.

Suehiro, A. (1989). *Capital accumulation in Thailand, 1855–1985*. UNESCO The Center for East Asian Cultural Studies.

Suehiro, A. (1992). Capitalist development in post-war Thailand: Commercial bankers, industrial elite, and agribusiness groups. In R. McVey (Ed.), *Southeast Asian capitalists* (Chapter 2, pp. 35–64). Cornell University Press.

Suehiro, A. (2009). *Tai: Chuushinkoku no mosaku (Thailand: Challenge a middle-income country)*. Iwanami (In Japanese).

Suehiro, A. (2014). *Shinkou ajia keizai-ron: Kyacchi-appu wo koete (Newly emerging Asian economies: Beyond the catch-up industrialization approach)*. Iwanami (In Japanese).

Suehiro, A. (2019). Responses to the middle-income trap in China, Malaysia, and Thailand. In K. Tsunekawa & Y. Todo (Eds.), *Emerging states at crossroads* (Chapter 2, pp. 27–47). Springer.

Suehiro, A., & Wailerdsak, N. (2004). Family business in Thailand: Its management, governance, and future challenges. *ASEAN Economic Bulletin*, *21*(1), 81.

Wailerdsak, N. (2005). *Managerial careers in Thailand and Japan*. Silkworm Books.

Wailerdsak, N. (2008). Companies in crisis. In P. Phongpaichit & C. Baker (Eds.), *Thai capital after the 1997 crisis* (Chapter 1, pp. 17–57). Silkworm Books.

Wailerdsak, N., & Siengthai, S. (2016). Business network in Thailand: From import substitution, export oriented to expansion in AEC. In J. Nolan, C. Rowley, & M. Warner (Eds.), *Business networks in East Asian capitalisms: Enduring trends, emerging patterns*. Chandos Publishing, Elsevier.

Warr, P. (2008). Trade policy and the structure of incentives in Thai agriculture. *ASEAN Economic Bulletin*, *25*(3), 249–270.

World Bank. (2017). *Special economic zones: An operational review of their impacts*. The World Bank Group.

Yusuf, S. (Ed.). (2003). *Innovative East Asia: The future of growth*. The World Bank Group.

Yusuf, S. (2017). Middle-income countries: Trapped or merely slowing? *Asian-Pacific Economic Literature*, *31*(2), 19–29.

Yusuf, S., & Evenett, S. J. (2002). *Can East Asia compete? Innovation for global markets*. The World Bank Group.

Zeng, D. Z. (2021). The past, present, and future of special economic zones and their impact. *Journal of International Economic Law*, *24*(2), 259–275.

Chapter 6

High-income development model

6.1 The 2000s–2010s economic revitalization and ASEAN Economic Community

After 1997, Thailand's economic growth averaged 3 percent, with a nadir of –7.6 percent in 1998. It surmounted adversities, including the global financial crisis in 2008 (–0.7 percent), followed by devastating floods in Bangkok and central Thailand in 2011 causing closure of factories and necessitating a rehabilitation budget (0.8 percent). Exports plummeted drastically. In 2014, political turmoil and the National Council for Peace and Order (NCPO) coup occurred (1.0 percent) (Ouyyanont, 2019).

From 1998 to 2008, Thai business groups had yearly growth rates of 10 percent in international trade, but this rate dropped to 0.9 percent between 2011 and 2016. Absence of modern technology prevented Thailand's manufacturing sector, its main export route and source of prosperity, from advancing. This trap illustrated the law of diminishing returns and the Lewis turning point, when economic gains from exploiting local labour and imported technology decline. This ended a paradigm of low-cost advantage and input/resource-driven economic growth (World Bank, 2016; Suehiro, 2019).

By contrast, in late 2015 the AEC created a window of opportunity for Thai business group investment, particularly in Cambodia, Laos, Myanmar, and Vietnam (CLMV nations). This involved forming new businesses, mergers, and acquisitions, as well as the phenomenon of Thai firm acquisition in industrialized nations. In 2008, after the global financial crisis (GFC), it was decided to support expansion of ASEAN and Chinese markets instead of the home market.

The IMF and World Bank first embraced Anglo-American corporate governance in the Thai capital market. They directed listed companies to operate fairly, transparently, and without corruption. Large owners exploiting minority shareholders and others were diminished. In 1999, the Institute of Directors (IOD) was founded, with Charnchai Charuvastr serving as first leader. The IOD trains directors to oversee management to benefit all shareholders, not just a single group. It recommended at least three independent directors

DOI: 10.4324/9781003370536-9

Table 6.1 Evolution of business groups in Thailand: 2000s–2020s

Period	*2000s–2010s*	*2020s–present*
Strategy	Build-up of the 1997 crisis and recovery, global crises, and floods	Moderate growth, political uncertainty, cost-push inflation
Economic development	Asian financial crisis 1997 with structural weakness (weak mid- and high-skills, rising wages) Some relocation to CLMV initiated Export and FDI promotion Sufficiency economy Frequent political change, floods with somewhat limited economic impact	Moderate growth and expected recession due to COVID-19 outbreak Policy emphasis on inclusive/regional growth Demographic change, rising labour costs Subsidies to poor along with mega infrastructure
Business networks	*Diversified business groups (holding companies, cross shareholding)* Local capitalists Foreign MNCs Government SMEs	*Diversified business groups (holding companies, cross shareholding, synergy with partners)* Local capitalists Foreign MNCs Government SMEs, Tech-startups
Market	Overseas markets (China, ASEAN, US, EU, Japan) and domestic market M&A in overseas and domestic markets	Overseas markets (China, ASEAN, US, EU, Japan) and domestic market M&A in overseas and domestic markets
Finance	Listed on the stock exchange and pyramidal shareholdings Corporate bond Infrastructure fund, property fund Loan from commercial banks	Listed on the stock exchange and pyramidal shareholdings Corporate bond, perpetual bond Infrastructure fund, property fund Loan from commercial banks Venture capital
Technology	Joint ventures with foreign MNCs Rising corporate R&D	Joint ventures with foreign MNCs Rising corporate R&D
Human resources	Talent management International human resource management	Global HR, global managers, global citizens Education of board directors

Table 6.2 List of companies investing in ASEAN countries

Myanmar: **Ratchaburi Electricity Holdings-** distributing gas, LNG gas, and hydro-electricity energy **Millcon Steel** – construction materials **General Engineering** – construction materials **Italian-Thai** – construction sub-contracting **SCG** – construction materials **Advanced Information Technology** – communication systems set up **Thonburi Hospital** – hospital and health care **Sahapatanapibul** – garments, ready-made noodles, cosmetics **Modernform** – establishing a furniture manufacturing plant **Double A** – pulp and paper	**Lao PDR:** **Ratchaburi Electricity Holdings** – distributing gas, LNG gas, and hydro-electricity energy **Banpu** – hydro-electricity generating plant **CK Power** – hydro-electricity generating plant **SCG** – construction materials **Sor. Khonkaen Foods** – food processing **Demco** – infrastructure system **Major cineplex** – movie theatre **Mitr Phol** – sugar **TOA** – paint
Indonesia **Ichitan** – beverage **SCG** – construction materials, petrochemical **Plam B** – advertising billboards **Central** – department store **Thai Summit** – automotive parts **Banpu** – coal mining **Osotspa** – groceries and related products **CP** – food processing	**Cambodia** **Group Leasing** – motorcycle leasing **CP** – food processing **Mega Life Sciences** – manufacturing and distribution of drugs (medical) and health-related products **Major cineplex** – movie theatre **SCG** – construction materials **Central** – department store
Singapore **Thai Bev** – alcohol and non-alcohol beverages **Minor Food** – Thai Express restaurant **S&P** – restaurant **Gunkul International** – engineering procurement and construction **Thai Union** – food-tech startup **Jasmine Technology Solution** – Cloud AI, fintech	**Vietnam** **CP** – food processing **SCG** – construction materials, petrochemical **M-Link Asia Corporation** – telecommunications products **Oishi** – food **Thonburi Hospital** – salinated water, drug manufacturing plant, hospital **SriThai Superware** – melamine factory, plastic packaging **Central** – department store **Berli Jucker** – trading, manufacturing **TOA** – paint

as well as audit and nominating committees. Later, more directors attended courses, especially the director certification program (DCP), and joined the IOD's House of Directors to learn to cope with business group governance structures in which major shareholders wish to influence decision-making and prioritize their own interests.

Thai business groups valued leadership development courses that built relationships between the military, civil servants, and the private sector over human resource development. Consequently, the internal labour market system was strengthened, modern technology and innovation managed, and on-premises technological infrastructure proactively built. Six prominent courses were quickly reserved (Treerat & Vanichaka, 2016). These classes were related to financial market institutions, the Ministry of Justice, and House of Representatives. It reflects Thai business group efforts to expand business dominance after the military coup and half-democratic regimes with independent military-appointed judicial bodies, rather than promoting research and development (R&D) to boost global market competitiveness.

6.2 The 2020s economic rearrangement to identify a high-income nation model

The rise of diversified business groups explains early and rapid compressed industrialization of middle-income countries. Business groups can finance high-value-added investments based on off-the-shelf technologies, particularly in the low-cost, labour-intensive sectors of clothing, textiles, footwear, agribusiness, and processed foods, as well as the high-tech automotive industry and electronic joint ventures with foreign partners. A controlling shareholder instructs group member firms to profit from a monopoly or monopsony. Activities of the controlling shareholder may represent excellent business group governance, defined as maximizing overall company group value. This indicates an escape route from the low-income trap (Dau et al., 2021a; Sturgeon & Whittaker, 2019; Whittaker et al., 2020).

However, from low-cost to high-value growth, or from catch-up to high-income growth, business group governance must be abandoned in favour of corporate governance. High-income growth is characterized by creative destruction or disruption of legacy technology firms. Entrenched business groups dislike innovation (Dau et al., 2021b). Overall, Thailand is highly inactive in R&D. The greatest obstacle is the paucity of Thai companies capable of producing innovative products or technology. Thai companies lack a foundation for social capability and human resource development required to create sophisticated technology (Wongpunya, 2016).

Instead, Thai business groups have shifted their focus from manufacturing to service and hospitality. Rather than building advanced manufacturing techniques, they invest in innovation to produce niche market goods and services. For example, improved productivity of renewable energy such as ethanol, housing construction for middle- and low-income consumers, developing shopping malls and community malls to fulfil the needs of younger customers and foreign tourists, and launching new businesses in health care and tourism for foreigners (Cuervo-Cazurra & Montoya, 2021; Makohin et al., 2020). On the negative side, Thai business groups deindustrialized prematurely (Chuntongvirat, 2020). On the positive side, they opted to grow into areas where competitive advantage was possible by using Thainess, a conceptual identity associated with the quality of being Thai.

Since the early 2010s, the BOT and other government institutions were aware of Thailand's middle-income trap problem. As a result, governments constantly implemented measures to stimulate the Thai economy. Under the administration of Prime Minister Thaksin Shinawatra (February 2001–September 2006), the National Competitiveness Plan 2005 was formulated on the basis of public-private partnerships totalling 1.8 trillion baht and with participation from foreign companies (Doner et al., 2009). This plan is comparable to China's 13th National Economic and Social Development Plan, Made in China 2025 (2016–2021), intended to advance the Chinese manufacturing sector to Industry 4.0 standards. In September 2006, Thaksin's regime was overthrown by a military coup, and the growth plan scrapped (Connors, 2008).

Later, the Abhisit Vejjajiva administration (December 2008–July 2011) introduced the Creative Economy and Strong Thai Action Plan policies (Termpittayapaisith, 2008, 2011). Overall expenditure of 1.4 trillion baht consisted entirely of loans to assist the Thai economy to recover from the 2008 GEC, although the Abhisit government was accused of misconduct.

The Yingluck Shinawatra government (August 2011–May 2014) implemented a Knowledge-Based Economy and a 2 Trillion Baht Mega Investment Project in Infrastructure to be spent on high-speed train projects costing 783 billion baht and flood-control efforts costing 350 billion baht. However, the Constitutional Court voided the program adopted by the House and Senate, calling it legally unconstitutional. After the military coup led by General Prayut Chan-ocha in May 2014, the idea was abandoned.

While the administration of General Prayut (May 2014 to the present) restored political stability, economic recovery has been slow. In May 2015, Prayut appointed Dr. Somkid Jatusripitak as deputy prime minister for economic affairs and promoted the Digital Economy and Thailand 4.0 policies, which have partly revived former Prime Minister Yingluck Shinawatra's transportation and infrastructure development megaproject (Anuroj, 2018; Desatova, 2018). In May 2016, a 20-year national strategy (2018–2037) was announced, focusing on creating sectors that employ sophisticated technology and innovation rather than social development (Jones & Pimdee, 2017; Vimolsiri, 2017). Thailand is expected to attain an annual growth rate of 4–5 percent.

The Eastern Economic Corridor (EEC) Development Plan, a continuation of the successful Eastern Seaboard Development Program, comprises 15 large-scale investment schemes, including infrastructure and 12 target industries, at a value of 1.7 trillion baht ($49 billion). It exceeds Thai private firm financial and technological resources. Thai government expects indigenous and foreign investment (Ministry of Industry, 2016). However, the novel coronavirus 2019 (COVID-19) pandemic affected the plan, which may be delayed, and the Thailand 4.0 proposal may meet the same fate as previous ones, in the worst-case scenario.

Despite lacking the power to steer future sectors, Thai business groups have chosen competitive areas over the government-supported national innovation system. Five dimensions of change (distinct industries, markets, partners, finance technique, and senior executives) include the following:

- Over the past decade, Thailand's economic expansion was driven by export-oriented industrialization (EOI) such as automobiles and auto components, electrical and electronic items. These high-tech industrial capitals are run by MNCs. The Thai business group is a major participant in monopoly industry capital (petrochemicals, renewable energy, and utilities), agricultural and food capital (most farmers have political stances), and service capital concentrating on local markets and international visitors (finance, insurance, tourism, modern retail, hospitals, real estate, and entertainment).

  Mainstream business groups are forming new partnerships to recover from COVID-19 pandemic repercussions. TCC/ThaiBev Group's Asset World Corporation (AWC), a real estate holding business, teamed with Walt Disney to restore Bangkok's Asiatique the Riverfront, reviving tourism in Thailand.

  Thai business groups began to flourish in future-oriented sectors, such as the Pure Energy Group, which transitioned from renewable energy generation to electric vehicle manufacturing, and Gulf Energy Group, which moved from power plants to purchasing shares in digital firms. Even PTT, a state-owned enterprise that dominates the oil and refining industries, ventured into retail, while Siam Cement Group/SCG, a leading conglomerate, expanded into pharmaceuticals. Complex, interrelated s-curve industries were focused on along the value chain.

  Only Thailand's startup development remained minimal compared to other ASEAN countries. Thailand had varied unicorn companies in 2021, including Ascend Money in fintech, Flash Express in logistics, Lineman Wongnai in food platform (ASEAN Secretariat, 2022).[1]
- Thai business groups expanded in the home market and large markets such as the United States, Europe, and Japan, as well as China and the ASEAN community. The AEC was founded in 2015, allowing Thailand to expand its market and boost investment. As a result, accelerating international trade discussions, including multilateral negotiations with individual states, a Comprehensive and Progressive Agreement of Trans-Pacific Partnership (CPTPP), and the Thailand Plus One strategy adopted by Japan all remain options.

- Joint ventures were formed with increasingly prominent Chinese companies to build new manufacturing (such as automobiles, tires, IT goods) and service industries (e-commerce, logistics, real estate). Thai companies no longer relied on Japanese or Western MNCs as in former days. Meanwhile, Japanese companies were locked into a domestic growth trajectory. New industries to boost Japanese growth through two lost decades have yet to be identified. As Thai wages soared, Japan relocated manufacturing bases to neighbouring nations, amassing assets in identical industries, although Japanese annual investment in Thailand remains constant.

  In cutting-edge industries such as electric automobiles, more Chinese companies have constructed factories and exported goods to Thailand. Meanwhile, Japanese companies are evaluating competitiveness on the American market, as they are captivated by the success of gasoline-powered automobiles. The Japanese e-commerce site Rakuten.com has declined. Japan concedes that it cannot generate as many high-quality digital and information technology (IT) professionals as China.
- Fund-raising is evolving. Thai business groups historically relied on short-term loans from international financial institutions and the SET. They have shifted to issue conventional and perpetual debentures, using real estate funds, real estate investment trusts (REITs), infrastructure fund (IFF), and commercial bank loan applications with yearly appreciating land as collateral. All this can help monopolized business groups enhance monopolistic power.

  On the other hand, Fintech has been used to help commercial banks and non-bank firms grow exponentially. Fintech facilitates SMEs and retail borrowers' access to credit sources while minimizing financial institution vulnerabilities. It represents an additional opportunity for the Thai financial industry.
- In terms of human resources, professional chief executive officers (CEOs) who were not ownership family members were chosen by Thai business groups, including Kasikorn Bank and Osotspa. Many groups, such as B. Grimm Power and Banpu, have maintained some older operations while diversifying into more promising ones, such as renewable energy. ASEAN expansion has forced many corporations to reorganize. Companies who wish to be listed on the Dow Jones Sustainability Index (DJSI) will want to fully employ Anglo-American corporate governance frameworks.

  There is a phenomenon of actively appointing independent directors characterized by increased acceptability by foreign investors, eliminating directors with hidden ties to major shareholders, and substituting directors with real expertise and freedom to comment on management. Although qualified independent directors remain scarce, some firms engage in image-building exercises with officers noted within industries who hold roles in multiple firms, exceeding individual capacities and scheduling possibilities.

Although manufacturing employment traditionally declines in middle-income and developed economies, it is essential for catch-up industrialization and prosperity. A vibrant manufacturing sector enhances living conditions for citizens and national worldwide influence, insofar as manufacturing is a significant technical accomplishment. Industrial policy is central to economic and social policy throughout structural change. Without structural change and manufacturing upgrading, no nation can transcend poverty or change its relative income status from low to medium or middle to high. Equally, the decline of nations is often related to missing structural change, to premature deindustrialization, or overreliance on inward investment and foreign technology (Aiginger & Rodrik, 2020; Sturgeon & Whittaker, 2019; Whittaker et al., 2020).

In general, manufacturing may be seen as a grimy sector with high carbon emissions. It is also prone to business instability, resulting in temporary waves of unemployment. Paradoxically, manufacturing is also associated with great employment opportunities and a substantial middle class (Cuervo-Cazurra & Montoya, 2021). The manufacturing industry offers several technological choices for cleaner, carbon neutrality production, and interplay between manufacturing and services typically results in well-paying, stable employment. Possibilities include the bio-circular-green (BCG) economic model or new industrial policy steered by job concerns. The motto "inclusive growth, green growth, and sustainable growth" attempts to combine these goals (Ouyyanont, 2019; Suehiro, 2019).

The key to success lies in each nation's social capability to acquire, employ, and improve imported technology. However, industrial monopolies and entrenched family business traps limit social capabilities of Thai companies. Switching to corporate governance, including diluting major large company shareholding, separating ownership from control, encouraging formation of managerial enterprises, as well as boosting disruptive startups, are all essential. These themes will be examined in the final chapter.

Thais who aspire to become rank alongside the Four Asian Tigers as an ASEAN fifth tiger have faced several obstacles over the past quarter century, including ten regimes and eight general elections and two coups d'état (Connors, 2008; Connors & Pathmanand, 2021). What is the difference between a national per capita income of $20,000 (1990 PPP) (high-income status) and $12,000 (middle-income status)? Income disparities may have to widen to attain a $20,000 per capita income rate. Rivalry and pressure add societal strain and friction. In addition to increasing social and environmental consequences, would economic monopolies held by a few clans and business groups, or by a few MNCs, be worth the effort?

Thailand must prioritize between economic and social development. Thailand can remain an upper-middle-income nation instead of seeking competitive high-income nation status. A middle-income nation may still benefit while eradicating inequality and balancing extreme societal inequities (Benyaapikul,

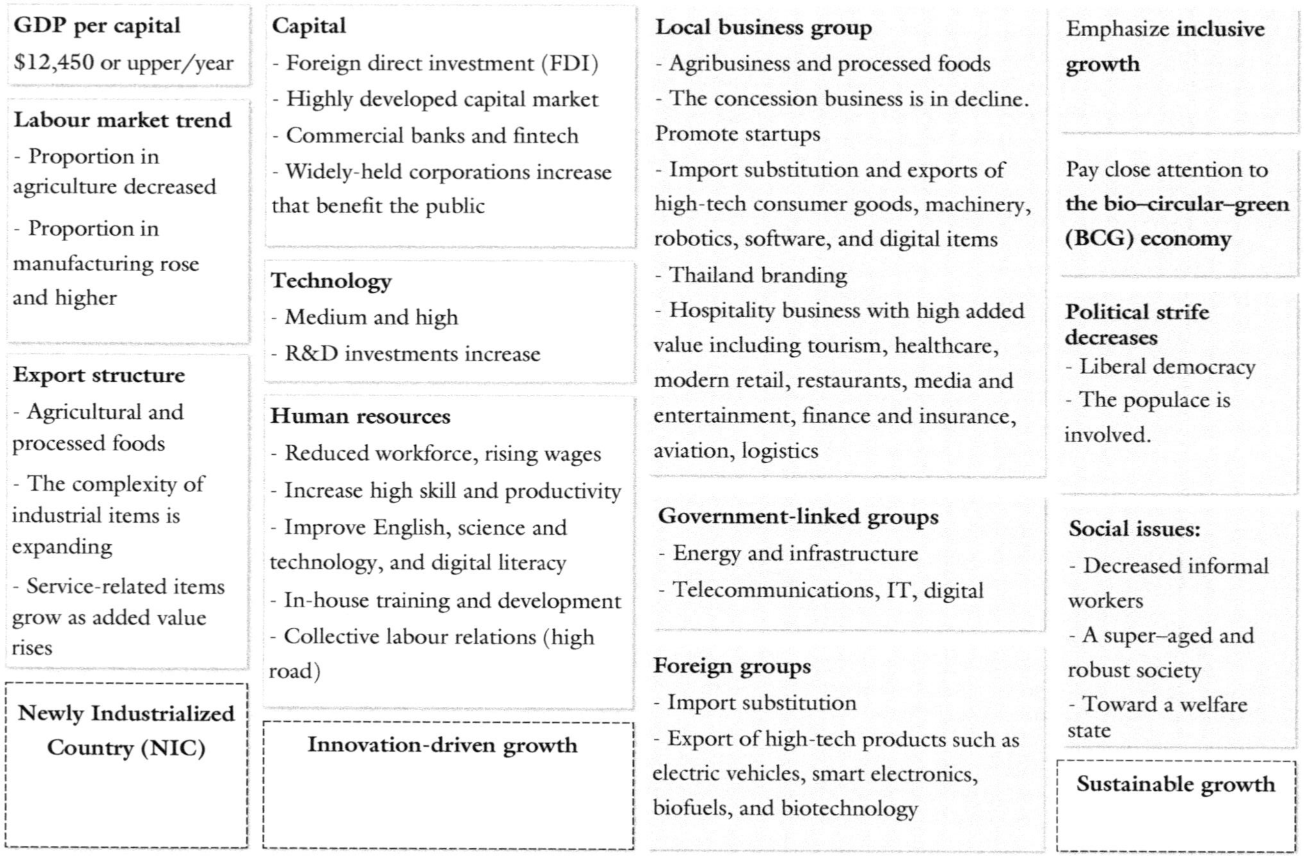

Figure 6.1 High-income model of Thailand

2021; Chiengkul, 2019). This strategy is more viable and less burdensome for Thais, based on the sufficiency economy philosophy (Jitsuchon, 2019). Upper-middle income nations may not be required to progress to high-income status.

6.3 From creative economy to new S-curves

6.3.1 *Creative economy*

Thai economic policies are in constant flux, depending on which political party forms a government as protagonist for a given policy followed by the word economy. For example, the industrial economy of the Chatchai government (August 1988 to February 1991) was followed by the dual-track economy of the Thaksin government (February 2001 to April 2006), sufficiency economy of the Surayud government (October 2006 to January 2008), creative economy and Thai Khem Kheng (Strong Thailand) economy of the Abhisit government (December 2008 to July 2011), the knowledge-based economy of the Yingluck government (August 2011 to May 2014), and Thailand 4.0 and digital economy, followed by the bio-circular-green (BCG) economy by the Prayut government (May 2014 to the present).

Thai economist technocrats[2] are aware of drawbacks to low-cost input-driven growth, accepting Thai economy structural flaws and economic hazards of remaining in a middle-income status for long intervals (Charoenporn, 2017; Jitsuchon, 2012). For example, the Abhisit government launched a creative economy (*settakit sangsan*) program in 2009, with details released in March 2011, to revitalize the national economy. Arkhom Termpittayapaisith, then secretary-general of the NESDC, explained the following (Termpittayapaisith, 2011):

> Thailand's past economy was divided into three stages. First, Thailand's economic development from the 1960s to the 1980s emphasized growth strategies based on low-cost inputs of production and resources (input/resource-driven economy) because it was a period in which competition must establish a comparative advantage, which was once thought to be effective.
>
> Economic development policy in the second stage switched to an efficiency/productivity driven economy strategy, or the competitive advantage era. Then to a higher level, the third stage implemented an innovative and creative growth strategy (innovation/creativity-driven economy), which overlapped with the transition from the middle-income trap. It may be claimed that Thailand's economic development in the past was guided by development plans compiled by the NESDC, and in accordance with the ideas from international organizations.
>
> (Termpittayapaisith, 2011)

Later, in drafting the 11th National Economic and Social Development Plan (2012–2016), the NESDB summarized results from the first to tenth editions of the National Economic and Social Development Plan by examining a traditional development paradigm through mass production and low-cost manufacturing sectors (factor-driven industries). Thailand is caught in three traps causing economic downturn: the middle-income trap, the economic inequality trap, and the misalignment of economic growth and environmental protection trap (Chiengkul, 2019; Ministry of Industry, 2016).

Therefore, Thailand requires a new economic development strategy based on these three supports to construct growth strategy to bring society closer to equilibrium and sustainability:

- A knowledge-based economy involving communication and information technologies, R&D, and creativity/innovation-driven growth to escape the middle-income trap.
- Inclusive growth and social development to alleviate the problem of economic disparity.
- Environmentally friendly and green growth to emerge from the economic development imbalance and environmental concern trap.

Consequently, in conjunction with the knowledge-based economy, the term creative economy was protagonist in the 11th National Economic and Social Development Plan, for four distinctive targeted industries (Termpittayapaisith, 2011):

- Industries exploiting cultural heritage and natural resources such as crafts and handicrafts, Thai traditional medical services, Thai food, spas, cultural tourism, and biodiversity.
- Cultural industries such as performing arts (traditional dancing), visual and graphic arts, architecture, painting, and sculpture.
- Media industries such as film and video, publishing, television, radio, music, and animation.
- Functionally creative industries such as advertising, design, fashion, and architecture (urban planning, landscape architecture, interior design, and decorative arts).

Notably, the automotive or electrical and electronic industry went unmentioned despite being Thailand's largest industry in GDP value. No local Thai companies exist in these fields, demonstrating that this program prominently highlighted a development goal shift from manufacturing industries relying on low-cost advantages (low-cost inputs, low wages) to service industries capitalizing on Thailand's national characteristics of hospitality, or so-called Thainess (Makohin et al., 2020; Suehiro, 2019).

6.3.2 Thailand 4.0 and new S-curves

From 2006 to 2015, the Thai manufacturing sector endured low-level growth: annual growth rates were 3.0 percent for manufacturing industries, 2.0 percent for investments in these industries, and 5.4 percent for manufactured exports despite rising exports of autos and auto components, and only 0.7 percent for total factor productivity (TFP). These reflected a loss of economic opportunity and to decreasing national competitiveness inadequate for driving the economy to its next phase.

In May 2014, a Thai military group launched a coup d'état to halt unproductive political conflict between pro- and anti-Thaksin groups that began in 2013. Under the government of General Prayut Chan-ocha (former army commander-in-chief), a special economic team led by Deputy Prime Minister Somkid Jatusripitak and the Ministry of Industry reorganized previous policies to provide a new long-term national strategy for conquering the middle-income trap (Connors & Pathmanand, 2021). This national strategy, Thailand 4.0, redirected economic policy to innovation-based development (Jones & Pimdee, 2017).

Thailand 4.0 combines NESDC creative economy, digital economy promotion,[3] and next-generation industries proposed by the Board of Investment (BOI) as new growth engines, with rehabilitating Eastern Seaboard Development Program (later known as the Eastern Economic Corridor (EEC)) as a new growth hub joining the ADB's Greater Mekong Subregion (GMS) project, covering the Rayong, Chonburi, and Chachoengsao Province automobile clusters (Anuroj, 2018; Desatova, 2018). In July 2016, Thailand 4.0 was officially announced on broadcast and internet channels.

The Royal Thai Army-based government ambitiously predicted that this developmental model would drive Thailand's annual economic growth rate to 4–5 percent, annual investment growth rate to 10 percent, annual export growth rate to 8 percent, annual total factor productivity (TFP) growth rate to 2 percent, over the next 20 years (Eastern Economic Corridor Office, 2019, p. 15). This will boost Thailand to high-income or developed nation status by 2032 (GDP per capita US$12,450) (Maesincee, 2016), in contrast to the "balanced society and reduced inequality" previously evoked by Arkhom.

In July 2017, to implement the Thailand 4.0 policy, the Prayut government enacted a National Strategies Preparation Act, empowering political leaders to manage national matters over the next 20 years (2018–2037) beyond the individual authority of each cabinet organized after general elections (Vimolsiri, 2017). National strategy committee members comprise the prime minister (chairperson); two deputy prime ministers (vice chairpersons); National Security Council chair; army, navy, and air force commanders; business association representatives, including the Thai Federation of Industries; and leaders of major corporations such as the Charoen Pokphand Group and Siam Cement Group.[4] This act clearly indicates that the Prayut government aims for strong state economic leadership, following the Chinese model of state intervention or group C discussed in Chapter 3.

On 17 November 2015, the cabinet accepted five existing (First S-curve) and five prospective industries (New S-curve) as next-generation industrial targets. Development of high-tech industries such as next-generation automotive, smart electronics, robots, biochemicals, and the digital economy were heavily

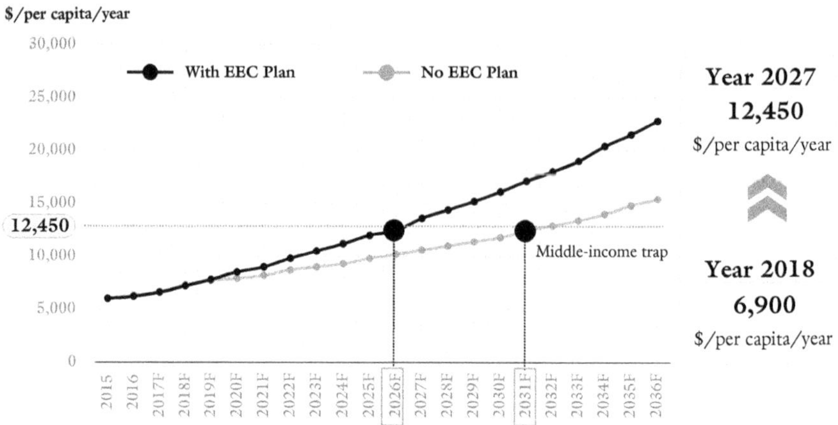

Figure 6.2 EEC plan and escaping the middle-income trap

Source: Author's compilation based on data provided by the Eastern Economic Corridor Office of Thailand (July 2019; p. 76)

influenced by MNC regional strategy and investment decisions in Thailand. Local firms were to use regional advantages in medical and wellness tourism, agriculture and biotechnology, and food innovations to sell products, despite lacking self-sustaining abilities and knowledge about key industrial innovation (Maesincee, 2016; Makohin et al., 2020). Later, two further industries were added: defence as well as education and human resource development.[5]

Careful examination reveals that implementation of the long-term strategy is directly linked to following five events occurring at home and abroad:

Firstly, the Thailand 4.0 policy was established by the National Strategies Preparation Act, B.E. 2560 (2017) and National Reform Plans and Procedures Act, B.E. 2560 (2017), both deriving from the Constitution of the Kingdom of Thailand, B.E. 2560 (2017) to serve as instruments for determining national long-range development (Lee et al., 2020). So for the next two decades, this this strategy must remain the national goal even if general elections result in changes of government (four-year terms).[6]

Secondly, the EEC[7] project is a significant government initiative that is in accordance with the country's policy priorities. This project expanded on the Eastern Seaboard Development Program (Eastern Seaboard, ESDP), which started in 1981 as part of the fifth Economic and Social Development Plan of Thailand (1982–1986) during the Prem Tinsulanonda administration. Simultaneously, this EEC initiative strives to unite past regional development programs and industry promotion policies. In 2017, two major laws were revised to comply with the Eastern Special Development Zone Act, B.E. 2561 (2018)[8] (proclaimed on 14 May 2018), including Investment Promotion Act (No.4), B.E. 2560 (2017), and National Competitiveness Enhancement for Targeted Industries Act, B.E. 2560 (2017).

In fact, the NCPO authorized management of the EEC project to the Eastern Special Development Zone Policy Committee. The Eastern Special Development Zone Act, B.E. 2561 (2018),[9] was enacted by the government to assure domestic and foreign investors that the project would continue, rather than being cancelled or abridged as usual by political crises or changes in government. The economic team, as a working ensemble, mandated this condition (from the interview).

Thirdly, the EEC initiative was tied to the ASEAN Economic Community (AEC) goal, starting in January 2016, to make Thailand's eastern region the ASEAN Gateway to Asia. Most Thais consider Thailand's geographic location to be one of its greatest assets. Myanmar and India are to the west, with Cambodia and Vietnam, as well as Japan and the United States, to the east. ASEAN nations are to the south, and China to the north. Thailand's central location promotes interconnection with other regions.

Fourthly, it is related to China. This strategy is founded on the notion of fostering collaboration through the Twenty-First Century Silk Road Strategy, known as the One Belt, One Road Initiative (OBOR) and Made in China 2025 policy (MIC 2025). This was confirmed by General Prayut during the Ninth Brazil, Russia, India, China, and South Africa (BRICS) Summit, bringing together leaders of the BRICS countries and the Emerging Markets and Developing Countries Dialogue (EMDCD) with Egypt, Mexico, Guinea, and Tajikistan. The summit was held from 4 to 5 September 2017 on the invitation of the Chinese government in Xiamen, southern Fujian Province. General Prayut met for bilateral talks with President Xi Jinping to reaffirm the two nations' strong partnership through Chinese support for Thai national reforms as part of the Thailand 4.0 program, as well as Thai support for the Chinese 21st Century Maritime Silk Road (MSR) initiative.[10]

Fifthly, this project depends on significant Thai and foreign capital groups, which may result in a Thai economic monopoly that will increase over time, especially in critical industries. The state has fully intervened in allocating and using national resources, as well as selecting the private groups to have the authority to do so. Who will be responsible for investing in this mega-project remains a moot point. PPP investment in primary infrastructure such as deep seaports, high-speed trains, aviation industries, tourism, and new cities is worth up to 650 billion baht, with the state investing 200 billion baht (32 percent), and the private sector investing 450 billion baht (68 percent). The state has received a 450 billion baht refund (Eastern Economic Corridor Office, 2019, p. 31).

The Asian Infrastructure Investment Bank (AIIB), backed by the Chinese government and other Chinese financial institutions, are projected to contribute to the government's budget (public loans). The Thai government has urged significant Thai large firms to participate in the project and attract foreign investment. Both the promotion of next-generation industries and the EEC project are closely connected with state leadership, as well as the movement of local large firms and MNCs. If large Thai firms advance into fields such as high-speed trains, next-generation automotive, robotics, and the digital economy, they require full investment and technological support from Japanese, Western, and Chinese MNCs. This differs from China, where the government aims to promote self-reliance in scientific and technological development.

6.3.3 BCG economy and ESG

A notable feature of Thai economic development policies is the emphasis on growth goals (higher GDP per capita), relying mostly on FDI, despite occasional reassessment and recognition of the need for balanced social goals (reducing inequality) and sufficiency economy dependent on the competitiveness of domestic Thai companies. Thailand habitually shifts the target back and forth between growth and balancing goals (Benyaapikul, 2021; Jitsuchon, 2019).

While Thailand advances with the Thailand 4.0 policy supporting high-tech industries, a global trend of change seeks to halt environmentally harmful development. Thailand's return to a balanced economy in the 13th National Economic and Social Development Plan with the BCG economic policy follows United Nations (UN) Sustainable Development Goals (SDGs), Global Capital Market Environmental, Social, Governance (ESG), and the 2021 United Nations Framework Convention on Climate Change Conference of the Parties (UNFCCC COP26) in Glasgow, the United Kingdom, to prevent global warming and to achieve the net-zero goal of balancing between greenhouse gas emissions and absorption (Jamprasert et al., 2020; Maesincee, 2016; Termpittayapaisith, 2022).

The bio-circular-green (BCG) economy is expected to be important for the future of manufacturing in low- and middle-income countries. The COVID-19 pandemic has seen an acceleration of digitization and automation. The fourth wave of technological advancement in manufacturing, referred to as Industry 4.0, has been linked to the development of the BCG economy. In Thailand, combining these two approaches can help to reduce material intensity of manufacturing, waste reduction from industry, and improve industrial innovation. A large fraction of municipal solid waste is organic. There are also significant amounts of agricultural residues and growing amounts of byproducts from food processing. These material streams have great potential for circularity and can, when properly managed, contribute to improved agricultural productivity and reduced dependence on costly synthetic fertilizers, among other benefits (Jamprasert et al., 2020; Termpittayapaisith, 2022).

To stimulate investment, Thai government organizations and institutions funded by the Japanese government have organized a number of seminars concerning the BCG economy in Thailand (Nation Group, 2021; JETRO Thailand, 2022).

Thailand must also address increasing societal issues such as rising economic inequities, rapid transition to a super-aged society, and a deteriorating environment. To escape the middle-income trap, Thailand is expected to pursue an inclusive and a green growth plan, as well as an innovation-led growth strategy. This policy option was expressed in the NESDC's 20-year national strategy (2017–2036) published in May 2016. This plan takes a different path than Thailand 4.0, which emphasizes industrial over social development (NESDC, 2016, 2022; Wongpunya, 2016). Thailand will struggle to attain the 4.5 percent growth target set in the Thailand 4.0 policy with the dual structure for national targets (Lee et al., 2020).

This fact shows that Thailand is pursuing a different path than China, by remaining an upper-middle-income country with a moderate GDP growth rate rather than becoming a high-income country with a comparatively rapid growth rate. The former is a more feasible national path and places less burden on Thai citizens.

Even though Thailand's income stagnates at upper-middle-income status (about $13,000), Thai citizens would be fairly well served if Thailand can carve a niche for itself in Asian markets and use that position for social advancement. Ultimately, progress is contingent on whether a new generation of Thais prioritize upper-middle-income nation status or finding new growth paths to escape from the middle-income trap.

Notes

1 A unicorn is a privately owned startup with a valuation of $1 billion or more. According to the ASEAN Investment Report (2022), there are 46 ASEAN unicorns, for example, in Indonesia (JD.ID, Ajaib, Blibli, J&T Express, Kredivo, Kopi Kenangan, Ruangguru, Sicepat, Tiket.com, Xendit), in Singapore (PropertyGuru, One Championship, V3, Advance Intelligence Group, Bolttech, Carro, Carousell, JustCo, Matrixport, Moglix, Ninja Van, NIUM, Patsnap, SecretLab), in Vietnam (VinaPay, Momo, Sky Mavis), in Malaysia (Air Asia Digital, Carsome, Edotco), and in the Philippines (Mynt).

2 Technocratic government officials participating in development initiatives are officials from the Bank of Thailand, the Budget Office of the Ministry of Finance, the Office of the National Economic and Social Development Council (NESDC), and the Board of Investment (BOI). The latter two agencies were set up with the First National Economic Development Plan, as recommended by the World Bank team in the 1960s. Meanwhile, economists from the Thailand Development Research Institute (TDRI), a public policy research institute established in 1984, and from research centers of main commercial banks, private institutions, and academics will criticize the governmental economic policies.

3 The Ministry of Digital Economy and Society (DES), reshuffled in September 2016, originally known as the Ministry of Information and Communication Technology (ICT), was founded in October 2002. It is responsible for the following major projects: Net Pracharat, Smart City, Cyber Clean, ASEAN Digital Hub, Anti-Fake News Center, and Community Digital Center (www.mdes.go.th).

4 See "Prarachabanyat Kan Jat-tham Yutthasat Chat" in Rachakichanubeksa (Government Gazette) 134, no. 79, Ko, 31 July 2017, p. 112.

5 On 22 November 2017, at the third meeting of the Eastern Economic Development Policy Committee, chaired by General Prayut, the defense industry was

designated as the eleventh target industry to concentrate on developing individual cutting-edge technologies, decrease reliance on foreign investors, and recruit and develop high-level specialists. Within a decade, the air force plans to spend from 5 to 60 billion baht to purchase weaponry (see "the Defense Industry can Grow in the EEC," *Krungthep Turakij*, 3 September 2020).

6 Some Thai political researchers argue that the 20-year National Strategic Plan of the Prayut government is a byproduct of a military regime to usurp prime ministerial power for the military. This strategy is defined by a compulsory law ensuring that in Thailand, future politics and direction must follow the path set by the 2014 coup d'état until 2037. It simultaneously promotes large capital groups that aim to monopolize national economic power (Bamrungsuk, 2020).

7 Special economic zones (SEZs) are geographically distinctive areas where governments apply policies to develop industries and support infrastructure differently than in other areas through investment, taxation, employment, and technology and innovation development. These are widely used in both emerging countries and developed countries to attract foreign investors and boost national competitiveness. Chapter IV of the United Nations Conference on Trade and Development (UNCTAD) World Investment Report 2019 enumerated 5,383 SEZs globally. Nations with the most SEZs were China with 2,543, Philippines with 528, India with 373, North America with 262, Russia with 130, Turkey with 102, and Thailand with 74. The EEC was also designed as a world class economic zone.

8 See details on the website of the Office of the Eastern Special Development Zone Policy Committee in Thai, English, Chinese, and Japanese versions (www.eeco.th).

9 General Prayut Chan-ocha was named prime minister by the Palang Pracharat Party, which earned the second most votes after the Pheu Thai Party in the March 2019 general election. On June 11 of that year, he was elected prime minister with the votes of the ruling coalition and 250 senators nominated by the National Council for Peace and Order. General Prayut affirmed that the EEC project would continue in his policy announcement of July 25th.

10 The signing of four agreements between the Thai and Chinese governments is the crux of the matter.

First contract: Phase 1 of the project design contract for constructing the Sino-Thai high-speed railway system connecting Bangkok and Nakhon Ratchasima (the 253-kilometre project is worth 5.2 billion baht).

Second contract: Phase 1 of the project consultant contract for construction, supervision, and development of the Sino-Thai high-speed railway system connecting Bangkok and Nakhon Ratchasima.

Third contract: The Joint Plan of Action on Thailand-China Strategic Cooperation (2017–2021).

Fourth contract: A Memorandum of Understanding on Cooperation within the Framework of Silk Road Economic Belt and the 21st Century Maritime Silk Road initiative.

References

Aiginger, K., & Rodrik, D. (2020). Rebirth of industrial policy and an agenda for the twenty-first century. *Journal of Industry, Competition and Trade, 20*, 189–207.

Anuroj, B. (2018). *Thailand 4.0 – a new value-based economy*. Board of Investment.

ASEAN Secretariat. (2022, August). *ASEAN investment report 2022: Pandemic recovery and investment facilitation*. ASEAN Secretariat.

Bamrungsuk, S. (2020, May 21). 10 pii lom prab, 10 pii rathaprahan! (10 years of siege, 6 years of coup!). *Matichon* (In Thai).

Benyaapikul, P. (2021). Thailand's path to economic recovery and advancement: Diagnostic study on the middle income trap and prospects for post-covid economic growth. *Thammasat Review of Economic and Social Policy*, *7*(2), 34–79.
Charoenporn, P. (2017, October 10). *Seminar on Thailand and overcoming the middle-income trap*. At Faculty of Economics, Thammasat University (In Thai).
Chiengkul, P. (2019). Uneven development, inequality and concentration of power: A critique of Thailand 4.0. *Third World Quarterly*, *40*(9), 1689–1707.
Chuntongvirat, K. (2020). A study of deindustrialization and its implications on Thailand's private investment. *Focused and Quick*, *66*.
Connors, M. K. (2008). Thailand-four elections and a coup. *Australian Journal of International Affairs*, *62*(4), 478–496.
Connors, M. K., & Pathmanand, U. (Eds.). (2021). *Thai politics in translation: Monarchy, democracy and the supra-constitution*. NIAS Press.
Cuervo-Cazurra, A., & Montoya, M. (Eds.). (2021). *Innovating for the middle of the pyramid in emerging countries*. Cambridge University Press.
Dau, L. A., Morck, R. K., & Yeung, B. (2021a). Corporate governance versus business group governance, part 1: The low-income trap. In K. Sogner & A. Colli (Eds.), *The emergence of corporate governance: People, power, and performance* (Chapter 6, pp. 103–120). Routledge.
Dau, L. A., Morck, R. K., & Yeung, B. (2021b). Corporate governance versus business group governance, part 2: The middle-income trap. In K. Sogner & A. Colli (Eds.), *The emergence of corporate governance: People, power, and performance* (Chapter 7, pp. 121–134). Routledge.
Desatova, P. (2018). Thailand 4.0 and the internal focus of nation branding. *Asian Studies Review*, *42*(4), 682–700.
Doner, R. F., Hicken, A., & Ritchie, B. K. (2009). Political challenges of innovation in the developing world. *Review of Policy Research*, *26*(1–2), 151–171.
Eastern Economic Corridor Office. (2019, July). *2 Years of EEC: Connecting the world to promote Thailand's prosperity*. Eastern Economic Corridor Office.
Jamprasert, N., Kuwalairat, P., Srivisal, N., & Sthienchoak, J. (2020). *ESG and creditworthiness: Two contrary evidence from major Asian markets*. Discussion Paper No. 129. Puey Ungphakorn Institute for Economic Research.
JETRO Thailand. (2022, February 7). *Thailand-Japan sustainable business seminar for carbon neutrality*. Online seminar held by JETRO Thailand and EEC Office (In Thai and Japanese).
Jitsuchon, S. (2012). Thailand in a middle-income trap. *TDRI Quarterly Review*, *27*(2), 13–20.
Jitsuchon, S. (2019). Thailand's sufficiency economy philosophy as an alternative path to sustainable development. *European Journal of Sustainable Development*, *8*(2), 191–191.
Jones, C., & Pimdee, P. (2017). Innovative ideas: Thailand 4.0 and the fourth industrial revolution. *Asian International Journal of Social Sciences*, *17*(1), 4–35.
Lee, K., Wong, C., Intarakumnerd, P., & Limapornvanich, C. (2020). Is the fourth industrial revolution a window of opportunity for upgrading or reinforcing the middle-income trap? Asian model of development in Southeast Asia. *Journal of Economic Policy Reform*, *23*(4), 408–425.
Maesincee, S. (2016). *Thailand 4.0: Will it move the country out of its 'lost decade'?* Asian Institute of Technology (In Thai).

Makohin, Z., Atamanchuk, Z., & Mitiushkina, K. (2020). The role of tourism in escaping the middle-income trap. *Management Theory and Studies for Rural Business and Infrastructure Development*, *42*(3), 295–302.

Ministry of Industry. (2016, October). *Yuthasad kan pattana udsahakam thai 4.0 raya 20 pii (2560–2579) (The strategies for industrial development in Thailand 4.0 20 years period (2017–2036)*. Ministry of Industry (In Thai).

Nation Group. (2021, October 28). *Thailand next episode 3: Circular economy, innovation for the future.* Virtual Forum held by the Nation Group (In Thai).

Office of the National Economic and Social Development Board. (2012). *The eleventh national economic and social development plan (2012–2016)*. NESDB (In Thai).

Office of the National Economic and Social Development Council (NESDC). (2016). *Thailand's 20-year national strategy 2018–2037.* http://nscr.nesdc.go.th/ns/

Office of the National Economic and Social Development Council. (2022). *The thirteenth national economic and social development plan (2017–2021)*. NESDC (In Thai).

Ouyyanont, P. (2019). Thai economic growth: Retrospect and prospect. In M. J. Montesano, T. Chong, & M. Heng (Eds.), *After the coup: The National council for peace and order era and the future of Thailand* (Chapter 13, pp. 335–356). ISEAS Publishing.

Sturgeon, T. J., & Whittaker, D. H. (2019). Compressed development. In S. Ponte, G. Gereffi, & G. Raj-Reichert (Eds.), *Handbook on global value chains* (Chapter 28, pp. 452–465). Edward Elgar.

Suehiro, A. (2019). Responses to the middle-income trap in China, Malaysia, and Thailand. In K. Tsunekawa & Y. Todo (Eds.), *Emerging states at crossroads* (Chapter 2, pp. 27–47). Springer.

Termpittayapaisith, A. (2008). *The 10th national economic and social development plan and creative economy.* Office of the National Economic and Social Development Board (In Thai).

Termpittayapaisith, A. (2011). *Settakit sangsan khong thai (Thailand's creative economy)*. Office of the National Economic and Social Development Board (NESDB) (In Thai).

Termpittayapaisith, A. (2022, August 17). *Thidthang longtun thai, watachak dokbia khaa khun (Direction of Thai investment, growing interest rates)*. Seminar on Decoding the Rising Interest Rate Era of Investments, held by Prachachat Turakit (In Thai).

Treerat, N., & Vanichaka, P. (2016). Elite networking through special executive courses. In P. Phongpaichit & C. Baker (Eds.), *Unequal Thailand: Aspects of income, wealth, and power* (Chapter 5, pp. 73–96). National University of Singapore Press.

UNCTAD. (2020). *World investment report 2019.* UNCTAD.

Vimolsiri, P. (2017). *Thailand 20-year strategic plan and reform.* National Economic and Social Development Council (NESDC).

Whittaker, D. H., Sturgeon, T., Okita, T., & Zhu, T. (2020). *Compressed development: Time and timing in economic and social development.* Oxford University Press.

Wongpunya, N. (2016, October). *What Thailand needs to do to become a high-income country.* ISEAS – Yusof Ishak Institute.

World Bank. (2016). *Getting back on track: Reviving growth and securing prosperity for all, Thailand systematic country diagnostic.* The World Bank Group.

Chapter 7

EEC plan and foreign investors

7.1 Eastern Economic Corridor Plan

7.1.1 *Background*

The EEC plan developed from a desire to revitalize the Eastern Seaboard Development Program approved by the cabinet in 1981 to exploit natural gas deposits discovered in the Gulf of Thailand in 1973. Over the past 35 years, it has transformed Thailand's economy from import-substitution to export-oriented growth (Sangsubhan, 2017).

Despite initial conflict between the World Bank and Thai government, the Eatern Seaboard Development Program was seen as a megaproject, featuring two deep-sea ports: Map Ta Phut Industrial Area in Rayong Province, focusing on the petrochemical industry while endangering the environment, and Laem Chabang Industrial Area in Chonburi Province, devoted to light industry for export. Investments followed in Laem Chabang from the Siam Cement Group (SCG), Mitsubishi Motors Corporation (MMC) Sittipol, and other automotive manufacturers and distributors. It replaced the previously planned light industry as a production base for the automobile, electrical equipment, mechanical, and petrochemical sectors (Sangsubhan, 2017, 2021).

The Eastern Seaboard Development Program was entirely funded and technologically supported by Japan's Overseas Economic Cooperation Fund (OECF), later renamed the Japan Bank for International Cooperation (JBIC). It is among the most significant projects that Japan has undertaken for Thailand. Sixteen infrastructure projects, including roads and ports, received Japanese government financing. Without deductions, it was worth 1.8 million yen, or 21 percent of the total loan value of 8.4 billion yen that Japan extended to Thailand over 12 years from 1982 to 1993 (Suehiro, 2017).

On 17 January 2017 at a cabinet meeting, Eastern Special Development Zone (ESDZ) supervisory organizations were established by related royal decrees, divided into three hierarchies (EEC Office, 2019):

1) Eastern Special Development Zone Policy Committee ("Policy Committee") chaired by the prime minister to indicate ESDZ development policies.

DOI: 10.4324/9781003370536-10

2) EEC Project Management Committee with the minister of industry as chair, seconding the Policy Committee.
3) Eastern Economic Corridor Office of Thailand (EEC Office or So.Ko. Po.Or.) to implement policy set by the Policy Committee.

The EEC Office has six divisions: policy and planning, area and community, special economic promotional zone, infrastructure investment, foreign affairs, and organizational optimization. The office was formerly housed in a building of the Industrial Estate Authority of Thailand near Makkasan railway station that was formerly the National Economic and Social Development Board (NESDB)'s Eastern Seaboard Development Program Office, before being relocated to the CAT Telecom Building on Charoen Krung Road (Suehiro, 2020).

The Prayut government exploited the interim constitution's emergency powers to realize the EEC plan. Starting in 2016, the following 15 projects in four groups (see Figure 7.1) received investments (EEC Office, 2019):

1) Infrastructure development, including these seven projects:

- U-Tapao International Airport Development Project and Eastern Airport City. U-Tapao Airport served as a US airbase during the Vietnam War. It was built in an environmentally responsible manner but was abandoned after American forces were evacuated in 1975. As the third international airport, it will process up to 30 million travellers annually, with the Navy's Sattahip commercial port renovation project. After completion in 2025, it will also serve as an Asia-wide maintenance, repair, and overhaul (MRO) facility.[1]
- Map Ta Phut Port Development Project, Phase 3.
- Laem Chabang Port Development Project Phase 3 (Terminal F) to improve the two deteriorating port facilities. Previously planned, the first and second phases are scheduled to open in 2025 and 2029, respectively. Together they will handle four million 20-foot equivalent units (TEU) annually.[2]
- A high-speed railway linking three airports (Don Mueang, Suvarnabhumi, and U-Tapao) project was intended to be built on the Eastern Seaboard but never materialized. A high-speed train would reduce travel time between Bangkok and U-Tapao to 45 minutes, improving transportation speed and efficiency (Lauridsen, 2020).
- A double-track railway project.
- Construction of an intercity highway (motorway road) to supplement an expressway currently connecting Bangkok and Rayong.

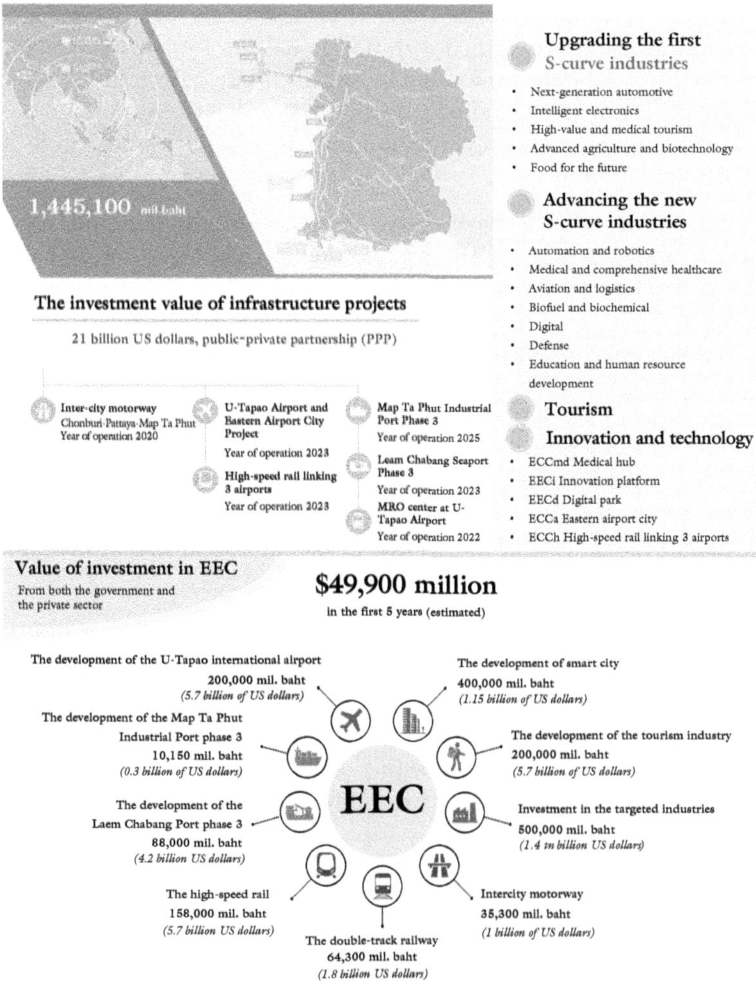

Figure 7.1 The value of investment in EEC

Source: Compiled by the author based on *2 years of EEC* (EEC, 2019, pp. 20–23, 30–31)

Note: Total value of investment at $49,900 million or 1,600,000 million baht

These projects, totalling 650 billion baht in investment and representing one third of the total investment value of 1.7 trillion baht, aim to develop the eastern region's transportation and logistics infrastructure.

2) New target industries, with four projects (seven industries) for projected investment value of 500 billion baht.

- Modern automotive sector (electric vehicles) currently housed in older industrial estates combined with traditional automobile manufacturers.
- Petrochemical industry located in Map Ta Phut Industrial Estate.
- Aircraft maintenance industry located near U-Tapao Airport.
- Intelligent electronics and medical hub manufacturing base in Si Racha District, Chonburi.

3) Tourist industry. Since the Vietnam War era, Eastern Thailand, especially Pattaya, has been a popular tourist destination for American soldiers. The goal is to develop a tourism industry using all available resources and expertise.
4) Industrial innovation with Smart New City Development (Smart City), focusing on the digital economy and environmentally friendly renewable energy. Smart City supports the creation of new lifestyles for about one million workers who will move to the EEC area during the next decade or two and provides business opportunities for many small- and medium-sized firms (Keeranan, 2022; Sathapholdeja, 2019). Green space must account for 30 percent of the entire area, as well as transit to connect the infrastructure system to a distance of 30 kilometres.

Total value of the four projects was US$49.9 billion, or 1.7 trillion baht. In 2017, this amount accounted for 61 percent of Thailand's annual budget of 2.7 trillion baht, more than three times the value of 5.43 billion baht economic investment in normal budget planning. This mandates strong commitment to large-scale investment initiatives, with the ECC plan as the centrepiece for escaping the middle-income trap (EEC Office, 2019; Phuangketkeow, 2020).

7.1.2 *Implementation challenges and obstacles*

The EEC plan may be hampered by six challenges and impediments (Suehiro, 2020):[3]

1) How to raise the substantial funding required.

Government policy relies on PPP investments. The government is intended to invest 30 percent, the private sector 60 percent, and state-owned enterprises 10 percent, according to the Public-Private Partnership Act, B.E. 2562. (2019). Government debt limited to 60 percent of statutory GDP is referred to as government investment. As a result, rather than spending money from the Thailand Future Fund (TFIF), the Prayut government will first use the PPP law as a shield, enlisting help from private businesses (Board of Investment, 2020).

Obviously, domestic capital will be insufficient. Over half of the funds must be borrowed from third-party financial institutions, such as Japan's Asian Development Bank (ADB) and International Cooperation Agency (JICA),

China's Industrial and Commercial Bank (ICBC) and Asian Infrastructure Investment Bank (AIIB). China established new financial institutions linked to the Belt and Road Initiative (BRI) with the US$100 billion AIIB and US$40 billion New Silk Road Fund (NSRF). Thailand's engagement with China's new Silk Road strategy should be substantial (Chirathivat et al., 2022; Sangsubhan, 2018, 2021).

2) Assigning responsibility for 15 investment projects, especially the 12 target industries.

Health care & tourism, agriculture & biotechnology, and food processing are three fields in which Thai companies are potentially competitive. Foreign companies are essential for developing the remaining seven industries. Whether MNCs see Thailand as a production base for each industry depends on their regional goals. Military and education industries, ranked eleventh and twelfth, tend to rely on collaborating with leading international educational institutions as well as attracting foreign company investment.

The Thai government encourages leading MNCs to invest in each industry, emphasizing national reliance on them. As the EEC office lacks international branches, Thai ambassadors are issued lists of sought-after companies from the EEC office, which they will contact for potential investments. Foreign corporations such as Mercedes-Benz, BMW, Ford, Toyota, SAIC Motor, Great Wall Motors, and Skywell are sought for constructing new hybrid and electric cars, while Seagate Technology, Samsung, Midea, and Haier are in demand for developing smart electronics. For manufacture of robots and medical equipment, Hirata, Baxter Manufacturing, and Xiasan Robots and Automation are needed. In the digital industry, 5G technology has enticed Chinese and American firms such as Huawei and Alibaba, as well as Microsoft, Google, and VMware, to invest in personnel and create businesses in Thailand (Sangsubhan, 2021).

Before the EEC plan was announced, US Goodyear developed a new aviation tire facility near an old manufacturing area in Pathum Thani Province. The largest privately held freight and postal corporation in the United States, United Parcel Service (UPS), was also asked to invest in the transportation and logistics market.

Thai Airways International PLC must construct an MRO facility at U-Tapao Airport in Rayong Province in collaboration with Airbus France, Boeing, Senior Aerospace, and SAAP of the United States, as well as Air Asia, a Malaysian budget airline, and Mitsubishi Motors of Japan. With Asian air travel business decreasing due to the COVID-19 pandemic, Thai Airways filed for bankruptcy and reorganization in September 2020. The carrier's intention to develop an aircraft maintenance yard was jeopardized when partner Airbus cancelled a contract signed in 2017, imperilling Thai Airways' recovery scheme.

In addition, 31 companies from seven countries have expressed interest in development of the high-speed rail linking three airports. In December 2018, the Charoen Pokphand Group – led consortium consisting of China Trust Company (CI TIC), China Railway Construction Group (CRCC), Ch. Karnchang PLC, and Bangkok Expressway and Metro PLC – was awarded the contract with a 224 billion baht bid.

Table 7.1 Thai business groups and foreign investors in EEC

	Sector	*Country (Company)*
	Infrastructure	Utapao airport and Eastern airport city: Thailand (Royal Thai Navy, BBS-consortium: Bangkok Airways, BTS Group, and Sino-Thai Engineering and Construction) High-speed rail linking three airports: Thailand (State Railway of Thailand, Bangkok Expressway and Metro, Italian-Thai Development, and CH Karnchang), China (China Railway Construction)
		Laem Chabang seaport phase 3: Thailand (Port Authority of Thailand, GPC joint venture: Gulf Energy Development, PTT Tank Terminal), China (China Harbor Engineering)
		Map Ta Phut industrial port phase 3: Thailand (Industrial Estate Authority of Thailand, Gulf MTP LNG Terminal, a joint venture of Gulf Energy Development and PTT Tank Terminal)
		MOR center at U-Tapao airport: Thailand (Thai Airways) and other aviation companies
	Industrial estates in EEC	Thailand (WHA Group, Amata City, Pinthong, Rojna, CPGC: C.P. Land and China Guangxi Construction Engineering)
Upgrading the first-S-curve industries		
1	Next-generation automotive	Thailand (Energy Absolute, Thonburi Automotive, Thai Summit), China (SAIC Motor-CP, Beiqi Foton – CP, Jiangte Joylong, Great Wall, Anhui Ankai, BYD, Holley), EU (Mercedes Benz, BMW, Scania), Japan (Toyota, Isuzu, Mitsubishi, Nissan, Honda, Mazda, FOMM, Subaru, Mitsubishi Fusho), Malaysia (Tan Chong), US (GM)

(*Continued*)

Table 7.1 (Continued)

	Sector	*Country (Company)*
2	Intelligent electronics	Canada (Celestica), EU (ETA, BHS, Stiebel Eltron, NXP, ABB, Fasco Motor, Schneider, MPO Asia), Japan (HA, OA: Panasonic, Daikin, Canon, Sharp, Hitachi, Mitsubishi Electric, Toshiba; HDD & Parts: HGST, Toshiba, Nidec, TDK, AGC, NHK; Semiconductor: Rohm, Oki, Sanyo, Stanley, Shindengen; PCB: CMK, NOK; EMS, PCBA: SIIX, Kaga, Katata, Katolec, Eiwa, Alpine; Electronic parts: Fujikura, Minebea, Murata, Seiko), Korea (LG, Samsung, KEC, Haeng Sung, Hansol, Dongjin, Duck Sung, Sung In, Yoowon), Taiwan (CAL-COMP), US (Seagate, Western Digital, Donaldson, Hutchison, Maxim, Microchip, Spansion, Honeywell, Innovex, Sanmina-SCI, Benchmark)
3	High-value and medical tourism	Thailand (Tourism Authority of Thailand, Minor International, Bamrungrad Hospital, Samitivej Hospital, MQDC, Siam Wellness), Canada (Baycrest Global Solutions)
4	Advanced agriculture and biotechnology	Thailand (CP, Mitr Phol, Srithai Agro), China (Yellow Sea Fisheries Research Institute, Light Industry Research Institute of Guangxi, Nanning Wanyu Foods, Beijing Genomic Institute)
5	Food for future	Thailand (Betagro, SCG, CPF, Mitr Phol, Thai Union, Malee, ThaiBev, UFC, Bangchak, TVO, Medi Foods, Thai President Foods, Boon Rawd)
Advancing the new S-curve industries		
6	Automation and robotics	Thailand (Gravity Game Tech, HDP, PMP, Maxtech, Femtobit, Aerial, A. L. Tech, CT Asia, Anchi, Eureka, ABB, Abiz, Brainworks, NKE, Fersmek), China (Siasun), Japan (Hirata, OJ System)
7	Medical and comprehensive health care	Thailand (Food and Drug Administration, BDMS, Chulabhorn Royal Academy, Bamrungrad, Thonburi, Mega Lifesciences, Siam Pharmaceutical, Biolab, Better Pharma, OLIC), Belgium (Janssen-Cilag), China (BGI-Shenzhen, KBIC), German (Berlin Pharmaceutical Industry), France (Sanofi), Japan (Meiji, Takeda, Hakuzo Medical), UK (GSK, Astrazeneca), US (Merck, Pfizer), Switzerland (Novartis, Roche)

(*Continued*)

Table 7.1 (Continued)

	Sector	*Country (Company)*
8	Aviation and logistics	Thailand (AOT, CAAT, Bangkok Airways, Thai Airways, Nok Air, Thai Smile), China (China Aerospace Science and Technology, China National Aviation, China Eastern Air, Wuhan optic valley, NWIEE, CNSO, DJI), France (Michelin, Safran, Revima, Airbus Helicopters), German (Helix Composite, Leistritz, AVIA Satcom), Hong Kong (East Asia Composite), Indonesia (Thai Lion Air), Japan (Senko Logistics), Malaysia (Air Asia), Netherland (Aeroworks, Aeroworks Composites, Chromalloy), US (Ducommun Technologies, Senior Aerospace, Triumph Structures), Vietnam (Vietjet Air)
9	Biofuel and biochemical	Thailand (PTT MCC Biochem, SCG Chemical, Mitr Phol, TRR, KTIS, KSL, Patum, AIE, EA, Thai Ethoxylate, TOL, NatureWorks, Polyplex, HMC Polymers), China (Niran), Japan (Ajinomoto, Kuraray), Netherlands (Corbion Purac), Taiwan (Pure & Chem, UNIC Technology), US (Ingredion)
10	Digital	Thailand (CAT Telecom, AIS, True-D, Sahapat, Omise, aCommerce, Pomelo Fashion), China (Huawei, Alibaba, Tencent, Kingsoft, JD.com, China Unicom, China Mobile International, CAC Telecom, Hong Kong Cable, Tus-Holdings Company, ZTE), France (Schneider Electric), German (Bosch), Japan (NEC, Furukawa, Epson, Toyocom, Kyocera), Singapore (Singtel), Switzerland (Schaffner EMC)
11	Defence	US, China, Turkey
12	Education and human resource development	Thailand (Amata University, King Mongkut's Institute of Technology Ladkrabang), Switzerland (Les Roches Institution), Taiwan (National Taiwan University), US (Carnegie Mellon University)

The EEC plan is entirely reliant on foreign technology partnership. Without foreign investment and assistance from foreign government financial institutions, the project could not attain completion. In every sense, the Thaksin government's 2005 megaproject, the so-called "Kingdom of Thailand Modernization Framework," is comparable to the present one.[4]

While China's long-term national science and technology development plan 2006–2020 establishes basic aims to "create innovation for ourselves" and lessen reliance on foreign technology, Thailand 4.0 clearly relies on others. Proof of this was seen when an economic team led by Deputy Prime Minister Somkid Jatusripitak[5] actively sought investment from Japan and China.

The EEC office urges local Thai companies to actively boost competitiveness. If the plan succeeds in attracting foreign investors due to EEC office skilled promotion, Thai companies must be prepared. No achievement is possible without willingness to develop, self-empower, absorb, and transfer technology. Building individual Thai company technology and branding must be set aside for a willingness to follow international standards in accounting, legislation, manufacturing, and human resource development. Those who have lost interest in the EEC endeavour have negative views of it, although this type of special economic zone is seen internationally.[6]

3) Issues resulting from Prayut's use of exceptional powers to support the EEC plan (supreme legal authority under Article 44 of the Interim Constitution).

Thai strategy comprises listening to diverse opinions and examining environmental impacts on economic growth plans closely linked to local communities, especially after the 1997 Asian financial crisis, when Chuan Leekpai was prime minister. Thaksin Shinawatra and Yingluck Shinawatra later became prime ministers, but public hearings, while continuing, became less prominent.

Many EEC operational plans rely on emergency powers and obligatory special laws. Meanwhile, the EEC office was appointed, wielding more authority than the law would normally allow. Such tactics accelerate activity, and after the political situation has stabilized, local residents are likely to complain and seek new public hearings and environmental impact analysis. In 2009, a series of lawsuits about pollution management in development zones along the eastern shore provided a precedent.

While some residents of other areas may hope that their own province follows in the path of the EEC, EEC citizens share similar concerns: what benefits will the EEC provide to their homes, towns, and provinces? Negative stories about the EEC are rife, including major corporation favouritism, and concerns about rapid development, air and noise pollution, water scarcity, industrial waste, higher living costs, and community congestion (Tontisirin & Anantsuksomsri, 2021).

Ownership distribution is particularly lacking in the land governance framework for development. Large capitalists and houses are also favoured. The EEC office is attempting to create a regulatory framework to diversify ownership, generate knowledge, and interact inclusively with area residents. But the effort will take time, and land interests are being pursued by several government authorities[7] (Keeranan, 2022; Tontisirin & Anantsuksomsri, 2021).

4) Dissatisfaction with governmental policy of concentrating resources solely on Thailand's eastern area, as well as political pressure from other regions.

No opposition currently exists to the policy focused on Thailand's eastern region. Thaksin supporters in the north and northeast of Thailand have no means of resisting the plan. The Japanese Chamber of Commerce and Industry requested that the high-speed railway starting station be expanded to connect industrial estates in Ayutthaya, the centre of Japanese electrical and electronic companies, with Rayong Province. But in July 2017, the proposal was rejected by Prayut on the grounds that current law only permitted development in three eastern region provinces. One day, perhaps, why only the eastern part of Thailand has been granted these privileges may become a topic of discord (Suehiro, 2020).

To counter such protests in advance, the government declared that advantages were not limited to three provinces. The EEC plan is considered a sandbox or test project. If it succeeds, similar projects will follow, such as the Northern Economic Corridor (NEC-Creative LANNA), Northeastern Economic Corridor (NeEC-Bioeconomy), Central-Western Economic Corridor (CWEC), and Southern Economic Corridor (SEC) (Keeranan, 2022; Phuangketkeow, 2020). But progress on these appears glacial compared to the EEC, with no concrete details, action plans, or even defined framework formulated as yet.[8]

There have also been suggestions that the zone be expanded into adjacent provinces. For example, the State Railway of Thailand would extend phase 2 of the high-speed train linking three airports project from Rayong to Chanthaburi and Trat Provinces. The Southern Economic Bridge Project (Land Bridge) would also connect Ranong and Satun Provinces in the Western Andaman Sea with Chumphon, Songkhla, and Nakhon Si Thammarat in the Gulf of Thailand. The project is anticipated to cost 1.5 trillion baht and has been in the works since Thaksin's administration.

5) Whether Thais, especially engineers and middle-level executives, are willing to work in rural provinces outside of Bangkok.

The three eastern Thai provinces are proud of having a national GDP per capita higher than Bangkok's. But this figure is calculated by dividing the total value added by the region's population. The disparity between Bangkok and the three provinces remains apparent when it comes to educational possibilities (recognized high schools, universities, and tutoring establishments), housing conditions, and transportation. Finding skilled Thai engineers and families is challenging, but attitudes may change as regional digital economy develops and institutions of higher education expand to the east.

Rather than being an industrial zone, the EEC plan aspires to construct a city. The area between Chonburi and Rayong is being developed into Chachoengsao as a residence site for EEC workers to achieve a balance between life and work for the new generation (Sangsubhan, 2021). The EEC Office summarized the demand for manpower in the EEC area over five years from 2019 to 2023, with 475,674 skilled jobs. The top three industries with highest labour demands are digital (24 percent), logistics (23 percent), and smart electronics (12 percent).

6) Project continuity, which could be jeopardized by diverse factors.

Economic repercussions of the COVID-19 pandemic may impede Thailand's ambition to become a high-income, innovation-driven nation by 2037. The Thai economy is primarily reliant on global value chains (GVCs), halted in different sectors in early 2020 due to the COVID-19 pandemic, which, according to all analyses, affected it the most in the ASEAN region.

Nonetheless, COVID-19 has scarcely impacted infrastructure development so far, according to Kanit Sangsubhan, secretary-general of the EEC office. Because all projects were either in planning phases or seeking investors before the pandemic, everything remains within the framework of parameters. By using videoconferencing technology, stakeholders were able to continue discussions about the projects during the pandemic (Sangsubhan, 2022).

Although Somkid and Minister of Industry and Finance Uttama Savanayana, the project's two founders, resigned from the cabinet in 2020, the EEC working team has remained intact. The Eastern Special Development Zone Act, B.E. 2561 (2018), is also in effect, with a ruling committee chaired by the prime minister. When major potential investors arrive in Thailand, they meet with the prime minister to ensure that the project receives sufficient attention. However, the Nikkei Asian Review has noted Somkid's longstanding relationship with Japan, where investors prize credit and personal relationships. His departure may prove to be a turning point leading to slowdown or withdrawal from the EEC plan (Toru, 2020; Yuda, 2020).

7.2 Belt Road Initiative of China

7.2.1 21st Century Silk Road

On 7 September 2013, Xi Jinping, China's leader, spoke about the Silk Road Economic Belt[9] at Nazarbayev University in Astana, Kazakhstan, formally launching China's 21st Century Silk Road program. Just over a year later, on 3 October 2014, during a tour to Association of Southeast Asian Nations (ASEAN) nations, he announced the Marine Silk Road project[10] at the Indonesian House of Representatives in Jakarta. In March 2015, China published a paper, "Vision and Actions for Jointly Building the Silk Road Economic Belt and the 21st Century Maritime Silk Road," that became part of Chinese foreign policy (Aoyama, 2016; Li et al., 2022).

The BRI concept projects building a massive infrastructure network comprising roads, railways, elevated tracks, ports, oil pipelines, and telecommunications, as well as special economic zones, to connect economies of over 60 countries across three connected continents. BRI connects 30 percent of the world's GDP, 62 percent of its population, and 75 percent of its energy (Ngampramuan, 2021; Sangsubhan, 2018).

The strategy's objectives include strengthening connections with neighbours, acquiring natural resources in Central Asia, removing surplus supply in the Chinese steel industry through infrastructure projects, and accessing the Indian Ocean and South China Sea (Jones & Hameiri, 2020). Chinese resolve to impose global influence are mirrored, implying a shift in economic and political power balance from West to East (Aoyama, 2016; Li et al., 2022).

Unlike the contemporaneous Brexit, or withdrawal of the United Kingdom (UK) from the European Union (EU) on 31 January 2020, or the America First platform of former United States President Donald Trump, BRI plans include creation of a framework to advance the digital economy (Ito, 2020). More than merely exporting commodities, capital, and tourism, China is also the source of such internet phenomena as Lazada, TikTok, and WeChat. It is also experimenting to make the digital yuan the world's most widely used currency.

The Chinese government has linked the BRI plan to the Silk Road Fund and Asian Infrastructure Investment Bank (AIIB), with combined capital of $55 billion and $100 billion, respectively. China's five largest banks – Industrial and Commercial Bank of China (ICBC), China Development Bank (CDB), New Development Bank, People's Bank of China (PBoC), and The Export – Import Bank of China (Chexim – China Exim Bank) – have committed a collective $285 billion to the BRI. In collaborating with this project, neighbouring nations will have access to loans from these funds. In this way, China has become a decisive source of EEC funding[11] (Jones & Hameiri, 2020; Ngampramuan, 2021).

7.2.2 *Chinese southward movement and the EEC*

The future of the EEC project is not assured. Foreign investors may abandon the project outright, as they did with former Prime Minister Thaksin's Kingdom of Thailand Modernization Framework (KTMF). Even if the National Strategies Preparation Act, BE 2560 (2017) and Eastern Special Development Zone Act BE 2561 (2018) are followed to the letter, investments may soon diminish.

Two characteristics distinguish the EEC from the KTMF. The first is the September 2017 agreement on national strategic collaboration signed by Prayut and Xi. The second is the readiness of Chinese companies to collaborate with the EEC, as seen in a 19 April 2018 memorandum of understanding (MoU) between the Prayut government and Jack Ma, billionaire chairman of Alibaba Group Holding Limited, for the Electronic Trading Complex (EC Park) in Si Racha District, Chonburi Province (Nidhiprabha, 2019).

The MoU specifies: (1) delivery of Thai agricultural commodities to Chinese cities by e-commerce, (2) collaboration on developing digital and e-commerce skills, (3) establishing a digital tourism platform, and (4) investment in the EEC Smart Digital Hub. Collaboration with Alibaba, which holds vast consumer data in China, was significant. The day before the MoU was signed, sales of Thai durian fruit began on Tmall.com, and 80,000 transactions were completed in one minute.

China's BRI strategy includes the land Silk Road connecting Kunming City to Bangkok and Singapore through Laos. EEC expansion establishes connections with Cambodia and Vietnam to reach the East China Sea, accessible from the eastern Thailand ports of Laem Chabang and Sattahip. Kunming is also included in EEC Policy Steering Committee investment strategy papers (Chirathivat et al., 2022).

The Charoen Pokphand Group (CP) is central to the EEC goal of converting Thailand's eastern shore into a digital hotspot with bullet trains, 5G networks, and smart vehicle manufacturers. A consortium led by CP, including China Railway Construction Corporation Limited (CRCC) and CITIC Group Corporation Ltd., was the lowest bidder for a 255 billion baht contract to build a 200 km rail network connecting three airports (Lauridsen, 2020). The director appointed by CITIC Limited, a part of CITIC Group, as vice chairman and chief executive officer of CPG China, mentioned a "One Belt, One Road Economic Corridor." According to this concept, the Chinese government is represented by CITIC and the BRI plan, whereas the Thai government is represented by the CP Group and the EEC project (Suehiro, 2020).

Chinese officials are also focusing on the "maritime base" concept, intended to financially assist Laem Chabang, Sattahip, and Map Ta Phut ports in Thailand. The ports of Sihanoukville in Cambodia and Vung Tau in Vietnam would also be implicated. China favoured Thailand as a strategic base for South China Sea growth, just as it selected Sri Lanka as strategic base for Indian Ocean development (Sangsubhan, 2018).

By 2018, China's investment in Thailand had increased significantly, surpassing Japan and Singapore as the third largest source of permitted foreign direct investment (FDI). In 2019, Chinese and Taiwanese investment projects more than doubled the rate of Japanese projects. However, manufacturing businesses favoured light industry and low- and moderate-value-added sectors such as metal processing over 5S curve industries. Since 2015, an increase in Chinese visitors led to increased service sector investment in real estate, hotels, retail, and e-commerce (Nidhiprabha, 2019).

7.3 Japan and Thailand plus one

7.3.1 *Greasing the wheels of commerce*

Thailand's Eastern Seaboard Development Program (ESDP), initiated as part of the 5th Economic and Social Development Plan of Thailand (1982–1986), developing the Eastern Seaboard to promote industrial growth and decentralize economic and population growth, with Japanese assistance. In 1985, currency rates were manipulated by weakening the US dollar against the Japanese yen in the Plaza Accord, a joint agreement signed between France, West Germany, Japan, the United Kingdom, and the United States. To avoid international political upheaval, Japanese companies migrated to Thailand, Singapore, Indonesia, Malaysia, and the Philippines, where they could manufacture locally and export to the United States and European Union (EU) markets.

From 1988 to 1991, while governments of neighbouring countries were preoccupied with internal political issues, the Thai government led by Chatichai Choonhavan proclaimed a strategy of "converting the battlefield into the commercial field." In what was declared an "economic miracle" in the "Fifth Tiger of Asia," Thailand was bolstered by governmental acceptance of Japanese foreign direct investment (FDI), to facilitate commerce (Braudel & Reynold, 1992). Due to this precedent, some Thai observers today expect a comparable windfall if Japanese and other multinational corporations (MNCs) accept the EEC as an innovation and high-technology destination (Tangkitvanich, 2019).

The EEC plan is divided into two main investments: infrastructure and 12 target industries. Most infrastructure projects were organized through competitive bidding from Thai-Chinese joint ventures. After conducting feasibility assessments, Japan deemed these plans difficult to fund. As public-private partnerships (PPPs), private joint ventures face a possibility of insolvency or loss. Japanese investors withdrew from the bidding process when the Thai government declined their requests for guarantee in the event of loss (Suehiro, 2020).

Thailand's objective is to escape the middle-income trap before it is expected to become a super-aged society in in 2031, adding substantial fiscal burdens. Chinese companies are willing to participate in the infrastructure plan to comply with the Belt and Road Initiative (BRI) and avert a trade war with the United States (Ngampramuan, 2021). Nevertheless, Japanese companies see four major obstacles to long-term EEC success (JETRO Thailand, 2019):[12]

- Human capital: Thailand has repeatedly noted an absence of technical vocational education and training (TVET) students, while Japanese investors complain about a lack of experienced Thai engineers. Japanese stakeholders see Thai engineers as overly prideful (*hana ga takai*), work-shy about visiting arduous sites, and unmotivated. These objections suggest that Thailand's Ministry of Labour should be proactive in developing the national industrial qualification system.
- Transport issues: Thailand hopes that constructing a one-hour bullet train linking the EEC and Bangkok would facilitate recruitment of skilled engineers and managerial class employees with families (Sangsubhan, 2022).

Japanese investors, who have extensive high-speed train experience, disagree and fear that emphasizing infrastructure while disregarding investment in people will result in income distribution deterioration.

- Crowding-out effect: Thailand may be overconfident about EEC plans, anticipating that foreign MNCs and major domestic investors will flood the region. In reality, Thailand will continue to compete with international exporters who produce comparable items but pay higher wages to workers. Increased public spending will result in reducing or eliminating private sector expenditures as opportunity cost and interest rates for loans increase.
- Chinese and Japanese rivalry: Thailand prefers fierce bidding as seen in Phase 1 of infrastructure investment but must avoid escalating rivalries between two main MNCs to the point both desist. Ensuring that Chinese and Japanese investors actively engage in the EEC plan beyond individual competition is essential for its success (Pavlicevic, 2017).

7.3.2 *Ranking in the Japanese flying geese paradigm*

Thailand may serve as a profitable market and efficient manufacturing base for Japanese companies. Japan is Thailand's largest investor, but Thailand has never experienced a positive trade balance with Japan. Thailand receives only 3.6 percent of Japanese total exports (sixth largest exporter) and only 2.9 percent of total imports (tenth largest importer).[13]

Thailand offers the following advantages and disadvantages: Firstly, it has a stronger manufacturing base than surrounding developing countries, with deep-sea ports, airports, transportation infrastructure, and accumulated industrial clusters. There is also less vividly remembered trauma in amnesiac Thailand than elsewhere in the Association of Southeast Asian Nations (ASEAN) of the cruelties of Japanese military occupation during World War II. Also, entrepreneurs in Thailand tend to be less energetic about accessing foreign technology through industrial espionage than those in other Asian nations (Tangkitvanich, 2019).

Nevertheless, Thailand's growth rate is approaching saturation. Apart from the EEC, Thailand has no significant investment initiatives. Economic income and wealth are concentrated, and ownership is distributed unequally. It is a top-down dictatorship through a bureaucracy, state-owned enterprises, and large capital groups, leading to difficulties in expanding the economy (Phuangketkeow, 2020).

In market terms, Thailand's annual automobile output surpassed two million vehicles, one million of which were sold domestically and the remainder exported. According to Sathapholdeja (2019), Thailand has a strong automobile market and production base, which comprises a diverse array of SMEs in supporting industry. High-speed trains and the Bangkok mass transportation system project are examples of infrastructure needs. They're in heavy reliance on Japanese loans to construct motorways, bridges over the Chao Phraya and Mekong Rivers, electric trains, and other projects.

This concurs with the High-Quality Infrastructure Export Expansion Initiative, launched in 2013 as part of economic policies implemented by the Government of Japan led by Shinzō Abe, informally referred to as Abenomics. Japan focused on physical and non-physical infrastructure, including by enhancing connectivity and reducing disparities and assisting ASEAN countries escape the middle-income trap, which China is also attempting to achieve (Doner, 2018).

Japanese investment in service businesses such as tourism, outdoor restaurants, and cultural venues is a growing trend. Approximately 1.3 million Thais visit Japan annually, and Japanese companies seek to profit from this market (Tangkitvanich, 2019). By 2022, Thailand had 73,000 Japanese residents, of whom 53,000 lived in Bangkok, making it Asia's largest Japanese metropolis outside Japan. Now 5,400 Japanese companies operate in Thailand.

Politically, despite economic success during the 1980s and 1990s, Thai government coalition administrations were unstable and short-lived. But policies remained stable, despite governance uncertainties. During the Thaksin regime from 2001 to 2006, the government appeared more stable, although policies were increasingly shifting. Thai politics became destabilized during an era of one-party state stability. Elections alternated with coups, creating a vicious leadership cycle.

During Prayut's coup followed by a disputed election, despite the backing of the Thai monarchy, the political scene has degraded to an unstable government with shifting policies. A coalition government reliant on small factions inspired waves of street protestors, including youths calling for democracy, constitutional reform, dissolution of parliament, and monarchic reform, a previously taboo subject (Kongkirati & Kanchoochat, 2018).

By contrast, Vietnam is attracting manufacturing operations due to geographic advantages and lower costs, with an export basket comparable to China's. While its politics remain stagnant, Vietnam is a vast market with a youthful population. Vietnam has access to the Comprehensive and Progressive Agreement for Trans-Pacific Partnership (CPTTP), the EU-Vietnam Free Trade Agreement (EVFTA), and the EU's generalized system of preferences (GSP). Since 2015, Thailand has been refused GSP status, and trade privileges with other countries, notably the EU, are relatively limited.

Finally, Thailand will soon transition to a super-aged society.[14] It faces acute labour shortages and must import workers from neighbouring countries. As a result, relying on local market returns for investment may not be an ideal option. Thai employees desire stability and high competence levels, yet advanced skilled labour remains scare. For these reasons, Japanese investment has dwindled significantly after the 2011 Thailand floods.

7.3.3 *Thailand plus one strategy*

The China-US trade war and the COVID-19 pandemic have demonstrated the need for companies to diversify supply chains outside of China, leading to a so-called "China Plus One" strategy, in which MNFs move to other countries in addition to China. Japanese investors, too, have sought alternatives over the past decade to replace China as a source of intermediated products imported from Japan and as a manufacturing base for finished export items. Japanese companies strive to lessen the reliance on China due to uncertainties about the Japan-China political relationship.

Previously, Japanese investors relocated manufacturing bases to ASEAN countries, another trend linked to China. As Japan-ASEAN trade reduced, China-ASEAN trade expanded, facilitated by Japanese companies. Later, the China Plus One plan emerged in reaction to soaring wages and living costs in Chinese industrial cities, stringent Chinese government regulations, and the US-China trade war (JETRO Thailand, 2015, 2019).

"Thailand Plus One" was also launched during the 2011 Thailand floods to reduce dependency on a single country, with Japanese international labour division diversifying risks connected with Thailand's industrial supply chain. The approach sought to safeguard Thailand's major industrial hubs, apart from labour-intensive, low-cost, low-technology manufacturing work outsourced to Cambodia, Laos, Myanmar, and Vietnam (the CLMV countries) (Ishida et al., 2017; JETRO Thailand, 2015).

From the Japanese viewpoint, the Asian supply chain offers little prima facie evidence that production bases for major capital-intensive commodities exported from China to Thailand (10 percent of total imports), such as mobile phones, personal computers, electric and electronic (E&E) equipment and machinery, and steel, will be relocated to Thailand. HP, Dell, and their EMS subcontractors have heavily invested in China and are expanding operations into Vietnam and India, sustaining the overall reliance on China.

Despite Japan's substantial industrial clusters in Thailand, Japanese companies continue to purchase locally at a rate under 60 percent. Local procurement of hard commodities such as electric cars, high-value-added electronic devices, and robot manufacturing in Thailand will remain limited until industrial agglomerations develop. Thai imports from Japan are increasing in accord with Japanese FDI accumulation (JETRO Thailand, 2019).

Thailand's primary exports to China are soft commodities or agricultural products, used for final consumption such as rice and fruit, animal feed, and intermediate manufactured products such as natural and synthetic rubber. These are relatively low-value-added goods. China retains the manufacturing base for vehicle tires and high-value-added industrial components.

However, the Chinese share of trade and inbound investment may surpass Japan due to increased liberalization in the manufacturing and service sectors, including logistics, e-commerce, real estate, and tech startups. This may change if Thailand introduces regulations significantly increasing the proportion of electric vehicles and intensifies encouragement of artificial intelligence (AI), automation and robotics, and digital technology.

Meanwhile, Japan has studied Thailand's demographic shift and seeks a "Thai model" for the first developing nation to become a super-aged society, facing a "poor and old" (PO) future, along with China (Sasiwongsaroj & Burasit, 2019). This includes developing nation welfare state formats, universal coverage or a 30 baht charge for all medical treatment, long-term care, as well as NGO and community volunteer roles. If the relatively low-cost "Thai model" proves superior to the high-cost "Japanese model," it may benefit other developing latecomers, striving to catch up with industrialization.

Finally, due to Japan's lost decades and the rise of China, some observers have overlooked the former's enduring importance in Asia. Japan has established relationships through a long history of private and public regional investment, making it a formidable rival to China. By contrast, China still must prove its potential for overtaking Japan as leader of the flying geese paradigm in Asia (Ito, 2020).

Notes

1 The project on a 6,500-rai site costs 290 billion baht. BBS joint venture group, including Bangkok Airways PLC (45 percent), BTS Group Holdings PLC (35 percent), Sino-Thai Engineering and Construction PLC (20 percent), hired Narita International Airport Corporation (Japan), which won the auction and signed a contract on 19 June 2020 to deliver the best return to the state during the concession's 50-year term (current value 305,555 million baht).

2 In November 2021, GPC International Terminal Ltd. (GPC) signed a public-private partnership (PPP) contract with the Port Authority of Thailand (PAT) to develop and operate Laem Chabang Port Phase 3, a Terminal F project in Chonburi Province. PTT Tank Terminal Company Limited (PTT Group), Gulf Energy Development PLC, and China Harbor Engineering Company Ltd hold 30, 30, and 40 percent stakes in GPC, respectively. The GPC proposal (1.2 billion baht) underbid the cabinet resolution's median price of 3.2 billion baht. NPC, a rival organization, submitted a 2.7 billion baht bid packet earlier but was disqualified by the Supreme Administrative Court. Later, PAT negotiations with the GPC increased the return to 2.9 billion baht (see "Timeline 2 years 7 months 12 days to close Laem Chabang Phase 3 joint venture deal," *Krungthep Turakit,* 14 November 2021).

3 Summarized from an interview by the author and Professor Dr. Akira Suehiro with Dr. Kanit Sangsubhan, secretary-general of the EEC Office, on 22 August 2017.

4 In June 2005, the Cabinet authorized KTMF, a 1.8 trillion-baht investment initiative, including energy, transportation, mass transit networks, residential housing, and water resources. But foreign investors were not attracted by the proposal. The project was later postponed and eventually vanished after a coup d'état in September 2006.

5 Somkid stated during an opposition debate in parliament on economics that the root of disparity was the low value of Thai goods and services, and low-earning farmers. Because the private sector is unwilling to invest, workers are unable to

augment earnings. In addition to high-tech industries, the EEC effort focuses on agriculture, biotechnology, and tourism. The project acts as a sandbox for future growth of these industries. Thai workers lack skills and training. So the project must unite foreign investors with experience in each of these fields. To entice investment requires major infrastructure and digital commitments and BOI initiatives (see "Somkid pointed to the economy growing, but not spreading quickly, hoping to use the EEC to pull off, refuse to accept the capitalist's favor," *Thairath*, 24 February 2020).

6 Interview by the author with Dr. Cholachit Vorawangso Virakul, executive director attached to secretary general, Office of the Secretary General, Eastern Economic Corridor Office of Thailand on 11 March 2020.

7 Chaiyon Praditsil and his team (2021) investigated land management conflicts in the EEC project. Case studies are available in a variety of formats and sizes.

8 For example, Udon Thani Industrial Estate, which would be the first industrial estate in upper Isan, Thailand's populous Northeastern region, located at the crossroads of the dual-track high-speed train connecting Bangkok and Nong Khai Provinces. It may transport goods between Thailand, Laos, and southern China, as well as to Laem Chabang Port and the EEC. To encourage foreign investment, it sought special BOI incentives comparable to those granted by the EEC (Board of Investment, 2020) (see "First phase of Udon Thani industrial estate to be ready next year" *The Nation* 14 September 2020).

9 Updating the historical Silk Road, today's land route connects China and Europe through China's high-speed rail network to the heart of Central Asia, through Kazakhstan and Iran, the Middle East through Turkey, and Europe through Frankfurt, Venice, and Amsterdam. These cities and ports are all significant international economic and industrial centres (Button, 2017).

10 The marine route connects major Chinese ports such as Shanghai, Tianjin, and Fuzhou, down to the South China Sea, through ASEAN nations, across the Straits of Malacca into the Indian Ocean, and into the Middle East, where parts of the route enter West Africa through the Persian Gulf and Suez Canal before entering the Mediterranean and heading to Europe. This path is traced to recall the significance of ancient Chinese trade routes.

11 Unlike the Marshall Plan, a US-sponsored program which primarily distributed aid in the form of non-repayable grants, China frequently lends money at commercial interest rates. Japan, in turn, uses the Japan International Cooperation Agency (JICA) and Japan Bank for International Cooperation (JBIC) to offer technical support, official development assistance (ODA), and concessional loans to developing nations.

12 Interview by the author with Japanese executives of the AMEICC Bangkok (AEM-METI ASEAN-JAPAN Economic & Industrial Cooperation Committee) and a Japanese consultant of Nomura Research Institute Thailand, on 30 January 2020, and Japanese investors attending the 3rd River Forum in Sriracha, on 29 May 2019.

13 Japan recognized that promoting industrialization in Asia's less developed countries could open up new markets for Japanese companies, strengthen political influence in strategically important countries, and facilitate access to much-needed natural resources to fuel rapid growth. Japan, as described in the flying geese growth paradigm, would lead its neighbours in transitioning to more profitable economic sectors, thereby increasing its own wealth (Doner, 2018; Hayter & Edgington, 2004). Thailand might apply the successful aspects of this paradigm when expanding economically into its own neighbouring countries.

14 Thailand's aging population is accelerating with the fastest rate in Asia. In 2015, the proportion of those over 60 years old attained 16.3 percent and is projected

to approach 25 percent by 2028. Total fertility rate is less than 1.5 children per female of childbearing age (Sasiwongsaroj & Burasit, 2019). Thailand lacks explicit policies addressing root causes of aging societies, preferring to address policy issues relating to older citizen. By contrast, in May 2021, China imposed a three-child policy to boost the national birth rate and avoiding aging society status.

References

Aoyama, R. (2016). One belt, one road: China's new global strategy. *Journal of Contemporary East Asia Studies*, *5*(2), 3–22.

Board of Investment. (2020). *Investment promotion measures in the Eastern Economic Corridor (EEC)*. Board of Investment.

Braudel, F., & Reynold, S. (1992). *The wheels of commerce Vol. II: Civilization and capitalism 15th–18th century*. Harper & Row.

Button, K. (2017, March). *High-speed railways: Do they produce economic growth?* Mercatus Research, Mercatus Center at George Mason University.

Chirathivat, S., Rutchatorn, B., & Devendrakumar, A. (Eds.). (2022). *China's belt and road initiative in ASEAN: Growing presence, recent progress and future challenges*. World Scientific Publishing.

Doner, R. F. (2018). Japan in East Asia: Institutions and regional leadership. In P. J. Katzenstein & T. Shiraishi (Eds.), *Network power: Japan and Asia* (Chapter 6, pp. 197–233). Cornell University Press.

Eastern Economic Corridor Office. (2019, July). *2 years of EEC: Connecting to the world to promote Thailand's prosperity*. Eastern Economic Corridor Office.

Hayter, R., & Edgington, D. W. (2004). Flying geese in Asia: The impacts of Japanese MNCs as a source of industrial learning. *Journal of Economic & Social Geography*, *95*(1), 3–26.

Ishida, M., Umezaki, S., & Yamada, Y. (Eds.). (2017). *Tai purasu wan no kigyo senryaku (Corporate strategy with Thailand Plus One)*. Keiso Shobo (In Japanese).

Ito, A. (2020). China reshaping Asia: Economic transition and the rise of an economic superpower. In K. Goto, T. Endo, & A. Ito (Eds.), *The Asian economy: Contemporary issues and challenges* (Chapter 3, pp. 48–66). Routledge.

JETRO Thailand. (2015). *Cambodia, Laos and Myanmar: Plus one investment destinations*. A seminar co-hosted by JETRO Thailand and the Board of Investment, at the Pullman Bangkok Grand Sukhumvit (In Thai and Japanese).

JETRO Thailand. (2019). *Survey of business circumstance on Japanese corporation in Thailand by Japanese Chamber of Commerce in Bangkok, Thailand*. Japan External Trade Organization (JETRO) (In Japanese).

Jones, L., & Hameiri, S. (2020). *Debunking the myth of debt-trap diplomacy: How recipient countries shape China's belt and road initiative*. Chatham House.

Keeranan, S. (2022, October 15). Santi pad EEC ua thunyai (Santi denies EEC support for major capitals). *Krungthep Turakit* (In Thai).

Kongkirati, P., & Kanchoochat, V. (2018). The Prayuth regime: Embedded military and hierarchical capitalism in Thailand. *TRaNS (Trans Regional and National Studies of Southeast Asia)*, *6*(2), 279–305.

Lauridsen, L. S. (2020). Drivers of China's regional infrastructure diplomacy: The case of the Sino-Thai railway project. *Journal of Contemporary Asia*, *50*(3), 380–406.

Li, J., Qian, G., Zhou, K. Z., Lu, J., & Liu, B. (2022). Belt and road Initiative, globalization and institutional changes: Implications for firms in Asia. *Asia Pacific Journal of Management, 39*(3), 843–856.

Ngampramuan, S. (2021). Thailand's 4.0 development strategy in the context of the Belt and Road Initiative. In C. Ploberger, S. Ngampamuan, & T. Song (Eds.), *China's belt and road initiative* (Chapter 5, pp. 77–92). Routledge.

Nidhiprabha, B. (2019). China's business cycle and impacts on Thailand. In *Macroeconomic policy for emerging markets: Lessons from Thailand* (Chapter 10, pp. 173–194). Routledge.

Pavlicevic, D., & Kratz, A. (2017, April). Implications of Sino Japanese rivalry in high-speed railways for Southeast Asia. *East Asian Policy*, pp. 15–25.

Phuangketkeow, S. (2020). Thailand's Eastern economic corridor: A bold strategic move. *ISEAS Perspective, 13*, 1–11.

Praditsil, C., et al. (2021, December 15). *Kanchai amnadrat naikan catrabob thiidin khong rabiengsettakitpiset phaktawanook (The use of state authority in the Eastern Economic Corridor's land governance system)*. A presentation given at the 3rd progress report conference, land governance system for development, land use alternatives and policies for the next 20 years. At SM Tower, Office of Science, Research, and Innovation Promotion Commission (In Thai).

Sangsubhan, K. (2017, November 16). *Industry 4.0 and investment in EEC towards Thailand 4.0*. A speech at the 4th Ship Technology for the Next decade: Ship tech IV, at Royal Cliff Beach Hotel, Pattaya, Chonburi (In Thai).

Sangsubhan, K. (2018, August 25). *Thailand and China BRI connectivity for the future*. A speech at the seminar on EEC the prime gateway to Asia, at Pattaya, Chonburi (In Thai).

Sangsubhan, K. (2021, October 18). *EEC future: 5G infrastructure will boost Thailand's potential to compete on a global scale*. A speech at the virtual seminar held by Krungthep Turakit (In Thai).

Sangsubhan, K. (2022, August 17). *Next chapter of EEC*. A speech at the seminar on EEC new chapter new economy, at Grand Hyatt Erawan Hotel, Bangkok (In Thai).

Sasiwongsaroj, K., & Burasit, Y. (2019). Features and challenges of an ageing population in Thailand. In M. J. Montesano, T. Chong, & M. Heng (Eds.), *After the coup: The National council for peace and order era and the future of Thailand* (Chapter 14, pp. 357–380). ISEAS – Yusof Ishak Institute.

Sathapholdeja, N. (2019, March 18). TMB analytics tang khamtham promkaang khoomoon SMEs thai yuu trong nai nai EEC-talaad look (Ask questions and unfold the data. Where do Thailand's SMEs stand in the EEC-global market?). *Thaipublica* (In Thai).

Suehiro, A. (2017). China's offensive in Southeast Asia: Regional architecture and the process of Sinicization. *Journal of Contemporary East Asia Studies, 6*(2), 107–131.

Suehiro, A. (2020). Eastern economic corridor and strategic alliances with China. In A. Suehiro et al. (Eds.), *New regional order and overlapping strategies in Asia: Thailand in connection with CLMV, China, and Japan* (Chapter 3, pp. 61–90). Institute of Social Science, The University of Tokyo (In Japanese).

Tangkitvanich, S. (2019, May 29). *Thailand routes in political, economic, and social contexts*. A speech for the 3rd River Forum in Sriracha, at Building C, Samitiveth Hospital Sriracha (In Thai).

Tontisirin, N., & Anantsuksomsri, S. (2021). Economic development policies and land use changes in Thailand: From the eastern seaboard to the eastern economic corridor. *Sustainability, 13*(11), 6153.

Toru, T. (2020, August 30). Thailand's economic wizard throws in the towel. *Nikkei Asian Review.*

Yuda, M. (2020, July 16). Thailand's economic ministers quit amid coronavirus crisis. *Nikkei Asian Review.*

Part III

Thai business groups approaching the middle-income trap

Chapter 8

Business concentration

8.1 Distinctive characteristics of Thai business groups

Thai business groups have five distinguishing characteristics: As discussed in Chapter 3, large corporations in Thailand and other emerging countries are sustained by three fully diverse forms of capital: state enterprises, foreign companies or multinational corporations (MNCs), and local private enterprises. This is referred to as a tripod structure of industrial organization (Suehiro, 1989; Suehiro & Wailerdsak, 2004; Wailerdsak & Suehiro, 2010), which directs the economy and industry.

Secondly, controlling shareholders control all significant firms, whether state-owned, family-owned, or MNCs. These large shareholders also control management (Phipatseritham, 1981; Wailerdsak, 2006, 2008b). This is true for both private and public enterprises registered on the Stock Exchange of Thailand (SET). US or UK companies with dispersed shares or no identifiable major shareholder capable of taking control are extremely rare.

Thirdly, almost every family in Thailand's private sector is of Chinese origin (descendants of Chinese immigrants to Thailand).[1] Of the leading 50 business groups, four are state-related entities (Krung Thai Bank, TMB Bank, PTT, and Thai Airways), four genuine Thai entities (Siam Cement of the Crown Property Bureau, Jasmine of the Potharamik family, Boon Rawd Brewery of the Bhirombhakdi family, and Italthai of the Karnasuta family), and two business entities with Indian ancestry (Siam Vidhya of the Chansrichawla family and Indorama Ventures of the Lohia family). The remaining 40 have Sino-Thai support. Most ethnic Chinese in Thailand were born in the Kingdom, have Thai nationality, and speak Thai language. This research classifies them as indigenous or Thai businesspeople.[2]

Fourthly, rather than establishing a standalone firm, Thai family businesses prefer to build a group or conglomerate under the *kongsi* management structure, a process by which a family consolidates its business (wealth) under a single umbrella overseen by the founder. As a result, the founder's sons/daughters and subsequent generations diversify into varied linked businesses. This is especially true when extended family is involved. The technique is used

DOI: 10.4324/9781003370536-12

in Chinese-Thai society to distribute wealth among family members (Wailerdsak, 2008b; Wailerdsak & Suehiro, 2014).

Finally, as primary or related firms, most of these business groups were previously listed on the SET. From the late 1980s, when Thailand enjoyed an unparalleled economic boom, the stock market rose quickly. After the 1997 crisis, the Thai government enhanced disclosure and corporate governance, focusing mainly on publicly listed companies. Comparatively few foreign companies are listed on the SET (Wangwan & Leemakdej, 2022).

8.2 Industry monopoly

8.2.1 *Top 100 Thai business groups*

In Thailand, the distribution of income and wealth has long been highly skewed (Phongpaichit, 2016; Hewison, 2006, 2021). According to the Credit Suisse Research Institute's annual Global Wealth Databook, Thailand's wealth concentration is among the greatest in the world, ranking first in 2018. Less than 1 percent of the population owns 66.9 percent of the country's total wealth. The richest 10 percent possess 85.7 percent of the wealth, while the other 90 percent own just 14.3 percent. This illustrates the wealth divide, defined by the Global Wealth Databook as "rich concentration against poor dispersion (*ruai krajuk jon krajai*)" (Credit Suisse, 2018).

Likewise, manufacturing goods and services is often a large-scale enterprise requiring sophisticated technology and production techniques. In this way, business or ownership concentration, as well as industry monopolies, are easily established (Phipatseritham, 1981; Kanchoochat, 2022).

Historically, the Thai government fostered industry through state-owned enterprises and nationalist economic principles. Later, the government sought to diminish the influence of state-owned enterprises by focusing on private businesses through a series of national economic and social development plans (Suehiro, 1992, 2009, 2014). Legislation was enacted to promote foreign investment by offering varied types of assistance and special privileges. While such initiatives accelerated industrial sector growth, they also established economic monopolies (Suehiro, 2019; Kanchoochat, 2022). Private firms became increasingly important for resource allocation, job creation, money distribution, economic stabilization, and political involvement.

If a single manufacturer exists, the value in gauging business concentration is monopolized. However, in an industry where the actual number of manufacturers is unknown, business concentration rates cannot be quantified. In such cases, a large manufacturer's role in the sector is determined by production capacity, assets, sales, revenue, and related factors.

To examine business concentration, Table 8.1 indicates the proportion of Thailand's leading 100 business groups (excluding gold trading firms), and Table 8.2 provides the proportion of Thailand's 100 major business groups

Table 8.1 Top 100 Thai business groups by ownership patterns, 1989–2018 (excluding gold trading firms)

Ownership pattern	*1989*		*1997*		*2000*		*2004*		*2010*		*2013*		*2018*	
		%		%		%		%		%		%		%
(1) Number of firms (total = 100)	100	*100*	100	*100*	100	*100*	100	*100*	100	*100*	100	*100*	100	*100*
Government-linked companies	5	*5.0*	9	*9.0*	13	*13.0*	14	*14.0*	11	*11.0*	14	*14.0*	11	*11.0*
The Crown Property Bureau*	7	*7.0*	5	*5.0*	5	*5.0*	7	*7.0*	3	*3.0*	3	*3.0*	3	*3.0*
Family-owned firms	50	*50.0*	46	*46.0*	32	*32.0*	19	*19.0*	21	*21.0*	26	*26.0*	27	*27.0*
Widely held firms	3	*3.0*	5	*5.0*	3	*3.0*	5	*5.0*	6	*6.0*	3	*3.0*	5	*5.0*
Foreign firms (MNCs)	33	*33.0*	30	*30.0*	47	*47.0*	55	*55.0*	59	*59.0*	54	*54.0*	54	*54.0*
(Japanese firms)	17	*17.0*	18	*18.0*	20	*20.0*	28	*28.0*	29	*29.0*	25	*25.0*	23	*23.0*
(2) Distribution of revenue		%		%		%		%		%		%		%
Combined revenues (mil. of baht)	719,145	*100*	2,439,113	*100*	2,847,566	*100*	4,979,761	*100*	10,503,753	*100*	14,169,693	*100*	15,702,861	*100*
Government-linked companies	107,153	*14.9*	382,941	*15.7*	549,580	*19.3*	1,628,382	*32.7*	3,407,253	*32.4*	5,145,811	*36.3*	4,337,207	*27.6*
The Crown Property Bureau	53,936	*7.5*	114,638	*4.7*	133,836	*4.7*	239,029	*4.8*	447,671	*4.3*	670,420	*4.7*	735,728	*4.7*
Family-owned firms	306,356	*42.6*	1,178,092	*48.3*	794,471	*27.9*	577,652	*11.6*	1,590,587	*15.1*	2,264,652	*16.0*	3,677,133	*23.4*
Widely held firms	21,574	*3.0*	51,221	*2.1*	34,171	*1.2*	139,433	*2.8*	386,492	*3.7*	446,876	*3.2*	724,658	*4.6*
Foreign firms (MNCs)	230,126	*32.0*	712,221	*29.2*	1,335,508	*46.9*	2,395,265	*48.1*	4,671,750	*44.5*	5,641,934	*39.8*	6,228,135	*39.7*
(Japanese firms)	106,433	*14.8*	448,797	*18.4*	467,001	*16.4*	1,200,122	*24.1*	2,448,803	*23.3*	2,985,642	*21.1*	2,921,941	*18.6*

Sources: (1) Database of Akira Suehiro covering 1989–2013 (2) Database compiled by the author and Akira Suehiro for 2018
Based on several sources such as Top 1,000 Companies of *Business+ Magazine*, listed company information of the SET website

Note
(1) Top 100 business groups were selected by revenue and categorized by 20 percent cut-off ownership rule.
(2) *Includes the Siam Cement Group (SCG) and the Siam Commercial Bank Group (SCB).

Table 8.2 Top 100 Thai business groups by ownership patterns, 1989–2018 (including gold trading firms)

Ownership pattern	*1989*		*1997*		*2000*		*2004*		*2010*		*2013*		*2018*	
		%		%		%		%		%		%		%
(1) Number of firms (total = 100)	100	*100*	100	*100*	100	*100*	100	*100*	100	*100*	100	*100*	100	*100*
Government-linked companies	5	*5.0*	9	*9.0*	13	*13.0*	14	*14.0*	10	*10.0*	13	*13.0*	11	*11.0*
The Crown Property Bureau*	7	*7.0*	5	*5.0*	5	*5.0*	7	*7.0*	3	*3.0*	3	*3.0*	3	*3.0*
Family -owned firms	50	*50.0*	46	*46.0*	32	*32.0*	19	*19.0*	25	*21.0*	30	*30.0*	31	*31.0*
Widely held firms	3	*3.0*	5	*5.0*	3	*3.0*	5	*5.0*	6	*6.0*	3	*3.0*	5	*5.0*
Foreign firms (MNCs)	33	*33.0*	30	*30.0*	47	*47.0*	55	*55.0*	56	*56.0*	51	*51.0*	50	*50.0*
(Japanese firms)	17	*17.0*	18	*18.0*	20	*20.0*	28	*28.0*	28	*28.0*	23	*23.0*	21	*21.0*
*Gold trading firms	N.A.		N.A.		N.A.		N.A.		4	*4.0*	5	*5.0*	8	*8.0*
(2) Distribution of revenue		%		%		%		%		%		%		%
Combined revenues (millions of baht)	719,145	*100*	2,439,113	*100*	2,847,566	*100*	4,979,761	*100*	11,296,856	*100*	15,420,265	*100*	17,165,774	*100*
Government-linked companies	107,153	*14.9*	382,941	*15.7*	549,580	*19.3*	1,628,382	*32.7*	3,366,254	*29.8*	5,102,334	*33.1*	4,337,207	*25.3*
The Crown Property Bureau	53,936	*7.5*	114,638	*4.7*	133,836	*4.7*	239,029	*4.8*	447,671	*4.0*	670,420	*4.3*	735,728	*4.3*
Family -owned firms	306,356	*42.6*	1,178,092	*48.3*	794,471	*27.9*	577,652	*11.6*	2,100,985	*18.6*	3,141,846	*20.4*	4,984,555	*29.0*
Widely held firms	21,574	*3.0*	51,221	*2.1*	34,171	*1.2*	139,433	*2.8*	386,492	*3.4*	446,876	*2.9*	724,658	*4.2*
Foreign firms (MNCs)	230,126	*32.0*	712,221	*29.2*	1,335,508	*46.9*	2,395,265	*48.1*	4,995,454	*44.2*	6,058,789	*39.3*	6,383,625	*37.2*
(Japanese firms)	106,433	*14.8*	448,797	*18.4*	467,001	*16.4*	1,200,122	*24.1*	2,421,776	*21.4*	2,921,509	*18.9*	2,836,453	*16.5*
*Gold trading firms	N.A.		N.A.		N.A.		N.A.		914,656	*8.1*	1,454,438	*9.4*	1,484,315	*8.6*

Sources: (1) Database of Akira Suehiro covering 1989–2013 (2) Database compiled by the author and Akira Suehiro for 2018
Based on several sources such as Top 1,000 Companies of *Business+ Magazine*, listed company information of the SET website

Note
(1) Top 100 business groups were selected by revenue and categorized by 20 percent cut-off ownership rule.
(2) *Includes the Siam Cement Group (SCG) and the Siam Commercial Bank Group (SCB).

(including gold trading firms) by total sales/revenue from 1989 to 2018. In addition, they are categorized into five types based on ownership pattern:

- Government-linked companies (GLCs). Most of these companies, including PTT PLC and Thai Airways International PLC, were previously state-owned.
- The Crown Property Office is a significant investor in several companies, including Siam Cement Group (SCG) PLC and Siam Commercial Bank (SCB) PLC.
- A family business, owned and operated by a single family.
- Thai firms with dispersed ownership with no significant shareholders.
- Foreign-owned companies, particularly MNCs (Japanese nationality and others).

This database (including Thai and English corporate names, business types, sales/revenue, and assets) was collected from two sources:

1) Databases of 1,000 leading companies featured in the Top 1,000 Companies special issue of *Business+ Magazine* published by ARIP Company.
2) Securities and Exchange Commission (SEC) website information about companies publicly traded on the SET (www.sec.or.th).

After data is entered on an Excel sheet, major shareholdings in each company are analysed. Following World Bank criteria, controlling shareholders are defined as owning over 20 percent of company equity. When fewer than 0.5 percent of shares are distributed, major shareholders cannot be identified, and the corporation is designated as widely held (Wailerdsak, 2006).

Commercial banks and gold trading firms are not included on this 1989–2004 list. After 2010, *Business+*'s Top 1,000 Companies Database comprised Ministry of Commerce data, including for commercial banks and gold trading firms. In 2018, the database listed eight gold trading firms, seven of which are family-owned. As family businesses increasingly thrive, rising gold prices appear to further boost family business prosperity.

Since 2010, the Ministry of Commerce has requested that private businesses provide individual data (separate subsidiaries). By contrast, the SET requires listed companies to report with consolidated financial statements (Wailerdsak & Suehiro, 2014). As a result, statistics from these two sources are not identical. For example, according to Business+, PTT's earnings total 1.471 trillion baht. The SET reported earnings for the same corporation of 2.368 trillion baht. Charoen Pokphand Foods revenue statistics are cited as 47.6 billion and 56.8 billion baht by Business+ and the SET, respectively. SCG has revenues of 33.9 billion baht according to Business+, but 55.3 billion baht by SET data. As a result, ranks in the present table are mostly based on consolidated data from subsidiaries in compliance with SET requirements.

Data revealed that after the Asian financial crisis, government-linked companies and foreign companies grew in number and revenue. The sales/revenue proportion of government-linked companies increased from 15.7 percent in 1997 to 32.7 percent in 2004 and by 27.6 percent in 2018. During these same years, foreign company shares of total sales/revenue climbed from 29.2 percent to 48.1 percent and 39.7 percent, respectively, accounting for about half of the total. Privatization and stock market listings are associated with business concentration development by government-linked companies. The Finance Ministry holds a sizable interest (O'neill et al., 2004; Satitniramai, 2013; Wailerdsak, 2008a).

It was determined that business concentration in large production-based industries such as oil and gas, petrochemical, cement, steel, and electricity would result in a high degree of economic concentration or monopoly. With the growth of the PTT group, there are now six large publicly traded companies involved in oil refining, natural gas exploration, renewable energy, and petrochemicals[3] (see Table 8.3).

On the other hand, the number of family-owned businesses in the 100 leading business groups declined from 46 in 1997 to 19 in 2004, rising again to 27 in 2018. Their proportion of total sales/revenue for these years decreased from 48.3 percent to 11.6 percent, before doubling to 23.4 percent, respectively. The share of family businesses is rapidly declining, owing to the loss of many well-known family businesses during the 1997 Asian financial crisis. Large family-owned enterprises in the automobile, steel, and petrochemical industries were compelled to close or sell their operations to foreign partners (Wailerdsak, 2008a).

Tellingly, family firms (including gold trading firms) recovered to 18.6 percent of total sales/revenue in 2010 and increased to 20.4 percent in 2013 and again to 29.0 percent in 2018. If these data really reflect a recovery for family businesses in Thailand, these firms must be identified, classified as established or new, and examined in terms of their expanding sectors.

Only three to six businesses, fewer than 1 percent, with dispersed shares or so-called managerial enterprises with diverse ownership and management remain that are not controlled by a single shareholder. This reflects Thai economic corporate concentration and monopolies, dominated by government-linked companies, a few business dynasties, and MNCs[4] (Kanchoochat & Intarakumnerd, 2014; Kanchootchat et al., 2021).

Foreign company proportions have continued to grow in the economy. During the past few decades, it may be said that encouraging foreign investment has failed in terms of technology transfer. In all MNCs equipped with cutting-edge production and managerial technology, Thai manufacturing ability for learning has been restricted. As a result, there is continued dependence on foreign companies operating in the sector. Thailand's ongoing task is to elevate domestic industry to a playing field level with international competitors (Ouyyanont, 2019).

Table 8.3 Industrial monopoly of the PTT group

SET Name	*Full name*	*Business type*	*Shareholding %*
PTT	Petroleum Authority of Thailand PLC	Natural gas, oil, petrochemicals	–
PTTEP	PTT Exploration & Production PLC	Oil and gas exploration	PTT 34.71%
TOP	Thai Oil PLC	Oil refinery and sales	PTT 51.97%
PTTGC	PTT Global Chemical PLC	Petrochemicals	PTT 51.82%
IRPC	Integrated Refinery and Petrochemical Complex PLC	Oil refinery and sales	PTT 51.95%
GPSC	Global Power Synergy PLC	Electricity, steam, industrial water	PTT 24.77%
OR	PTT Oil and Retail Business PLC	Oil and retail businesses	PTT 25.00%

	2008	2010	2012	2014	2017	2021
No. of listed firms	463	455	469	526	566	593
Profit of PTT group	88.2	153.9	211.6	838.0	237.0	280.5
Profit (%)	28.7	25.1	29.1	11.9	24.1	28.5
Revenue of PTT group	2,999	2,826	4,480	4,576	3,383	4,167
Revenue (%)	41.0	38.7	43.1	39.7	30.7	31.7
Total Assets of PTT group	1,555	2,065	3,052	3,384	3,822	3,764
Total Assets (%)	10.9	12.2	13.6	12.6	11.8	11.7

Remark: 2008–2017 featured PTT6, whilst 2021 included PTT7. GPSC was founded in 2013. OR was founded in 2018.

Source: Author's compilation based on the PTT Financial Reports; number of listed companies from SET website's Company Focus; overall listed companies financial results by industry group (total) from SET website's Market Statistics

Note: Proportions of the PTT Group (7 firms) of the total 593 listed firms in 2021, accounted for 30 percent (billions of baht, %)

8.2.2 *20 leading Thai business groups*

Later, dominant sectors shifted over time, as seen in Table 8.4, comparing the 20 major Thai business groups in 1979, 1980, 1997, 2010, and 2018, respectively. Thai business groups may be classified into five categories based on origins and core businesses.

Table 8.4 Top 20 business groups in Thailand, 1997, 2010, and 2018

Rank	*1997*		*2010*		*2018*			
	Group name	*Revenue*	*Group name*	*Revenue*	*Group name*	*Core business type*	*No. of firms*	*Revenue*
1	Siam Cement	213,346	Siam Cement	839,309	PTT	energy, oil refining	8 (28)	3,788,521
2	Bangkok Bank	194,999	Charoen Pokphand (CP)	644,823	Charoen Pokphand (CP)	agrobusiness, retails, telecom	9 (25)	1,529,579
3	Charoen Pokphand (CP)	141,145	Indorama Ventures	272,568	Crown Property Bureau	construction materials, petrochemical	6 (31)	760,057
4	Thai Farmers Bank*	139,279	TCC	264,887	TCC	beer, beverages, real estates, glass	15 (38)	562,515
5	Siam Commercial Bank	125,983	Hua Seng Heng	206,892	Hua Seng Heng	gold trading	1	436,707
6	TCC	117,942	Bangkok Bank	161,364	Mea Thong Suk	gold trading	1	353,899
7	Bank of Ayudhya	91,741	Boon Rawd Brewery	149,512	Indrorama Ventures	petrochemical, chemical products	1 (8)	352,471
8	Boon Rawd Brewery	78,763	Banpu/Mitr Phol	131,798	Munkong Kehakarn/ Supalai	real estates	2	330,522
9	TPI*	67,816	Central	130,485	Central	retails, hotel	13	287,111
10	Central	48,676	Siam Commercial Bank	125,983	Krungthai Bank	finance	3	238,458
11	Shin Corporation	48,584	Thai Union Frozen	113,359	Thai Airways	airways	4	235,196
12	Sahapat	46,458	Sahaviriya	112,087	Boon Rawd Brewery	beer, beverages, real estates	7	207,446
13	UCOM*	41,764	Sritang Agro	97,059	PTG Energy	Energy	2	199,760
14	Itathai	40,821	Land and House	77,505	Land and House	real estates, housing	7	176,807
15	MMC Sitthipol*	38,555	Sahapat	74,900	Thai Union	agro-business (canned tuna)	2	160,849

(*Continued*)

Table 8.4 (Continued)

Rank	*1997*		*2010*		*2018*			
	Group name	*Revenue*	*Group name*	*Revenue*	*Group name*	*Core business type*	*No. of firms*	*Revenue*
16	Siam Motors Nissan*	35,851	SMC Polymer	73,286	Shining Gold	gold trading	2	148,260
17	Metro#	35,325	Betagro	62,059	BDMS	medical, health care, airways	5	146,100
18	Soon Hua Seng#	34,859	BDMS	54,424	GCAP	gold trading	1	121,367
19	Bangkok Metropolitan#	32,971	Muangthai Insurance	54,147	Muangthai Insurance	finance, insurance	2	117,823
20	Osotspa	32,227	TFI/Nestcafe	49,149	EGCO	energy	3	110,193

Sources: Top 1,000 companies database of Akira Suehiro for 1997 and 2010; and Top 1,045 companies database prepared by the author and Akira Suehiro for 2018 from sources like TOP 1000 COMPANIES 2019–2020, ARIP, and SET website

Note
(1) # shows business groups that dissolved after 1997 Asian financial crisis, whereas * shows shrunk business groups.
(2) This ranking of the top 20 from a database of the top 200 groups including both family businesses and state-owned corporations.
(3) In 2018, Bangkok Bank, KBank, and Banpu groups are classified as widely held corporations.
(4) Some groups are ranked when revenue is considered, but not when market capitalization is included, because their shares are held by investment or holding companies rather than individual shareholders.

The first is rice-trading empires that were established from the 1910s to the 1930s. They engage in rice milling/export, shipping, insurance, money exchange, and remittance services for overseas Chinese while establishing extensive networks with Hong Kong and Singapore. These groups include Wanglee (Poon Phol), Bulsook (Serm Suk/MC Thai), Bulakul (Mah Boonkrong/Chokchai), Iamsuri (Kamol Kij), Lamsam (Kasikornbank), Saetthapakdi and Bunyarat families (Suehiro, 1989, pp. 110–111).

In the 1940s and 1950s, a second business group was established, specializing in commercial banking, insurance, import/export, sugar milling, and brewing. Military and political leaders openly participated in commercial and public business during this era. Participation took two forms: incorporating new state-sponsored companies and reorganizing ownership and management of extant Chinese-owned corporations. Military commanders and other high-ranking officials were invited to serve on boards of both entities. These groups include the Asia Trust (Bangkok Bank), Thai-Hua (Keng Hua/U Chu Liang), Ayudhya, and Mahakhun (Suehiro, 1989, pp. 137, 157; Baker & Phongpaichit, 2014).

A third group was formed in the 1960s, when Thailand's government supported industrialization by using private capital from domestic and foreign sources. Three subdivisions exist within this category, for financial, industrial, and agricultural conglomerates (O'neill et al., 2004; Suehiro, 1992). In the 1950s, four substantial financial conglomerates were formed from commercial banking groups: the Sophonpanich family's Bangkok Bank, the Lamsam family's Kasikornbank, the Tejapaibul family's Bangkok Metropolitan Bank, and the Ratanarak family's Bank of Ayudhya. Apart from the Tejapaibul family, other groups are believed to significantly influence Thailand's financial sector, despite group shareholding reductions after the 1997 crisis (Satitniramai, 2013; Wailerdsak, 2006).

Industrial groups focus on import-substitution industries such as textiles (the Phothirattanangkun family's Sukree/TBI and the Darakananda family's Saha Union), electric appliances (the Karnchanachari family's Siew National), automobile assembly (the Phornprapha family's Siam Motors and the Sukosol family's Kamol Sukosol), chemical fertilizer (the Srifuengfung family's THASCO Chemical), and consumer goods (the Chokwatana family's Sahapat) in close coordination with foreign capital, mostly through joint ventures with Japanese firms.

An agribusiness group originated in the late 1970s, swiftly spreading by combining agricultural exports with industrial activities for products such as broiler chickens, hatchery shrimp, and canned tuna. Examples include the Chearavanont family's CP group, the Dumnernchanvanit family's Soon Hua Seng/Kaset Rung Ruang, and the Kanathanavanich family's Laemthong/Metro. For over half a century, agricultural exports have meaningfully contributed to Thailand's economic growth.

In the late 1980s, a fourth category of new capitalists arose quickly due to modernization of heavy and chemical industries, financial deregulation, and the stock market and real estate booms. Television broadcasting and

CD-making core companies are featured in addition to steel, petrochemical, telecommunication sectors, and property development. Some benefit from an ability to win governmental concessions for providing services or manufacturing certain products (Suehiro, 2008; Wailerdsak, 2008a). These business groups originally traded on the SET and sold shares to the general public. The Shinawatra family's Shin group, the Leophairatana family's TPI, the Asavabhokhin family's Land and Houses, the Maleenont's BEC World, and the Damrongchaitham family's GMM Grammy belong to this category.

The fifth category comprises business groups that expanded after the 1997 Asian financial crisis for two primary reasons. Firstly, the private sector was encouraged to join in energy and petrochemical production and distribution, relieving the burden on government investment. New business groups emerged, such as Indorama Ventures, a petrochemical and chemical venture of the Lohia family; the EGCO Group, Thailand's first major private power generator, owned by Thailand's Electricity Generating Authority, and TEPDIA Generating B.V., a Japanese joint venture; and PTG Energy of the Ratchakitprakarn family, a distributor of gasoline and liquefied petroleum gas (LPG) for automobiles.

Secondly, a growing middle class seeks to invest in gold, health, and life insurance. As a result of online trading and gold futures investment, gold trading firms are augmenting rapidly. For example, the Pasawong family's Hua Seng Heng, the Hiranyasiri family's Mae Thong Suk (MTS Gold), the Tanachon family's Shining Gold, and the Khuhapremkit family's GCAP. Health insurance is gaining popularity as the social welfare system struggles to keep up with demand. Examples include Bangkok Dusit Medical Service controlled by the Prasarttong-osoth family and Muang Thai Life Assurance owned by the Lamsam family.

In sum, Thai business groups have changed continually in response to rapid national economic growth and changing environments. However, corporate organizations have propelled Thailand's economic growth and industrialization to its upper-middle-income status. The inverse effect is business concentration and industrial monopolies, existing in practically every key sector, including energy, finance, and consumer goods (Kanchoochat, 2015, 2018; Suehiro, 2019). The question arises whether to continue expanding into a developed country, or how can Thailand ease national business concentration and economic monopoly?

8.2.3 *Wealthy stockholding families and investor perspectives*

Figure 8.1 and Tables 8.6 to 8.9 profile 20 leading families owning billions of baht worth of stocks by market value of holdings and core business activities. A special December issue of *Money and Banking* (Kan Ngoen Kan Thanakan) magazine about wealthy stockholding families in Thailand has been published

Figure 8.1 Wealthy stockholding families and business type, 2021

Source: *Money and Banking* magazine, December 2021 p. 185

Note

* The new owner families who contributed to the economy in the post-1997 Asian Financial Crisis

since 1994, with rankings established by annual SET share distribution report as of 30 September, using the third-quarter share price.

The following table compares four years over a 25-year interval:

- 1994, when Thailand's stock market peaked before the 1997 Asian financial crisis.
- 2003, when most Thai firms finally recovered from the Asian financial crisis.

Table 8.5 Top 20 wealthy stockholding families, 2019

	Family name	*Group name*	*Business type*	*Business details*	*Market cap.*
1	**Ratanavadi****	Gulf Energy	manufacturing	Power plant	120,959
2	**Prasarttong-osoth***	BGH	service	Bangkok Group Hospital, Bangkok Airways	88,197
3	**Osathanugrah**	Osotspa	service	Consumer products	82,271
4	**Petaumpai****	Muangthai Capital	finance	Motorcycle leasing, Nano finance	82,122
5	**Tangkaravakoon**	TOA Paint, STARK	manufacturing	Building paint, electric wire	63,560
6	**Kanjanapas**	Bangkok Land, BTS	service	Real estates, BTS	58,461
7	**Chirathivat**	Central, CPN	service	Department store, hotel, retail, restaurant	57,048
8	**Ahunai***	Energy Absolute	manufacturing	Renewable energy, biodiesel	45,257
9	**Thirakomen***	MK Restaurant	service	Restaurant	35,146
10	**Bodharamik**	Jamine, MONO	service	Telco, data services	32,596
11	**Asavabhokhin**	Land & Houses	service	Real estates, housing	32,237
12	**Link**	B.Grimm Power	energy	Power plant	28,657
13	**Vijitpongpun***	Pruksa Real Estate Houlding (PSH)	service	Real estates, housing	26,278
14	**Harnpanich**	Bangkok Chain Hospital	service	Hospital	24,807
15	**Thongtang***	BDMS	service	Hospital	24,707
16	**Kaewbootta***	Srisawad	finance	Leasing	23,023
17	**Suriyawanakul***	Global House	service	Housing materials	22,872
18	**Thianvon***	CP (CPALL, CPF)	manufacturing, service	Retails, processed food	21,722
19	**Sirivadhanabhakdi**	TCC, Thai Beverage	manufacturing, service	Beverages, insurance, real estates	20,661
20	**Prakitchaiwattana****	Krungthai Card	service	Personal loan	19,845

Source: Money and Banking, December 2019, p. 201
(Unit: million baht)

Notes: *New owner families who contributed to the economy in the post-1997 Asian Financial Crisis
**New owner families who contribute to the economy after 2010

Table 8.6 Top 20 wealthy stockholding families, 2010

	Family name	*Group name*	*Business type*	*Business details*	*Market cap.*
1	**Maleenont**	BEC World	service	TV 3	44,176
2	**Vijitpongpun***	Pruksa Real Estate Houlding (PSH)	service	Real estates, housing	37,618
3	**Asavabhokhin**	Land & Houses	service	Real estates, housing	21,868
4	**Kanjanapas**	Bangkok Land, BTS	service	Real estates, BTS	20,269
5	**Chirathivat**	Central, CPN	service	Department store, hotel, retail, restaurant	18,325
6	**Vongkusolkit**	Banpu, Mitr Phol	manufacturing	Coal, sugar	12,757
7	**Chansiri**	Thai Union Frozen	manufacturing	Canned tuna	12,669
8	**Weeraborwongpong**	Siam Gas (SGP)	manufacturing	LPG gas	10,845
9	**Sophonpanich**	Bangkok Bank (BBL)	finance	Commercial bank, finance	10,001
10	**Mahagitsiri**	Thainox, Thai Film Industries	manufacturing	Steel, Nescafé	8,405
11	**Osathanugrah**	Osotspa	service	Consumer products	8,124
12	**Prasarttong-osoth***	BGH	service	Bangkok Group Hospital, Bangkok Airways	8,012
13	**Saengsastra**	Dynasty Ceramic	manufacturing	Construction materials	7,423
14	**Poolvoralaks**	EGV	service	Cinema	6,872
15	**Punsak-udomsin**	Sahapat (ICC)	manufacturing	Consumer products	6,831
16	**Vitayanagorn**	Thai Vegetable Oil	manufacturing	Vegetable oil "agun brand"	6,501
17	**Thanalongkorn**	Sabina	manufacturing	Lingerie	6,328
18	**Tangmatitham**	Spasi, Mankong Kehakan	service	Real estates, housing	6,300
19	**Heineicke**	Minor International	service	Hotel, restaurant	6,215
20	**Leophairatana**	TPI	manufacturing	Cement, petrochemical	6,193

Source: *Money and Banking* magazine, December 2010, p. 209
(Unit: million baht)

Table 8.7 Top 20 wealthy stockholding families, 2003

	Family name	*Group name*	*Business type*	*Business details*	*Market cap.*
1	**Maleenont**	BEC World	service	TV 3	26,711
2	**Assavabhokhin**	Land & Houses	service	Real estates, housing	19,880
3	**Shinawatra**	Shin Corp.	service	Telco, real estates	18,543
4	**Damapong**	Shin Corp.	service	Telco, real estates	9,382
5	**Chirathivat**	Central, CPN	service	Department store, hotel, retail, restaurant	7,545
6	**Karnasuta**	Italthai, ITD	manufacturing	Construction contractor	6,701
7	**Chansiri**	Thai Union Frozen	manufacturing	Canned tuna	6,053
8	**Damrongchaitam**	GMM Grammy	service	Song, entertainment	5,534
9	**Pha-oenchoke**	Thai Rung Union	Manufacturing	Modified cars	4,507
10	**Vitayanagorn**	Thai Vegetable Oil	Manufacturing	Vegetable oil "agun brand"	4,076
11	**Leophairatana**	TPI	Manufacturing	Cement, petrochemical	3,896
12	**Charanachitta**	Italthai, ITD	Manufacturing	Construction contractor	3,886
13	**Mahagitsiri**	Thainox, Thai Film Industries	Manufacturing	Steel, Nescafé	3,717
14	**Mankongcharoen**	Natural Park, changed to U City	Service	Real estates	3,456
15	**Leeissaranukul**	Thai Stanly, Inoue Rubber	Manufacturing	Auto parts	3,441
16	**Kromdit**	Amata City	Service	Industrial estate	3,135
17	**Bodharamik**	Jamine, MONO	Service	Telco, data services	3,031
18	**Vongkusolkit**	Banpu, Mitr Phol	Manufacturing	Coal, sugar	2,681
19	**Chetchotisak**	RS	service	Song, entertainment	2,612
20	**Wattanavekin**	Kiatnakin Phatra (KKP)	manufacturing finance	Sugar, commercial bank	2,189

Source: *Money and Banking* magazine, December 2003, p. 234
(Unit: million baht)

Table 8.8 Top 20 wealthy stockholding families, 1994

	Family name	*Group name*	*Business type*	*Business details*	*Market cap.*
1	**Shinawatra**	Shin Corp.	service	Telco, real estates	38,820
2	**Assavabhokhin**	Land & Houses	service	Real estates, housing	25,688
3	**Kanjanapas**	Bangkok Land, BTS	service	Real estates, BTS	7,915
4	**Horrungruang**	NTS, Hemraj	manufacturing	Steel, industrial estate	7,443
5	**Srivikorn**	Srivikorn	manufacturing	Thailand Carpet manufacturing, hotel	5,154
6	**Sophonpanich**	Bangkok Bank (BBL)	finance	Commercial bank, finance	4,954
7	**Tangmatitham**	Spasi, Mankong Kehakan	service	Real estates, housing	4,925
8	**Chearavanont**	CP	manufacturing	Processed food, telco	4,830
9	**Phornprapha**	Thitikorn, Siam Konlakan	manufacturing	Motorcycle leasing, auto parts, music school	4,307
10	**Sirivadhanabhakdi**	TCC, Thai Beverage	manufacturing, service	Beverages, insurance, real estates	4,295
11	**Chiangpruk**	Shin corp.	service	Shareholders	4,289
12	**Vongkusolkit**	Banpu, Mitr Phol	Manufacturing	Coal, sugar	4,059
13	**Harnpanich**	Land & Houses	service	Shareholders, real estates	3,792
14	**Lertsumitkul**	Srithai Superware	manufacturing	Melanin container	3,786
15	**Wattanavekin**	Kiatnakin Phatra (KKP)	manufacturing finance	Sugar, commercial bank	3,769
16	**Srifuengfung**	Thai-Asahi Glass	manufacturing	Glass, chemicals, insurance	3,745
17	**Bencharongkul**	UCOM, changed to DTAC	service	Telco	3,740
18	**Ngoe-sirimanee**	Property Perfect	service	Real estates, housing	3,729
19	**Wongpakdee**	Shin Corp.	service	Shareholders	3,348
20	**Mahadamrongkul**	C. Thong Panich	service	Imported watches, hotel	3,164

Source: *Money and Banking* magazine, December 1994, p. 160
(Unit: million baht)

Despite the impact of the European debt crisis, SET valuation rebounded from 45 billion baht one year before to 63 billion baht.

- 2010, after former Prime Minister Dr. Thaksin Shinawatra sold his Shin Corporation shares, removing himself from rankings of Thai billionaire shareholders.
- 2021, with Thailand experiencing a recession due to the novel coronavirus 2019 (COVID-19) pandemic.

Table 8.6 to 8.9 are noteworthy as a proxy indicator of local and foreign investor confidence in competitiveness of specific families and business types, as well as company growth potential. Yet this table contains three significant flaws.

Firstly, data is included only about SET-listed firms, excluding families who do not sell shares to the general public, such as the Bhirombhakdi family of Singha Beer.

Secondly, the list is based on stockholder market values, not real economic performance (such as sales or profits), and therefore fails to reflect complete family assets. To determine each family's total revenue, Table 8.4 of Thailand's top 20 business groups must be consulted.

Thirdly, because the list only includes families who own individual shares in listed companies, any family that owns a listed company indirectly through a family-owned holding or investment company will automatically be omitted. For example, the Chearavanont family of the CP group, Thailand's second biggest family business, are not included in the list because family members do not directly own shares in the three listed companies (CP Foods, CP All, and True Corporation). Instead, they indirectly own shares through family-owned holding companies such as Charoen Pokphand Group Co., Ltd.; C.P. Interfood (Thailand) Co., Ltd.; and C.P. Holding (Thailand) Co., Ltd. (Wailerdsak, 2020).

Similarly, the Sirivadhanabhakdi family of the T.C.C. or ThaiBev group controls listed companies such as Berli Jucker (BJC), Frasers Property (Thailand), Sermsuk, Oishi, Golden Land Property, and Univentures through family investment companies such as T.C.C. Corporation Co., Ltd.; T.C.C. Wengnakornkhasem Co., Ltd.; Siriwana Co., Ltd.; and Wattanapakdee Co., Ltd. Therefore, if share value is calculated according to market price that the family company has invested, they would immediately rise to first and second position in listings.

In 2021, research revealed that half the 20 leading groups were affiliated with well-established families who were dominant before the 1997 Asian financial crisis. The remainder are newcomers to extreme wealth and power. Intriguingly, 11 families work in service industries, including finance and leasing. Three dominate the energy sector: Gulf Energy, owned by the first-ranked Ratanavadi family, specializes in power plant operations; the fourth-ranked

Ahunai family owns Energy Absolute, focusing on renewable energy and biodiesel; while B. Grim Power, owned by the eighth-ranked Link family, is a prominent regional player in renewable energy.

Only three families are manufacturers: the third-ranked Osathanugrah family of Osotspa, producing the popular M-150, Shark, and M-Strom energy drinks; the seventh-ranked Tangkaravakoon family of TOA, producing building paint and electrical wire; and the ninth-ranked Thanombooncharoen family of Carabao, manufacturing the Carabao Dang energy drink.

By comparison, only six families were associated with the ten future target industries prioritized by the Thailand 4.0 policy: three aforementioned groups in the energy industry and the remainder in hospital and medical services: the second-ranked Prasarttong-osoth family of Bangkok Dusit Medical Services (BDMS), eleventh-ranked Wittayakom family of Bamrungrad Hospital, and sixteenth-ranked Harnpanich family of Bangkok Chain/Kasemrad Hospital.

The remaining 11 groups are involved in non-banking financial institutions (NBFIs), providing vehicle title loans and personal loans (for example, Chuchat and Daonapa Petampai's Muangthai Capital, and the Kaewbootta family's Srisawad); modern retail, particularly chain stores selling information technology (IT) products and home décor (for example, COM-7, JMART, Dohome, and Homepro); and real estate development (such as the Kanjanapas family's BTS Group Holding, Asavabhokhin family's Land & House, and Wijitpongpan family's Pruksa Holding).

Previously, stock billionaires were all founders or controlling shareholders actively involved in management. By 2021, four billionaire stockholders (Niti Osathanugrah, Pongsak Thammathataree, Thaveechat Jurangkool, and Mongkol Prakitchaiwattana) were neither founders nor managers of companies in which they were stockholders. The list indicates a rise in domestic investors enriched from capital market investment.

The leading 20 families owning billions of baht worth of stock classified by service business: manufacturing/agriculture: construction and real estate, dating back to 1994, during the economic bubble (6:9:5), in 2003, after the Asian financial crisis (9:7:4), 2010 (6:10:4), and 2021 (9:8:3).

Before the Asian financial crisis, investors showed interest in manufacturers of textiles, electrical appliances, autos, and steel, while agribusinesses drew attention after the crisis. Later, middle-class expansion occurred simultaneously with service business growth of hospital and medical services, real estate development, NBFIs, shopping malls, convenience shops, fast-food chains, restaurants, and entertainment (Suehiro, 2014; Wailerdsak & Siengthai, 2016). This accelerated deindustrialization.

These findings suggest that investors saw Thai business group competitiveness as distinct from Industry 4.0 manufacturing technologies. Investors preferred Thai energy and market-focused services companies over Thai industrial conglomerates. Were the rising strength of Thai business groups aligned with

Philip Kotler's Marketing 4.0, rather than Industry 4.0 presentations, a wider perspective would become visible (Kotler et al., 2016).

8.3 Competitiveness

8.3.1 *Industry 4.0*

The Thailand 4.0 Policy was first mentioned by the media on 26 May 2015, in "Thailand 4.0: Whether this approach will help Thailand escape its lost decade," an opinion piece by Suttichai Yun, editorial director of the Nation newspaper. Suttichai asked if Thailand 4.0 was a viable long-term approach for a nation seeking to escape the middle-income trap. He explicitly attributed the policy to Dr. Suvit Maesincee, advisor to Dr. Somkid Jatusripitak, deputy prime minister for Economic Affairs, noting that it cohered with the substance of the Ministry of Industry's Thai Industry 4.0 statement.

However, four stages of development outlined in Thailand 4.0 by Dr. Suvit Maesincee and the National Economic and Social Development Council (NESDC) comprised value-added creation in past production structures (Maesincee, 2016; NESDC, 2016):

- Investments during Thailand 1.0 centred on agribusiness such as crops, livestock, horticulture, rice exports, teak, and tin. Rural society and domestic industry were inextricably linked.
- Thailand 2.0 began creating light industries, including clothes, footwear, and handbags, as well as import substitution profiting from natural resources and an abundant supply of cheap labour.
- Thailand 3.0 was centred on heavy industry, labour-intensive product exports, and encouraging foreign investment, using cutting-edge technologies such as integrated circuits and automotive parts.
- Thailand 4.0 focused on new S-curve industries to create long-term value through bio-circular-green (BCG) economy.

Otherwise expressed, Thailand 4.0 was unrelated to Klaus Schwab's description of the *Fourth Industrial Revolution* (2017), considering industrial system changes in energy sources and production systems from phases 1.0 to 3.0.[5] In Thailand 4.0, governmental economic policies and industry growth methodology changes were addressed, substituting production for imports and exports. For this reason, describing Thailand's manufacturing system as Thailand 3.0 may be deceptive, insofar as it is situated midway between Industry 2.0 and Industry 3.0. No industrial base exists to enable Industry 4.0.

Thai business groups focusing on Industry 4.0 according to the German model, a key influence on Thailand 4.0, are frequently capital-intensive and subject to strict government regulation. As a result, they require political ties for collecting economic rents, including the following (see Table 8.9):

Table 8.9 Major business groups in manufacturing industry (Industry 4.0)

Category	*Type of business*	*Name of group*
Energy*	Oil, refinery, and petrochemical	PTT and subsidiaries, Indorama Venture, Vinythai, SCG, EGCO, RATCH, GPSC, B.Grimm Power
	Electric power plant, renewable energy	Gulf Energy, Banpu, Glow, National Power Supply, Gunkul, Energy Absolute, Mitr Phol Bio Power
	Solar energy	SPCG, Thai Solar Energy, Super
Construction Materials	Cement	Siam Cement, Siam City Cement, Asia Cement
	Construction materials	Thai Watsadu, Siam Global House, Dynasty Ceramics, Dcon Products, TOA Paint, Vanachai
	Steel and iron	Sahaviriya Steel Industries (SSI), Asia Metal, Posco-Thainox, TMM Steel, Millcon Steel, Chow Steel
Transportation	Expressway and public transportation	BTS, Bangkok Expressway and Metro (BEM)
	Marine	Prima Marine, Asia Marine, Biotech, Precious Shipping, Thoresen Thai
	Airline	Bangkok Airways
High-tech	Electronics	KEC International, Tanin Elna, SVI
	Electric appliances	Tasaki, Saijo-Denki, UNI-Aire, Central Air, Hatari, Accord, Master Kool
	Auto parts	Thai Summit, Stanley Electrics
	Electric vehicle	Pronprapa (BYD), Energy Absolute, Mahakitsiri (P80GO)
Consumer Goods	Consumer goods	Sahapat and subsidiaries, Moshi, Ocean Glass
	Personal products (health, beauty), pharmaceutical	SmoothE, Asian Phytoceuticals, Do Day Dream, Jack Chia, Rojukiss, Nova Organic, Thai Optical, Beauty
	Furniture	Modernform, TCM
	Jewellery	Pranda Jewelry, Jubilee, Creative James & Jewelry

Sources: As of 2022, the author's compilation based on field research; statistics from each industry associations and the Stock Exchange of Thailand's website

Notes

(1) The list includes only Thai-majority-owned businesses and excludes foreign-owned businesses.

(2) Most energy companies operate in the oil, power plant, renewable, and solar sectors. They are grouped by the companies for which they excel.

- Energy groups, consisting of oil refineries, natural gas, and petrochemicals controlled by PTT (government-related companies), and Siam Cement Group (SCG) in petrochemicals.
- Renewable energy and biotechnology groups, including Gulf Energy, Absolute Energy, B. Grimm Power, the Dhumrongpiyawut family's Gunkul Engineering group, the Khunchornyakong family's SPCG, and others. Due to government incentives, these groups have dramatically developed over the past decade and are now actively investing in the Eastern Economic Corridor (EEC).
- Business groups in industries governed by the state: steel, construction contracting, airline services, real estate development, telecommunications, and banking and finance, as well as life and health insurance. Thai and foreign companies competing in these markets must adhere to governmental rules as well as contend with disruptive digital innovations.
- Business groups producing and exporting high-tech products: electric vehicles, smart electronic components, and sustainable businesses for carbon neutrality, as well as tech start-ups. Most are multinational corporations (MNCs) with modern production technology, stringent product quality control, large fixed expenses, and research and development (R&D) investment, with worldwide market knowledge.

8.3.2 Newly agro-industrialized country (NAIC)

This business group developed in the 1980s as a result of newly agro-industrialized country (NAIC) development strategy, seen as a growth group with a competitive advantage gained by use of indigenous resources and market experience (see Table 8.10).

- Agrobusiness groups, growing from import substitution policies in the 1970s and 1980s and export-oriented manufacturing policies of the 1990s: the Chiaravanont family's CP, operating integrated agro-industrial and food businesses, owning hypermarket Makro and Lotus, and 7–11 convenience stores; the Taepaisitphongse family's Betagro, the Chotitawan family's Saha Farms, the Teawsomboonkit family's Thaifoods in food products, the Chansiri family's Thai Union in canned tuna; the Vongkusolkit family's Mitr Phol/Banpu in sugar and coal mining; and the Sincharoenkul family's Sri Trang Agro in natural rubber.
- Consumer goods groups, developing in the 1970s and 1980s due to import substitution policies and further expanded by a growing middle class: the Chokwatana family's Sahapat, Thailand's largest consumer products conglomerate and owner of Saha Lawson convenience stores, the

Bhirombhakdi family's Boon Rawd Brewery, owner of Singha Beer and bottled water, the Sirivadhanabhakdi family's TCC (Berli Jucker, ThaiBev), owner of Chang Beer and Big C Supercenter supermarket operator, as well as energy drink sectors such as the Osathanugrah family's Osotspa and the Yoovidhya family's Krating Daeng (Red Bull).

In an interview, Thai Union officials claimed to be the world's top exporter of canned fish.[6] Thailand's food manufacturing firms are well-known globally

Table 8.10 Major business groups in agro-industry (NAIC)

Category	*Type of business*	*Name of group*
Agribusiness	Broiler chickens	CP (CP Foods), Betagro, Laemthong, GFPT, Thaifoods
	Rice, tapioca, palm/ vegetable oil, corn	CP (CP Intertrade), Capital Rice, Asian Golden Rice, Patum Rice Mill (Mah Boonkrong), United Flour Mill, Thai Wah, United Palm Oil, Lam Soon, Univanich, Vichibhan, Agripure, Thai Vegetable Oil
	Sugar, ethanol	Mitr Phol, Buriram Sugar, Kaset Thai International Sugar (KTIS), Thai Roong Ruang, Khon Kaen Sugar, Kwang Soon Lee
	Natural rubber	Thai Hua Rubber, Sri Trang Agro, Sri Trang Gloves, Wongbandit, Southland Rubber, Shun Thai, Northeast Rubber
	Fruit juice, functional drink	Malee, Tipco, Royal Plus, Sappe
	Animal feed	Lee Feedmill, United Feedmill, Thai Union Feedmill
	Canned tuna, frozen shrimp	Thai Union (TU), Seafresh, Tropical Canning
Foods and drinks	Energy drink	Osotspa (M150), Red Bull, Carabao Deang
	Beer and soft drink	TCC (Sermsuk, Oishi), Boon Rawd Brewery (Singha), Ichitan
	Food seasoning, sauce, traditional Thai food, frozen food, snack	JD Food, Premier, Thaitheparos, S.Khonkaen, Surapon Foods, Thai President Foods, Taokaenoi, Nescafé coffee
	Bakery	President Bakery (Farmhouse), UFM, Srifa Bakery

Sources: As of 2022, the author's compilation based on field research; statistics from each industry associations and the Stock Exchange of Thailand's website

Note: The list includes only Thai-majority-owned businesses and excludes foreign-owned businesses.

by the marketing slogan as kitchen of the world. Despite crises, food enterprises may continue to expand sales and acquisitions domestically and abroad since food is a necessary and obviously beneficial product, consumed deliberately.

Historically, food manufacturing and exporting were formerly unprofitable. Then businesses shifted their focus to innovative food R&D, investing in large food startups focused on insect food, fish protein meals, and plant-based meats, as well as branding. Consequently, globally recognized brands were developed. Thai Union acquired global status in less than a decade (Wailerdsak, 2020).

Over 45,000 operational employees are prioritized (35,000 in Thailand, mostly labourers from Myanmar, down from 52,000). Catching and canning fish is difficult, demanding toil, but workers may adapt to their surroundings and organizational needs. Thai food manufacture cannot rely on typical mass production methods. But a high-value, premium production method with automation and robots must be established. A leaner workforce and more diverse innovative product offerings help maintain an environmentally and socially responsible corporate strategy (Wailerdsak, 2020).

However, Thai business groups have a stronger and more distinct competitive edge in agribusinesses and consumer goods. Despite an effort in new sectors such as high-speed rail, artificial intelligence (AI), robotics, the internet of things (IoT), 3D printing, nanotechnology, biotechnology, materials science, and quantum computing, Thailand lacks high-tech competitiveness compared to Malaysia and Asian newly industrialized economies (NIEs). All technologies require consistent foreign assistance, with each new circumstance needing capital and technological support. This contrasts with Chinese dedication to self-sufficient science and technology development (Suehiro, 2019).

8.3.3 Marketing 4.0

Thailand 4.0 blends Germany's Industry 4.0 concept with Marketing 4.0, as pioneered by Philip Kotler. Thailand 4.0 prioritizes two main pillars: the digital economy and 12 target industries. The digital economy is referred to as Marketing 4.0, while smart factories are associated with Industry 4.0. In Thailand, smart factories encompass smart agriculture, smart small- and medium-sized enterprises (SMEs), smart tourism, smart homes, smart cities, and smart services, all incorporating marketing and urban planning elements.

Thai business group growth from domestic demand (demand-driven growth) and competitiveness created with the Made in Thailand brand followed the 2000s creative economy policy until it was accepted by investors as cohering with the Marketing 4.0 strategy based on the concept of Philip Kotler (Kotler et al., 2010, 2016, 2021) (see Table 8.11):

- Modern retail groups catering to Asian lifestyles, enjoying dining, shopping, socializing with family and friends, e-commerce, and logistics. For

Table 8.11 Major business groups in service industry (Marketing 4.0)

Category	*Type of business*	*Name of group*
Property, housing, and industrial estates	Construction	Italian-Thai Development, Ch. Karnchang, Sino-Thai, Team Group
	Property development	CP (CP Land, Magnolia Quality), TCC (Univentures, TCC Land, Frasers Property), Bangkok Land
	Housing	Land & Houses, Pruksa Real Estate, Supalai, Quality House, Mankong Kehakan, Ananda, Sansiri, AP
	Industrial estate	Sahapat, Amata Corp., Hemaraj, WHA
Health care and wellness	Hospital, healthcare services	BDMS (Bangkok Dusit Medical Service), BCH (Bangkok Chain Hospital), Bamrungrad Hospital, Thonburi Hospital, Vimut Hospital (Pruksa Real Estate)
	Spa and wellness	Siam Wellness, Veranda Resort, Chivasom
Hotel and restaurant	Hotel services	Central (CENTEL), CP (CP Land), Dusit Thani, MINT (Avani, Anantara), Eastin
	Fast-food chain, restaurant	MINT (Pizza Company, Swensen's, Sizzlers), Central (CRC), MK Restaurant, S&P, BarBQ Plaza, Greyhound, After You, Ohkajuu
Entertainment	Cinema	Major Cineplex, SF Cinema
	TV programs, media	BEC World, GMM Grammy, Kantana, Workpoint, JKN
Commerce	Online shopping, TV shopping	Central (JD.com), Sea (Shopee Singapore), RS
	Modern retail stores, Omni-channel	Berli Jucker, Jmart/Singer, Com7, Kamart
	Bookstore, publishing	Central/COL (B2S, OfficeMate), Se-ed, Amarin Book Center, Matichon
Modern retail and shopping mall	Department store	Central (Central, Robinson), The Mall (The Mall, Emporium, Emquartia, Emsphere), Icon Siam, Siam Piwat (Siam Paragon), TCC (Asiatique), SF (Mega Bangna, Esplanard, LaVilla, J Evenue)
	Supermarket, C&C	CP (Tesco Stores, Siam Makro), Central (CPN, CRC, Tops), Siam Future, TCC (Big C)
	Convenience store	CP (CP ALL, 7-Eleven), Central (Familymart), Sahapat (Lawson)
	Furniture and interior decoration	Central (Baan & Beyond, Thai Wasadu), Index Living Mall, SB Furniture, Homepro, Dohome

(Continued)

Table 8.11 (Continued)

Category	*Type of business*	*Name of group*
Nonbank	Personal loan, leasing	Muangthai Capital, Srisawad, Ngen Tid Loo, Tisco, Micro Leasing
	Insurance	Thai Insurance, Muangthai Insurance, Bangkok Insurance, Thai Marine Insurance
Telecommunications	Phone/internet provider	AIS, DTAC, TRUE, NT
	IT	Loxley, Jasmine, Yip In Soi

Sources: As of 2022, the author's compilation based on field research; statistics from each industry associations and the Stock Exchange of Thailand's website

Note: Marketing 4.0 enterprises grew with the urban middle class.

example, the Chirathivat family's Central; the Umpujh family's The Mall and Siam Paragon; and Chearavanont family's Icon Siam, as well as dozens of small, green open-air community malls built by new family owners in the Bangkok Metropolitan Area. All have developed e-commerce websites and formed partnership with logistic firms (Banomyong, 2017).

- Service-oriented groups expanding alongside the urban middle class: convenience stores (CP, 7-Eleven); restaurants (MK Suki, S&P, Oishi, and Barbecue Plaza); hotels (Minor International and Dusit Thani); real estate development (Bangkok Land, Land & House, BTS Holding, Sansiri, Pruksa Holding, and WHA); entertainment and media (Grammy, BEC World, and Workpoint); movie theatres (Major Cineplex, SF Cinema); exhibition centres (BITEC Bangna, Muang Thong Thani, Queen Sirikit Center); health centres (BDMS, Bamrungrad Hospital, Bangkok Chain/Kasemrad Hospital); international schools (219 companies with 4,114 private schools in 2020); and telecommunications (AIS, DTAC, True).
- Commercial banks, finance companies, and insurance companies. In these sectors, Thai companies must compete with foreign competitors.

In 2015, after the Association of Southeast Asian Nations established an ASEAN community consisting of economic, political security, and social cultural aspects, several firms catering to Thai lifestyle and hospitality have been permitted to expand and invest energetically in the ASEAN region. This has been particularly prevalent in Cambodia, Laos, Myanmar, and Vietnam (CLMV countries) and Chinese markets with comparable lifestyles (Wailerdsak & Siengthai, 2016).

These companies are continually on the lookout for new non-manufacturing business prospects. In addition, they engage in new ventures and retain trade ties with major Japanese and Chinese companies. For example, Central Department Stores launched over 50 businesses in the ASEAN community, in addition to European acquisitions. Japan's Jasco Department Store extended into over 30 supermarkets in ASEAN countries through partnerships with Thai chain store restaurants and cinema complexes (Suehiro, 2014).

Local businesses fall into three categories: Industry 4.0, NAIC, and Marketing 4.0. Thailand achieved upper-middle-income status by benefiting from labour-intensive agricultural, food, and industrial exports. Today, the Kingdom requires new approaches to achieve high-income nation status. Most Thai industry groups have ignored the government's industrial policies and arguments by international organizations about the national innovation system and technology upgrading in manufacturing. They are now competing in a global market, calling for new strategies in non-manufacturing industries to be able to grow alongside the ASEAN community and China.

Notes

1 In Thailand, ethnic Chinese constitute a demographic minority (10 percent of the population). Numerous dialects of Teochew, Hainanese, and Hakka are spoken. Hokkien and Cantonese, which are widely spoken in other Southeast Asian commercial settings, are comparatively minor (Brooker Group, 2003).
2 See Esho (2015) for Indian business groups in Thailand.
3 By the end of 2021, six PTT groups had total assets of 4 trillion baht, including PTT (a holding company and natural gas business) with 2,419,144 million baht, Petroleum Exploration and Production (PTTEP) with 606,861 million baht, Petrochemical and refining groups, including PTT Global Chemical (PTTGC) with 452,565 million baht and Thai Oil (TOP), 255,862 million. In addition, Oil and Retail (OR) was listed on the SET in 2020 (Refer to *PTT Annual Report*, March 2022).
4 Listed companies are highly concentrated. The ten major owners possess over 60 percent of the stock in 304 (or 75.5 percent) of the 403 listed companies surveyed. The ten leading shareholders own virtually all the stock in many public firms. Each listed company also has a certain number of stockholders. Of 403 listed firms polled, 144 (or 35.7 percent) had fewer than 1,000 shareholders.
5 The first industrial revolution spanned from about 1760 to around 1840. Triggered by construction of railroads and the steam engine, it ushered in mechanical production. The second industrial revolution, which started in the late nineteenth century and into the early twentieth century, made mass production possible, fostered by the advent of electricity and the assembly line. The third industrial revolution began in the 1960s. It is usually called the computer or digital revolution because it was catalysed by the development of semiconductors, mainframe computing (1960s), personal computing (1970s and 1980s), and the internet (1990s).
6 Interview by the author with an executive of Thai Union PLC, on 23 April 2021.

References

Baker, C., & Phongpaichit, P. (2014). *A history of Thailand* (3rd ed.). Cambridge University Press.

Banomyong, R. (2017). Logistics services liberalization in Thailand. In S. Tham & S. Basu Das (Eds.), *Services liberalization in ASEAN: Foreign direct investment in logistics* (Chapter 6, pp. 181–211). ISEAS – Yusof Ishak Institute.

Brooker Group. (2003). *Thai business groups: A unique guide to who owns what.* Brooker Group.

Credit Suisse. (2018). *Global wealth databook 2018.* Credit Suisse Research Institute.

Esho, H. (2015). Economic activities of Indian business groups in Thailand: Continuity and discontinuity. *The Hosei University Economic Review*, *8*(1–2), 51–104.
Hewison, K. (2006). Thailand: Boom, bust and recovery. In G. Rodan, K. Hewison, & R. Robison (Eds.), *The political economy of South-East Asia: Markets, power and contestation* (Chapter 3, pp. 72–106). Oxford University Press.
Hewison, K. (2021). Crazy rich Thais: Thailand's capitalist class, 1980–2019. *Journal of Contemporary Asia*, *51*(2), 262–277.
Kanchoochat, V. (2015). The middle-income trap and East Asian miracle lessons. In A. Calcagno et al. (Eds.), *Rethinking development strategies after the financial crisis, Vol. 1: Making the case for policy space* (pp. 55–66). United Nations.
Kanchoochat, V. (2018). Thailand trapped: Catch-up legacies and contemporary malaise. *TRaNS: Trans-Regional and -National Studies of Southeast Asia*, *6*(2), 253–277.
Kanchoochat, V. (2022). Siamese twin troubles: Structural and regulatory transformations in unequal Thailand. *Asian Economic Policy Review*, *18*(1), 1–22.
Kanchoochat, V., Aiyara, T., & Ngamarunchot, B. (2021). Sick tiger: Social conflict, state – business relations and exclusive growth in Thailand. *Journal of Contemporary Asia*, *51*(5), 737–758.
Kanchoochat, V., & Intarakumnerd, P. (2014). *Tigers trapped: Tracing the middle-income trap through the East and Southeast Asian experience*. Working Paper No. 04/2014, Berlin Working Papers on Money, Finance, Trade and Development. University of Applied Science.
Kotler, P., Kartajaya, H., & Setiawan, I. (2010). *Marketing 3.0: From products to customers to the human spirit*. John Wiley & Sons.
Kotler, P., Kartajaya, H., & Setiawan, I. (2016). *Marketing 4.0: Moving from traditional to digital*. John Wiley & Sons.
Kotler, P., Kartajaya, H., & Setiawan, I. (2021). *Marketing 5.0: Technology for humanity*. John Wiley & Sons.
Maesincee, S. (2016). *Thailand 4.0: Will it move the country out of its 'lost decade'?* Asian Institute of Technology (In Thai).
Office of the National Economic and Social Development Council (NESDC). (2016). *Thailand's 20-year national strategy 2018–2037*. http://nscr.nesdc.go.th/ns/
O'neill, H. M., Rondinelli, D. A., & Wattanakul, T. (2004). Ownership and its impact on coping with financial crisis: Differences in state-, mixed-, and privately-owned enterprises in Thailand. *Asia Pacific Journal of Management*, *21*(1), 49–74.
Ouyyanont, P. (2019). Thai economic growth: Retrospect and prospect. In M. J. Montesano, T. Chong, & M. Heng (Eds.), *After the coup: The National council for peace and order era and the future of Thailand* (Chapter 13, pp. 335–356). ISEAS Publishing.
Phipatseritham, K. (1981). *Wikrao laksana kanpen chaokhong turakit khanaadyai nai prathedthai* (*Analysing the ownership structure of the Thai big business groups*). Thammasart University Press (In Thai).
Phongpaichit, P. (2016). Inequality, wealth and Thailand's politics. *Journal of Contemporary Asia*, *46*(3), 405–424.
Satitniramai, A. (2013). *Rat Thai kab kan patiroop settakit: Chak kamnerd toonniyom nai tanakaan tung wikrit settakit 2540 (The Thai state and economic reform: From the establishment of banking capitalism to the Asian financial crisis)*. Same Sky Books (In Thai).
Schwab, K. (2017). *The fourth industrial revolution*. Portfolio Penguin.

Suehiro, A. (1989). *Capital accumulation in Thailand, 1855–1985*. UNESCO The Center for East Asian Cultural Studies.

Suehiro, A. (1992). Capitalist development in post-war Thailand: Commercial bankers, industrial elite, and agribusiness groups. In R. McVey (Ed.), *Southeast Asian capitalists* (Chapter 2, pp. 35–64). Cornell University Press.

Suehiro, A. (2008). *Catch-up industrialization: The trajectory and prospects of East Asian economies*. National University of Singapore Press.

Suehiro, A. (2009). *Tai: Chuushinkoku no mosaku (Thailand: Challenge a middle-income country)*. Iwanami (In Japanese).

Suehiro, A. (2014). *Shinkou ajia keizai-ron: Kyacchi-appu wo koete (Newly emerging Asian economies: Beyond the catch-up industrialization approach)*. Iwanami (In Japanese).

Suehiro, A. (2019). Responses to the middle-income trap in China, Malaysia, and Thailand. In K. Tsunekawa & Y. Todo (Eds.), *Emerging states at crossroads* (Chapter 2, pp. 27–47). Springer.

Suehiro, A., & Wailersak, N. (2004). Family business in Thailand: Its management, governance, and future challenges. *ASEAN Economic Bulletin, 21*(1), 81–93.

Wailerdsak, N. (2006). *Klumthun turakit krubkruathai koon lae lang wikrit pii 2540 (Thai family-owned business groups before and after the 1997 crisis)*. BrandAge Books (In Thai).

Wailerdsak, N. (2008a). Companies in crisis. In P. Phongpaichit & C. Baker (Eds.), *Thai capital after the 1997 crisis* (Chapter 1, pp. 17–57). Silkworm Books.

Wailerdsak, N. (2008b). Family business in Thailand: Ownership structures and stock market. In V. Gupta, N. Levenberg, L. Moore, J. Motwani, & T. Schwarz (Eds.), *Culturally-sensitive models of family business in Southern Asia: A compendium using the GLOBE paradigm* (Chapter 5, pp. 108–136). ICFAI University Press.

Wailerdsak, N. (2020). *Kanborihaan daoden lae senthang suu phuuborihaan radabsuung nai mitithang settasad (Talent management and paths to the top in economic dimension)*. Institute for Continuing Education and Human Resources, Thammasat University (In Thai).

Wailerdsak, N., & Siengthai, S. (2016). Business network in Thailand: From import substitution, export oriented to expansion in AEC. In J. Nolan, C. Rowley, & M. Warner (Eds.), *Business networks in East Asian capitalisms: Enduring trends, emerging patterns* (Chapter 10, pp. 211–233). Chandos Publishing, Elsevier.

Wailerdsak, N., & Suehiro, A. (2010). Business groups in Thailand. In A. Colpan, T. Hikino, J. Lincoln, & D. Musson (Eds.). *Oxford handbook of business groups* (Chapter 9, pp. 237–266). Oxford University Press.

Wailerdsak, N., & Suehiro, A. (2014). Family business groups in Thailand: Coping with management critical points. *Asia Pacific Journal of Management, 31*(4), 997–1018.

Wangwan, N., & Leemakdej, A. (2022). *Hidden ownership and corporate governance*. SET Research Scholarship 2021–2022, The Stock Exchange of Thailand.

Chapter 9

Expanding business power

9.1 Selection and specialization

After the Plaza Accord in 1985, the Thai economy grew at the fastest pace among the World Bank's eight high-performing East Asian economies (HPAEs).[1] Annual real gross domestic product (GDP) growth rate was 8.2 percent. Between 1987 and 1990, Thailand's GDP increased by 9.5, 13.2, 12.2, and 11.6 percent, respectively (Phongpaichit & Baker, 1996). After joining Japanese production networks for export-oriented manufacturing of electronics and other labour-intensive products and import-substituting industries, most notably automotive assembly, Thailand experienced a decade of rapid investment, export, and output growth. This was due to job creation coupled with productivity growth dynamics (Phongpaichit & Baker, 1998).

However, the 1997 Asian financial crisis revised the situation. The Thai government eased restrictions on foreign ownership. Many Thai companies were obliged to sell shares to foreign partners and raise funds due to currency rate fluctuations and post-crisis economic slump losses[2] (Wailerdsak, 2006, 2008). Even in the oil and refining industries, only the defunct state-enterprise PTT survived, which had to be listed on the SET.

Thailand's GDP per capita could have reached $17,000 had it sustained high manufacturing output and productivity growth rates throughout the twenty-first century. But the GDP per capita fell well short of the US$7,000 threshold from 2000 to 2022. The nation has not yet reverted to pre-crisis prosperity levels.

To keep up with Thai economic restructuring and compete with foreign companies, Thai business groups eschewed business diversification in favour of selection and specialization. They intensified involvement in the energy, natural resource, agro-industrial, and service industries. In Thailand, service industries range from finance and luxury tourism to low-wage employment for seasonal migrants. Premature deindustrialization is associated with a rise in the middle class, changing consumer preferences, and increasing foreign tourist visits (Endo & Oizumi, 2020; Makohin et al., 2020).

DOI: 10.4324/9781003370536-13

Several attempts have been made in the agriculture and service industries to develop specific innovations and boost productivity. For instance, the CP group is a market leader in agro-industry (Charoen Pokphand Foods), convenience stores (CP All is the parent company of CP 7-Eleven), and telecoms (True Corporation). CP Foods is one of Thailand's leading agricultural firms and a significant supplier of frozen chicken and shrimp to Asia.

Along with conventional seed trading since the 1970s, CP Foods and CP Intertrade (the CP group's international trading arm) have expanded into new niche-type markets, such as natural rubber products and packaged rice for export. Both businesses target mainland China. A new industrial estate development business was also launched to entice Chinese investors, demonstrating the company's focus on the Chinese market and investors.

Meanwhile, in 1998 CP All opened the first CP 7-Eleven. By 2018, Thailand's CP 7-Eleven (10,500 outlets) overtook American (8,421 stores) and South Korean (9,200 stores) presence, and is currently second only to Japan (20,033 stores). The rapid company growth and enhancement of high-quality services and new products are noteworthy. The 7-Eleven in Thailand rebranded itself as "convenient eating stores" with the advertising slogan: "Stop by whenever you're hungry." In 2007, the CP Group opened Panyapiwat Institute of Management (PIM) to train workers for convenience shops and agro-industry; 5,000 students have been educated to play supporting roles. By contrast, CP All and its affiliates have a *Little Toagae* entrepreneurship development program and exacting performance appraisal system to motivated young staff to undertake difficult work challenges[3] (Wailerdsak, 2020).

Thai hospital groups, a rising niche market, can expand business power because of three factors (Rompho et al., 2021):[4]

- Development of the middle class and private health insurance systems which serve domestic patients in an increasing number of hospital branches.
- Welcoming foreign patients by catering to the halal dietary code of Muslim patients and families, despite Thailand's status as a predominantly Buddhist country. Middle Eastern patients reportedly prefer to land at Bangkok's Suvarnabhumi Airport instead of Tokyo's Narita Airport due to superior medical and tourism services at the former.
- Hospital development in neighbouring countries, especially Myanmar, Laos, and Cambodia, to cater to increasing numbers of high-budget customers.

The need for innovation, organizational capacity building, and new job creation in highly competitive agriculture, retail, and medical industries has become a substantial engine of GDP growth. This is in addition to the state's national innovation system and the industrial R&D drawn on endogenous growth theory and orthodox economic policies (Suehiro, 2008, pp. 64–71).

9.2 Leveraging political influence

Thai business groups leverage political clout for expansion. Starting with the 1960s industrialization drive, the nation was ruled by politicians and high-ranking military officials who became private company chairpersons, directors, or shareholders. Then came a call for democratic governance and reform of political malfeasance. Politicians, government officials, and elite military capitalists no longer participate publicly in different company activities. But economic and political elites coordinate in more intricate ways. Major business groups routinely sponsor and fund political parties to promote company activities (Bunkanwanicha & Wiwattanakantang, 2009).

This occurred in 1992, in response to an urban middle class demand for democracy, leading to political violence in May of that year. As a condition of obtaining the 1997 Constitution, a group of corporate capitalists were permitted to participate in full-fledged political activity. Business monopolies were highly active during the Thaksin administration, from 2001 to 2006, establishing political parties, contesting and winning elections, and forming a government comprising representatives from principal business groups (Hewison, 2010). Cabinet members are considered as representing capitalist regimes characterized by cronyism and bribed through financial politics (*tanakit kanmuang*) (Bunkanwanicha & Wiwattanakantang, 2009).

In the late 2010s, General Prayut's military regime restored the Joint Public and Private Sector Consultative Committee (JPPSCC) model pioneered by General Prem Tinsulanonda in the late 1980s. Also, the *pracharat* (people-state) campaign sought to combine military, business, governmental, and civil societies.

Between 2020 and 2022, to combat the novel coronavirus 2019 (COVID-19) pandemic, the opposition party attacked stimulus measures as "capitalist policies by capitalists for capitalists." Their complaint was that large business groups were replacing small traders by closing flea markets and restaurants as precautionary measures, but not shopping malls, despite the fact that the latter were closed, with air circulating indoors as a health risk. Retail groups benefited from cabinet measures such as Tasting, Shopping, Using (*Chim Shop Chai*); Shopping with Refunds (*Shop Dee Mee Kuen*); and Shopping Subsidy (*Kon La Kreung*) schemes. A We Travel Together (*Rao Tiew Duay Kan*) scheme favours major hotel chains over small resorts (Nikomborirak, 2021).

These included earlier efforts to situate well-ventilated sales booths and sidewalk venues, disproportionately affecting small merchants who lack brick and mortar locations like convenience stores. The government increased community taxes on white liquor, rendering small outlets uncompetitive, with the alleged goal of reducing alcoholism in Thailand. The Eastern Economic Corridor (EEC) Development Plan favouring Chinese business groups does not generate new innovations but invests in distribution hubs such as Alibaba. Others blame monopolistic capitalists intertwined with the state for inequities.

Leveraging political influence may be an ideal way to build upper-middle-income countries, allowing major capital-intensive companies to attain economies of scale and accelerate local content requirements. But governmental intervention may lead to corruption or domestic market distortion. Domestic political instability has persisted, necessitating more market liberalization to achieve a high-income status.

9.3 Mergers and acquisitions

Another stage of power expansion for Thai business groups is in a growing capacity for M&A to extend operations. Acquisitive growth is a means to obtain productive services and knowledge a firm requires to enter a new field (Penrose, 1959, p. 126). The main advantage of acquisitive, over organic, growth is the ability to purchase relatively quickly what Penrose (1959) called a bundle of resources (often firm-specific, such as tacit knowledge). This advantage prompts emerging economy firms to pursue domestic and international acquisitions (in emerging and developed economies) (Lebedev et al., 2015; Peng et al., 2018).

Thailand has undergone three M&A booms over the past three decades (Figure 9.1):

- During the economic boom of the early 1990s.
- Between 1997 and 2004 post-Asian financial crises.
- Starting in 2010.

(Unit: millions of US dollar)

Year	2003	2004	2005	2006	2007	2008	2009	2010	2011	2012	2013	2014	2015	2016	2017	2018	2019	2020	2021
Net purchases of M&A	18	-7	-203	88	42	1,339	865	2,810	4,569	5,659	9,602	-718	437	4,483	2,693	3,623	5,141	6,581	12,319
OFDI	615	72	529	968	3,003	4,057	4,172	8,162	6,258	10,597	11,679	5,575	1,687	12,367	14,217	17,373	10,395	18,999	17,303
Net Sales of M&A	1,150	216	-632	3,771	1,991	150	351	461	954	- 65	14	448	-892	-1795	-22	-930	-315	-9826	-11.9

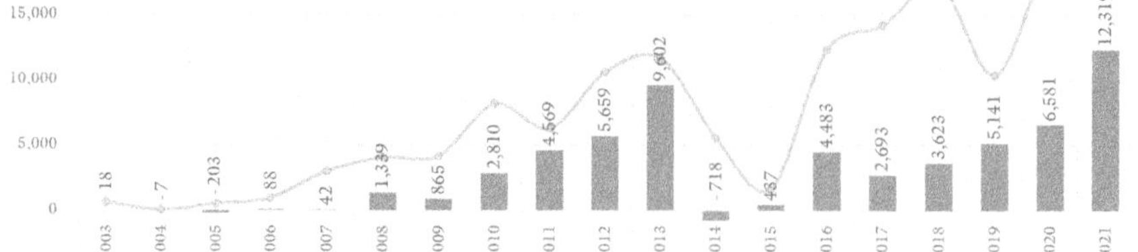

Figure 9.1 Mergers and acquisitions values of Thailand, 2003–2021

Source: Compiled by the author from UNCTAD, World Investment Report 2022, Annex Table 5 Value of cross-border M&A net purchases, by region/economy of seller/purchasers, 1990–2021

Since the 2008 global financial crisis, there has been a wave of acquisitions of domestic competitors in food and beverages, health care, modern retail, real estate, and digital television. This is due to the expansion of urban areas and the middle class, as well as the trend of Thai business groups making cross-border acquisitions with large capital, such as coal, canned tuna, hotels, petrochemicals, food and beverages, and modern retail (Endo & Oizumi, 2020).

This phenomenon was once deemed unachievable and not developing globally. Figure 9.1 displays the value of cross-border M&As (bar graph) and Thai outward FDI. The 2016 survey conducted by Willis Towers Watson called multinational Thai and Asian companies who make cross-border acquisitions "Asia Trailblazers."[5] The term was coined in recognition of these firms' pioneering spirit and ambition to go beyond their local markets and successfully grow their businesses abroad.

Previous business expansion approaches were used to diversify into unrelated businesses, improve stock market value, and reduce business risk, or establish subsidiaries as part of a production chain governed under one pyramidal umbrella. However, M&As are currently a primary growth vehicle for acquiring strategic assets such as product brands, distribution networks, technical secrets, and critical assets of local firms, rather than starting from scratch (Greenfield FDI), which is more expensive and time-consuming (Jongwanich et al., 2013; Pananond, 2011). Significantly, share prices of affiliated firms listed on the Stock Exchange of Thailand (SET) jumped at the announcement of acquisitions, comparable to reactions in the United States for a previously unknown effective way of raising extensive capital.

Table 9.1 shows that Thai business groups undertook a record number of domestic acquisitions. In response to the ASEAN Economic Community (AEC) opening in 2015, regional M&As increased. French Casino sold ThaiBev of the TCC Group, a majority stake in Big C, for $3.46 billion. Central Group purchased interests in Vietnam's Big C. Table 9.1 displays deals over $3 billion. Several purchases also occurred of lesser value.

Table 9.1 Mergers and acquisitions deal of Thai business groups, 2010–2022

Date	*Group name*	*Acquired company*	*Sector*	*Value of investment/ acquisition* Millions of dollars
July 2010	Banpu	Centennial Coal, the largest coal company in New South Wales, Australia	Coal	1,905
July 2010	Thai Union	MWBrands SAS, the largest tuna canned producer in France; purchased from Lehman Brothers	Tuna canned	884

(*Continued*)

Table 9.1 (Continued)

Date	*Group name*	*Acquired company*	*Sector*	*Value of investment/ acquisition* Millions of dollars
Aug. 2010	Sahaviriya	Blast furnace division of Corus Group, England	Blast furnace	469
Nov. 2010	Indorama	INVISTA, a subsidiary of Koch Group, Petroleum department, the US	Polymer	420
Dec. 2010	BGH	Health Network (seven hospitals, such as Phayathai, Paolo Memorial)	Hospital	317
Sep. 2011	Central	La Rinascente SpA, an old chain department store having 11 branches in Italy	Retail	372
Sep. 2011	TCC	Serm Suk (Pepsi Co.), Thailand's largest beverage producer	Beverages	314
Sep. 2011	SCG	PT. Chandra Asri Petrochemical, Indonesia	Petrochemical	425
Feb. 2012	Indorama	Chemical division of Old World Industries, LLC, the US	Ethylene	795
July 2012	TCC	Fraser & Neave Ltd., Singapore's largest beverage producer owned by Lee Guanyu's brother	Beverages	2,210
Sep. 2012	TCC	Golden Land Property, Thailand	Property	340
Dec. 2012	CP	Ping An Insurance (2nd largest in China) 15%	Insurance	9,386
Apr. 2013	CP All	Siam Makro, purchased from SHV Holdings, Netherlands	Cash & Carry	6,600
Dec. 2013	MUFG	Mitsubishi UFJ Financial Group Inc., Japan purchased 76.88% stake of Bank of Ayudhya from GE Group	Bank	5,310
Apr. 2014	TCC/Berli Jucker	Metro Cash & Carry in Vietnam (German)	Cash & Carry	650 Euro
Nov. 2014	WHA Corp.	Hemaraj Land & Development, Thailand	Industrial land developer	1,340

(Continued)

Table 9.1 (Continued)

Date	*Group name*	*Acquired company*	*Sector*	*Value of investment/ acquisition*
				Millions of dollars
Feb. 2016	TCC	Big C Supercenter (Casino group of France)	Supermarket	3,460
Sep. 2016	BDMS	Nai Lert Park Hotel (former Hilton Hotel) on wireless road	From hotel to health centre	370
Nov. 2016	CPF	Bercio Parent, the US	Frozen foods	1,075
Apr. 2017	CPF	Westbridge Food Group, the US	Food	60 Pound
Feb. 2019	TMB Bank	Thanachart Bank (TBank)	Bank	4,470
Dec. 2019	Bangkok Bank	PT Permata TBK, Indonesia	Bank	2,674
Jan. 2020	Asset World Corp	12 hotels and mixed-use projects	Real Estate	870
Mar. 2020	CPF	Tesco Asia, Malaysia	Supermarket	1,500
Apr. 2021	Gulf Energy	Advanced Info Service (59.6%)	Telco	11,862
Apr. 2021	Gulf Energy	Intouch Holdings	Telco	5,731.5 Millions of dollars
Apr. 2021	PTT, Siam Management	Global Power Synergy	Energy	800.6
July 2021	PTTGC	Allenex Holding Gmb	Coating resins, additives	4,002.2 ml EURO
July 2021	Central World	Siam Future Development	Real Estate	399.1
Aug. 2021	U City and VGI	Jay Mart	Telco	317.0
Oct. 2021	Morgan Stanley	Asian Aviation	Transport and logistics	329.7
Oct. 2021	Univenture BGP	Eastern Cogeneration	Energy	373.6
Oct. 2021	CP Mechandi-sing	Siam Makro (3.4%)	Food and beverage	434.8
Nov. 2021	True Corp.	Total Access Communication (DTAC), No.2 and No.3 mobile operators in Thailand.	Telco	4,205.3
May 2022	Kiatnakin Phatra Securities	Bamrungrad Hospital (9.0%)	Health care	357.5
July 2022	Advanced Wireless Network	Jasmine Broadband Internet	Telco	362.0

(Continued)

Table 9.1 (Continued)

Date	*Group name*	*Acquired company*	*Sector*	*Value of investment/ acquisition* Millions of dollars
July 2022	Advanced Wireless Network	Triple T Broadband	Telco	546.2
Aug. 2022	RATCH Group	NEXIF Energy	Energy	605.0
Aug. 2022	CP	Metro Cash & Carry, India	Cash & Carry	1,000.0
Nov. 2022	Central and Signa	Selfridges Group, UK	Department store	5,370.0

Source: Compiled by the author based on (1) UNCTAD, *World Investment Report, Annex Table 9.5: Cross-border M&As deals worth over $ 3 billion completed, various years;* (2) KPMG M&A trends in Thailand, 2019–2022; and annual report of each company

Note: BDMS: Bangkok Dusit Medical Services; BGH: Bangkok General Hospital; CP: Charoen Pokphand; SCG: Siam Cement Group; TCC: Thai Charoen Corporation

Some researchers argue that Thai firms seek substantial capital market funds to expand abroad. The Thai capital market has grown by listing a parent firm or subsidiary on the SET and issuing common shares or debt securities (debentures) (Jongwanich et al., 2013). However, when examining private financial data in Thailand, it may be discouraging to note that SET fund-raising, despite some increases, is still inferior to commercial bank loans. Historically, the Thai capital market has not developed sufficiently to finance the private sector.

Why do domestic and international banks lend to Thai firms? Major companies in Thailand use land holdings as loan collateral (Suehiro, 2014), so few small- and medium-sized enterprises (SMEs) are able to invest abroad. High borrowing rates and credit restrictions impede obtaining and using the system's financial services. SMEs cannot raise long-term money on the Thai capital market due to lack of the confidence and collateral assets possessed by large corporations.

Before land prices rose, land assets were almost insignificant, and banks refused land as collateral. After the 1997 Asian financial crisis, real estate became the most significant mortgage collateral and accumulating land assets a sure-fire method to secure bank loans. Land and buildings may be securitized as securitization assets and used to raise funds on the SET. With this strategy, businesses may develop exponentially (Laovakul, 2016).

In addition, the key differences between the current M&A boom and previous ones are substantial increases in costs, a greater use of property funds,[6] and increased amount of M&A undertaken outside Thailand. Increased M&A costs are inextricably linked to rising land prices in the Bangkok Metropolitan Area (BMA). The price of land climbed 45 times from 1985 to 2013 (Pomchokchai, 2014). Growing land value provided expansion opportunities for family business groups with extensive land holdings. Land acquisition became a guarantor for bank lending. Notably, land and buildings were securitized assets for raising capital on the stock market (Laovakul, 2016).

Financial instruments, including property funds, infrastructure funds, and real estate investment trusts (REIT), were used by the CP and WHA group. CP Land, a property business subsidiary of CP group, owned CP Tower I on Silom Road and CP Tower II (Fortune Tower) on Rachadapisek Road. When the company launched a condominium development business, it securitized three buildings to establish a property fund. Ten billion baht obtained from this property fund were immediately mobilized as investment for constructing a new condominium.

WHA group established two real estate investment trusts (REITs) – WHA Premium Growth Freehold and Leasehold Real Estate Investment Trust (WHART) and Hemaraj Leasehold Real Estate Investment Trust (HREIT) – by selling assets to the respective funds and then listing them on the Stock Exchange of Thailand (SET). In this way, WHA raised sufficient capital to purchase Hemaraj Land and Development PLC, which owned major industrial estates in the EEC.[7]

In 2021, TRUE and DTAC (Total Access Communication PLC) formally announced merger plans, suggesting a domestic growth slowdown. If the merger succeeds, it will reduce the telecom industry to two players (including AIS), strengthening the present monopoly. True is a Chearavanont family company. DTAC is owned by Telenor Asia Pte Ltd. of Norway (42.62 percent) and Thai Telco Holdings Limited of the Bencharongkul family (22.43 percent). Because the telecom industry provides a foundation for other businesses, the government should support shareholder distribution and administration by professional managers. They should be examined to ensure they are serving society rather than just their owners. This topic will be explored in Chapter 11.

Indeed, most recent M&A deals (Table 9.1) were done outside of Thailand. For example, in 2010 Thai Union Frozen Products of the Chansiri family, Thailand's largest canned tuna maker, purchased MW Brands SAS, France's largest canned tuna manufacturer. In 2012, the TCC group of the Sirivadhanabhakdi family, Thailand's largest beverage industry corporation, acquired Singapore's Fraser & Neave Ltd. Central Department Store, and the Chirathivat family, Thailand's largest department store chain owners, bought the United Kingdom's Selfridges luxury department store from the Weston family in 2022, raising its total European store count to 39.

Thai business groups believe that horizontal M&A saves time and money compared to starting a new brand, in addition to offering rapid access to innovations amassed by acquiring foreign companies. These M&A deals promote cross-regional knowledge sharing and cultivate global competitive advantage. This form of M&A-based R&D is distinct from the manufacturing industry as defined by catch-up industrialization theory.

9.4 Overseas investment

Latecomers confront new economic challenges and opportunities in the globalized era. Globalization compels emerging countries to modify their expansion strategies. Some "passive receivers" of foreign investment must now actively seek new markets and technologies abroad (Pananond, 2011). The global value chain strengthens OFDI from emerging economies and improve intercontinental relations. OFDI and MNCs from emerging economies, notably BRICS (Brazil, Russia, India, China, and South Africa), have grown in the past decade. This new trend of rising international investment in emerging countries can be explained by the notion of compressed development (Hamilton-Hart & Yeung, 2021; Lee & Sermcheep, 2017; Li & Zhang, 2021).

Previous research indicates that internationalization may be motivated by a firm's desire to capitalize on R&D skills and recoup previous R&D investment. Effective R&D requires skilled personnel to generate novel concepts and translate them into useable technology, products, marketing programs, and services, with sufficient funding for ongoing R&D. Many businesses invest in international expansion or entrepreneurship to boost competitiveness. Internationalization can lead to efficiency in integrating global operations and exploiting economic and institutional characteristics and opportunities of international markets, including cheap labour, an abundance of financial and natural resources, alliance partners, and conquering institutional irregularities and limitations (Carney et al., 2017; Fang et al., 2018; Lin & Wang, 2021).

A similar pattern is visible for Thai OFDI. It is noteworthy that in 2011, Thailand's OFDI began to outpace IFDI in value (see Figure 9.2). Since the mid-2000s in the ASEAN Economic Community (AEC), investments by Thailand's Big Four (PTT, SCG, CP, and TCC groups) have expanded. Thai and foreign firms prefer CLMV over other Asian nations for three main reasons (Moeller, 2021; Wailerdsak, 2013):

- Geography (transport connections and long-term accumulation of economic trade).
- A positive forecast for future CLMV market growth.
- Slowing growth and risk distribution of local markets as a motivating factor for the Thailand Plus One policy.

Since the Asian Economic Community (AEC) debuted in 2015, Thai business groups and the Thai government have been particularly active. After the May 2014 coup, the military government prioritized border economies. This idea was inextricably linked to ambitions to connect the Greater Mekong Subregion's economic corridors. Thailand also pursued deeper integration into regional production networks to boost exports, signing many overlapping regional and bilateral trade and investment agreements. Thai companies are focusing efforts on regional, instead of local, growth (see Table 9.2 to 9.5).

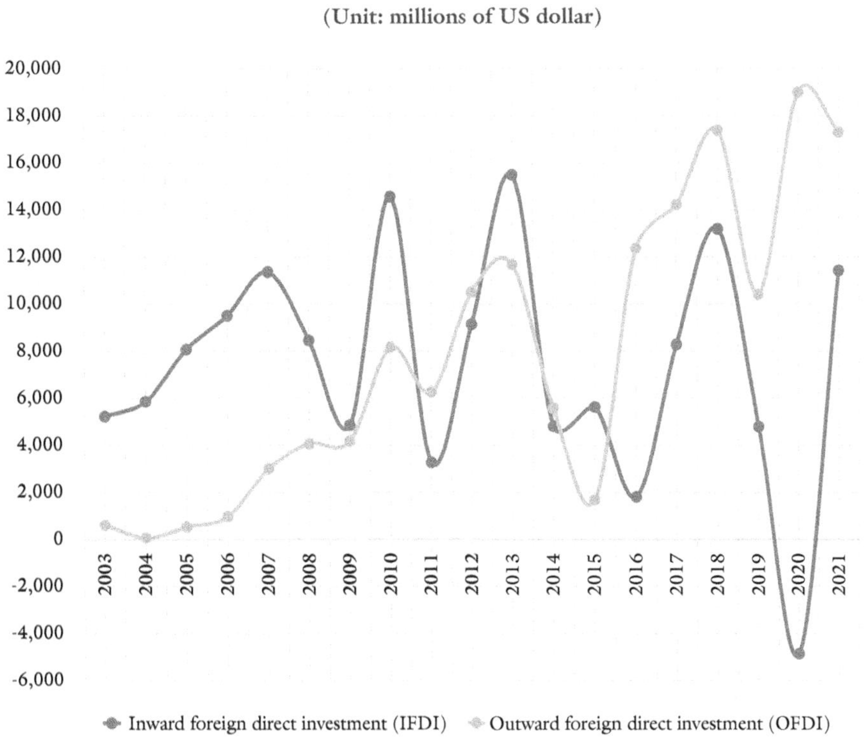

Figure 9.2 Outward foreign direct investment of Thailand, 2003–2021

Source: Author's compilation from UNCTAD, World Investment Report 2016, Annex Table 9.1 FDI flows, by region and economy, 2010–2011, p. 198

UNCTAD, World Investment Report 2018, Annex Table 9.1 FDI flows, by region and economy, 2012–2017, p. 186

UNCTAD, World Investment Report 2022, Annex Table 9.2 FDI flows, by region and economy, 2016–2021, p. 212

Even Central Department Store group entered ASEAN, while maintaining upscale department stores in Europe.

According to the *ASEAN Investment Report*, the extensive ASEAN market and strong regional integration make it a key FDI destination for the developing world, second only to China, and will potentially drive global economic recovery. Intra-ASEAN FDI continues to be an important source of FDI and establishing regional production networks motivated by potential electric vehicle (EV), electronic, digital economy, and green technology markets. Startups,[8] especially unicorns, have driven these new trends and contributed to the ASEAN Industry 4.0 revolution (ASEAN Secretariat, 2022).

Table 9.2 OFDI stock classified by country (value), 2006–2021

Year	*World*	*Asia*	*ASEAN*	*CLMV*	*China and Hong Kong*	*EU*	*Free Tax*
2006	8,756	5,810	3,502	1,437	1,530	323	1,967
2007	9,889	5,811	3,265	945	1,947	661	2,124
2008	12,677	7,773	4,685	1,326	2,237	712	2,679
2009	18,035	11,265	6,128	1,884	3,224	1,008	3,933
2010	24,581	15,543	9,558	2,404	3,912	1,583	4,481
2011	42,054	25,907	14,872	4,096	6,704	2,679	6,820
2012	57,063	32,740	16,990	4,741	9,184	4,967	10,417
2013	66,354	36,773	17,757	5,887	9,366	5,364	14,874
2014	68,521	39,094	19,355	6,669	9,767	4,927	17,409
2015	76,012	43,371	21,438	8,572	11,197	7,888	19,426
2016	95,236	55,731	28,523	11,506	14,752	9,148	20,426
2017	116,527	66,550	34,595	14,187	19,522	15,154	21,710
2018	135,920	72,669	40,069	16,350	24,156	20,823	21,642
2019	146,989	83,282	44,735	18,738	29,876	23,450	18,732
2020	173,437	102,730	59,537	21,700	31,836	25,324	21,700
2021	179,577	101,825	59,552	22,098	32,579	30,220	22,098

Source: Compiled by the author based on the Bank of Thailand website, Statistics, External Sector – >International Investment Position – >Thai Direct Investment Position Classified by Country (EC_XT_064)

Note: *Free tax area means British Virgin, Cayman, Mauritius Islands
(Unit: million of US dollar)

Table 9.3 OFDI stock classified by country (%), 2006–2021

Year	*World*	*Asia*	*ASEAN*	*CLMV*	*China & Hong Kong*	*EU*	*Free Tax*
2006	100.0	66.4	40.0	16.4	17.5	3.7	22.5
2007	100.0	58.8	33.0	9.6	19.7	6.7	21.5
2008	100.0	61.3	37.0	10.5	17.6	5.6	21.1
2009	100.0	62.5	34.0	10.4	17.9	5.6	21.8
2010	100.0	63.2	38.9	9.8	15.9	6.4	18.2
2011	100.0	61.6	35.4	9.7	15.9	6.4	16.2
2012	100.0	57.4	29.8	8.3	16.1	8.7	18.3
2013	100.0	55.4	26.8	8.9	14.1	8.1	22.4
2014	100.0	57.1	28.2	9.7	14.3	7.2	25.4
2015	100.0	57.1	28.2	11.3	14.7	10.4	25.6
2016	100.0	58.5	29.9	12.1	15.5	9.6	21.4
2017	100.0	57.1	29.7	12.2	16.8	13.0	18.6
2018	100.0	62.4	34.4	14.0	20.7	17.9	18.6
2019	100.0	56.7	30.4	12.7	20.3	15.9	12.7
2020	100.0	59.2	34.3	12.5	18.4	14.6	12.5
2021	100.0	56.7	33.2	12.3	18.1	16.8	12.3

Source: Compiled by the author based on the Bank of Thailand website, Statistics, External Sector – >International Investment Position – >Thai Direct Investment Position Classified by Country (EC_XT_064)

Note: *Free tax area means British Virgin, Cayman, Moritious Islands

Table 9.4 OFDI stock classified by business sector (value), 2006–2021

Year	*World*	*Manufacturing*	*Foods and drink*	*Chemicals*	*Auto*	*Wholesale and retail*	*Finance and insurance*
2006	8,756	4,011	1,504	578	184	441	1,456
2007	9,889	3,199	980	325	165	499	2,389
2008	12,677	4,184	1,228	566	253	742	2,228
2009	18,035	5,429	1,324	807	738	1,569	3,108
2010	24,581	7,290	1,380	1,138	648	2,501	2,875
2011	42,054	8,735	1,564	1,396	463	3,480	6,822
2012	57,063	15,253	5,894	1,715	870	4,599	8,032
2013	66,354	16,930	6,815	1,897	1,007	6,906	8,365
2014	68,521	16,244	5,393	1,502	2,379	6,764	10,225
2015	76,012	19,998	7,752	2,086	1,016	8,691	11,060
2016	95,236	26,996	12,309	2,454	2,511	10,734	16,544
2017	116,527	35,239	17,294	2,930	3,379	13,509	18,355
2018	135,920	44,900	21,169	3,138	3,216	16,602	19,325
2019	146,990	49,440	22,558	3,373	4,235	18,623	18,025
2020	173,437	58,373	25,536	3,590	5,966	19,821	27,867
2021	179,577	59,886	23,296	3,691	5,063	19,260	28,862

Source: Compiled by the author based on the Bank of Thailand website, Statistics, External Sector – >International Investment Position – >Thai Direct Investment Position Abroad Classified by Business Sector of Thai Investors (EC_XT_068)

(Unit: million of US dollar)

Table 9.5 OFDI stock classified by business sector (%), 2006–2021

Year	*World*	*Manufacturing*	*Foods and drink*	*Chemicals*	*Auto*	*Wholesale and retail*	*Finance and insurance*
2006	100.0	45.8	17.2	6.6	2.1	5.0	16.6
2007	100.0	32.3	9.9	3.3	1.7	5.0	24.2
2008	100.0	33.0	9.7	4.5	2.0	5.9	17.6
2009	100.0	30.1	7.3	4.5	4.1	8.7	17.2
2010	100.0	29.7	5.6	4.6	2.6	10.2	11.7
2011	100.0	20.8	3.7	3.3	1.1	8.3	16.2
2012	100.0	26.7	10.3	3.0	1.5	8.1	14.1
2013	100.0	25.5	10.3	2.9	1.5	10.4	12.6
2014	100.0	23.7	7.9	2.2	3.5	9.9	14.9
2015	100.0	26.3	10.2	2.7	1.3	11.4	14.6
2016	100.0	28.3	12.9	2.6	2.6	11.3	17.4
2017	100.0	30.2	14.8	2.5	2.9	11.6	15.8
2018	100.0	38.5	18.2	2.7	2.8	14.2	16.6
2019	100.0	33.6	15.3	2.3	2.9	12.7	12.3
2020	100.0	33.7	14.7	2.1	3.4	11.4	16.1
2021	100.0	33.3	13.0	2.1	2.8	10.7	16.1

Source: Compiled by the author based on the Bank of Thailand website, Statistics, External Sector – >International Investment Position – >Thai Direct Investment Position Abroad Classified by Business Sector of Thai Investors (EC_XT_068)

9.4.1 Central department store group of the Chirathivat family

Unlike other Thai business families (*Teochew*), the Chirathivat family of Central Department Store (Central) is of Hainanese origin. In 1925, the patriarch Tiang moved to Bangkok and opened a shop, Keng Seng Lee, near the Oriental Hotel (now the Mandarin Oriental) with his eldest son, Samrit, in 1947. Central, Thailand's first department store, opened in 1956 in Chinatown. Today, the 75-year-old company operates over 60 department stores (Central, Robinson, Zen, Power Buy, and Super Sports) and shopping centres across Thailand as well as 5,000 hotels and restaurants. According to Forbes (2021), the Chirathivat family is Thailand's fourth wealthiest, with a net worth of US$11.6 billion.

The group is Thailand's largest retailer. As early as the 1990s, it decided to list its hotels (Central Plaza Hotel, CENTEL), property development (Central Pattana, CPN), and later in 2020, modern retail (Central Retail Corporation, CRC) on the Stock Exchange of Thailand (SET). However, they decided not to list three flagship firms: Central Trading (1954), Hang Central Department Store (1968), and Central Department Store (1974). These firms are privately controlled by the Chirathivat family (Endo, 2013) (see Figure 9.3).

A rising economy and burgeoning middle class helped expand their empire in scale and scope. However, since the 2010s, Thailand has an aging population that spends more resources abroad. Domestic demand stalled as competition intensified (Ono, 2017). The group focused on overseas markets, particularly fast-growing Vietnam, which is geographically closer to Thailand and has similar customer habits. The Vietnamese economy rises by up to 7 percent annually. Central has been in Vietnam for almost a decade, starting as a fashion service provider. In 2015, it became associated with Nguyen Kim and Lanchi Mart, and by 2020, Central Vietnam had 35 shopping malls and over 230 merchants in 63 provinces, encompassing 1.08 million square meters and generating 3.7 billion baht annually.

Central is now Vietnam's largest global retailer, serving over 12 million customers daily. Within five years, the company seeks to expand to 55 provinces, requiring more investment than in Thailand. Due to rapid expansion in Vietnam, an M&A strategy was used to find prospective acquisition opportunities. Managing Vietnamese staff of acquired companies was essential. Due to time constraints, building a business culture and integrating Thai and Vietnamese retail practices proved difficult. This signified that Thai business groups have demonstrated innovation in international human resource management.[9]

Additionally, the European market is a focus for Thai and Chinese visitors eager to purchase brand-name items. The group has continued to purchase European luxury department stores, including Italy's La Rinascente, German's KaDeWe, and England's Selfridges. International operations generate roughly 30 percent of group revenue. Despite Central's failure in 2011 to

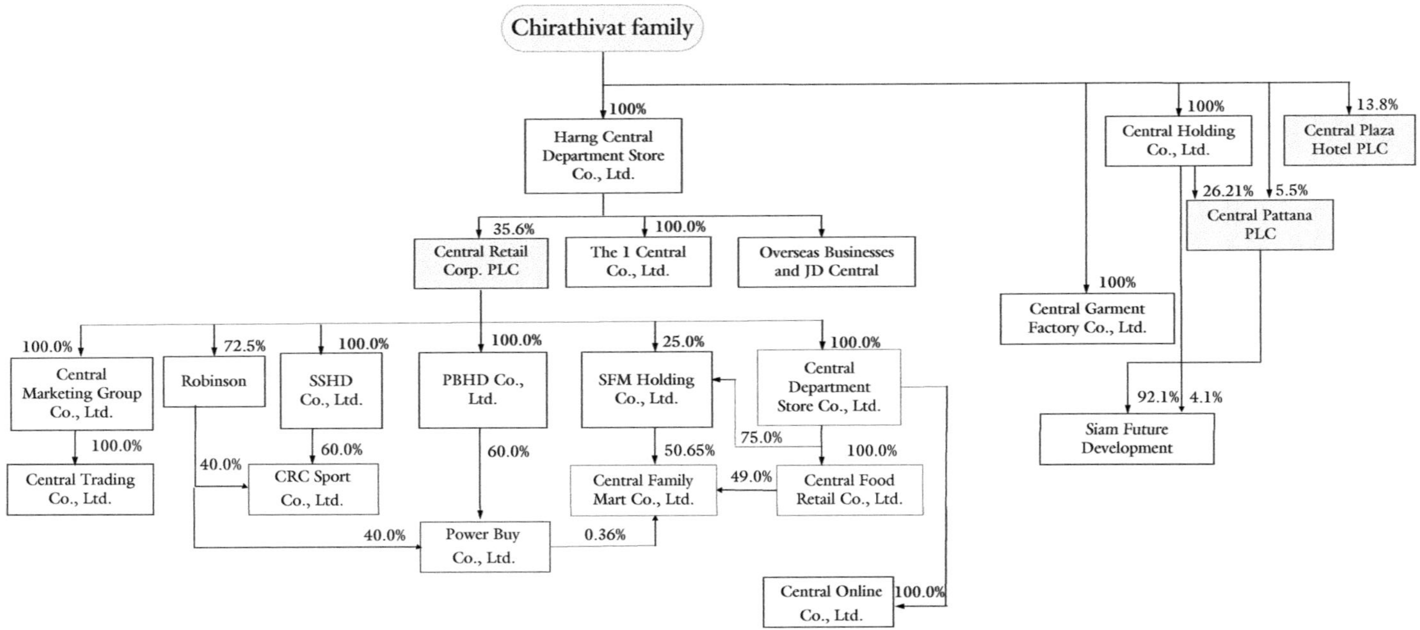

Figure 9.3 Pyramidal ownership structure of the Central group

Sources: Author's compilation based on the annual reports of listed companies belonging to the Central groups as of December 2021

Table 9.6 Domestic and international expansion of the Central group, 1982–2022

Date	*Region*	*Province/City*
Central in Thailand		
Dec. 1982	Bangkok	Central Ladprao
Nov. 1993	Bangkok	Central Ramindra
Mar. 1995	Bangkok	Central Pinklao
Oct. 1997	Bangkok	Central Rama 3
Dec. 2001	Bangkok	Central Bangna
Dec. 2002	Bangkok	Central Rama 2, Central World
Dec. 2003	Bangkok	Central Ratanathibet
Nov. 2008	Bangkok	Central Chaengwattana
2009	Eastern, Northeast	Central Pattaya (Jan.), Central Udon (Apr.), Central Chonburi (May), Central Khonkaen (Dec.)
2011	North, Bangkok	Central Chiangrai (Mar.), Central Phitsanulok (Oct.), Central Rama 9
2012	South, North	Central Suratthani (Oct.), Central Lampang (Nov.)
2013	North, Northeast, South	Central Ubon (Apr.), Central Chiangmai (Nov.), Central Hatyai (Dec.)
2014	South	Central Samui (Mar.), Central Salaya (Aug.)
2014	Vietnam	Robinson department store
2014	Indonesia	Central department store
2015	Eastern, South, Bangkok	Central Rayong (May), Central Phuket (Jun.), Central Westgate (Aug.), Central Eastville (Nov.)
2016	South	Central Nakhon Si (July)
2017	Northeast	Central Korat (Nov.), Central Mahachai (Nov.)
2019	Bangkok	Central i-City (Mar.), Central Village (Aug.)
2021	Eastern, Central	Central Si Racha (Oct.), Central Ayutthaya (Nov.)
2022	Eastern	Central Chonburi
Central in Europe		
2011	Italy	La Rinascente
2013	Denmark	Illum
2015	Germany	KaDeWe (Berlin), Alsterhaus (Humbrug), Oberpollinger (Munich)
2020	Switzerland	Globus, Switzerland
2022	UK	Selfridges & Co.

Sources: Author's compilation based on the Central Pattana annual report 2021 and various newspaper

Notes

(1) Information is limited to Central Plaza, which was constructed and refurbished by Central Pattana PLC (real estate development) and Central Retail Corporation PLC (CRC), excluding Central Department Store and Robinson Department Store.

(2) Target customers include not only Thais but also neighbouring countries such as Myanmar, Laos, Cambodia, Malaysia, Vietnam, as well as Chinese tourists.

Table 9.7 Central Group of Companies (CGC) CEO Management Board, 2013

No.	*Name*	*Family relationships*	*Positions*	*Group in-charge sector*
1	Sudhitham	Tiang's 8th son	Chairman	Take whole-group responsibility, director of CENTEL
2	Suthilaksh	Tiang's 11th son	Executive Director	Strategic management and organizational structure of the group
3	Prin	Samrit's 5th son	Executive Director	Finance
4	Tos	Samrit's 6th son	Executive Director	CEO of CRC (Central Retail Corporation Ltd.), retail and department stores
5	Kobchai	Wanchai's 2nd son	Executive Director	CEO of CPN (Central Pattana PLC), real estate development
6	Pichai	Wanchai's 4th son	Executive Director	CEO of CMG, trading and management
7	Thiradej	Suthikiat's 1st son	Executive Director	CEO of CRG (Central Restaurants Group), restaurant management
8	Thirayuth	Suthikiat's 2nd son	Executive Director	CEO of CHR (Central Hotels and Resorts), hotels and resorts

Source: www.centralgroup.com/ceoManagementBoard.html (accessed 26 October 2013)

Notes

(1) Tiang was the founder of Central group. Samrit was Tiang's oldest son. Wanchai was Tiang's second son. Suthikiat was Tiang's fourth son.
(2) All management board are members of the Chirathivat family.

open branches in China due to inability to compete with domestic rivals, it still seeks to tackle Chinese online markets through a Chinese-language version of a website, Aux Villes du Monde, and partnership with JD.com, a Chinese competitor of Alibaba, a multinational technology company specializing in e-commerce, retail, Internet, and technology. After leaving China 90 years ago, the Chirathivat family is returning to its ethnic roots to court future progress.

Previously, family members occupied all 15 board and 7 executive seats, making Central one of Thailand's most family-dominated conglomerates. In 2013, Tos Chirathivat, Samrit's youngest son, became chief executive officer (CEO). In 2016, the group began recruiting non-family executives into top management roles, for the first time creating an outsider-dominated team. Nicolo Galante, a former McKinsey consultant who overhauled online operations and established new marketing channels for European retailers, was appointed group chief operating officer (COO). Edwin Yap Hawson, a former Johnson & Johnson (J&J) China and IHG (Intercontinental Hotel Group) executive, was named president of the Central Marketing Group. Yol Phokasub, former head of Siam Commercial Bank

Table 9.8 Central Group of Companies (CGC) CEO Management Board, 2022

No.	*Name*	*Family relationships*	*Positions*
Executive committee			
1	Tos Chirathivat	Samrit's 6th son	Executive Chairman and CEO Central Group
2	Prin Chirathivat	Samrit's 5th son	Executive Director and Deputy Group CEO
3	Dr. Suthiphand Chirathivat	Tiang's 10th son	Executive Director
4	Suthilaksh Chirathivat	Tiang's 11th son	Executive Director
5	Narongrit Chirathivat	Suthipong's 1st son	Executive Director
6	Pichai Chirathivat	Wanchai's 4th son	Executive Director
7	Thiradej Chirathivat	Suthikiati's 1st son	Executive Director
Management team			
8	Pandit Mongkolkun		Co-Group CFO Central Group
9	Wallaya Chirathivat		CEO of Central Pattana
10	Thirayuth Chirathivat		CEO of Centara Hotels & Resorts
11	Yol Phokasub		CEO Central Retail
12	Ty Chirathivat		CFO Central Retail
13	Oliver Langlet		CEO Central Retail Vietnam
14	Stefano Della Valle		CEO Central Group Europe

Source: www.centralgroup.com/en/management (accessed November 4, 2022)

Notes

(1) Tiang was the founder of Central group. Samrit was Tiang's oldest son. Wanchai was Tiang's second son. Suthipong was Tiang's third son. Suthikiat was Tiang's fourth son.
(2) The Central group started to employ non-family professional managers, including foreigners.

(SCB), was hired as CEO of Central Retail Corporation (CRC), listed in 2020. Prasarn Trairatvorakul, former governor of the Bank of Thailand, is a senior advisor. The group has engaged diverse experts and foreign executives under the leadership of Tos. Using only insiders may have constrained group developmental capacity.

Central Group serves as a model for creating comprehensive family constitutions, councils, and offices. The Chirathivat family is ardently dedicated to transmitting their businesses to future generations (Endo, 2013). In the context of a changing retail market today, transitioning from a third to fourth generation, they might be confronting the so-called "Buddenbrooks Syndrome," cited by business historians (Rose, 1995) to explain an inability of family firms to survive beyond the third generation. It remains possible, if unlikely, for a Thai retail giant to conquer the global retail market if a family business can transform into a managerial enterprise through digital technology and market competition.

9.4.2 *Overseas earnings*

Thai business groups divide revenue streams into three sources: local, export, and international. They have begun to express a wish for increased foreign revenue, with decreased home revenue. For instance, domestic income for Charoen Pokphand Foods (CPF) accounted for 68 percent of total income in 2008, while exports and overseas projects accounted for 16 percent (see Figure 9.4). In late 2012, exports fell with foreign income exceeding domestic revenue. By 2022, foreign income accounted for 68 percent of overall revenue, inverting the 2008 ratio. The case of Siam Cement Group/SCG also revealed a phenomenon of actively investing in foreign countries, particularly ASEAN (see Figure 9.5 and Table 9.9).

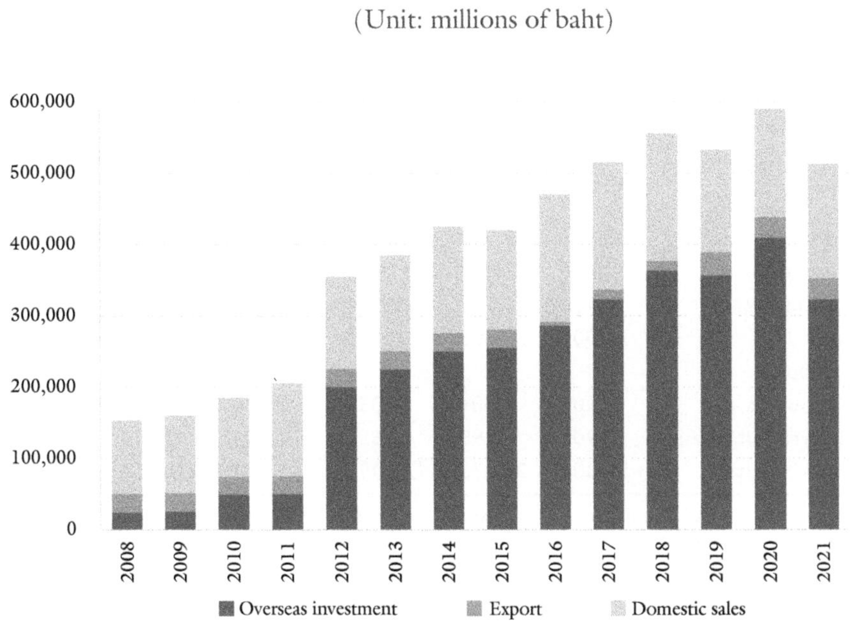

Figure 9.4 Overseas earnings of the CPF, 2008–2021

Sources: Author's compilation from the annual reports of Charoen Pokphand Foods PLC., various years

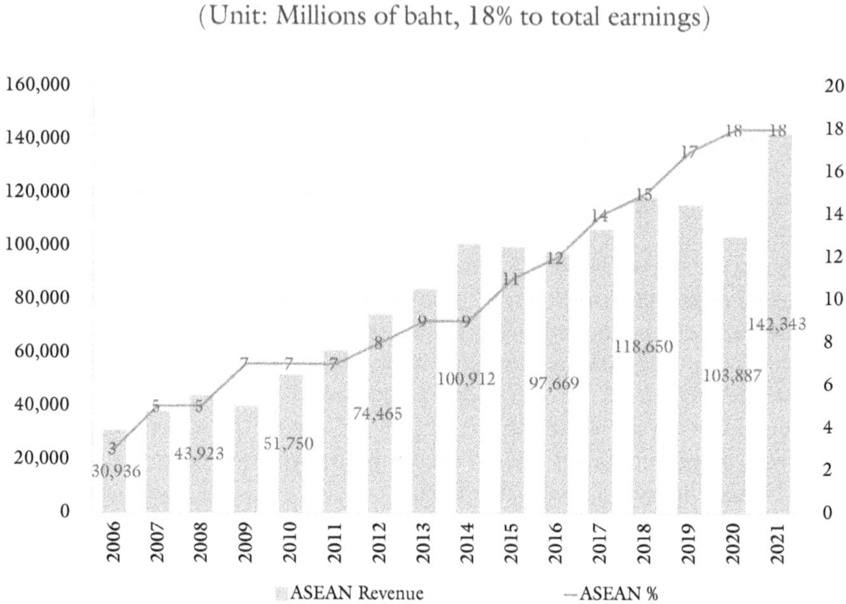

Figure 9.5 Overseas earnings of the SCG, 2006–2021

Sources: Author's compilation from the annual reports of SCG PLC., various years

Table 9.9 SCG regional operation and ASEAN: Assets

Country	*2012*	*2014*	*2016*	*2018*	*2020*	*2021*
Indonesia	30,100	39,303	50,253	51,580	36,093	120,354
Vietnam	12,600	22,662	33,780	67,893	144,247	215,054
Myanmar	100	6,521	12,700	11,134	10,590	–
Laos	4,000	8,686	10,358	11,499	11,281	11,352
Cambodia			11,280	11,299	12,278	15,087
Philippines	7,600	7,004	7,032	7,805	11,652	12,937
Malaysia/Singapore	900	699	652	2,101	2,313	8,944
ASEAN Total	55,300	84,875	126,055	163,311	228,454	383,728

Sources: Author's compilation from the annual reports of Siam Cement Group, various years (Unit: million of baht)

9.5 Foreign strategic alliances

9.5.1 *Alliance with Japan and the West*

Thai business groups have traditionally formed joint ventures with foreign partners, especially Japan and the West, when seeking expansion into new areas. But as a result of the Asian financial crisis and the early 1990s prolonged recession in Japan, China simultaneously became the benchmark for low-cost production and upgraded its managerial and technological capabilities across a broad range of industries. In terms of labour-intensive industries, Thailand was priced out of the market and unable to compete with China's drive into capital- and technology-intensive operations.

But most Thai businesses appear to view China as a strategic ally, not a competitor. Thai businesses remain optimistic about the Chinese market as China expands its investment in tourist sectors and public and private Thai-Chinese joint ventures expand. Thailand's business leaders believe that by forging strategic alliances with Chinese companies and reengineering their growth strategies, domestic value added can be boosted and market reach broadened for sophisticated manufacturing goods.

Due to a reluctance of Thai-Japanese or Western joint ventures to transfer technology to Thai companies, many multinational corporations (MNCs) have historically failed to develop R&D facilities in Thailand, despite Thai government efforts. MNCs often cite a scarcity of highly qualified employees as an excuse, and that knowledge spillovers have never worked in Thailand due to supply constraints. An absence of major indigenous high-tech companies and reliance on MNCs for technology and market access has impeded Thailand's productivity growth.

However, Thai-Chinese strategic alliances have transferred technology to local partners, including in the electric auto, tire, biotechnology, finance, and insurance industries (as discussed in Chapter 7). For the first time, Thai companies will be permitted to create their own manufacturing base. If these initiatives succeed, the Thailand 4.0 policy anticipates moving into technologically intensive manufacturing and setting new productivity standards by stressing digital technology.

9.5.2 *Thai-Chinese alliance*

Table 9.10 details joint investments and strategic alliances between Thai and Chinese companies between 2007 and 2022. These public and private connections are growing in number and broadening across business sectors.

The Chearavanont family's CP Group made an unprecedented contribution as primary conduit for Chinese investment in the EEC. Their commercial interests diversified beyond agriculture to include vehicle assembly, information communication, online commerce, real estate development, industrial park construction, and life insurance. The CP Group will apparently continue to play a crucial role in establishing strong business connections with China (Suehiro, 2017).

For instance, in 2012 SAIC-CP was established as a joint venture between CP and Shanghai Automotive Industry Corporation (SAIC). SAIC is the seventh largest automobile manufacturer in the world and the second largest in China. The company produces and distributes passenger cars in Thailand and internationally under the MG brand, acquired from England. In the real estate

Table 9.10 Thai-Chinese strategic alliances, 2007–2022

Type of Business	*Year/Month*		*Country*	*Thai firm*	*Chinese firm*
(1) Energy, natural resources					
Atomic power plant	Oct. 2007	Tech. assistance	Thailand	EGCO	CLP Power, Cantong
Undersea oil	Feb. 2008	Alliance	Myanmar	PTT Group	CNOOC (SE)
Biomass	May 2010	Joint venture	China	Mitr Phol Sugar	Funan Sugar
Solar power plant	May 2014	Construction	Thailand	EGAT	Consosium
Energy	Jan. 2017	MOU	Thailand	B.Grimm	CEEC
Energy	Mar. 2018	EPC Contract	Thailand	PTT Group	Sinopec
(2) Automobiles, tyre					
Compact car	Jan. 2009	Joint venture	Thailand	CP Group	Chery Auto
Tyre	Dec. 2010	Joint venture	Thailand	Thai Hua Rubber	Hangzhou Rubber
Automobile	Dec. 2014	Joint venture	Thailand	CP Group	SAIC Motor
Automobile	Sep. 2022	Investment	Thailand	Rever Automotive	BYD
(3) Information communications technology					
Home appliance	Apr. 2007	Acquisition	Thailand	Sanyo Universal	Hier
Communications	Dec. 2013	Planning	Thailand		Baidu
Communications	July 2014	Alliance	Thailand	CP Group	China Mobile
Communications	Oct. 2019	MOU	Thailand	Ministry of Digital	Huawei, Alibaba, JD.com
(4) Property development, industrial estates					
Industrial estate	Mar. 2011	Joint venture	Thailand	Amata Corporation	Holy Group
Property business	Apr. 2013	Joint venture	Thailand	CP Group	Greenland (Shanghai)
Property business	Jan. 2015	Investment	China	CP Group	CITIC
Industrial estate	Aug. 2018	Joint venture	Thailand	CP Land	Guangxi Construction
(5) Banking, insurance					
Banking	Jan. 2010	Alliance	China/ Thailand	Kasikorn Bank	China Minsheng Banking Corp.
Banking	Mar. 2011	Alliance	China/ Thailand	Bangkok Bank	ICBC
Life insurance	Dec. 2012	Investment	China	CP Group	Ping An Insurance
Finance	Feb. 2018	Investment	Thailand	CT Bright (CP)	HNA Innovation

Source: Compiled by the author based on Akira Suehiro (2017) for 2007–2015 and various newspapers

sector, CP Land teamed with Guangxi Construction Engineering Group to establish a 3,068-rai (490.5-hectare) industrial park in Bankhai, Rayong, targeted at Chinese investors.

CP-backed True Corporation PLC is collaborating with Huawei Technologies Co., Ltd. to establish an Internet of things (IoT) laboratory and recently became Thailand's first 4G operator using Huawei equipment. While the United States seeks allies in prohibiting Huawei from developing 5G networks, the company is investing in Thailand's first 5G testbed. In addition, CP has a joint venture with Jack Ma's Ant Group, which has a 20 percent stake in Ascend Group, a Thai electronic wallet and microloan startup. The deal, not part of the EEC, uses CP's 7-Eleven convenience store network.[10]

In 2016, Foton Motor Group and Bangchan General Assembly Co., Ltd. launched a joint venture to manufacture pickup vehicles for consumers in Thailand and abroad. Thai Hua Rubber, the nation's second largest supplier of natural rubber, and Chinese tire manufacturer Qin Hua Rubber Co., Ltd. have created a joint venture to manufacture passenger vehicle and light truck (PVLT) tires.

If these projects are realized, for the first time, Thai enterprises will establish a manufacturing base in the automobile sector. This approach to core manufacturing industry innovation differs from typical strategies to entice Japanese and Western MNC R&D departments to Thailand. As latecomers to technology, Chinese companies are eager to share cutting-edge innovation with local partners in developing nations.

Consequently, even if Japan and the United States express reservations about joining the EEC, China will continue to promote the BRI and use AIIB and China Development Bank financing. The EEC will not need to reinvent itself if Chinese tech titans such as Alibaba and Huawei[11] actively engage in creating a digital economy as EEC cornerstone. Accordingly, the EEC's future direction depends on the world economic order and environment imposed by China's Southward Movement, with Thailand serving as a significant test case for ASEAN national development.

Although Thailand benefits significantly from Chinese trade and investment, Thai citizens continue to harbour misgivings about China. The Sino-Thai high-speed railway project connecting Vientiane (Laos), Nong Khai, and Bangkok exemplifies this discord. In December 2021, Laos opened the US$6 billion Boten–Vientiane railway, but in Thailand, the corresponding project has stalled due to concern about widening trade imbalances with China, a flood of cheap Chinese goods and immigrants, a possible debt trap, and what is seen as a potential new threat of colonialism due to Sino-Thai investment policies (Lauridsen, 2020).

Thailand may not completely benefit from the so-called China model since it may potentially erode the stability of Thai small- and mid-size enterprises (SMEs). China's investment approach includes importing Chinese staff at all levels, from supervisors and plant managers to general workers. The theory is that other domestic employees and suppliers are unable to compete. Chinese exports can be sold at a discount on the global market due to government subsidies and bulk manufacturing.

Thailand is also apprehensive that Chinese investment in Thailand helped avert a US-China trade war by substituting Thailand for China as an industrial export base. But the United States and its trade partners are boosting anti-dumping and countervailing tariffs (CVD) to cut subsidies and have sanctioned China for its low-cost manufacturing in Thailand. This is detrimental to other Thai exports to the United States.

Thailand has a long history of positive interactions with international superpowers such as the United States, China, and Japan, all of which seek to expand their sphere of influence in Southeast Asia. With these three adversaries, Thailand has sought a middle ground while also trying to lead the area in post-World War II conflict resolution and economic prosperity. The EEC project fits into the jigsaw puzzle of Thai strategy, associated with ambitious expectations of collaboration with China, which boosts its regional influence through expanded technological and economic capacity.

In summary, since the 2010s, domestic growth rates have remained low due to a reliance on low-value-added exports and energy, intermediate product, and machinery import. It is still impossible to shift to higher-value-added exports. As a result, Thailand has been forced to increase its reliance on tourism and services (Makohin et al., 2020). Businesses are making it more difficult for people to earn money by working at home, and most Thais believe that their life is not improving.

Many Thai businesses invest in the fast-growing ASEAN region as Thai business leaders earn exorbitant sums due to special state economic assistance. However, Thai business group relocation to other countries is a time-honoured option for escaping the middle-income trap by diversifying markets, investing overseas, and establishing new business partners, especially China, to compensate for a sluggish home market, rising wages, and an aging population.

Notes

1 The *East Asian miracle: Economic growth and public policy* (1993), a study completed by the World Bank, reported that East Asia has a remarkable record of high and sustained economic growth. From 1965 to 1990, its 23 economies grew faster than those of all other regions. Most of this achievement is attributable to seemingly miraculous growth in just eight high performing Asian economies (HPASs) – Japan; the four Asian tigers (Hong Kong, the Republic of Korea, Singapore, and Taiwan); and the three newly industrializing economies (NIEs) of Southeast Asia, Indonesia, Malaysia, and Thailand.

2 For example, the Phornprapha family's Siam Motors joint venture with Nissan Motor and the Leeissaranukul family's MMC Sitthipol joint venture with Mitsubishi Motors. Both families exited the automobile assembly sector and subsequently departed from lists of 50 wealthiest families in Thailand. Despite aspirations to build Thailand's first national car, the Siam Cement Group (SCG) also was forced to abandon the industry in the aftermath of the Asian financial crisis.

3 Over 15 phases of the promotional ladder are accessible at CP ALL, according to an interview by the author with executives of CP ALL PLC. A corporate "treadmill for talent" has been planned to reward good performance trimestrially to sustain employee motivation more intensely than average company annual performance reviews (Wailerdsak, 2020).
4 Interview by the author with executives of Bamrungrat Hospital on 2 September 2021.
5 Asian trailblazers are first- and second-tier Asian multinational corporations (MNCs) (Willis Towers Watson, 2016).
6 In 2013, the SET (excluding the MAI market) actively added 23 new firms, with 13 continuing to operate normally. Seven others were real estate funds, and the remaining three infrastructure funds (Suehiro, 2017, p. 59).
7 Interview by the author with an executive of WHA Corporation PLC on 28 May 2021.
8 Interestingly, the ASEAN is a prolific producer of unicorns, ranking behind only the United States, China, and India. ASEAN unicorns increased from 2 in 2014 to 10 in 2018 and 46 in 2021. Depending on market conditions, the region's expanding digital economy might yield other unicorns over the next few years. The majority of ASEAN unicorns (38 of 46) invest internationally in a variety of nations within the region and beyond. Twenty-eight unicorns have grown internationally via FDI, 16 via cross-border M&As, and 33 via joint ventures, strategic alliances, or partnerships with foreign MNCs or startups. Unicorns in the region acquire strategic assets (technology) to complement existing businesses or to diversify into new business areas (ASEAN Secretariat, 2022).
9 Interview by the author with an executive of Central Group on 1 June 2020.
10 Interview by the author with an executive of True Corporation PLC on 18 May 2021.
11 In March 2021, the Huawei ASEAN Academy (Thailand) EEC branch opened in Chonburi, representing a new model of Chinese-Thai digital economy cooperation. The EEC plans to offer digital development courses with a goal of training 6,000 students and IT-related professionals by 2021 and 30,000 by 2024, respectively.

Reference list

ASEAN Secretariat. (2022, August). *ASEAN investment report 2022 – Pandemic recovery and investment facilitation*. ASEAN Secretariat.

Bunkanwanicha, P., & Wiwattanakantang, Y. (2009). Big business owners in politics. *The Review of Financial Studies*, *22*(6), 2133–2168.

Carney, M., Duran, P., van Essen, M., & Shapiro, D. (2017). Family firms, internationalization, and national competitiveness: Does family firm prevalence matter? *Journal of Family Business Strategy*, *8*(3), 123–136.

Endo, G. (2013). *Diversifying retail and distribution in Thailand*. Silkworm Books.

Endo, T., & Oizumi, K. (2020). Urbanizing Asia: Cities transforming into mega-regions. In K. Goto, T. Endo, & A. Ito (Eds.), *The Asian economy: Contemporary issues and challenges* (Chapter 8, pp. 147–168). Routledge.

Fang, H., Kotlar, J., Memili, E., Chrisman, J. J., & Massis, D. (2018). The pursuit of international opportunities in family firms: Generational differences and the role of knowledge-based resources. *Global Strategy Journal*, *8*(1), 136–157.

Hamilton-Hart, N., & Yeung, H. W. (2021). Institutions under pressure: East Asian states, global markets and national firms. *Review of International Political Economy*, *28*(1), 11–35.

Hewison, K. (2010). Thaksin Shinawatra and the reshaping of Thai politics. *Contemporary Politics*, *16*(2), 119–133.

Jongwanich, J., Brooks, D. H., & Kohpaiboon, A. (2013). Cross-border mergers and acquisitions and financial development: Evidence from emerging Asia. *Asian Economic Journal*, *27*(3), 265–284.

Laovakul, D. (2016). Concentration of land and other wealth in Thailand. In P. Phongpaichit & C. Baker (Eds.), *Unequal Thailand: Aspects of income, wealth, and power* (Chapter 2, pp. 32–42). National University of Singapore Press.

Lauridsen, L. S. (2020). Drivers of China's regional infrastructure diplomacy: The case of the Sino-Thai railway project. *Journal of Contemporary Asia*, *50*(3), 380–406.

Lebedev, S., Peng, M. W., Xie, E., & Stevens, C. E. (2015). Mergers and acquisitions in and out of emerging economies. *Journal of World Business*, *50*, 651–662.

Lee, C., & Sermcheep, S. (2017). *Outward foreign direct investment in ASEAN*. Cambridge University Press.

Li, D., & Zhang, Y. (2021). Compressed development of outward foreign direct investment: New challenges to the Chinese government. *Journal of Asian and African Studies*, *56*(2), 335–351.

Lin, W. T., & Wang, L. C. (2021). Family firms, R&D, and internationalization: The stewardship and socio-emotional wealth perspectives. *Asia Pacific Journal of Management*, *38*(1), 91–119.

Makohin, Z., Atamanchuk, Z., & Mitiushkina, K. (2020). The role of tourism in escaping the middle-income trap. *Management Theory and Studies for Rural Business and Infrastructure Development*, *42*(3), 295–302.

Moeller, J. (2021). *Asia's transformation: From economic globalization to regionalization*. ISEAS – Yusof Ishak Institute.

Nikomborirak, D. (2021). Thailand's policy challenges. *Asian Economic Policy Review*, *15*, 284–300.

Ono, Y. (2017, September 18–24). Outsiders in: To tackle e-commerce Thailand's Central Group look beyond the family circle for management talent. *Nikkei Asian Review*.

Pananond, P. (2011). The global value chains of Thai multinationals: Evidence from listed firms in Thailand. *Economics, Management, and Financial markets*, *6*(1), 98–141.

Peng, M. W., Lebedev, S., Vlas, C. O., Wang, J. C., & Shay, J. S. (2018). The growth of the firm in (and out of) emerging economies. *Asia Pacific Journal of Management*, *35*(4), 829–857.

Penrose, E. T. (1959) *The theory of the growth of the firm*. John Wiley & Sons.

Phongpaichit, P., & Baker, C. (1996). *Thailand: Economy and politics*. Oxford University Press.

Phongpaichit, P., & Baker, C. (1998). *Thailand's boom and bust: Revised edition*. Silkworm Books.

Pomchokchai, S. (2014). *An analysis of land prices in Bangkok, 1994–2013*. Agency for Real Estate Affairs, Thailand.

Rompho, N., Boon-Itt, S., & Vinayavekhin, S. (2021). Business start-up survey for the healthcare industry in Thailand. In S. Teerakapibal, N. Rompho, A. Tanvisuth, & O. Komazawa (Eds.), *Population ageing in Thailand: Business opportunities in the era of population ageing*, Vol. 4 (Chapter 2, pp. 12–28). ERIA Research Project Report FY2021 No. 06d.

Rose, M. B. (1995). *Family business.* Edward Elgar.

Suehiro, A. (2008). *Catch-up industrialization: The trajectory and prospects of East Asian economies.* National University of Singapore Press.

Suehiro, A. (2014). *Shinkou ajia keizai-ron: Kyacchi-appu wo koete (Newly emerging Asian economies: Beyond the catch-up industrialization approach).* Iwanami (In Japanese).

Suehiro, A. (2017). New growth strategies of Thailand's big firms in the ASEAN economic community era. In K. B. Teik, K. Tsunekawa, & M. Kawano (Eds.), *Southeast Asia beyond crisis and traps: Economic growth and upgrading* (Chapter 2, pp. 35–70). Palgrave Macmillan.

United Nations Conference on Trade and Development. (various years). *World investment report.* UNCTAC.

Wailerdsak, N. (2006). *Klumthun turakit krubkruathai koon lae lang wikrit pii 2540 (Thai family-owned business groups before and after the 1997 crisis).* BrandAge Books (In Thai).

Wailerdsak, N. (2008). Companies in crisis. In P. Phongpaichit & C. Baker (Eds.), *Thai capital after the 1997 crisis* (Chapter 1, pp. 17–57). Silkworm Books.

Wailerdsak, N. (2013). Impacts of the ASEAN (Association of South East Asian Nations) Economic Community on labour market and human resource management in Thailand. *South East Asia Journal of Contemporary Business, Economics and Law,* *2*(2), 1–10.

Wailerdsak, N. (2020). *Kanborihaan daoden lae senthang suu phuuborihaan radabsuung nai mitithang settasad (Talent management and paths to the top in economic dimension).* Institute for Continuing Education and Human Resources, Thammasat University (In Thai).

Willis Towers Watson. (2016). *2016 Asian trailblazers study: Masters of multitasking and transformation.* www.wtwco.com

World Bank. (1993). *East Asian miracle: Economic growth and public policy.* The World Bank Group.

Chapter 10

Family business trap

10.1 Tunnelling and expropriation of minority shareholders

Until now, there are several theoretical perspectives on business group development: institutional theory, market failure theory, transaction cost theory, resource-based theory, social capital theory, and principal-principal agency theory (Dela Rama, 2012; Djankov et al., 2008; Guillén, 2000; Hu & Sun, 2019; La Porta et al., 2000; Peng et al., 2018; Peng & Sauerwald, 2013; Young et al., 2008).

Institutional theory asserts that highly diversified business groups create value by compensating for inefficient national capital, labour, and product markets.

Market failure theory, in accordance with institutional theory, asserts that external markets might collapse due to inefficient market mechanisms, legal impediments, and lack of trust.

Transaction cost theory argues that internal business transactions lower transaction costs by eliminating costs associated with contracts, negotiations, and contract enforcements.

Resource-based theory claims that group-affiliated firms have opportunities to acquire and accumulate valuable resources, such as trained employees, and skills related to industry entry, management, and exports, giving them resource advantages over non-affiliated firms.

Social capital theory proposes that intra-firm networks such as group companies constitute social capital facilitating value creation.

Principal-principal (PP) agency theory argues that PP conflicts are a major concern of corporate governance in emerging economies, rather than traditional principal – agent (PA) conflicts. PP conflicts between controlling and minority shareholders result from concentrated ownership, extensive family ownership and control, business group structures, and weak legal minority shareholder protections.[2]

The 1997 Asian financial crisis exposed many instances of looting of firms by controlling shareholders. International researchers examined

DOI: 10.4324/9781003370536-14

family-owned and managed business groups. Two major factors triggered the crisis:

- Tunnelling conduct, which involves removing assets through an underground tunnel from companies, syphoning profits to avoid creditors, and using loan guarantees by other listed group members to bolster troubled firms in the group.
- Expropriating minority shareholders to benefit controlling shareholders.

Tunnelling refers to the transfer of resources from a firm to its controlling shareholder (usually also top management).[3] It has two forms: firstly, a controlling shareholder might self-deal through transactions, diverting resources from the firm for personal profit. Such transactions include outright theft or fraud, universally considered illegal although often undetected and unpunished. Other techniques include asset sales and contracts such as transfer pricing favouring the controlling shareholder, transfer of assets from a firm to its controlling shareholder at nonmarket prices, excessive executive compensation, loan guarantees using firm assets as collateral, and expropriation of corporate opportunities (Johnson et al., 2000; Hu & Sun, 2019; Purkayastha & Gupta, 2022; Wangwan & Leemakdej, 2022).

Secondly, controlling shareholders may increase their share of the firm without transferring assets through dilutive share issues (as the number of shares issued increases, share prices decrease), minority freeze-outs, insider trading, creeping acquisitions, or other financial transactions discriminating against minorities.

This occurs frequently in countries with inadequate law enforcement protection for minority shareholders and creditors. Due to excessive tunnelling, substantial resources are lost due to incapacities in legal systems. Reducing tunnelling by legal reform becomes a critical component for boosting financial and economic development (Claessens & Fan, 2002; Johnson et al., 2000).

After the Asian financial crisis, listed companies were required to follow Good Corporate Governance Principles. New corporate governance regulations, including establishment of audit, nominating, and compensation committees as well as independent directors were intended to increase security and diminish the prominence of family ownership and management. Yet the opposite has occurred. In Thailand, FBGs continue to rely on concentrated ownership through holding companies, cross shareholdings, and interlocking directorates. Independent directors and subcommittees are closely related to major shareholders (Khanthavit et al., 2004; Bunkanwanicha & Wiwattanakantang, 2008; Nikomborirak, 2004; Wailerdsak, 2008a; Wangwan & Leemakdej, 2022).

Insider trading revelations about well-known shareholders or senior executives of listed companies are commonplace, even those consistently awarded for complying with international norms for corporate governance standards. For instance, in December 2015, Thailand's Security and Exchange Commission (SEC) fined Korsak Chairasmisak and other CP ALL management team members for using insider information to purchase Siam Makro shares during negotiations with SHV Netherland B.V., which formerly held them. After the acquisition deal was signed, the CP ALL management team benefitted from the sale of shares.

In April 2022, Kraisorn Chansiri, founder and chairman of Thailand-based Thai Union, one of the world's largest seafood companies, resigned after being sanctioned for alleged insider trading. Nine shareholders were accused of insider trading between October and November 2017, before the company announced a large increase in profits for the third quarter of 2017. Kraisorn and others bought Thai Union stock in anticipation of the profit boost. They also passed the insider information along to family members and others who purchased Thai Union shares.

On a regular basis, the SET enables family companies to seek funds from the public. Large shareholders and management purposefully cheated on loans, filed for bankruptcy, and removed the company from the market, significantly impacting creditors and minority shareholders. Among these firms in 2021–2022 were Energy Earth controlled by the Phihakendr family, Polaris Capital controlled by the Nanavaratorn family, and Inter Far East Energy Corporation controlled by the Techanawakul family.

10.2 No separation of ownership and control – interlocking directorates

According to business history research, transition from family capitalism to managerial capitalism required mass production, marketing, and transportation, as family businesses cede to modern enterprises run by managerial specialists. This transformation was termed a managerial revolution by Alfred D. Chandler Jr. (Chandler, 1977, 1990). This is consistent with Berle and Means' proposal (1932) for separating ownership and control, or emergence of widely held corporations.

Later, Useem (1984) condemned family capitalism as an anti-industrial culture, insofar as its inner circle (groups supported and selected by family networks) exploit firms to accumulate family wealth rather than company wealth, as opposed to firms controlled by professional managers who receive salaries and bonuses. As firm scales expand, control over day-to-day operations and final decision-making is transferred from founding families to professional managers. The advent of professional managers and formation of complex occupational stratification marks a new threshold of managerial enterprise.

By contrast, studies conducted in the late 1990s (La Porta et al., 1999; Faccio & Lang, 1999) suggested that managerial enterprises that are widely held corporations are exceptional in the United States, the United Kingdom, and Japan. In Europe, Latin America, and Asia, most listed companies remain family-owned and managed.

In addition, economic history indicates that large, highly diversified FBGs contributed much to rapid Asian catch-up industrialization. FBGs can make decisions more quickly than joint-stock companies, with diversification leading to economies with scale and scope, and a network of affiliated enterprises helped contend with pervasive "network externality" issues (Chung, 2013; Chung & Chan, 2012; Liebowitz & Margolis, 1994).[4] While capital markets are still developing, FBGs can redistribute capital from profitable firms to support expansion and high-value-added projects. Therefore, tycoons and dynasties dominating these groups had some cause to depict themselves as nation-builders in addition to their personal acquisitiveness (Dela Rama, 2012; Kock & Guillén, 2001).

However, recent research (Dau et al., 2020, 2021a, 2021b) posits that business group tasks are complete after they build a network of firms, each generating positive network externalities for others. In economies rising to high-income levels, business group governance cedes to corporation governance. To transition from catch-up to high-income growth, business group governance must be abandoned in favour of corporate governance. High-income economies thrive from creative destruction. Innovative firms create breakthrough technologies that obliterate or disrupt legacy firms while elevating economy-wide productivity.

Dismantling business groups is one way to switch engines and reignite growth by creative destruction. As part of the New Deal, the US disbanded business groups, ushering in an unprecedented age of trade barriers and state intervention. The 1933 Glass-Steagall Act separated commercial and investment banking activities, splitting the industry leader J.P. Morgan & Co.'s commercial banking and securities activities into the investment bank Morgan Stanley and commercial bank JP Morgan. The Public Utilities Holding Companies Act of 1933 barred the operation of excessively large business groups in the public utility sector. Successive Income Tax Acts imposed and enhanced intercorporate dividend levies, sanctioning firms that owned shares in other firms. The 1940 Investment Companies Act regulated the organization of companies, including mutual funds, engaging primarily in investing, reinvesting, and trading securities, and whose own securities are offered to the investing public (Collis et al., 2018; Hamdani et al., 2020).

This approach to diminishing business groups considered inordinately large and market dominating was internationalized in Japan by the post-war US military government. Zaibatsu, a Japanese term meaning wealthy clique, were large capitalist enterprises of Japan before World War II, similar to cartels or trusts but usually organized around a single family. They helped construct the first Asian industrial economy in the 1920s. From 1945 to 1952, Japan was a US military protectorate, and some American bureaucrats, with experience in gradually disbanding US cartels, attempted a comparable societal reform in post-war Japan. By the US withdrawal in 1952, zaibatsu had evolved into self-contained firms, widely held and professionally managed, comparable to the United States (Hamdani et al., 2020; Wailerdsak, 2004b). Legislative reforms of business groups occurred in a context of public outrage at abuses by business elites. Such approaches may be unworkable in countries where business lobbying remains influential (Collis et al., 2018; Morck & Nakamura, 2007; Morck & Yeung, 2018).

In Thailand, ownership and control are separated in a handful of state enterprises with the Ministry of Finance as principal shareholder and Crown Property Bureau–owned firms.[5] Almost all large companies may be traced back to closely held firms (Khanthavit et al., 2004). Small stock markets controlled by legacy firms have potential to restrict access by new rivals to finance and retain controlling blocks within legacy business groups, including banks. Industrial policies prioritizing access to subsidies and regulatory favours have reenergized business groups. A regional embrace of import substitution has limited local startup access to foreign business partners and capital, reinforcing legacy firm ability to block disruptive innovators (Nikomborirak, 2004; Wailerdsak & Suehiro, 2010).

Some economists believed that enhancing economic openness through economic integration, bilateral and multilateral trade, and capital barrier reductions may encourage innovation-led growth by reducing the power of domestic legacy firms (and business groups) to stymie incumbents. Comparing the TCC and Osotspa groups, a generational shift and acquiescence by owner families may also help diffuse ownership concentration.

10.2.1 TCC group of the Sirivadhanabhakdi family

Notably, in Thailand, FBG tycoons tend to be polygamous in terms of personal relationships, resulting in unusually large families. For example, the founder of Central Department Store fathered 14 sons and 12 daughters with three wives. Of an extended family of 220 offspring, about 50 are involved in the business. Due to lack of primogeniture norms in contemporary Chinese families, the most talented member of any generation (whether eldest son, daughter, or in-law) is awarded leadership roles in groups. In this way, Thai Chinese families have access to a wide choice of executive talent through kinship and affinity (Wailerdsak, 2020a, 2021).

There are many examples of FBG owner sons, daughter, or sons-in-law succeeding in businesses unrelated to the main family firm. The TCC group depicted in Figure 10.1 is an example of how first to second generational transfer tends to foster business diversification within FBGs.

10.2.2 Osotspa group of the Osathanugrah family

The Premier group descends from Pe Osathanugrah, who started Osotspa (Teck Heng Yoo) Co., Ltd. in 1930 as an importer and distributor of medical Chinese herbs. After World War II, the firm moved into manufacturing and sales of Western pharmaceuticals as the result of a technological partnership

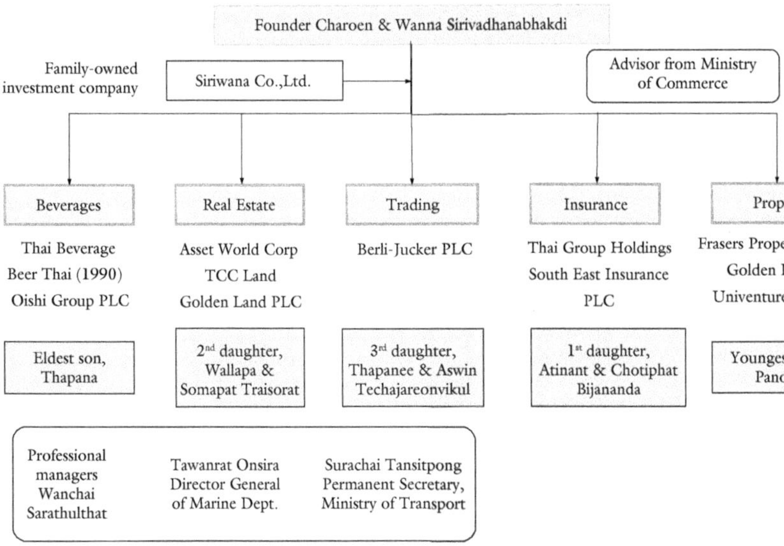

Figure 10.1 **Business diversification of the TCC/Thai Bev group**

Source: Author's compilation from the annual reports in 2021 of publicly traded TCC group firms and Akira Suehiro's database

with Japan's Taisho Pharmaceutical Co., Ltd. to produce a vitamin elixir. This enterprise laid the groundwork for the subsequent handover of the Osotspa group to the founder's son, Sawat.

The group began diversifying into leasing, banking, real estate, and export-oriented manufacturing during the third generation of Sawat's sons and daughters (processed food, sport shoes, luggage, shrimp, and personal and healthcare products). While maintaining primary businesses in pharmaceuticals (including the M-150 energy drinks and non-alcoholic beverages), this new generation of owner/managers focused on investing in Thailand's emerging sectors. As seen in the business diversification of the Osospa/Premier group illustrated in Figure 10.2, they separated Premier and GF Holdings new businesses from parent companies. A new generation of FBG owner/managers responded to Thailand's rapidly expanding and transforming economy by assembling a conglomerate.

The Osathanugrah family was ranked eighth on the Forbes list of Thailand's top 50 wealthiest families in 2021. Petch Osathanugrah, Surat's eldest son and CEO of Osotspa since 2010, decided to list Osotspa on the SET in 2018. Surin Osathanugrah (third generation) was appointed chairman of the board, Petch Osathanugrah was named vice chairman, Kannika Chalitaporn was selected as chairman of the executive committee, Thana Chaiprasit (fourth generation) became acting CEO, and Chatcharin Osathanugrah (fifth generation) vice chairman of the executive committee.

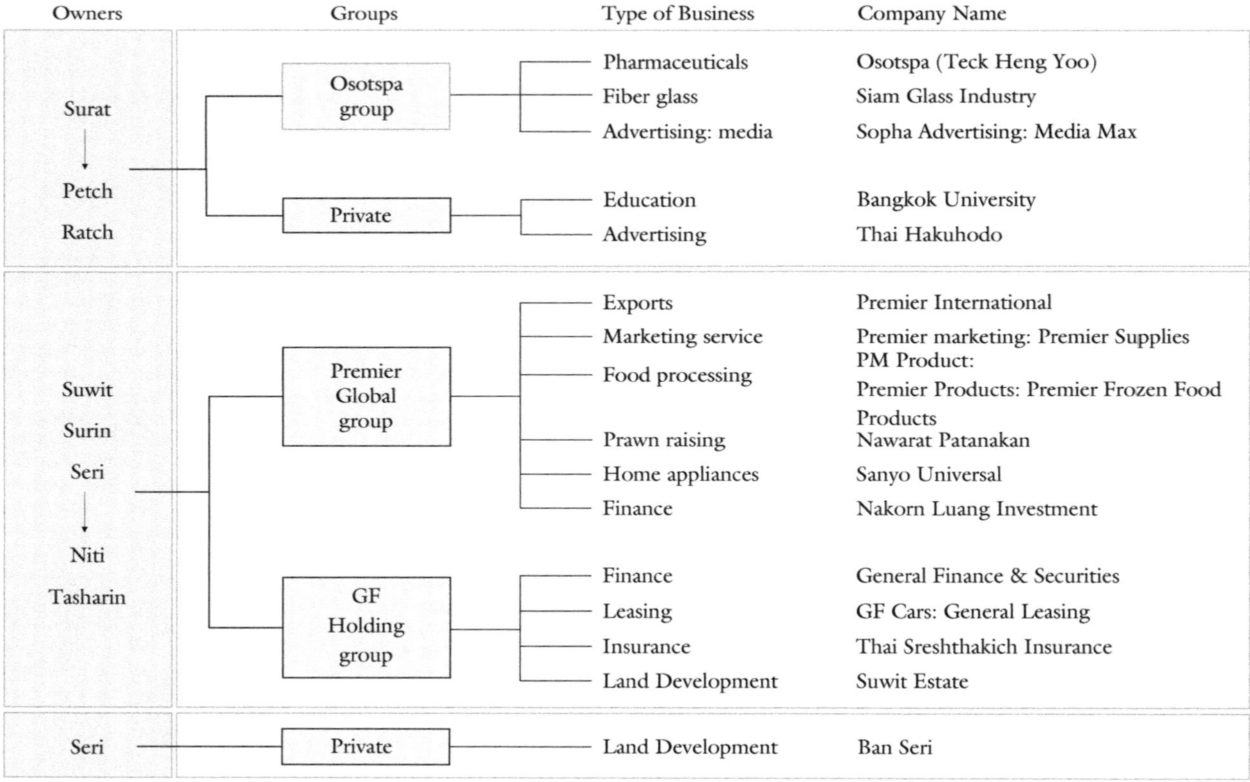

Figure 10.2 Business diversification of the Osotspa/Premier group

Source: Author's compilation from the *Phucatkan Monthly* magazine, March 1990, pp. 115–129 and Akira Suehiro's database

Note: Pe was the Osotspa founder. Sawat was Pe's second son, with one daughter (Pranee) and four sons (Surat, Suwit, Surin, Seri). Pranee married Thana Chaiprasit, having one son (Pratharn). Petch and Ratch are Surat's sons. Niti is Surin's son. Tasharin is Seri's son. All second- and third-generation members are members of the Osotspa's board of directors in 2021.

While the Osathanugrah family retains majority ownership and governs the Osotspa, they state clearly that professional management takes precedence over family control. The family aspires to develop and sustain the group through professional management and a shift from the image of a family business. It has recruited staff from the banking and consumer products worlds. Osotspa hires include Kannika Chalitaporn, former SCB and Unilever Group executive; Wannipa Bhaktabutr, former executive vice president of personal care product marketing at Unilever Thai Trading Co., Ltd.; and other former Unilever Group executives and employees.

Some Thai FBGs approach a fourth or fifth generation with the intent to split ownership and management and exit family businesses, although these remain in the minority. The Osotspa group's next major goal is to establish a human resource management system for senior executives, obviating any need for employing external leaders. This is vital for the business to mature into a full-fledged managerial enterprise.

10.3 Concentrated ownership – holding companies and cross shareholding

La Porta et al. (1999) detected pyramidal large FBGs throughout Asia. This indicates that a tycoon or business family owns an apex firm controlling a first tier of subsidiaries, each of which controls firms in a second tier, in turn individually controlling firms in the next lower tier. In the existing literature, there are two main views on why FBGs are using the pyramidal structure (Bunkanwanicha et al., 2006). Firstly, as mentioned earlier, pyramids are chosen to facilitate tunnelling (self-dealing to concentrate profits in companies owned directly by the controlling family). Pyramidal groups can raise considerable capital while maintaining effective business group governance. Cross shareholding structures are also employed to bolster central controller power (World Bank, 1998).

Secondly, pyramids are used for diversification and growth of entire groups. Families may use existing firms to set up new firms, thereby magnifying a family's actual wealth by controlling several firms (Almeida et al., 2015; Almeida & Wolfenzon, 2006; Morck et al., 2005). Also, a pyramid creates an internal capital market to help the family group overcome financial constraints and thereby expand their business.

It has been suggested that concentrated ownership and pyramidal control are a natural reaction to an unmodified institutional framework marked by ill-defined property rights, cronyism, undeveloped capital markets, lax or nonexistent product liability regulations, and management talent scarcity (Bunkanwanicha et al., 2006; La Porta et al., 1999). Significantly, this illustrates an intention by family owners to retain control of company wealth as family resources, regardless of business size. Two cases in point are the Charoen Pokphand (CP) and Sahapat Groups.

10.3.1 Charoen Pokphand (CP) group of the Chearavanont family

The Charoen Pokphand group, owned by the Chearavanont family, is Thailand's largest multinational agribusiness conglomerate. The first generation began by importing seeds. The second, under Dhanin Chearavanont (83), developed an integrated agribusiness conglomerate based on poultry, extending backwards to feedmills and forward to retail. The group became Asia's largest poultry producer and fourth largest supplier in the world.

By the 2020s, it had around a hundred companies spread across twenty countries with a workforce of over 120,000. Dhanin, the group head, and his family were ranked 387th in the 2022 Forbes World Billionaires' List (net worth US$1.7 billion), and as Southeast Asia's seventeenth richest businesspeople (net worth US$1.4 billion).

The group was severely affected by the 1997 Asian financial crisis. After commissioning a study from US consultants, it responded with a strategic decision to slim down to three core business areas in agribusiness, telecoms, and retail. Each of the three core businesses was reorganized under its own holding company, and the company structures below them were streamlined. More outsiders were invited as board directors to promote transparency and attract foreign capital. Institutional investment made up 22 percent of the agribusiness holding company, 22 percent of the telecom, and 32 percent of the retail firm.

Above the three divisional holding companies is an unlisted investment firm of which 89 percent is controlled by family members. Below them is an elaborate pyramid of firms knit together by cross shareholdings. In March 2022, the Chearavanont family circuitously owned 37.67 percent of CPF shares through family non-listed companies: Charoen Pokphand Holding Co., Ltd. (CPH), Charoen Pokphand Group Co., Ltd. (CPG), and other group companies.

The group also invested heavily in telecommunications, cable television, retailing (Siam Makro, Lotus, and 7-Eleven), and petrochemicals. These new firms were typically joint ventures with international partners that supplied technology and market access. True Corporation is the group's flagship telecom firm (TRUE, former TelecomAsia Corp: TA, listed in 1993). In November 2021, they agreed to explore a merger between Thailand's second and third largest telecom companies, TRUE and Total Access Communication (DTAC).

The Chearavanont family, led by Dhanin, sought to preserve control over CPF and TRUE through two holding companies: CPH and BTH, as well as the unlisted CPG, which has served as the CP Group's ultimate holding company and base since 1990. The CPG is owned by Chearavanont family members (84 percent), associated firms (5 percent), and long-term CP Group employees (11 percent).

Clearly, the CP Group sought to attract foreign investors to CPF and TRUE by simplifying primary business ownership structure and increasing managerial transparency. Restructuring the CP Group ownership structure strengthened CP Group voting rights for outside investors, exceeding cash-flow rights over several affiliated firms. Indeed, they succeeded in attracting

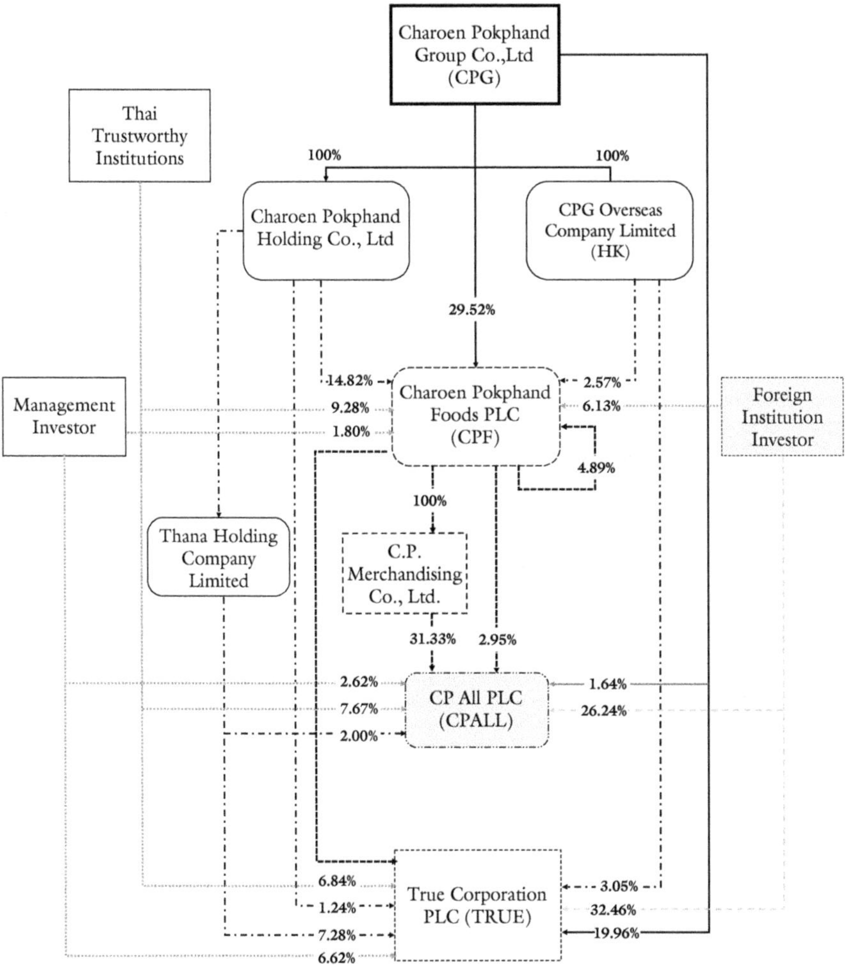

Figure 10.3 Pyramidal ownership structure of the CP group

Source: Tachakulchareon (2017), p. 34, based on the annual reports of listed companies belonging to the CP group as of December 2016 and see also Wailerdsak (2008b), p. 127

foreign institutional investors, whose combined percentages of total shareholdings climbed to 22.59 percent in CPF and 32.21 percent in TRUE following reorganization.

10.3.2 *Sahapat group of the Chokwatana family*

The Sahapat Group of the Chokwatana family is one of Thailand's most integrated production-marketing conglomerates, comprising about 40 manufacturing companies in four major industries: cosmetics, textiles, footwear, and food processing (including Mama instant noodles). It is known collectively as the Sahapathana or Sahapathanapibul Group (often abbreviated to Sahapat or Saha).

Thiam Chokwatana (Lee Heng Thiam), the group's founder, began as an importer of Chinese sundries, such as shirts. In 1962, he launched a joint venture with Japan's Lion Corporation to develop a detergent production and sales firm (Pao). From that point, the Sahapat group developed quickly due to a statewide network of traveling vendors selling Japanese products, such as Pias cosmetics. The business used the same network to advertise Wacoal women's underwear, which it began manufacturing in 1970.

The group exemplifies a family ownership structure in which the owner family chooses to list primary businesses and a significant number of related businesses on the SET. The group holding company is comprised of two flagship companies: Saha Pathana Inter-Holding PLC (SPI; founded in 1972 as Saha Pathana Investment Co., Ltd. and listed in 1977) and Saha Pathana Pibun PLC (SPC, listed in 1978). In addition, they have invested in a number of public and unlisted operational companies. The group constructed a highly complex stock pyramid and cross shareholding structure.

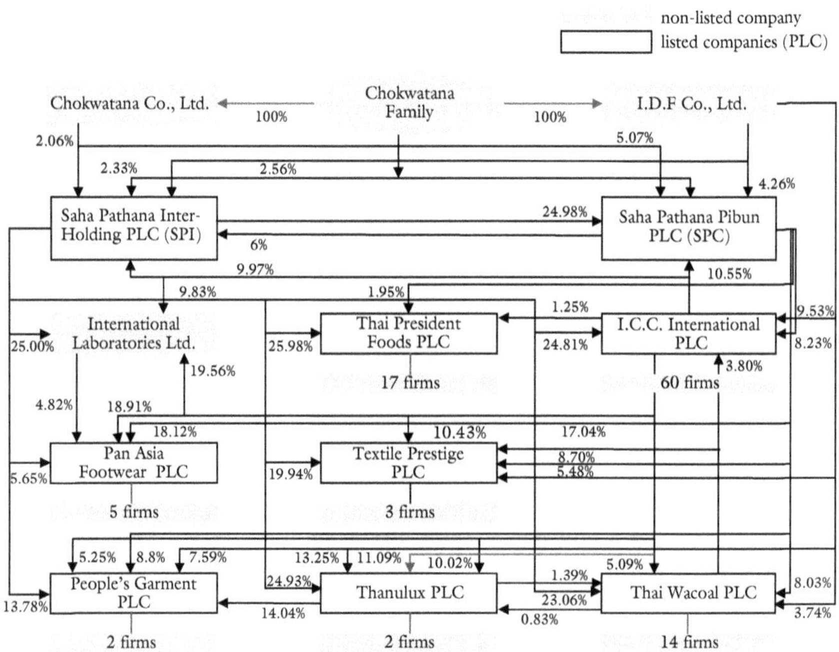

Figure 10.4 Pyramidal ownership structure of the Sahapat group

Source: Compiled by the author based on the annual reports of listed companies belonging to the Sahapat group as of December 2021 and see also Wailerdsak (2008b), p. 125

Although apparently the group makes key businesses accessible to foreign investors and has relatively little direct control, a closer investigation of ownership structure indicates that controlling shareholders are mostly owner family members. The family possesses a sizable majority of total shares in the two firms (about 34.23 percent in SPI and 43.64 percent in SPC). They own shares directly (through Chokwatana family members) and indirectly (through family-owned investment companies such as the Chokwatana Co., Ltd. and I.D.F. Co., Ltd., as well as a cross shareholding web).

These holding firms exert management control over investment strategy, staff, marketing strategy, and research and development (R&D). This time-honoured method might lead to widespread misperception that the firms exist to help a single family. Yet because the ultimate result is the broader welfare of society over time, it is essential that government authorities refrain from enforcing antitrust and concentrated ownership limitations.

Ownership concentration is faulted for encouraging dominant owners to expropriate other investors and stakeholders and pursue personal nonprofit maximization goals, as well as inhibiting the hiring of expert managers, who are increasingly needed as economies and enterprises grow and become more complicated (World Bank, 1998, p. 60). In recent years, these ownership systems have come under growing political and market pressure.

10.4 Managerial enterprise development

Typically, ownership and management of second and third generation Thai FBGs are intimately connected. Significant shareholders coexist alongside directors and other senior management positions. Almost all roles within affiliate firms are filled by siblings and children, including sons-in-law and daughters-in-law, who assist in managing businesses. Families often branch into new areas by indulging ambitions of children, especially those educated overseas, returning with new skills and visions of the future (Wailerdsak, 2020a, 2021; Wailerdsak & Suehiro, 2010, 2014). To strengthen bargaining power, they network mutually through marriage alliances, cross shareholdings, and cooperation in associations providing community welfare (Bertrand et al., 2008).[6] This is typically referred to as a closed family business.

By contrast, third and fourth generation FBGs cede control to non-family members. This often arises when large FBGs are unable to adequately employ family members or expand into more complex businesses. They require more capable managers while maintaining direct and indirect management oversight (Wailerdsak, 2003, 2004a, 2005; Wailerdsak & Suehiro, 2014). Generational shifts may redistribute family ownership, reducing ownership concentration. This has been observed in Osotspa, Central, and KBank.

Over the past decade, ownership and control of the Chinese corporate sector has finally begun to fundamentally differ from past socialist prototypes. With China on the verge of becoming a developed nation, apparently a managerial revolution has occurred (Walder, 2011; Warner, 1999).

Commercial bank sectors, hardest hit by the 1997 Asian financial crisis, reveal parallel alterations. Before the crisis, the government protected a cartel of around 16 domestic banks from any new entry or foreign competition. Prominence of financial conglomerates, with banks financing expansion of other group firms, although high interconnected debt of member firms proved financially unstable, was a distinctive feature of Thai capitalism in the pre-crisis era (Bunkanwanicha & Wiwattanakantang, 2008; Menkhoff & Suwanaporn, 2007).

Banks were forced to raise large amounts of new capital during the crisis to repair balance sheets and comply with new Basel capital adequacy and loan-loss provisional standards. The government promised to assist banks by recapitalization in exchange for restructuring corporate debt. Fearful of takeover, most major banks declined such offers. Due to a dearth of domestic funds, the government relaxed restrictions on foreign investment in banks (Menkhoff & Suwanaporn, 2007).

As a result, late in 1997, Chatri Sophonpanich, chairman of the board of directors of Bangkok Bank, held a reception for Thailand's tycoons affected by the crisis. At the start of 1997, Chatri's bank had been the largest private commercial bank in Southeast Asia. By 2019, after two decades of recovery, in terms of assets it ranked only third in Thailand (Hewison, 2021). The other three major family-owned commercial banks survived (Kasikornthai Bank of the Lamsam family, the SCB of the Crown Property Bureau, and Ayudhya Bank of Ratanarak family). But the family stake was slashed to under 5 percent.

By 2000, foreign stakes in major banks had increased significantly, although families retained management control. Both Bangkok Bank and Thai Farmers Bank were obliged to raise capital and accept over 48 percent of foreign investment. The royal family's Siam Commercial Bank recapitalized, accepting a 49 percent foreign stake. The Tejapaibul family's Bangkok Metropolitan Bank was taken over by the state. The Ratanarak family, founders of Bank of Ayudhya PLC, branded and commonly referred to as Krungsri, initially resisted state efforts to recapitalize but by 2000 had accepted a 40 percent foreign stake. Later, Bank of Ayudhya PLC was acquired by Bank of Tokyo-Mitsubishi UFJ (75 percent stake), with the Ratanarak family still retaining about 20 percent in 2017. Banks seen as having poor business group governance were obliged to restructure ownership and management.

10.4.1 Bangkok Bank of the Sophonpanich family

Figure 10.5 examines the total asset ratio for Thailand's five major commercial banks, comparing 1979 and 2022. Before the 1997 Asian financial crisis, Bangkok Bank was one of the Association of Southeast Asian Nations (ASEAN) largest banks. It is the largest commercial bank in Thailand in total assets, deposits, and total liabilities, with a market share of over 30 percent.

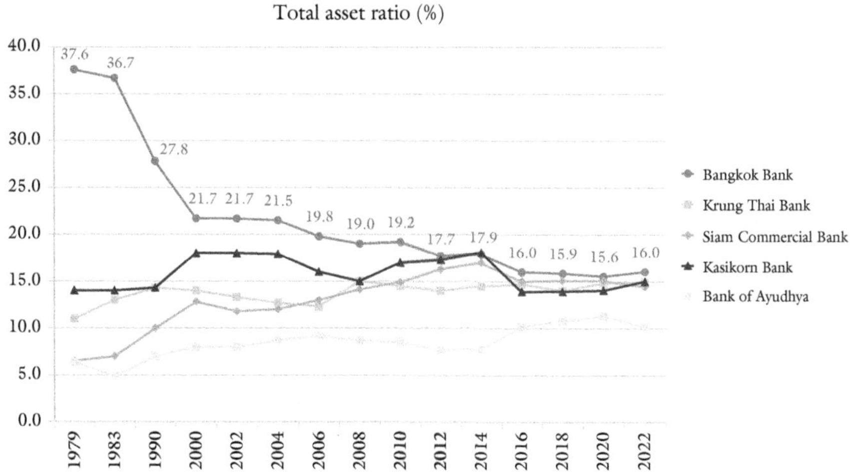

Figure 10.5 Total asset ratio of five major commercial banks, 1979–2022

Source: Author's compilation based on the Bank of Thailand website, (1) Financial Institutions>Summary Statement of Assets and Liabilities> Commercial Banks Registered in Thailand>Bank Name, browsed by year (December); (2) FI_CB_001 All commercial banks' assets and liabilities (1979–2022)

It has a long history of collaborating with governments and connecting significant clients to major infrastructure projects. It declined after the crisis, as a result of ardent competition from rival banks. In 2010, Krungthai Bank (KBank) overtook Bangkok Bank in terms of total liabilities, total assets, and deposits. In 2013, SCB outperformed Bangkok Bank in total liabilities. By 2022, the assets of Bangkok Bank as a percentage of the overall banking system would be less than 15 percent.

Table 10.1 lists Sophonpanich family executives who continue to hold key management positions at Bangkok Bank, Bangkok Insurance, and Bangkok Life Assurance. The group may include some non-family executives in a format peculiar to Bangkok Bank, relying on outsiders to assist when family members are unready due to excessive youth. However, it demonstrates a dedication to succession by the next generation, rather than any expected exit from the family business (Wailerdsak, 2005, 2008b). Therefore, it is still timely to monitor how family businesses and managerial enterprises perform in the Thai commercial banking industry.

Bangkok Bank has a longstanding history of international expansion, with branches in China, Hong Kong, Taiwan, Japan, Singapore, and Indonesia, as well as Cambodia, Laos, Myanmar, and Vietnam (the CLMV countries). It has been called the most innovative bank in the market but was hardest hit by the Asian financial crisis. It may also be unfavourably positioned for recovery due to the advent of digital technology, such as super applications (apps) used by many banks to respond to consumer needs for transactions involving gold

Table 10.1 The Sophonpanich family and directorship of the Bangkok Bank group

Positions	*Bangkok Bank*	*Bangkok Insurance*	*Bangkok Life Assurance*
Chairman of the Board of Directors	Piti Sithi-Amnuai	Chai Sophonpanich (Owner Chin's fifth son)	Siri Ganjarerndee
Chairman of the Board of Executive Directors	Deja Tulananda	–	–
CEO/President	Chartsiri Sophonpanich (Chatri's eldest son)	Apisit Anantanatarat	Chone Sophonpanich (Cheodchu's eldest son)
Director	Suvarn Thansathit	Panus Thiravanitkul	Savitri Ramyarupa
Director	Chansak Fuangfu	Suvarn Thansathit	Prapaivan Limsong
Director	Charamporn Jotikasthira	Supadis Disku	Chollada Sophonpanich (Cheodchu's eldest daughter)
Director	Boonsong Bunyasaranand	Nintira Sophonpanich (Chartsiri's wife)	Vetit Assawamangcla
Director	Thaweelap Rittapirom	Satoru Okura	Kazuyuki Saigo

Source: Author's compilation from the annual reports in 2021 of publicly traded Bangkok Bank group firms

Note: Chin was the Bangkok Bank co-founder. Chatri was Chin's second son. Cheodchu was Chin's sixth son.

trading, food delivery, and debentures. Among new approaches, for which Bangkok Bank has so far been outpaced by the competition, are adopting artificial intelligence and machine learning technology to increase productivity, valuing the environment and sustainability, and embracing cryptocurrency.

10.4.2 Siam Commercial Bank of the Crown Property Bureau

Siam Commercial Bank (SCB) was founded on 30 January 1906 by Royal Charter to serve as Thailand's first indigenous bank. Throughout its 115 years of operations, the bank has shaped the country's financial services landscape through countless business cycles and political shifts. Backed by the strong support of its major shareholders, the bank has navigated the ups and downs of these changes to become better and stronger.

SCB's major shareholders as of 30 December 2021 were His Majesty King Maha Vajiralongkorn Phra Vajiraklaochaoyuhua (23.35 percent), Ministry of Finance–owned Vayupak Fund 1 (23.10 percent), and Thai NVDR Co., Ltd.

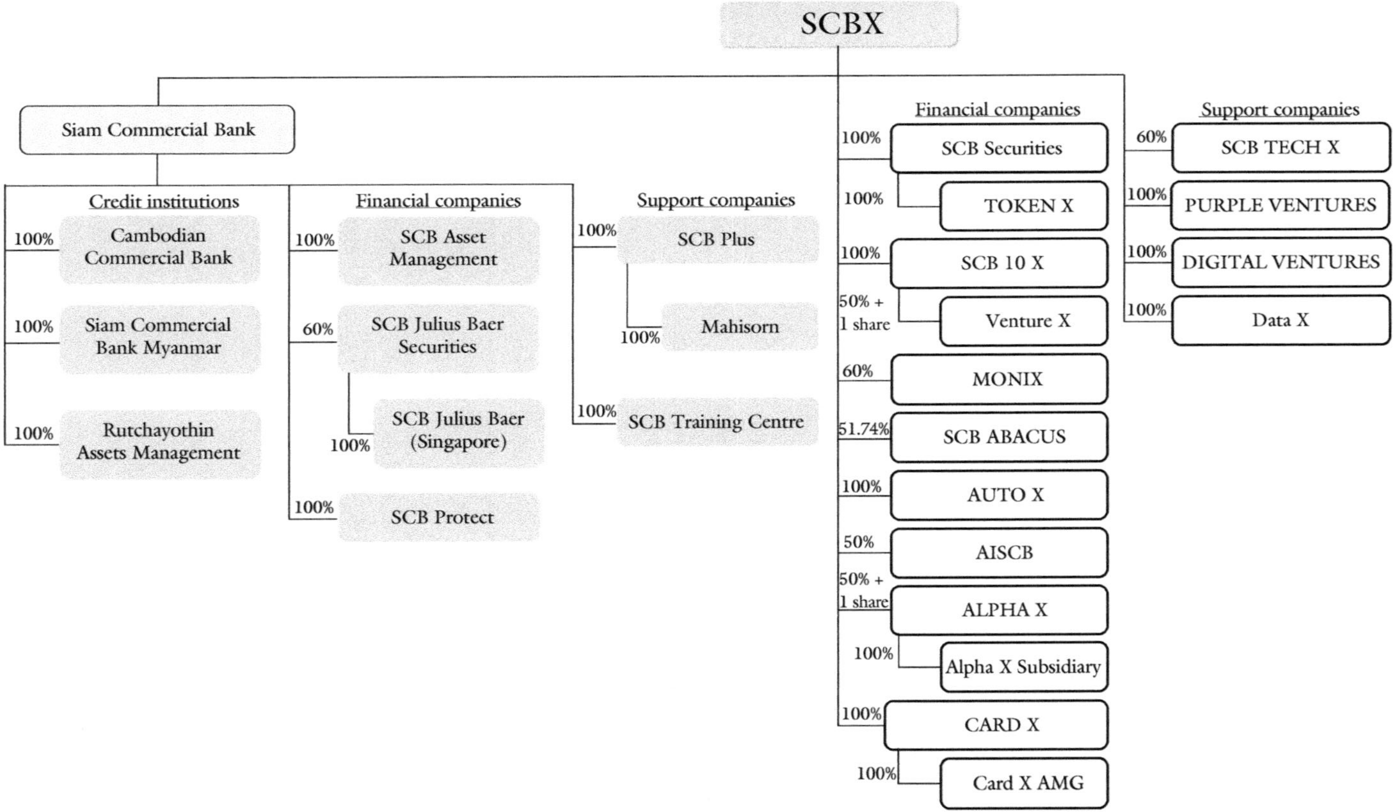

Figure 10.6 Pyramidal ownership structure of the Siam Commercial Bank group

Source: Author's compilation from the annual report in 2021 of publicly traded Siam Commercial Bank group firms

Table 10.2 Separation of ownership and control of the Siam Commercial Bank group

Board of Directors

Name	*Sex*	*Positions*	*Background*
Dr. Vichit Suraphongchai	M	Chairman	
ACM. Satitpong Sukvimol	M	Director	
Prasan Chuapanich	M	Independent Director	
Kan trakulhoon	M	Independent Director	
Krirk Vanikkul	M	Independent Director	
Dr. Thaweesak Koanantakool	M	Independent Director	
Pol. Col. Thumnithi Wanichthanom	M	Director	
Dr. Pasu Decharin	M	Independent Director	
Weerawong Chittmittrapap	M	Independent Director	
Chaovalit Ekabut	M	Independent Director	
Dr. Lackana Leelayouthayotin	F	Independent Director	
Dr. Pailin Chuchottaworn	M	Independent Director	
Jareeporn Jarukornsakul	F	Director	
Chakkrit Parapuntakul	M	Director	
Chunhachit Sungmai	F	Director	
Pantip Sripimol	F	Director	
Arthid nanthawithaya	M	Director, CEO	
Executives Committee			

Name	*Sex*	*Positions*	*Background*
Apiphan Charoenanusorn	F	President	Trueborn manager
Sarut Ruttanaporn	M	President	Trueborn manager
Dr. Arak Sutivong	M	President	Trueborn manager
Narong Srichukrin	M	SEVP	Trueborn manager
Dr. Yunyong Thaicharoen	M	SEVP	Trueborn manager
Poramasiri Manolamai	F	SEVP	Manager from outside
Auraratana Jutimitta	F	SEVP	Manager from outside
Vitoon Pornsakulvanich	M	SEVP	Trueborn manager
Pikun Srimahunt	F	SEVP	Trueborn manager
Wallaya Kaewrungruang	F	SEVP	Trueborn manager
Manop Sangiambut	M	SEVP	Trueborn manager
Sathian Leowarin	M	SEVP	Manager from outside
Krieng Wongnongtaey	M	SEVP	Trueborn manager
Voranuch Dejakaisaya	F	SEVP	Manager from outside

Board of Directors			
Name	*Sex*	*Positions*	*Background*
Dr. Chalee Asavathiratham	M	SEVP	Manager from outside
Patraporn Sirodom	F	SEVP	Manager from outside
M.L. Chiradej Chakrabandhu	M	SEVP	Trueborn manager

Sources: Siam Commercial Bank Annual Report 2021

Note: Trueborn managers mean those who have worked with the company in the lower management levels before being promoted to the top management levels

(8.44 percent). As one of Thailand's leading universal banking groups, the bank offers a wide array of financial products and services to varied customers. The bank's revenue came from corporate, SME, and retail and wealth. In 2021, the retail and wealth contributed more than half of the bank's revenue, followed by corporate and SME.

In addition to SCB Securities Co., Ltd. and SCB Asset Management Co., Ltd., the bank also has a subsidiary – namely, SCB 10X – that focuses on digital and data analytics and using cutting-edge technologies to improve the banking business. SCB 10X was founded in 2020 to build new growth sectors beyond banking.

SCBX aims to be "the Most Admired Financial Technology Group in ASEAN" with 200 million customers. M&A or partnerships with industry leaders will establish digital platforms and ecosystems to reach clients both in Thailand and the region.

SCBX will become the Group's mothership, while the Bank and other subsidiaries will become subsidiaries of SCBX. Certain existing subsidiaries and credit card and personal loan businesses will spin off from the Bank, with the new entities owned directly by SCBX. These subsidiaries will venture into businesses with growth, return and risk profiles distinct from the Bank, such as personal loans (e.g., title loan, luxury car hire purchase, credit card), unsecured personal loans, and innovative technology solution and digital platform businesses.

SCB (owned by CPB) recruited senior executives and aggressively formed collaborations with startups, establishing itself as a regional financial technology firm and transcending the paradigm of a commercial bank (Nanthawithaya, 2022).

10.4.3 *Kasikornthai Bank of the Lamsam family*

At the end of World War II, Kasikornthai Bank or KBank (formerly named the Thai Farmers Bank) was established on 8 June 1945 by Choti Lamsam and Thai-Chinese relatives. In early days, the bank focused on providing financial

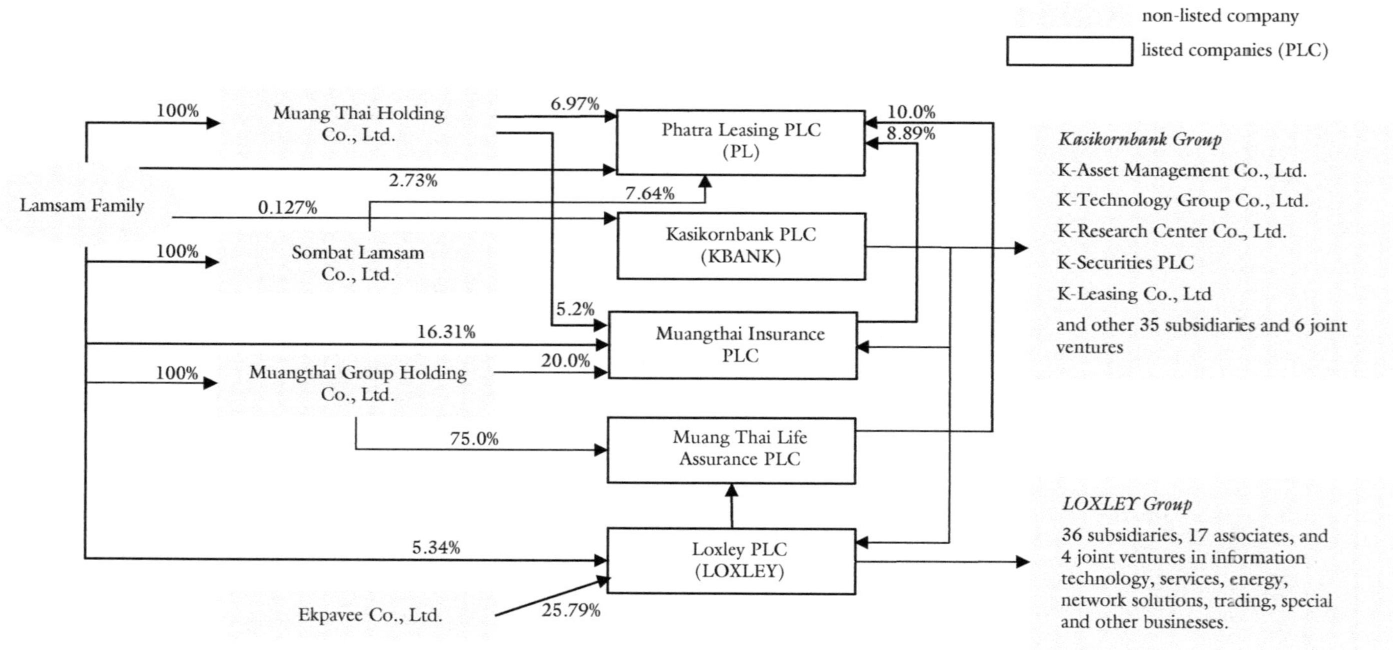

Figure 10.7 Pyramidal ownership structure of the KBank group

Source: Compiled by the author based on the annual reports of listed companies belonging to the KBank/Loxley groups as of December 2021 and see also Wailerdsak (2008b), p. 129

Note: The shareholders of Ekpavee Co., Ltd. consist of the Lamsam family (12 persons) and Lamsam Estate Co., Ltd. (64.01 percent), the Wanglee family (22 persons) (9.44 percent), and the Chatikavanij family (3 persons) (6.77 percent).

Table 10.3 Separation of ownership and control of the KBank group

Board of Directors			
Name	*Sex*	*Positions*	*Background*
Banyong Lamsam	M	Honorary Chairman	Owner family
Banthoon Lamsam	M	Chairman Emeritus	Owner family
1. Kobkarn Wattanavrangkul	F	Chairperson of the Board	Lead Independent Director
2. Sujitpan Lamsam	F	Vice Chairperson, Non-Executive Director	Member of the Risk Oversight Committee
3. Kattiya Indaravijaya	F	Chief Executive Officer, Executive Director	Member of the Risk Oversight Committee
4. Pipit Aneaknithi	M	President, Executive Director	Member of the Risk Oversight Committee
5. Patchara Samalapa	M	President, Executive Director	
6. Krit Jitjang	M	President, Executive Director	Member of the Risk Oversight Committee
7. Pipatpong Poshyanonda	M	President, Executive Director	
8. Sqn. Ldr. Nalinee Paiboon, MD	F	Independent Director	Chairperson of the Corporate Governance Committee
9. Saravoot Yoovidhya	M	Independent Director, Member of the Audit Committee	Member of the Risk Oversight Committee
10. Dr. Piyasvasti Amranand	M	Independent Director	Chairman of the Risk Oversight Committee
11. Kalin Sarasin	M	Independent Director, Chairman of the Audit Committee	Member of the Human Resources and Remuneration Committee
12. Wiboon Khusakul	M	Independent Director	Member of the Human Resources and Remuneration Committee, Member of the Corporate Governance Committee
13. Suphajee Suthumpun	F	Independent Director, Member of the Audit Committee	Chairperson of the Human Resources and Remuneration Committee, Member of the Risk Oversight Committee

(*Continued*)

Table 10.3 (Continued)

Board of Directors

Name	*Sex*	*Positions*	*Background*
14. Sara Lamsam	M	Non-Executive Director	Member of the Corporate Governance Committee
15. Chanin Donavanik	M	Independent Director	Member of the Corporate Governance Committee
16. Jainnisa Kuvinichkul Chakrabandhu Na Ayudhya	F	Independent Director, Member of the Audit Committee	Member of the Risk Oversight Committee
17. Chonchanum Soonthornsaratoon	F	Non-Executive Director and Legal Adviser	Member of the Corporate Governance Committee, Member of the Human Resources and Remuneration Committee
18. Suroj Lamsam	M	Non-Executive Director	Member of the Human Resources and Remuneration Committee

Executives Committee

Name	*Sex*	*Positions*	*Background*
19. Dr. Adit Laixuthai	M	Corporate Secretary, SEVP	Trueborn manager
20. Thiti Tantikulanan	M	Capital Markets Business Division Head	Trueborn manager
21. Jirawat Supornpaibul	M	Private Banking Group Head	Trueborn manager
22. Chongrak Rattanapian	M	CFO, SEVP, Finance and Control Division Head	Trueborn manager
23. Silawat Santivisat	M	SEVP	Trueborn manager
24. Wasana Surakit	F	SEVP	Trueborn manager
25. Natcha Argasreog	F	SEVP	Trueborn manager
26. Khajarin Maintaka	F	SEVP	Trueborn manager

Sources: Kasikorn Bank Annual Report 2021

Notes
(1) Trueborn managers mean those who have worked with the company in the lower management levels before being promoted to the top management levels.
(2) Only Ms. Sujitpan Lamsam (vice chairperson) holds 0.127 percent of total shares.

services to farmers, who comprised the majority of the Thai population. Such initiative kept the economy rolling despite the war's hardships. During the 1980s and 1990s, the bank was one of Thailand's most successful financial conglomerates. After the Asian financial crisis, the bank redefined its mission, values, and vision while undertaking a thorough renovation toward consumer banking. It adopted a new strategic direction and gained the leading position in the Thai financial institutions' good corporate governance system.

The bank has been dominated by the Lamsam family. It is a financial conglomerate consisting of four principal companies: KBank, Muangthai Insurance, Muang Thai Life Assurance, and Phatra Leasing. As with the CP group, the family interest is organized similarly, with a wholly owned investment arm, Sombat Lamsam Co., Ltd., Muang Thai Holding Co., Ltd., and Muang Thai Group Holding Co., Ltd., sitting atop a web of pyramidal and horizontal shareholdings. The family retains control through its 100 percent stake of these holding companies. Moreover, each listed firm possess stakes in another group's companies.

As with other banks that survived the crisis, KBank opened its doors to foreign investors. The Lamsam family experienced a large decline in their stock (to less than 1 percent) and a significant rise in foreign ownership, notably Thai NDVR Co., Ltd. (to 49 percent), although the family retains management control.

Loxley Rice, another flagship company, began operations in 1939. After listing in 1994, the company concentrated on import and sale of industrial and consumer goods. As a result, it was established as a significant player in Thailand's communication industry. In 2021, the Lamsam family held 31.13 percent of Loxley, directly and indirectly, through Ekpavee Co., Ltd. (25.79 percent).

KBank made the decision to transition from family-owned to managerial enterprise. The CEO and top management team are all industry professionals, no longer members of the Lamsam family. Specifically, KBank developed homegrown executives through company scholarships for study abroad and the internal labour market system and established corporate governance consistent with its sustainability goals. By contrast, Bangkok Bank remains alone in retaining a strong family ownership and management structure.

Generally, the family business trap represents a dearth of skilled leaders to take succession seriously. Typically, family businesses educate selected heirs to develop relationships with creditors and foreign partners. This limits management possibilities and contributes to a prevalence of family feuds. It is difficult to recruit talent if non-family member opportunities for managerial careers are limited. Employees lack a sense of urgency in developing new technology and innovations. To avoid falling into the family business trap, skilled non-family executives must be cultivated (Wailerdsak, 2020b; Yan & Yu, 2021). Current members of KBank's management team reflect an internal labour market success story.

In summary, Thai business groups are expanding slowly as a result of the family business trap concentrating ownership and the *kongsi* (benevolent organizations of popular origin found among overseas Chinese communities for individuals with the same surname) management style of Chinese-Thai society. This leads to tunnelling and expropriation of minority shareholder issues. Four areas must be cultivated to escape the family business trap and, consequently, from the middle-income trap (Wailerdsak, 2006, 2008b, 2020b):

- Dispersed ownership in major companies.
- Increased numbers of managerial enterprises.
- The rise of non-family professional managers.
- Sound corporate governance promotion.

Large companies, such as financial institutions and manufacturers, should establish separation of ownership and control. Their executives must be vetted for professionalism, experience, and morality by regulated, unbiased bodies. Large companies should be assisted to become more sustainable, in the public interest. In this way, skilled managers may advance in social status and stratification.

The SET, SEC, Thai Capital Market Business Council, and Bank of Thailand should all contribute to this process. Given that managerial enterprises contribute value and benefit to Thai society more than family-owned businesses do, nurturing managerial enterprises and creating solid corporate governance are essential markers of subsequent national growth stages toward high-income-country status.

Notes

1 The term "family business" refers to firms in which ownership and management are controlled by a nuclear or extended family kinship group and profits distributed among members (Suehiro, 1993). Chandler defined a family capitalism system as an economy or sector of an economy controlled by family businesses (Chandler, 1977).

2 Unlike PA conflicts, which feature managerial opportunism (Jensen & Meckling, 1976; Shleifer & Vishny, 1997), PP conflicts are characterized by owner opportunism manifested in different forms, such as appointment of unqualified cronies or family members as senior executives, and pursuing projects that advance private benefits of major shareholders (Chung, 2013; Hu & Sun, 2019; Schulze et al., 2001).

3 The term "tunnelling" does not cover other agency problems, such as incompetent management, placement of relatives in executive positions, excessive or insufficient investment, or resistance to value-increasing takeovers.

4 Institutional void theory has been used to explain FBG's growth in emerging countries. According to these studies, FBGS internalize in institutionally underdeveloped environments in order to acquire scale or scope advantages from internationalization through diversification. However, family businesses in developed economies contrast findings in emerging economies. That is, the controlling family of an FBG in an emerging economy does not pick risk-aversion strategies (such as low level of diversification) in the same manner as the controlling family in a developed county would choose. Instead, the controlling family in an emerging economy is likely to diversify into multiple industrial domains and retain control over affiliate firms through a pyramidal ownership structure and family management (Almeida et al., 2015; Almeida & Wolfenzon, 2006; Kock & Guillén, 2001; La Porta et al., 1999; Morck et al., 2005).

5 The Crown Property Bureau is an agency set up in 1936 to control holdings accumulated by the Thai royal family over many generations. The bureau invests in diverse businesses, notably Siam Cement Group (SCG), Siam Commercial Bank (SCB), and real estate. A distinct office, the Bureau of the Royal Household established in 1350, manages financial matters for the present monarch, HM King Rama X (Suehiro, 1993).

6 Currently, love marriages are more prevalent than arranged wedlock within family business networks. Yet weddings between descendants of renowned business families persist, reputed for amalgamating wealthy Thai families through admixture (*thong paen diew kan*) (Bertrand et al., 2008). For example, in 2021 Natee Osathanugrah, guitarist of Getsunova, a Thai band signed by GMM Grammy, married Ingfah Damrongchaitham, eldest daughter of Grammy CEO Paiboon Damrongchaitham; in 2022, Chanon Sophonpanich, eldest son of Chartsiri Sophonpanich, President of Bangkok Bank, married Kamolnan Chearavanont, daughter of Supachai Chearavanont, Charoen Pokhpand Group CEO.

Reference list

Almeida, H., Kim, C. S., & Kim, H. B. (2015). Internal capital markets in business groups: Evidence from the Asian financial crisis. *The Journal of Finance, 70*(6), 2539–2586.

Almeida, H. V., & Wolfenzon, D. (2006). A theory of pyramidal ownership and family business groups. *The Journal of Finance, 61*(6), 2637–2680.

Berle, A. A., & Means, G. C. (1932). *The modern corporation and private property.* Commerce Clearing House.

Bertrand, M., Johnson, S., Samphantharak, K., & Schoar, A. (2008). Mixing family with business: A study of Thai business groups and the families behind them. *Journal of financial Economics, 88*(3), 466–498.

Bunkanwanicha, P., Gupta, J., & Wiwattanakantang, Y. (2006). *Pyramiding of family-owned banks in emerging markets.* Center for Economic Institutions Working Paper Series No. 2006–4. Institute of Economic Research, Hitotsubashi University.

Bunkanwanicha, P., & Wiwattanakantang, Y. (2008). *Allocating risk across pyramidal tiers: Evidence from Thai business groups.* Center for Economic Institutions Working Paper Series No. 2007–14. Institute of Economic Research, Hitotsubashi

Chandler, A. D., Jr. (1977). *The visible hand: The managerial revolution in American business.* Belknap Press of Harvard University Press.

Chandler, A. D., Jr. (1990). *Scale and scope: The dynamics of industrial capitalism.* Belknap Press of Harvard University Press.

Chung, H. M. (2013). The role of family management and family ownership in diversification: The case of family business groups. *Asia Pacific Journal of Management, 30*(3), 871–891.

Chung, H. M., & Chan, S. T. (2012). Ownership structure, family leadership, and performance of affiliate firms in large family business groups. *Asia Pacific Journal of Management, 29*(2), 303–329.

Claessens, S., & Fan, J. P. (2002). Corporate governance in Asia: A survey. *International Review of Finance, 3*(2), 71–103.

Collis, D., Anand, B., & Cheng, Y. J. (2018). The United States in contemporary perspectives: Evolving forms, strategy, and performance. In A. M. Colpan & T. Hikino (Eds.), *Business groups in the West: Origins, evolution, and resilience* (Chapter 15, pp. 402–431). Oxford University Press.

Dau, L. A., Morck, R. K., & Yeung, B. (2020). *Corporate governance, business group governance and economic traps.* NBER Working Paper No. 28069. National Bureau of Economic Research.

Dau, L. A., Morck, R. K., & Yeung, B. (2021a). Corporate governance versus business group governance, part 1: The low-income trap. In K. Sogner & A. Colli (Eds.), *The emergence of corporate governance: People, power, and performance* (Chapter 6, pp. 103–120). Routledge.

Dau, L. A., Morck, R. K., & Yeung, B. (2021b). Corporate governance versus business group governance, part 2: The middle-income trap. In K. Sogner & A. Colli (Eds.), *The emergence of corporate governance: People, power, and performance* (Chapter 7, pp. 121–134). Routledge.

Dela Rama, M. (2012). Corporate governance and corruption: Ethical dilemmas of Asian business groups. *Journal of Business Ethics, 109*, 501–519.

Djankov, S., La Porta, R., Lopez-de-Silanes, F., & Shleifer, A. (2008). The law and economics of self-dealing. *Journal of Financial Economics, 88*(3), 430–465.

Guillén, M. F. (2000). Business groups in emerging economies: A resource-based view. *Academy of Management Journal, 43*(3), 362–380.

Hamdani, A., Kosenko, K., & Yafeh, Y. (2020). *Regulatory measures to dismantle pyramidal business groups: Evidence from the United States, Japan, Korea and Israel.* ECGI-Law Working Paper No. 542. The European Corporate Governance Institute.

Hewison, K. (2021). Crazy rich Thais: Thailand's capitalist class, 1980–2019. *Journal of Contemporary Asia, 51*(2), 262–277.

Hu, H. W., & Sun, P. (2019). What determines the severity of tunnelling in China? *Asia Pacific Journal of Management, 36*(1), 161–184.

Jensen, M. C., & Meckling, W. H. (1976). Theory of the firm: Managerial behaviour, agency costs, and ownership structure. *Journal of Financial Economics, 3*(4), 305–360.

Johnson, S., La Porta, R., Lopez-de-Silanes, F., & Shleifer, A. (2000). Tunnelling. *American Economic Review, 90*(2), 22–27.

Khanthavit, A., Polsiri, P., & Wiwattanakantang, Y. (2004). *Did families lose or gain control after the East Asian financial crisis?* Center for Economic Institutions Working Paper Series No. 2003-1. Institute of Economic Research, Hitotsubashi University.

Kock, C. J., & Guillén, M. F. (2001). Strategy and structure in developing countries: Business groups as an evolutionary response to opportunities for unrelated diversification. *Industrial and Corporate Change, 10*(1), 77–113.

La Porta, R., Lopez-de-Silanes, F., & Shleifer, A. (1999). Corporate ownership around the world. *The Journal of Finance, 54*(2), 471–517.

La Porta, R., Lopez-de-Silanes, F., Shleifer, A., & Vishny, R. (2000). Investor protection and corporate governance. *Journal of Financial Economics, 58*(1–2), 3–27.

Liebowitz, S. J., & Margolis, S. E. (1994). Network externality: An uncommon tragedy. *Journal of Economic Perspectives, 8*(2), 133–150.

Menkhoff, L., & Suwanaporn, C. (2007). 10 years after the crisis: Thailand's financial system reform. *Journal of Asian Economics, 18*(1), 4–20.

Morck, R. (Ed.). (2005). *A history of corporate governance around the world: Family business groups to professional managers.* University of Chicago Press.

Morck, R., & Nakamura, M. (2007). Business groups and the big push: Meiji Japan's mass privatization and subsequent growth. *Enterprise & Society, 8*(3), 543–601.

Morck, R., & Yeung, B. (2018). East Asian financial and economic development. In T. Beck & R. Levine (Eds.), *Handbook of finance and development* (Chapter 7, pp. 194–241). Edward Elgar.

Nanthawithaya, A. (2022). *SCBX strategy is a big step towards becoming a tech company*. A seminar on Thailand Economic Outlook 2023, held by Krungthep Turakit, at the Renaissance Hotel, Bangkok, on 4 October.

Nikomborirak, D. (2004). Problems of corporate governance reform in Thailand. In F. Gul & J. Tsui (Eds.), *The governance of East Asian corporations: Post Asian financial crisis* (Chapter 11, pp. 216–235). Palgrave Macmillan.

Peng, M. W., & Sauerwald, S. (2013). Corporate governance and principal-principal conflicts. In M. Wright, D. S. Siegel, K. Keasey, & I. Filatotchev (Eds.), *The Oxford handbook of corporate governance* (Chapter 29, pp. 658–672). Oxford Academic.

Peng, M. W., Sun, W., Vlas, C., Minichilli, A., & Corbetta, G. (2018). An institution-based view of large family firms: A recap and overview. *Entrepreneurship Theory and Practice*, *42*(2), 187–205.

Purkayastha, A., & Gupta, V. K. (2022, February). Business group affiliation and entrepreneurial orientation: Contingent effect of level of internationalization and firm's performance. *Asia Pacific Journal of Management*, 1–30. https://doi.org/10.1007/s10490-022-09809-w

Schulze, W. S., Lubatkin, M. H., Dino, R., & Buchholtz, A. K. (2001). Agency relationships in family firms: Theory and evidence. *Organization Science*, *12*(2), 99–116.

Shleifer, A., & Vishny, R. W. (1997). A survey of corporate governance. *Journal of Finance*, *52*(2), 737–783.

Suehiro, A. (1993). Family business reassessed: Corporate structure and late-starting industrialization in Thailand. *Developing Economies*, *41*(4), 378–407.

Tachakulchareon, C. (2017). *Krongsang khwam pen chaokhong kap kankhayai kitchakan khong turakit krubkrua: Koranee suksa krua Charoen Pokphand (The ownership structure and the family business expansion: The case study of Charoen Pokphand Group)*. Independent Study. Thammasat Business School. (In Thai).

Useem, M. (1984). *The inner circle: Large corporations and the rise of business political activity in the US and the UK*. Oxford University Press.

Wailerdsak, N. (2003). Retaining and developing managers and professionals in a Thai telecommunications firm. *Journal of Asian Business*, *19*(1), 67–87.

Wailerdsak, N. (2004a). Promotion system and career development in Thailand: A case study of Siam Cement. *Journal of International Human Resource Management*, *15*(1), 196–218.

Wailerdsak, N. (2004b). Top executive origins: Comparative study between Japan and Thailand. *Journal of Asian Business & Management*, *3*(1), 85–104.

Wailerdsak, N. (2005). *Managerial careers in Thailand and Japan*. Silkworm Books.

Wailerdsak, N. (2006). *Klumthun turakit krubkruathai koon lae lang wikrit pii 2540 (Thai family-owned business groups before and after the 1997 crisis)*. BrandAge Books (In Thai).

Wailerdsak, N. (2008a). Companies in crisis. In P. Phongpaichit & C. Baker (Eds.), *Thai capital after the 1997 crisis* (Chapter 1, pp. 17–57). Silkworm Books.

Wailerdsak, N. (2008b). Family business in Thailand: Ownership structures and stock market. In V. Gupta, N. Levenberg, L. Moore, J. Motwani, & T. Schwarz (Eds.), *Culturally-sensitive models of family business in Southern Asia: A compendium using the GLOBE paradigm* (Chapter 5, pp. 108–136). ICFAI University Press.

Wailerdsak, N. (2020a). Women in business and management in Thailand: Transforming high participation without EEO. *Journal of Southeast Asian Economies, 37*(2), 163–180.

Wailerdsak, N. (2020b). *Kanborihaan daoden lae senthang suu phuuborihaan radabsuung nai mitithang settasad (Talent management and paths to the top in economic dimension)*. Institute for Continuing Education and Human Resources, Thammasat University (In Thai).

Wailerdsak, N. (2021). *Songphaan pheedaankaew: Phuuborihaanying kap Khwammaithaothiem thangpeed (Shining through the glass ceiling: Female managers and gender inequality)*. Institute for Continuing Education and Human Resources, Thammasat University (In Thai).

Wailerdsak, N., & Suehiro, A. (2010). Business groups in Thailand. In A. Colpan, T. Hikino, J. Lincoln, & D. Musson (Eds.), *Oxford handbook of business groups* (Chapter 9, pp. 237–266). Oxford University Press.

Wailerdsak, N., & Suehiro, A. (2014). Family business groups in Thailand: Coping with management critical points. *Asia Pacific Journal of Management, 31*(4), 997–1018.

Walder, A. (2011). From control to ownership: China's managerial revolution. *Management and Organization Review, 7*(1), 19–38.

Wangwan, N., & Leemakdej, A. (2022). *Hidden ownership and corporate governance*. SET Research Scholarship 2021–2022. The Stock Exchange of Thailand.

Warner, M. (1999). Introduction: China's managerial revolution. *Asia Pacific Business Review, 5*(3–4), 1–10.

World Bank. (1998). *East Asia: The road to recovery*. The World Bank Group.

Yan, H., & Yu, F. (2021). *The Routledge companion to Asian family business: Governance, succession, and challenges in the age of digital disruption*. Routledge.

Young, M. N., Peng, M. W., Ahlstrom, D., Bruton, G. D., & Jiang, Y. (2008). Corporate governance in emerging economies: A review of the principal-principal perspective. *Journal of Management Studies, 45*(1), 196–220.

Chapter 11

Conclusion and policy recommendations

11.1 Three prior work

Akira Suehiro's *Capital Accumulation in Thailand: 1855–1985* (1989) asserts that business groups are essential to emerging nation economic success, based on the tripod structure of business groups, including state, local, and foreign capital. Before the Siamese revolution of 1932, monarchs, nobles, and bureaucrats governed Thai capitalism. No indigenous or local capitalists were detectable. Later, in the 1960s, the Thai government promoted industrialization. State capital was mobilized to invest in utilities and dominate profitable industrial capital, including military- and politician-controlled petrochemicals, steel, and cement.

When the government began to support economic activities of Thais and foreigners in the 1970s, the local merchant class could swiftly accumulate capital while focusing on high-return businesses and ignoring technology. Financial and commercial capital outweighed industrial capital.[1] Foreign capital entered through joint ventures. Most supported light, labour-intensive indigenous import-substitution production. However, as the Thai market was small, exports also required boosting. Foreign capital helped remove obstacles to export and international business.

Suehiro's *Catch-up Industrialization: The Trajectory and Prospects of East Asian Economies* (2008) describes how East Asian caught up with industrialized nations in the 1970s and 1980s, due to developmental states with export-oriented industrial strategies and social capability. The Thai government launched the Eastern Seaboard project to push heavy industries and join newly industrialized countries (NICs). The business group was considered as a paragon for rapid industrialization during the economic boom. Excess profits were invested in industries offering decent jobs.

However, after the 1997 Asian financial crisis, business groups were accused of exploiting the nation for their own benefit, gaining special privileges and political favours without investing in high-performing industries. The low-cost advantage growth path that facilitated the East Asian economic miracle was later found to be inappropriate and achieving high-income nation status no longer prioritized.

DOI: 10.4324/9781003370536-15

My research, *Thai Family Business Groups before and after the 1997 Crisis* (Wailerdsak, 2006), describes the collapse of financial conglomerates, adaptations and failures of Thai business groups confronted by the 1997 Asian financial crisis, as well as World Bank and IMF efforts to implement an Anglo-American corporate governance system as well as accounting and auditing systems meeting international standards to oversee listed companies and benefit shareholders and society.

This book, *Business Groups and the Thailand Economy: Escaping the Middle-Income Trap*, follows the three aforementioned works. It underlines the importance of the business group through a case study of Thailand's entrapment among middle-income nations. Thailand previously adhered to the developmental state concept, in which the government directed targeted industrial policies. Meanwhile, Thai business groups used business group governance to ensure that such restrictions were followed effectively. This aided Thailand to attain upper-middle-income status by 2010, based on three primary levels: capital, technology, and human resources.

But financial markets failed to progress significantly in terms of fund-raising. Minority shareholders and creditors were not legally protected to the degree that they are in developed nations. The pyramidal ownership structure and subsidiary cross shareholding within groups, often known as the business group governance, can help groups acquire money and launch new enterprises (Wailerdsak, 2008).

Thai business groups lack proprietary technology, relying instead on joint ventures and strategic alliances with MNCs, which seek new regional production bases and customers. They can produce modern goods and services, partially substituting for imports while exporting. Although employing merely intermediate technology, this may contribute to Thailand's economic growth and employment creation through population dividends.

Typically, a Thai business group contains three categories of human resources:

- A family manager educated abroad, with a global perspective.
- So-called trueborn managers (or *luukmo* in Thai), management trainees who joined firms after graduation and formed a talent pool or internal labour market.
- Professional managers with proven records from other companies. Poaching non-family executives from Thailand-based MNCs and well-known corporations was commonplace.

Nevertheless, business group governance had its drawbacks. Since 1998, Thailand's growth rate stagnated,[2] a trend repeated by a series of crises and political upheavals. The next stage for middle-income countries would be to embrace the paradigm of corporate governance, implying capital accumulation by managerial enterprise with diversified ownership and key roles for senior executives (Dau et al., 2020, 2021a, 2021b; Inya et al., 2018). Therefore, human resource strategy should emphasize creating professional managers, not educational reform or scientific and technological progress (Morck, 2005; Morikawa, 1992).

11.2 Shift from family capitalism to managerial capitalism

According to catch-up industrialization theory, Japan is a paradigm of catch-up, with the potential to become Asia's first high-income country. At the start of the catch-up phase, Japan exploited family capitalism or zaibatsu corporate governance to diversify into family-owned and controlled large business groups with pyramidal structures with tiers of listed firms, as well as imported technology. Japan diligently pursued industrial policies based on governmental and private sector ties and a state-orchestrated Big Push[3] according to developmental state theory to identify target industries and drive growth to quickly overtake industrialized nations (Morck & Yeung, 2018).

Later, after the Great Depression decimated Western economies, Japan was severely affected by the global economic collapse. Its growth met difficulties, prompting Japanese nationalists and the military to gain power and conduct war to obtain natural resources. Military dictatorship lacked patience for market forces. A wartime economy was a command-and-control system with the military assigning each plant production quotas and using zaibatsu (industrial and financial vertically integrated business conglomerate) funding and management to support militarism approaching World War II (Morck & Yeung, 2018).

The American occupation after the Japanese defeat was a significant turning point that catalysed Japan's development. Under the US occupation, economic policy was mostly delegated to New Dealers weaned on extensive state intervention during successive Roosevelt administrations. New Deal economists Adolf Berle and Gardiner Means (1932) challenged large corporations to restore public trust in the economy. This approach hinged on a series of reforms to dismantle pyramidal business groups dominated by American robber barons (Hannah, 2021; Hamdani et al., 2020).

These 1930s New Deal corporate governance reforms included raising taxes on inter-corporate dividends and estates, banning large-scale business groups in public utilities and severing ties between major banks and industrial firms which they previously controlled (Kandel et al., 2017). These reforms subjected firms whose major assets were shares in other firms to regulation as mutual funds, limiting the number of pyramidal tiers among regulated public utilities. Together, by 1950 these reforms had rid the US of pyramidal business groups (Hamdani et al., 2020; Morck & Yeung, 2018).

In Japan, the Occupation government seized and reallocated zaibatsu family shares and intercorporate equity blocks holding their pyramidal groups together. When the US withdrew in 1952, it left a post–New Deal US corporate governance system in place (Morck & Nakamura, 2005; Franks et al., 2014). Most Japanese corporations had widely held share ownership and were run by salaried professional managers (*sarariman*). A so-called managerial capitalism was born (Morikawa, 1992).

However, owners of established firms produced by a successful Big Push rationally favoured the status quo, and corrupt government officials installed regulatory hurdles that prevented creative destruction[4] to achieve optimum return on investment (ROI). To attain the ranks of high-income countries, the middle-income trap must be avoided in which economic growth slows after an initial spurt of rapid development. Always developing but never developed, entrapped economy large business sectors are the domain of business dynasties descending from first-generation business elites who amassed wealth during early-stage development and used political influence to maintain a status quo favourable to them and their heirs (Rajan & Zingales, 2003a, 2003b; Morck et al., 2005). This is the explanation proposed by Haber (2005, 2013) for Latin American sluggish growth.

In the late 1940s, Japanese early-stage corporate elites were ousted by changes enacted under the US military occupation. Established company professionalized management and an influx of highly creative enterprises newly listed after World War II, including Casio, Honda, and Sony, accelerated Japanese productivity for decades (Mehrotra et al., 2011; Morikawa, 1992).

South Korean chaebol (large industrial conglomerates run and controlled by an individual or family) in the late 1970s followed suit. Like Japan's zaibatsu, Korea's notable chaebol groups attained full set diversification; each had at least one member firm for every significant high-tech manufacturing concern. Korean chaebol families have grown economically and politically powerful, wielding controversial influence over government policy.[5]

Nevertheless, Korean managerial and professional classes have emerged with a lifetime employment system, seniority-based wages, varied allowances, and extensive training at each career stage, including company-sponsored study aboard, to pursue long-term R&D objectives as a global player with top-quality products (Kim et al., 2004; Tung et al., 2013; Woo et al., 2020).

However, increasing negative publicity culminated in 2017 with the arrest of Samsung scion Lee Jae-yong, in a bribery scandal leading to the impeachment and arrest of President Park Geun-hye, the first female president popularly elected as head of state in East Asia. Chaebol reform became the top issue in the election to replace her, but scepticism remained. The chaebol may appear too powerful to fail, allowing member firms privileged access to debt financing and diverting capital allocation away from other firms (Jones, 2018; Morck & Yeung, 2018).

A comprehensive approach to improve chaebol was proposed. Firstly, strengthening international and domestic competition would oblige business groups to boost efficiency to survive. Stronger competition should include a more active market for corporate control and measures to address unfair subcontracting practices by business groups. Secondly, Korea needs a framework enhancing internal and external monitoring of business groups, including improved corporate governance and a larger role for institutional investors. Thirdly, more use of private remedies, including class action and derivative lawsuits, is needed to protect minority shareholder rights. Fourthly, group ownership structure should be revamped, prohibiting cross shareholding (imposed in April 1987), holding companies (April 1987), and new circular shareholding (July 2014) (in its simplest form, firm A holds shares in firm B, firm B holds shares in firm C and firm C owns shares in firm A) while also requiring disclosure of large-scale intra-group transactions (April 2000) (Jones, 2018; Jun et al., 2022).

As of 2020, China remains a middle-income nation, and descendants of its Communist-era revolutionary leaders enjoy privileged positions. Rent-seeking of Communist princelings may lock China in a middle-income trap to protect their wealth and power. Or China may follow in the footsteps of Japan or Korea by liberalizing and privatizing more broadly to avoid ensnarement in the trap. Its aging population and increasingly tight resource constraints may ultimately force the Chinese state to prefer the latter option. In December 2012, the Xi Jinping government launched an anti-corruption effort, potentially promoting market growth (Morck & Yeung, 2018).

Based on experiences of successful latecomer nations like Japan, South Korea, and China, how should Thailand proceed?

11.3 Policy recommendations

11.3.1 Industrial policy – eliminating industrial monopoly and promoting startups

In the 2020s, latecomer nations have encountered comparable circumstances. Rapid labour productivity growth in manufacturing and import competition led to a loss of production jobs and a move to services, with worsened wages and employment conditions. Automation, the knowledge economy, and digital technologies exacerbated the situation. Productivity impact of new technology was restricted to a few industries and urban areas, generating few good jobs, while the remainder of the economy was stagnant.

Therefore, the government's efforts to aggressively improve the entrepreneurial ecosystem and industrial policy was requested (Harrison et al., 2018). Although Thai companies may profit on backwardness through digital, industry 4.0, and green technologies, catching up with and even surpassing industrialized nations, latecomers like Thailand that once utilized the developmental state paradigm now must succumb to monopolies generating greater business power monopolies and extended authoritarian rule of centralized bureaucratic polity. The issue is how to escape this "monopolistic trap" (Nikomborirak, 2021).

In addition, the big push theory focuses principally on the industrial sector – capital products, consumer goods, and social overhead capital. Manufacturing is a superior motivator of economic growth (Murphy et al., 1989). But in emerging countries like Thailand, the most dominant sector consists of agricultural and primary production. For balanced economic growth, agriculture also demands a correspondingly big push. Any neglect of the agriculture sector in these countries would endanger the big push venture (Phongpaichit, 2022).

Problems	*Indicators*
Support two types of private companies: (1) import-substitution goods manufacturers, including electric, automobiles, smart electrical and electronic goods, machinery and equipment; and (2) export-competitive item manufacturers, while decreasing monopolies in nationally significant industries.	– Gross domestic product (GDP) value by industry – Export value by industry – Monopoly rate in different industries
Prioritize promoting businesses in which Thai companies are competitive, intricately interconnected with businesses such as integrated medical and health care, retail and food, banking and insurance.	– Industries where Thai companies are competitive – Complex industries linked to other industries
Promoting Thai company investment (1) in Thailand and (2) abroad. Initially, all nations preferred domestic investments. But overseas investment creates significant wealth. Obtaining cutting-edge technology may also be accomplished by international acquisitions. Therefore, it is essential to promote the role of Thai Overseas Investment Centers and Thailand's branding.	– Number of Thai-national MNCs – Number of Thai brands on a global scale
Promote investments in R&D to create new breakthroughs in manufacturing and services, leading to formation of corporate research centres or startup investments in partnership with academic institutions and linked networks, such as EdTech, FinTech, MedTech, BioTech, and FoodTech.	– R&D Investment Index – Number of startups – Number of unicorn companies

11.3.2 EEC plan – dispersion of ownership in large companies

As a sandbox of the big push, the EEC initiative intends to make Thailand the ASEAN centre for future high-tech sectors (Nikomborirak, 2021). Although EEC Office efforts to incorporate Thai business groups into PPP are energetic, the operation confronts some obstacles:

- Foreign investors are granted more investment privileges, with Thailand potentially competing with its neighbours for FDI. The administration was criticized for favouring foreign and major enterprises with government links, creating mistrust for state bias (Keeranan, 2022).
- A military-derived governmental image and consolidation of uneven administrative authority.
- Three eastern provinces ideal for manufacturing and export bases provide excellent agricultural regions and well-known tourist destinations, leaving collaboration with others difficult and conflict over resource allocation, such as for land.

Meanwhile, economic progress and monopolistic power in principal industrialized nations have evolved toward ownership and control separation. The government will establish the proportion of private equity for listed companies and implement measures to avoid integration or monopolistic power. However, for latecomers, it proved tough to oppose large corporations, and state authorities appeared to favour them (Hamilton-Hart & Yeung, 2021).

Problems	*Indicators*
The EEC must encourage Thai companies to acquire foreign technology and develop their own homegrown technology. While the EEC initiative was well-intentioned, one agency made all the decisions. In lieu of long-term concessions, resources and input should be allocated by fostering competition between Thai and foreign businesses.	– Number of Thai firms engaging in the EEC project – Number of Thai firms using high technology – Competitive intensity in each target industry
Diversified stock ownership should be mandated for major corporations in targeted industries. Ownership should not be concentrated in the hands of a single group.	– Number of widely held corporations

11.3.3 Investment fund – from family to managerial capitalism

In terms of capital, Thai companies should renounce family capitalism in which the owner and CEO are the same individual or group. This sort of business has limited social responsibility, since it strives only to maximize own profits. There should be a transition to managerial capitalism. Separation of owners and executives is said to increase company social responsibility. Since executives do not own the firm, they receive salary and bonuses and need to exploit others to maximize profit; instead, they will satisfy owners, themselves, and society (Phipatseritham, 1981).

Government agencies such as the Stock Exchange of Thailand, the Securities and Exchange Commission, Thailand, the Federation of Thai Capital Market Organizations (FETCO), the Institute of Directors (IOD),[6] and institutional investors should encourage investors to purchase shares of listed companies through education, as well as encourage listed companies to comply with international standards (Harrison et al., 2018). Hitherto, large companies have never been required to diversify shareholdings through cross-holding restrictions or using holding companies.

Problems	*Indicators*
Promoting Thai companies to transition from family businesses to managerial enterprises to benefit all stakeholders marks the start of societal egalitarian distribution by diversifying ownership of nationally essential companies.	– Number of managerial enterprises – Number of significant firms with concentrated ownership
Advancing Thai capital market expansion by increasing shareholder and institutional investor numbers to serve as a source of wealth rather than speculation. Financial literacy to monitor public company fair and transparent business practices.	– Capital market growth – Number of minority shareholders – Number of institutional investors

11.3.4 Technology – promoting sound labour relations

Technological development is concomitant with human development. Thai workers are mobile, and technology will follow them, hampering technology accumulation. To inspire workers to bond with businesses and transmit technology from one generation to the next, visionary leaders must create an internal labour market with positive employer-employee labour relations to improve social capability and eventually lead to creating native technology (Huneeus et al., 2021; Nikomborirak, 2021; Wailerdsak, 2003, 2004a, 2004b).

Problems	Indicators
Support Thai companies to boost employee output, with workers not seen as low-cost input readily replaced by migrant labour from neighbouring countries. A high-income nation must enhance productivity.	– Worker Productivity Index comparable to the United States
Improving labour productivity requires managers to interact with workers and maintain sound labour relations. Motivate workers to boost productivity and income, implicating democracy and workplace participation.	– Sound labour relations system
Promote human resource development at work by concentrating on internal labour market expansion, knowledge transfer, and technological invention.	– In-house training and development

11.3.5 Human resources – from family to professional management

In *The Visible Hand* (1977) and *Scale and Scope* (1990), Chandler notes that the market imperative compelled professional managers to replace family business owners. In Chandler's view, the extensive domestic market and technological progress encouraged large-scale enterprises beyond the capacity of a single family. Capital market development, the rise of professional management, and inheritance structural changes followed.

Chandler's other two factors – legal system constraints, whether the legal environment encourages or restrains adaptations by professional managers, and professional manager paraphernalia (prevalence of management-related associations, journals, training schools, and societal consultants) – point to institutional forces and social arrangements as determining family business professionalization (Zhang & Ma, 2009).

Therefore, market exigency pushes professionalization of family businesses. It is driven by the desire to capitalize on economic scale and scope during the global era, intensive market competition, and rapid technological innovation. These heighten the necessity for seeking more fine-grained information, rapider decision-making, and improved management (Inya et al., 2018).

A new group of professional managers has evolved economically. In certain industrialized nations, the government mandates that chief executive officers (CEOs) of major companies, such as large manufacturers, banks, and digital service providers be competent, ethical experts approved by impartial agencies, helping large companies to focus increasingly on social benefits and offering productive executives advancement and work-status opportunities to eliminate social stratification (Wailerdsak, 2020).

Basically, Thailand has exhibited a continuous improvement in the average ASEAN Corporate Governance Score (ACGS score) (Asian Development Bank, 2021). For an example, in 2021, the SEC determines that the chair of the board and chief executive officer (CEO) must not be the same person (no CEO duality) for companies issuing shares to the public. However, there are still challenges for improvement.

Problems	*Indicators*
Promote training and development of outside directors and professional executives who understand corporate governance, advanced technology, global markets, and societal sustainability.	– Number of professional outside directors – Number of professional executives
Promote the role of financial market bodies, including the Stock Exchange of Thailand (SET), Thai Capital Market Council, commercial banks, and professional institutions, offering executive monitoring mechanisms based on strong expertise and ethics.	– Number of charged executives – Number of administrative professional institutions

11.3.6 Other problems – building a good jobs economy[7]

Several issues not addressed here likewise prevent Thailand from escaping the middle-income trap: higher education – labour market imbalances, income inequality between formal and informal workers, unprogressive national innovation and R&D systems, social problems hindering economic growth, and labour market issues that accelerate the shift toward a super-aged society (Phongpaichit, 2022).

Catch-up industrialization and FDI, particularly from Japan over the past four decades, may propel Thailand to upper-middle-class status. Thai people had faith in the expertise and ambition of bureaucrats, governments, and business leaders since they contributed to the establishing good jobs economies, improving the quality of life and living standards.

But when the conventional, tried-and-tested model of catch-up industrialization became exhausted, Thailand was confined among middle-income nations, aggravating economic inequality, afflicting communities with poor social outcomes (health, education, crime) as well as social and political strife (populist backlashes, democratic malfunctioning). Business groups raise markups by permitting oligopolists or monopsonists to drive down wages.

Both political and commercial elite control national resources and power, eroding trust in elites, with a rise in populism and authoritarian politics. This is evident in political conflict dating back over a decade.

How can Thailand escape this predicament as a latecomer nation? By examining samples of industrialized nations and exploring the role of business groups and their leadership, indicates that to escape the middle-income trap, the trust of elites must be restored that they may regenerate a big push for high-tech and green industrialization and create a good jobs economy (Phipatseritham, 1981; Suehiro, 2008). The goal would be to establish a "mass meritocracy," empowering many individuals to thrive on individual capabilities and merits, surpassing class privilege and patronage systems (Wailerdsak, 2020).

Notes

1 Suehiro (1989) stated that compared to Japan, Thai business leaders were proficient in the use of modern technology, believing that tech companies could control the market. But Thai business leaders were marketing-focused, with scant interest in importing technology, deeming technological R&D wasteful and profit reducing. They believed that a market-dominated firm could occupy the industry. Despite evident differences, the goals were identical: to maximize profit and market share.

2 Thailand's economic growth rate averaged 1.7 percent during Prayut Chan-ocha's presidency (2014–2022). It attained a high of 4.2 percent in 2017 and a low of –6.2 percent in 2020.

3 Marginal increments in investment in unrelated parts of the economy are inadequate remedies, although simultaneous sizable investments may make a difference. If different economic sectors adopted increasing technological returns simultaneously, each might produce revenue fuelling a demand for goods in other sectors, expanding markets and making industrialization profitable. This notion of coordinated investment is the basis of the concept of the "big push," introduced by Rosenstein-Rodan (1943) and discussed by many others (Murphy et al., 1989).

4 A competitive business network may help a nation overtake other high-income economies. After that, growth must be sustained by continuing productivity improvement. In current high-income economies, disruptive innovation drives productivity growth (Fogel et al., 2008). Productivity growth is a process of creative destruction, in which new start-up companies emerge and partially destroy the value of old, existing firms (Schumpeter, 1911 [1934]). The financial industry's main societal purpose is to efficiently allocate capital to start-up innovators and away from comparatively sluggish existing companies.

5 Top 30 Korea's chaebols account for almost two thirds of exports in Korea's manufacturing and mining sector and a quarter of revenues in services. The groups consist of a large number of legally independent firms operating in a wide range of unrelated industries under the direction of owner families, whose control is cemented by equity holdings between the affiliated firms. The largest groups, Samsung, Hyundai Motor, SK, and LG, had an average of 70 firms in 2017 and accounted for nearly half of stock market capitalization (Jones, 2018; Jun et al., 2022).

6 The Thai Institute of Directors was assigned by the SEC to be a domestic ranking body to develop and review assessment criteria in the ASEAN CG Scorecard (ACGS) and disseminate the knowledge to Thai listed companies. The ACGS

training and seminars received a warm welcome from the listed companies and hence equipped them to effectively apply the governance principles (Asian Development Bank, 2021).

7 The definition of a good job is elusive, but primarily it requires steady, formal-sector employment with essential labour protections, including safe working conditions, collective bargaining rights, and arbitrary firing restrictions. A good job guarantees at least a middle-class existence with sufficient income for housing, food, transportation, education, and other family expenses, as well as some savings. More generally, good jobs provide career paths, self-development opportunities, flexibility, responsibility, and fulfilment (Rodrik & Sabel, 2022; Rodrik & Stantcheva, 2021).

References

Asian Development Bank. (2021). *ASEAN corporate governance scorecard country reports and assessments 2019*. Asian Development Bank.

Berle, A. A., & Means, G. C. (1932). *The modern corporation and private property*. Commerce Clearing House.

Chandler, A. D., Jr. (1977). *The visible hand: The managerial revolution in American business*. Belknap Press of Harvard University Press.

Chandler, A. D., Jr. (1990). *Scale and scope: The dynamics of industrial capitalism*. Belknap Press of Harvard University Press.

Dau, L. A., Morck, R. K., & Yeung, B. (2020). *Corporate governance, business group governance and economic traps*. NBER Working Paper No. 28069. National Bureau of Economic Research.

Dau, L. A., Morck, R., & Yeung, B. (2021a). Corporate governance versus business group governance, part 1: The low-income trap. In K. Sogner & A. Colli (Eds.), *The emergence of corporate governance: People, power, and performance* (Chapter 6, pp. 103–120). Routledge.

Dau, L. A., Morck, R. K., & Yeung, B. (2021b). Corporate governance versus business group governance, part 2: The middle-income trap. In K. Sogner & A. Colli (Eds.), *The emergence of corporate governance: People, power, and performance* (Chapter 7, pp. 121–134). Routledge.

Fogel, K., Morck, R., & Yeung, B. (2008). Big business stability and economic growth: Is what's good for General Motors good for America? *Journal of Financial Economics*, *89*(1), 83–108.

Franks, J., Mayer, C., & Miyajima, H. (2014). The ownership of Japanese corporations in the twentieth century. *Review of Financial Studies*, *27*(9), 2580–2625.

Haber, S. (2005). Mexico's experiment with bank privatization and liberalization, 1991–2004. *Journal of Banking and Finance*, *29*(8–9), 2325–2353.

Haber, S. (2013). *Crony capitalism and economic growth in Latin America: Theory and evidence*. Hoover Institution Press.

Hamdani, A., Kosenko, K., & Yafeh, Y. (2020). *Regulatory measures to dismantle pyramidal business groups: Evidence from the United States, Japan, Korea and Israel*. ECGI-Law Working Paper No. 542. European Corporate Governance Institute.

Hamilton-Hart, N., & Yeung, H. W. (2021). Institutions under pressure: East Asian states, global markets and national firms. *Review of International Political Economy*, *28*(1), 11–35.

Hannah, L. (2021). Managerial capitalism and corporate governance. In K. Sogner & A. Colli (Eds.), *The emergence of corporate governance* (Chapter 1, pp. 10–32). Routledge.

Harrison, R., Scheela, W., Lai, P. C., & Vivekarajah, S. (2018). Beyond institutional voids and the middle-income trap: The emerging business angel market in Malaysia. *Asia Pacific Journal of Management*, *35*(4), 965–991.

Huneeus, F., Larrain, B., Larrain, M., & Prem, M. (2021). The internal labour markets of business groups. *Journal of Corporate Finance*, *69*, 102017.

Inya, P., Psaros, J., & Seamer, M. (2018). The relevance of western corporate governance in mitigating management misconduct in Thailand. *Emerging Markets Finance and Trade*, *54*(6), 1425–1441.

Jones, R. S. (2018). *Reforming the large business groups to promote productivity and inclusion in Korea*. OECD Economics Department Working Papers No. 1509. OECD Publishing.

Jun, Y., Rowley, C., & Oh, I. (2022). Corporate governance reforms amidst economic maturation and democratization: The case of the Korean chaebol since the 1990s. *Asia Pacific Business Review*, *28*(1), 1–15.

Kandel, E., Kosenko, K., Morck, R., & Yafeh, Y. (2017). *The great pyramids of America: A revised history of US business groups, corporate ownership and regulation, 1930–1950*. NBER Working Paper No. 19691. National Bureau of Economic Research.

Keeranan, S. (2022, October 15). Santi pad EEC ua thunyai (Santi denies EEC support for major capitals). *Krungthep Turakit* (In Thai).

Kim, H., Hoskisson, R. E., Tihanyi, L., & Hong, J. (2004). The evolution and restructuring of diversified business groups in emerging markets: The lessons from Chaebols in Korea. *Asia Pacific Journal of Management*, *21*(1), 25–48.

Mehrotra, V., Van Schaik, D., Spronk, J., & Steenbeek, O. (2011). A creditor-focused corporate governance: Evidence from mergers and acquisitions in Japan. *Journal of Financial and Quantitative Analysis*, *46*(4), 1051–1072.

Morck, R. K. (Ed.). (2005). *A history of corporate governance around the world: Family business groups to professional managers*. University of Chicago Press.

Morck, R. K., & Nakamura, M. (2005). A frog in a well knows nothing of the ocean: A history of corporate ownership in Japan. In R. Morck (Ed.), *History of corporate governance around the world* (Chapter 7, pp. 367–465). University of Chicago Press.

Morck, R. K., Wolfenzon, D., & Yeung, B. (2005). Corporate governance, economic entrenchment and growth. *Journal of Economics Literature*, *43*(3), 657–722.

Morck, R. K., & Yeung, B. (2018). East Asian financial and economic development. In T. Beck & R. Levine (Eds.), *Handbook of finance and development* (Chapter 7, pp. 194–241). Edward Elgar.

Morikawa, H. (1992). *Zaibatsu: The rise and fall of family enterprise groups in Japan*. University of Tokyo Press.

Murphy, K. M., Shleifer, A., & Vishny, R. W. (1989). Industrialization and the big push. *Journal of Political Economy*, *97*(5), 1003–1026.

Nikomborirak, D. (2021). Thailand's policy challenges. *Asian Economic Policy Review*, *15*, 284–300.

Phipatseritham, K. (1981). *Wikrao laksana kanpen chaokhong turakit khanaadyai nai prathedthai (Analysing the ownership structure of the Thai big business groups)*. Thammasart University Press (In Thai).

Phongpaichit, P. (2022). *90 pii prachatipatai anakot ratsawadikan anakot sangkhomthai (90 years democracy, the future of the welfare state, the future of Thai society)* (In Thai). www.youtube.com/watch?v=VepYHD26XvU

Rajan, R. G., & Zingales, L. (2003a). *Saving capitalism from the capitalists*. Crown Business.

Rajan, R. G., & Zingales, L. (2003b). The great reversals: The politics of financial development in the twentieth century. *Journal of Financial Economics*, *69*(1), 5–50.

Rodrik, D., & Sabel, C. (2022). Building a good jobs economy. In D. Allen, Y. Benkler, L. Downey, R. Henderson, & J. Simons (Eds.), *A political economy of justice* (Chapter 2, pp. 61–95). University of Chicago Press.

Rodrik, D., & Stantcheva, S. (2021). Fixing capitalism's good jobs problem. *Oxford Review of Economic Policy*, *37*(4), 824–837.

Rosenstein-Rodan, P. N. (1943). Problems of industrialization of Eastern and South-eastern Europe. *Economic Journal*, *53*(210/211), 202–211.

Schumpeter, J. A. (1911 [1934]). *The theory of economic development*. Harvard University Press.

Suehiro, A. (1989). *Capital accumulation in Thailand, 1855–1985*. UNESCO The Centre for East Asian Cultural Studies.

Suehiro, A. (2008). *Catch-up industrialization: The trajectory and prospects of East Asian economies*. National University of Singapore Press.

Tung, R. S., Paik, Y., & Bae, J. (2013). Korean human resource management in the global context. *International Journal of Human Resource Management*, *24*(5), 905–921.

Wailerdsak, N. (2003). Retaining and developing managers and professionals in a Thai telecommunications firm. *Journal of Asian Business*, *19*(1), 67–87.

Wailerdsak, N. (2004a). Promotion system and career development in Thailand: A case study of Siam Cement. *Journal of International Human Resource Management*, *15*(1), 196–218.

Wailerdsak, N. (2004b). Top executive origins: Comparative study between Japan and Thailand. *Journal of Asian Business & Management*, *3*(1), 85–104.

Wailerdsak, N. (2006). *Klumthun turakit krubkruathai koon lae lang wikrit pii 2540 (Thai family-owned business groups before and after the 1997 crisis)*. BrandAge Books (In Thai).

Wailerdsak, N. (2008). Companies in crisis. In P. Phongpaichit & C. Baker (Eds.), *Thai capital after the 1997 crisis* (Chapter 1, pp. 17–57). Silkworm Books.

Wailerdsak, N. (2020). *Kanborihaan daoden lae senthang suu phuuborihaan radab-suung nai mitithang settasad (Talent management and paths to the top in economic dimension)*. Institute for Continuing Education and Human Resources, Thammasat University (In Thai).

Woo, Y., Choi, W., Min, I., & Jeong, M. (2020). Korean business groups and performance of group-affiliated professional sport teams: Focusing on the Asian financial crisis. *Sustainability*, *12*(17), 6888.

Zhang, J., & Ma, H. (2009). Adoption of professional management in Chinese family business: A multilevel analysis of impetuses and impediments. *Asia Pacific Journal of Management*, *26*(1), 119–139.

Index

Note: Page numbers in *italics* indicate a figure and page numbers in **bold** indicate a table on the corresponding page.

For Product Safety Concerns and Information please contact our EU representative GPSR@taylorandfrancis.com
Taylor & Francis Verlag GmbH, Kaufingerstraße 24, 80331 München, Germany

www.ingramcontent.com/pod-product-compliance
Ingram Content Group UK Ltd.
Pitfield, Milton Keynes, MK11 3LW, UK
UKHW022018230926
475702UK00029B/1863

* 9 7 8 1 0 3 2 4 4 1 1 5 3 *